THE PLAYS AND POEMS

OF RICHARD BRINSLEY SHERIDAN

THE SCREEN SCENE IN THE SCHOOL FOR SCANDAL

FROM A CONTEMPORARY PAINTING IN THE GARRICK CLUB LONDON

(Copyright. Garrick Club)

The PLAYS & POEMS *of*
RICHARD BRINSLEY
SHERIDAN

Edited with Introductions, Appendices
and Bibliographies by

R. CROMPTON RHODES

Author of The Stagery of Shakespeare
Shakespeare's First Folio
The Theatre Royal, Birmingham, 1774-1824
Black Sheep: a Comedy
Editor of Sheridan's Ode to Scandal

VOLUME II

NEW YORK

RUSSELL & RUSSELL · INC

1962

PUBLISHED, 1962, BY RUSSELL & RUSSELL, INC.

L. C. CATALOG CARD NO: 62-13850

PRINTED IN THE UNITED STATES OF AMERICA

TO SIR CHARLES HYDE, BART.

CONTENTS

vii

The School for Scandal, A Comedy

II. B

Note

THE SCHOOL FOR SCANDAL is here printed from a transcript made by THOMAS MOORE of the last complete revision of the comedy ever made by SHERIDAN and presented by him to Mrs. CREWE. The transcript, now in the Library of the Royal Irish Academy, Dublin, was made by altering a copy of the only authentic text printed in the author's lifetime:

"THE SCHOOL FOR SCANDAL, ... by RICHARD BRINSLEY SHERIDAN, ESQ., taken from a correct copy, performed at the Theatres, London and Dublin. Dublin: Printed and Sold by the Booksellers, 1799." This Edition was derived from the copy given by SHERIDAN to his sister (afterwards Mrs. LEFANU) and acted in Dublin by command of the Lord Lieutenant in January, 1778.

The Moore transcript, which neglected many small points, has been collated with the various editions from MS. including SHERIDAN's late draft (*circa* 1776-1777), as printed by FRASER RAE, and the London edition of 1826, as edited by GEORGE DANIEL, from the Drury Lane prompt-book.

R.C.R.

CONTENTS

Introduction

FROM his contemporaries *The School for Scandal* won for Sheridan the name of "the modern Congreve." It was the highest title they had to bestow upon a master of the comedy of manners. Sheridan had almost deliberately invited the comparison: one of his first plans on assuming the management of Drury Lane was to revive the comedies of Congreve, which, after some delay, he carried out—"deserving" (though not receiving) "the encouragement of the town, by the strength with which they were brought out, and the judicious—nay, masterly—manner in which the parts were cast."[1] In this way he had prepared his actors and his audience for the great comedy which, even then, was still uncompleted. He had turned aside in its composition to alter *The Relapse* into *A Trip to Scarborough*, seeking to add to the wit of Vanbrugh the quality of "grace," or at least to take away its "gracelessness." In his amendment of the character of Vanbrugh's Berinthia, he was determining the conduct of his own Lady Teazle: she was to be no sinner like the wanton wives of the older comedy, but one who "escapes—if only just—from her equivocal situation with her virtue." It was in this circumstance that he departed from the model of the older comedy: it was nevertheless to the earlier dramatists that his contemporaries went for their comparisons—"this excellent comedy is certainly the best that has appeared upon our stage since Congreve and Vanbrugh," declared *The Town and Country Magazine*,—"I have seen no comedy that comes near it since *The Provoked Husband*," wrote Horace Walpole to Robert Jephson.[2]

Of Vanbrugh's dialogue, as Moore said, Sheridan spoke always "with the warmest admiration," yet it was more natural to compare him with Congreve. One of the comedies that were re-

---

[1] *The London Magazine* for January, 1777.
[2] July 13th, 1777 (*Letters*, Vol. X, p. 82).

vived at Drury Lane was *The Double Dealer*, in which Sheridan
seemed to have been anticipated in some measure by the smart
malicious gossip of Lord Froth's house:—

Lord Froth. Hee, hee; my dear, have you done?—Won't
you join with us? We were laughing at my Lady Whifler and
Mr. Sneer.

Lady Froth. Ay, my dear,—Were you? Oh filthy Mr. Sneer!
he is a nauseous figure, a moſt fulsamick fop.—He spent two
days together in going about Covent Garden to suit the lining
of his coach with his complexion.

Lord Froth. O silly! yet his aunt is as fond of him, as if she
had brought the ape into the world herself.

Brisk. Who? my Lady Toothless? Oh, she 's a mortifying
speêtacle; she's always chewing the cud like an old ewe...

Lord Froth. Then she's always ready to laugh, when Sneer
offers to speak;—and sits in expeêtation of his no jeſt, with her
gums bare, and her mouth open——

Brisk. Like an oyſter at low ebb, egad—Ha, ha, ha!

Cynthia [*aside*]. Well, I find there are no fools so inconsid-
erable themselves, but they can render other people contemptible by exposing their infirmities.

Lady Froth. Then that t'other great ſtrapping Lady—I
can't hit off her name; the old fat fool, that paints so exorbi-
tantly.

Brisk. I know whom you mean—but, Deuce take her, I
can't hit off her name neither—Paints, d'ye say? Why she lays
it on with a trowel.—Then she has a great beard that briſtles
through it, and makes her look as if she was plaiſtered with
lime and hair, let me perish.[1]

It may be, as Moore said, that this has somewhat of a "parental
resemblance" to the conversations at Lady Sneerwell's, though
the more correêt phrase is "fraternal," while one muſt add with
him that it is "far inferior to them in delicacy and ingenuity." In
The School for Scandal, Sheridan vied with Congreve's maſter-
piece *The Way of the World*, yet unlike his illuſtrious predecessor

[1] *The Double Dealer*... As performed at the Theatre-Royal, Drury Lane. Regulated
from the Prompt-Book by Mr. Hopkins, Prompter. London. John Bell, 1777.

he wrote a play that succeeded in the theatre beyond all precedent
or expectation. Congreve was Sheridan's model so far as any
dramatist may be said to have been, always remembering the fine
saying that the great poets go to their predecessors only to confirm what is already in themselves.[1] But he could not altogether
escape from the influence of the sentimental comedy of his time.

In his essay on Comedy, Robert Heron summarized the considered verdict of his generation:

"In English comedy Congreve, I believe, stands without a
rival. His plots have great depth and art; perhaps too much:
his characters are new and strong; his wit genuine; and so ex-
uberant, that it has been alleged as his only fault, that he makes
all his characters inherit his own wit. Yet this fault will not be
imputed by adepts, who know that the dialogue of our comedy
cannot possibly be too spirited and epigrammatic, for it requires language as well as characters stronger than nature. . .

"By *The School for Scandal* the style of Congreve was again
brought into fashion; and sentiment made way for wit, and
delicate humour. That piece has indeed the beauties of Congreve's comedies, without their faults: its plot is deeply
enough perplexed, without forcing one to labour to unravel
it; its incidents sufficient, without being too numerous; its
wit pure; its situations truly dramatic. The characters however are not quite so strong as Congreve's; which may be regarded as the principal fault of this excellent piece."

It is not now the fashion to quote Macaulay, who coupled their
names as pre-eminent in his essay on *The Comic Dramatists of the
Restoration* (1840)—"the wit of Congreve far outshines that of
every other writer, except Sheridan, who has arisen within the
last two centuries." But in an earlier essay on *Machiavelli* he delivered an opinion that has long imposed itself upon critical
judgment:

"No writers have injured the comedy of England so deeply
as Congreve and Sheridan. Both were men of splendid wit and
polished taste. Unhappily they made all their characters in
their own likeness. Every fop, every boor, every valet, is a man

[1]Dramatists were still called "poets" in Sheridan's time.

of wit. The very butts and dupes, Tattle, Witwould, Acres, Puff, outshine the whole Hôtel de Rambouillet."

Yet this charge suffers, when applied to *The School for Scandal*, from exaggeration. There is a half-echo of this attitude in Mr. Allardyce Nicoll's complaint:

"Everyone in this world of refined manners is able to say something that is brilliant. Never for a moment does the sparkle disappear; so that sometimes we are inclined to be surfeited with too much of these intellectual fireworks. We pine occasionally for some of Goldsmith's 'humour' and 'homely nature,' feeling that this comedy of Sheridan's possesses that 'high' tone against which the former did battle."[1]

This common pitting of Goldsmith against Sheridan comes perilously near to a denial of the comedy of manners. It is true that Sheridan professed to be aware of his fault of endowing his characters with "an excessive opulence of wit." But, says Moore:

"That he had no such scruple, however, in writing it, appears evident from the pains which he took to string upon his new plot every bright thought and fancy which he had brought together for the two others; and it is not a little curious, in turning over his manuscript, to see how the outstanding jokes are kept in recollection upon the margin, till he can find some opportunity of funding them to advantage in the text. The consequence of all this is, that the dialogue, from beginning to end, is a continued sparkling of polish and point: and the whole of the Dramatis Personæ might be comprised under one common designation of Wits. Even Trip, the servant, is as pointed and shining as the rest, and has his master's wit, as he has his birth-day clothes, 'with the gloss on.' The only personage among them that shows any 'temperance in jesting,' is old Rowley; and he, too, in the original, had his share in the general largess of *bon-mots*—one of the liveliest in the piece being at first given to him, though afterwards transferred, with somewhat more fitness, to Sir Oliver. In short, the entire Comedy, is a sort of El-Dorado of wit, where the precious metal is

[1] *XVIII Century Comedy*, 1750-1800, p. 161.

thrown about by all classes, as carelessly as if they had not the least idea of its value."

Even at the risk of discontinuity, it is significant to pursue "Trip, the servant" with some pertinacity. He was the gentleman's gentleman, who exercised none of his wit upon his master, but exercised it lavishly "below stairs" upon the two money-lenders. In the presence of Charles, he was as formal as Joseph's servant, who had not the faintest glimmer of wit. Diggory might at a pinch leave his plough to wait at table in Mr. Hardcastle's antiquated mansion, but he would have not been tolerated for a moment in the fashionable house of a smart young man like Charles Surface. Trip belonged to an established type of comedy whose greatest representative is Figaro. But he had numerous English predecessors, among them Brush in *The Clandestine Marriage* and My Lord Duke in *High Life Below Stairs*. That he was the wittiest of them all since Jeremy in *Love for Love* is true for, in that "Temple of Dissipation," Charles's house, "the man was the shadow of the master." But there is something more to be said for Mr. Trip, something which lies below the surface of the printed page. If Sheridan had anticipated Mr. Shaw in the art of writing what are called "stage-directions," it would be realized that the character is entirely transformed by the manner in which Sheridan intended it to be acted, and in which it was acted by Lamash, with a mincing, drawling, affected manner. A passage in John Bernard's *Retrospections of the Stage* is eloquent in its suggestion. Once, in 1783, he says:

"I was surprised by a visit from La Mash, the fop-servant, who was passing through Belfast on his way to Scotland, accompanied by the well-known Kitty Frederick, a gay and graceful fair one, beautiful, vivacious, and extravagant. La Mash was naturally a fop, though not a polished one: he could not assume the gentleman, but the gentleman's gentleman fitted him like his clothes. This rendered him superior to Dodd, in My Lord Duke, and inferior in Sir Benjamin Backbite. But, like Edwin, and unlike Dodd, his acting was the counterpart of his daily deportment, and not the result of minute observation. One would have thought that his mother had been waiting-maid to the Duchess of Kingston, and his father the duster of Lord Chesterfield's clothes. Whilst at Drury Lane, Kitty Frederick had flopped her affections on him (he was the most elegantly made man I ever saw) and had run after him to Dublin. I could not, however, but express my surprise, that a person of notoriously expensive habits should have quitted the scene of her resources to join a penniless comedian.

" 'Whay, ay,' said he, 'eet ees vary remarkable, but eet ees vaary true; all the warld theenks there ees but one Frederick; and she theenks—ha! ha!—there ees but one La Mash.'

"He took a pinch of snuff in saying this, and his tone and manner, under other circumstances would, I am sure, have gained him a round of applause."

There lies the veritable Trip of the stage.

It is one of the curiosities of English criticism that so much time, and so little thought, has been devoted to denials of the originality of *The School for Scandal*. One would hesitate to venture into the atrocities of writing *scholia* upon *scholia*, except that the investigation throws, or may be made to throw, a new light upon the comedy. The silliest charge is that made by Sheridan's first biographer, Dr. Watkins, who asserted that *The School for Scandal* was written by "a young lady, the daughter of a merchant in Thames Street," who put her manuscript into the hands of Sheridan as manager of Drury Lane—"soon after which the fair writer, who was then in a stage of decline, went to Bristol Hot-Wells, where she died." The story is supposed to have been an old one: the Octogenarian who wrote *Sheridan and his Times* quotes some pleasantries of Garrick upon the subject, but no credence can be placed upon them. His explanation, however, is most likely the true one: the rumour was "probably set afloat by some wag for the mere jest of the thing." There is no doubt that Arthur Murphy's friends went about saying that Sheridan had stolen his ideas from the comedy of *Know Your Own Mind*, and it seems to me that some joker invented "the young lady of Thames Street" to cap and ridicule this calumny. No man with a sense of humour could ever have taken this egregious nonsense so seriously as Watkins did. But Murphy at least, as will be seen from his papers in Jesse Foot's *Life of Arthur Murphy*, had quite serious suspicions that Sheridan had ſtolen "some of his beſt thoughts" from *Know Your Own Mind*.[1]

George Daniel in his Preface to this comedy (1826) found the resemblance singular. "The charaƈters of Malvil and Joseph Surface are exaƈtly similar as regards their love of sentiment, their betrayal of friendship and their hypocritical slanders: and many of Bygrove's severe remarks upon Dashwood's passion for detraƈtion and caricature are very like Sir Peter's replies to the Scandalous College." Hazlitt in his *Leƈtures on the Comic Writers* (1819) had said that "some of the charaƈters in *The School for Scandal* were contained in Murphy's comedy of *Know Your Own Mind*. Yet they were buried in it for want of grouping and relief, like the colours of a well-drawn piƈture sunk in the canvas. Sheridan brought them out and exhibited them in all their glory. If that gem, the charaƈter of Joseph Surface, was Murphy's, the splendid and more valuable setting was Sheridan's. He took Murphy's Malvil from his lurking-place in the closet, and 'dragged the ſtruggling monſter into day' upon the ſtage. That is, he gave intereſt, life, aƈtion, in other words, its dramatic being, to the mere conception and written specimens of a charaƈter." Since *Know Your Own Mind* was performed on February 22nd and *The School for Scandal* on May 8th, of the same year, this is not merely a charge of academic plagiarism; it is an assertion of a direƈt piracy. It is, however, not to be thought that Garrick would have written the Prologue for Sheridan's play and the Epilogue for Murphy's, if such had been the case. Therefore it is quite safe to dismiss the resemblances as coincidences, accidental if curious. They are one more proof that scandal was a theme of the moment: if scandal is to be rebuked, the subſtance of the rebuke muſt be the same, whether the voice that speaks it belongs to Murphy's Bygrove or Sheridan's Sir Peter. Again, the resemblance between Malvil and Joseph Surface is one of type; both Sheridan and Murphy were depiƈting the hypocrite as sentimentaliſt—"Malvil," said *The London Magazine* in its notice of Mur-

---

[1] It may be observed, without developing the argument, that Sir Fretful Plagiary though a caricature of Cumberland, has at least some traits of Arthur Murphy.

phy's comedy, "is a character very common in real life, a man, who possessing the best sentiments, is continually plotting mischief." It is, in short, another reminder that Sheridan was an observer of life, not a thief of other people's plays.

Outside these two counts, the indictment against Sheridan contains many accusations of the crime of "plagiarism." Some of the instances are trivial: Percy Fitzgerald says somewhere that "little Premium" was borrowed from Foote's "little Transfer" in *The Minor*, though between the two moneylenders, the pretended and the actual, there is not the remotest resemblance except their label-names. And this usage is about the commonest device—literary, journalistic, and theatrical—of the period. To make a charge of such a nature is to display either ignorance, or carelessness.

At the first performance *The London Chronicle* described, by a suggestive analogy, Joseph and Charles as the Blifil and Tom Jones of the comedy; since when everybody has been called to give an opinion as to whether Sheridan did or did not plagiarize from Fielding. It is with some reluctance that it is now considered. The charge, in the end, amounts to no more than what Hazlitt said, "Joseph and Charles have a smack of Tom Jones and Blifil in their moral constitution." It would not matter very much if he had derived the germ of his characters from Fielding, yet it is most unlikely that anything of the sort occurred. The harm of a charge of this kind, is, however, that it very stupidly obscures the main issue. As Sheridan's father is reported to have said, by no means graciously, "Talk about the merit of Dick's comedy, there's nothing in it. He had but to dip in his own heart and find there the characters both of Joseph and Charles." *The London Magazine* of the day went farther; it laid down that "Every man under thirty is, indeed, in some measure, a Joseph or a Charles. He either acts up to some rules of prudential conduct, arising from native disposition or dictated by art; or he gives way to his passions; and, throwing off all restraint, stands confessed the gay, generous libertine, or the mere profligate sensualist." Of course, the writer was thinking of the young men of fashion, and that the name of Charles Surface was legion is testified by the *chronique scandaleuse* of the era. Moreover, *The London Magazine* hinted that the portrait might have been sat for by a young Member of Parliament, which, surely, was a suggestion that the model of Charles Surface was no other than Charles Fox. The young politician who owed £100,000 in 1773, and had nine executions in his house in that one year[1] must have contributed more traits to Charles Surface than are to be surmised from the most credulous study of *Tom Jones.*

"The origin of the scandal-scenes" is a theme which has excited the pertinacity of commentators, to the absolute neglect of a more important fact: Sheridan was pointing his satire against one of the greatest vices of the age. It was not merely gossip and slander and tale-bearing that prevailed, but a kind of "new journalism" which had been inaugurated by *The Town and Country Magazine*, founded in 1769, and *The Morning Post* founded in 1772. The magazine had confined its activities to a single monthly article, while every issue of the newspaper was filled with libellous paragraphs.

Sheridan began the first sheaf of jottings for his comedy, with the sentence, "Friendly caution to the newspapers." It survived through many phases of development to appear at last as the first words of *The School for Scandal* in the form "The paragraphs, you say, were all inserted." Although their exact purport is not defined, there can be no doubt that some of these paragraphs concerned "Sir P—— and Lady T——," while others hinted at an intrigue, or perhaps even a marriage, between "Mr. C——s S——ce and Lady Sn——ll." The matter is certainly obscured by the forged letters, but even at a very late stage of the play, in a line now deleted, Snake was intended to be labelled as a journalist—"There's a precious rogue for you: Yet that fellow is a Writer and Critic." Although the newspaper was not particularized, the application to *The Morning Post* is not to be doubted —"besides the general satire, which will hold good as long as the English language is read or understood, the particular application of it to a certain modern daily publication is logically true throughout, and ought to crimson with blushes every cheek

[1]Sichel, *Sheridan*, Vol. I, p. 149.

which has encouraged such a butchery of male and female reputations."[1]

The Town and Country Magazine is, of course, specifically named in the comedy. The chief department of this periodical was a series of "Memoirs" or "Histories" of some prominent man and his latest mistress, or some prominent woman and her latest lover, to which was annexed the "Tête-à-tête," a plate showing their portraits in vignette. The names of the parties were not given at length, but their identities were made obvious by the use of accepted soubriquets, or letters and dashes. There is no doubt that most of these scandalous chronicles were authentic, though not invariably so, for the Snakes and Sneerwells of the day favoured the Editor with their malicious communications; which, however, he professed to investigate before printing.[2] It seems to me that the "peculiar distinction" that Sheridan accorded to this periodical was due to the appearance of a Tête-à-tête-in January, 1777, four months before the performance of his comedy, giving the Memoirs of Malgrida and Thalia. Malgrida, "scholar, orator and politician" was the Earl of Shelburne; Thalia, described as "the wife of Mr. A———n, a musician," was no other than the original Lady Teazle, Mrs. Abington. It was not, however, the account of her latest intrigue which could have moved the lady to indignation, for this was known to all the world:[3] it was the revelation of the common profligacy of her youth, which she was eager to conceal. In any case, there is no doubt that the outline of her strange career and her romantic rise from sordid and profligate surroundings was correctly outlined in this Tête-à-tête. Yet no editor of Sheridan and no biographer

[1] *The London Magazine* for May, 1777.

[2] The Advertisement to this Magazine for January, 1770, said: "With respect to the History of Têtes-à-têtes, an article received with universal applause, we shall only remark, that it was not undertaken to gratify malignity, or to indulge impertinent curiosity, but to hold up a mirror to the *offending* parties by which they might see their own likeness reflected in such a manner, as to force them to renounce the *fashionable vices* of the age; a reformation much more likely to be effected by ridicule than sober reasoning." The *Advertisement*, January, 1771, testifies to "the menaces that have been used on the one hand, and the allurements and bribes which have offered on the other, to suppress the appearance of particular memoirs."

[3] "My lord Sh[elbur]ne, now Marquis of L[andsdow]ne allowed her fifty pounds a week, and gave her an elegant house, the corner of Clarges Street, Piccadilly."—*The Secret History of the Green Room*, (1792).

of Mrs. Abington has chanced upon it. To the charge (made with a "perhaps") againſt *The Town and Country Magazine*, the Editor replied:

"Mr. Sheridan, in his *School for Scandal* has thought proper to honour these Memoirs, with his particular attention: the Editor cannot, therefore, help thanking him in this place, for the peculiar diſtinction he has paid the Têtes-à-têtes in *The Town and Country Magazine*, as his comedy will probably have a very great run, and the author of this department be thereby immortalized upon the ſtage... But as Mr. Sheridan seems to hint that some of our characters, though blended in a Tête-à-tête have never seen each other, we entreat him before he pronounces sentence upon the present, to make use of his own recollection," that is, as to "the Amorous Juſtice and Miss L——n." The actress in the case was Mrs. Lessingham, and the Amorous Juſtice, being described as having altered Dryden's *Aurungzebe* for her benefit, is identified as Sir William Addington. But there is abundant evidence that scandal was a prevailing vice.[1] It was, however, in no sense, the motive of the main action of the play, so far as dramatic intereſt is considered.

It has even been claimed, in all solemnity and not as a piece of ironical impishness, that the fall of the screen in *The School for Scandal* was borrowed from the fall of the curtain in Moll Segrim's garret in *Tom Jones*. With the mention of that gem of ineptitude, one may dwell for a moment upon this scene, the moſt hackneyed yet ſtill the beſt, in the comedy. It is, in itself, detached from the play, the fineſt one-act play in the English language. The playwright, Reynolds, tells how, when a boy at Weſtminſter School, "on the firſt night of *The School for Scandal*, returning from Lincoln's Inn, about nine o'clock, from Vinegar Yard to Brydges Street," he heard such a tremendous noise over his head, that fearing the theatre was about to fall, he ran for his life. But next morning he learned that the noise was not that of the falling of the house but of "the prolonged, violent and tumultuous ap-plause" at the falling of the screen. The echoes are lingering ſtill.

[1] *E.g.*, an article on "Scandal, the fashion and propensity of these times," *The London Magazine*, for May, 1775.

Gifford, who had no glimmer of dramatic understanding, condemned the device as "unworthy of the dignity of comedy." This absurd contention is cited only for the pleasure of quoting Richard Cumberland, whose jealousy of Sheridan's comedy is supposed to have contributed to his appearance under the caricature of Sir Fretful Plagiary.

"I could name one now living, who has made such happy use of his screen in a comedy of the very first merit, that if Aristotle himself had written a whole chapter professedly against *screens*, and Jerry Collier had edited it with notes and illustrations, I would not have placed Lady Teazle out of ear-shot to have saved their ears from the pillory: but if either of these worthies could have pointed out an expedient to have got Joseph Surface off the stage, pending that scene, with any reasonable conformity to nature, they would have done more good to the drama than either of them have done harm; and that is saying a great deal."[1]

A glimpse of the "first night" is given in a letter of May 12th, 1777:

"Mr. Garrick's best wishes and compliments to Mr. Sheridan. How is the Saint[2] to-day? A gentleman who is as mad as myself about ye School remark'd, that the characters upon the stage at ye falling of the screen stand too long before they speak; —I thought so too ye first night:—he said it was the same on ye 2nd, and was remark'd by others;—tho' they should be astonish'd, and a little petrify'd, yet it may be carry'd to too great a length.—All praise at Lord Lucan's last night."

According to Arthur Murphy's *Life of David Garrick*, the old manager "read the play with close attention, and spoke of it in all companies with the highest approbation. He attended all the rehearsals and was never known, on any former occasion, to be more anxious for a favourite piece."

The School for Scandal was so well acted that its performance became a legend. "No piece," said Charles Lamb, long afterwards, "was ever so completely cast as this Manager's Comedy."

[1] *Memoirs of Richard Cumberland, Written by Himself* (1807), Vol. I. p. 303.
[2] The Saint was Mrs. Sheridan, Sir Joshua Reynolds's model for Saint Cecilia.

The phrase has a special meaning, for it was said at the time that for no other author than the manager would Dodd have played Backbite or Parsons played Crabtree. All "the strength of the company" was employed. As Walpole wrote to Jephson, two months after the first performance:

"To my great astonishment there were more parts performed admirably in *The School for Scandal*, than I almost ever saw in any play. Mrs. Abington was equal to the first of her profession, Yates (the husband), Parsons, Miss Pope, and Palmer, all shone. It seemed a marvellous resurrection of the stage."

The praise, however, was not everywhere so unqualified. Mrs. Abington and Smith, as Lady Teazle and Charles Surface, were the lady of quality and the man of fashion—she smart and vivacious, he easy and elegant, and both wanting nothing "but the fire and glow of youth." King was "admirable" as Peter. And so on. But "Mr. Parson's Crabtree was a horrid piece of playing. This favourite of the town should not abuse its indulgence, nor caricature everything, because some of his real caricatures have succeeded. We will venture to say that such hideous contortions of countenance, such horrid looks, upon so slight a provocation, were never exhibited at old Drury since it was built. He seemed to have copied his expressions of countenance from the *dramatis personæ* in the Dance of Furies in *The Christmas Tale*." Thus *The London Magazine*, and there is a convincing ring in the censure. Miss Hopkins, who played Maria instead of Mrs. Robinson, for whom Sheridan intended the part, was "not very striking": it is said that the author excused himself for not writing a love-scene for Maria and Charles because neither of them excelled in this style. One would rather believe that he did not write it because such a scene would have been out of keeping with the comedy of manners as exhibited by their characters, for they are no Mirabel and Millamant.

But James Boaden's testimony in *The Memoirs of Mrs. Siddons* represents the considered opinion:

"As Sheridan had built himself upon Congreve as to dialogue, so it was quite clear, that while composing, he meditated deeply how his thoughts were to be uttered, and his company fortunately possessed every variety of elocution. I think his comedy was better *spoken*, in all its parts, than any play that I have witnessed upon the ftage. And I can safely add that, as to the acting of it, every change, to the present hour, has been a sensible diminution of the original effect. The lingered sentiment of Palmer—the jovial smartness of Smith—the cauftic shyness of King—the brilliant loquacity of Abington—however congenial to the play, have long been silent. But as our ancient monafteries, at the revival of letters, when they obtained some fair and perfect manuscript of a great work, allowed surrounding foundations the advantage of a copy, and this copy again, in its turn, became an original to others; so the firft actors of *The School for Scandal* were imitated throughout the country, and some portion of *their* excellence, by frequent transmission, muft reach a diftant age."

The tradition, however, has not been preserved in this "diftant age."

Sheridan never authorized any edition of *The School for Scandal*, and the numerous early issues, with one exception, follow an excessively corrupt text. The one exception is a Dublin edition of 1799, which was printed from the prompt-book of the Theatre Royal, Dublin, where it was acted in January, 1778. It was derived from the copy presented by Sheridan to his sifter, Mrs. Lefanu. But Sheridan had previously corrected another MS. copy of *The School for Scandal*, which he sent with the poem called *A Portrait* to the beautiful Mrs. Crewe. It was in her hands in Auguft, 1777. Moore, who had cuftody of the Crewe MS. for a time, collated it carefully with a copy of the 1779 Edition. This, with the assiftance of Mr. W. J. Lawrence, I discovered in the Library of the Royal Irish Academy in Dublin. Moore's collation, however, was for his private information, not as a preparation to edit a classical text;—he ignored—no doubt as obvious—a number of misprints, verbal transpositions, and the like. Moreover, both copies omitted, for one reason or other, certain sentences which were (without doubt) spoken on the firft night at Drury Lane, and for fifty years afterwards. Accordingly, to the best of my judgment I restored the sentences accidentally omitted, and corrected the misprints, and gave my collation to Mr. Iolo A. Williams, who printed it in his edition of *Sheridan's Plays* (1926). The authority for these emendations was, without exception; the received text of the *Oxford Edition*[1]—which means, in fact, John Murray's edition of 1823, a reprint of the text in the *Collected Works* of 1821, for which Moore wrote a preface. It was natural to assume (i) that this had Moore's sanction, (ii) that it was transcribed from, or collated with, the Drury Lane prompt-book. But a subsequent deduction that John Cumberland's edition of 1826 was taken from that prompt-book, and the recognition that Moore had no responsibility whatever for any printed text, made a new collation imperative. Moreover, Moore assumed that the Crewe MS. belonged to (say) 1797, whereas in fact it belonged to 1777. Accordingly the late draft as printed by Fraser Rae, when corroborated by the Edition of 1826 took a new value in the detection of misprints, and the authority of the received text receded—it appears, in fact, to have been based upon the inaccurate prompt-book of Covent Garden—or the Haymarket. Lastly, the spurious Dublin Edition of 1781, though devoid of independent authority, had its corroborative value in many instances as to the use of phrases and sentences. Accordingly, on the basis of the Crewe text, as thus newly collated. I have endeavoured to recover the full and genuine text as it was spoken at Drury Lane on the first night, under the direction of Richard Brinsley Sheridan.

[1] Two excellent articles on " The Text of *The School for Scandal* " by Mr. M. J. Ryan, appeared in *The Times Literary Supplement* for March 22 & 29, 1928. It was not possible to deal with them in this edition, but they showed that my former reliance upon certain readings of the Oxford text was unjustified.

A Note on the Collations

The collation has been undertaken to justify or amend the Crewe MS. as transmitted by Moore. Where there have been reasonable doubts as to its correctness or completeness, the evidence for and against is given from other texts, but the collations are not exhaustive, and do not attempt to record the variations from the "received text" except in such cases as I previously accepted its authority as superior to that of the Moore transcript.

AUTHORITIES

CREWE. *Moore's alterations on a copy of the* 1799 *Edition, in accordance with the MS. given by Sheridan to Mrs. Crewe in the summer of* 1777. *The basic text.*

RAE. *Sheridan's late draft (circa* 1776-7*) as printed in* Sheridan's Plays as He Wrote Them (1902), *edited by Fraser Rae.*

> *The earliest authority for* 98 *verbal corrections mainly supported by the Edition of* 1826.

1799. Dublin: *"Taken from a Correct Copy," as acted at the Theatre Royal, Dublin, where it was first acted in* 1778 *from a MS. given by Sheridan to his sister Mrs. Lefanu.*

> *Many of the present emendations are of misprints ignored (perhaps as obvious) by Moore in his collation on his copy.*

1823. John Murray's *separate Edition, reprinting the text given in the Collected Works of* 1821, *and based (apparently) upon an inaccurate transcript used as the prompt-book at Covent Garden.*

> *The accepted text, as in the* Oxford Edition *for over a century, but quite unreliable. No single reading from it is here accepted without corroborative evidence.*

1826. John Cumberland's *Edition, "taken from the acting copy," no doubt of Drury Lane, Edited by George Daniell.*

> *An accurate and authoritative text, agreeing with this Edition, except for two passages then omitted as no longer intelligible—(on the Annuity Bill and on ladies' head dresses) and other small discrepancies.*
> *The chief corroboration of Rae, and the primary authority, with other evidence, for* 31 *corrections chiefly in passages where Rae had no MS. (Act III, scene iii and Act IV, scene i).*

1781. The Dublin Edition (*apparently a reprint from* 1780) *probably vamped from memory by an actor who had played under Sheridan's direction at Bath in* 1777. *While devoid of independent authority, it has a corroborative value, but the correspondences are not always literal.*

[Readings placed in brackets are those of the "received text" (i.e. 1823) formerly acepted by me but now rejected on the authority of the Crewe MS. when corroborated—unless otherwise stated—by either or both Rae and 1826.] *Om*—omitted, *Em*—Emendation.

Dramatis Personae[1]

As Acted at Drury Lane Theatre, May, 1777

SIR PETER TEAZLE	*Mr. King*
SIR OLIVER SURFACE	*Mr. Yates*
JOSEPH SURFACE	*Mr. Palmer*
CHARLES SURFACE	*Mr. Smith*
CRABTREE	*Mr. Parsons*
SIR BENJAMIN BACKBITE	*Mr. Dodd*
ROWLEY	*Mr. Aickin*
MOSES	*Mr. Baddeley*
TRIP	*Mr. LaMash*
SNAKE	*Mr. Packer*
CARELESS	*Mr. Farren*
SIR TOBY BUMPER[2]	*Mr. Gaudry*
LADY TEAZLE	*Mrs. Abington*
MARIA	*Miss P. Hopkins*
LADY SNEERWELL	*Miss Sherry*
MRS. CANDOUR	*Miss Pope*

[1]From *The Town and Country Magazine* for May, 1777.
[2]This character was not named on the early play bills.

21

Prologue[1]

Written by Mr. GARRICK

Spoken by Mr. KING

A SCHOOL for Scandal! Tell me, I beseech you,
Needs there a school—this modish art to teach you?
No need of lessons now;—the knowing think—
We might as well be taught to eat and drink;
Caus'd by a dearth of scandal, should the vapours
Distress our fair ones—let 'em read the papers;
Their powerful mixtures such disorders hit;
Crave what you will— there's *quantum sufficit.*
"Lord!" cries my Lady *Wormwood* (who loves tattle,
And puts much salt and pepper in her prattle),
Just ris'n at noon, all night at cards, when threshing
Strong tea and scandal—"Bless me, how refreshing!
"Give me the papers, *Lisp*—how bold and free! [*sips*]
"Last night Lord L. [*sips*] was caught with Lady D.
"For aching heads what charming *sal volatile!* [*sips*]
"If Mrs. B. will still continue flirting,
"We hope she'll *draw*, or we'll *undraw* the curtain.
"Fine satire, poz—in public all abuse it,
"But, by ourselves, [*sips*] our praise we can't refuse it.
"Now, *Lisp*, read you—there, at that dash and star."
"Yes, ma'am—A certain Lord had best beware,
"Who lives not twenty miles from Grosv'nor Square;
"For should he Lady W.—find willing,—
"*Wormwood* is bitter"—"Oh! that's me, the villain!
"Throw it behind the fire, and never more
'Let that vile paper *come within my door.*"

[1]Text from *The Town and Country Magazine* for June, 1777.

23

Thus at our friends we laugh, who feel the dart;
To reach *our* feelings, we ourselves muſt smart.
Is our young bard so young—to think that he
Can ſtop the full spring-tide of calumny?
Knows he the world so little, and its trade?
Alas! the devil's sooner *rais'd* than *laid*.
So ſtrong, so swift, the monſter there's no gagging:
Cut Scandal's head off, ſtill the tongue is wagging.
Proud of your smiles once lavishly beſtow'd,
Again our young Don Quixote takes the road;
To show his gratitude he draws his pen,
And seeks this Hydra, Scandal, in his den,
[From his fell gripe the frighted fair to save—
Tho' he should fall th' attempt muſt please the brave.][1]
For your applause all perils he would through—
He'll fight—that's write—a cavaliero true,
Till every drop of blood—that's ink—is spilt for you.

[1] *Om.*—1823: 1826

Act the First

SCENE I

LADY SNEERWELL'S *House*

LADY SNEERWELL *at the dressing-table*; MR. SNAKE *drinking chocolate.*

Lady Sneer. THE paragraphs, you say, Mr. Snake, were all inserted?

Snake. They were, madam; and as I copied them myself in a feigned hand, there can be no suspicion whence they came.

Lady Sneer. Did you circulate the report of Lady Brittle's intrigue with Captain Boastall?

Snake. That's in as fine a train as your ladyship could wish. In the common course of things, I think it must reach Mrs. Clackit's ears within four and twenty hours; and then, you know, the business is as good as done.

Lady Sneer. Why, truly, Mrs. Clackit has a very pretty talent, and a great deal of industry.

Snake. True, madam, and has been tolerably successful in her day. To my knowledge she has been the cause of six matches being broken off, and three sons disinherited; of four forced elopements, and as many close confinements; nine separate maintenances, and two divorces. Nay, I have more than once traced her causing a *tête-à-tête* in the *Town and Country Magazine,* when the parties, perhaps, had never seen each other's face before in the course of their lives.

Lady Sneer. She certainly has talents, but her manner is gross.

Snake. 'Tis very true.—She generally designs well, has a free tongue and a bold invention; but her colouring is too dark, and her outlines often extravagant. She wants that delicacy of tint, and mellowness of sneer, which diſtinguishes your ladyship's scandal.

Lady Sneer. You are partial, Snake.

Snake. Not in the leaſt—everybody allows that Lady Sneerwell can do more with a word or a look, than many can with the moſt laboured detail, even when they happen to have a little truth on their side to support it.

Lady Sneer. Yes, my dear Snake; and I am no hypocrite to deny the satisfaction I reap from the success of my efforts. Wounded myself in the early part of my life by the envenomed tongue of slander, I confess I have since known no pleasure equal to the reducing others to the level of my own injured reputation.

Snake. Nothing can be more natural. But, Lady Sneerwell, there is one affair in which you have lately employed me, wherein, I confess, I am at a loss to guess your motives.

Lady Sneer. I conceive you mean with respect to my neighbour, Sir Peter Teazle, and his family?

Snake. I do. Here are two young men, to whom Sir Peter has acted as a kind of guardian since their father's death; the eldeſt possessing the moſt amiable character, and universally well spoken of; the youngeſt, the moſt dissipated and extravagant young fellow in the kingdom, without friends or character: the former an avowed admirer of your ladyship's, and apparently your favourite; the latter attached to Maria, Sir Peter's ward, and confessedly beloved by her. Now, on the face of these circumſtances, it is utterly unaccountable to me, why you, the widow of a City knight, with a good jointure, should not close with the passion of a man of such character and expectations as Mr. Surface; and more so why you should be so uncommonly earneſt to deſtroy the mutual attachment subsiſting[1] between his brother Charles and Maria.

Lady Sneer. Then at once to unravel this myſtery, I muſt inform you, that love has no share whatever in the intercourse between Mr. Surface and me.

[1]attachment—1799. *Em.*—Crewe: Rae.

Snake. No!

Lady Sneer. His real attachment is to Maria, or her fortune; but finding in his brother a favoured rival, he has been obliged to mask his pretensions, and profit by my assistance.

Snake. Yet still I am more puzzled why you should interest yourself in his success.

Lady Sneer. How dull you are! Cannot you surmise the weakness which I hitherto, through shame, have concealed even from you? Must I confess, that Charles, that libertine, that extravagant, that bankrupt in fortune and reputation, that he it is for whom I'm thus anxious and malicious, and to gain whom I would sacrifice everything?

Snake. Now, indeed, your conduct appears consistent: but how came you and Mr. Surface so confidential?

Lady Sneer. For our mutual interest. I have found him out a long time since. I know him to be artful, selfish, and malicious—in short, a sentimental knave [while with Sir Peter, and indeed with all his acquaintance, he passes for a miracle of prudence, good sense, and benevolence.][1]

Snake. Yes; yet Sir Peter vows he has not his equal in England—and above all, he praises him as a man of sentiment.

Lady Sneer. True—and with the assistance of his sentiment and hypocrisy, he has brought Sir Peter entirely into his interest with regard to Maria [while poor Charles has no friend in the house, though, I fear, he has a powerful one in Maria's heart, against whom we must direct our schemes.][2]

Enter SERVANT.

Servant. Mr. Surface.

Lady Sneer. Show him up. [*Exit* SERVANT.] [He generally calls about this time. I don't wonder at people giving him to me for a lover.][3]

Enter JOSEPH SURFACE.

Joseph S. My dear Lady Sneerwell, how do you do to-day? Mr. Snake, your most obedient.

[1]*Om.*—Crewe. *Em.*—1799; Rae: (1781).   [2]*Om.*—Crewe. *Em.*—1799: Rae: (1781).
[3]*Om.*—Crewe: 1823. *Em.*—Rae: 1826: (1781).

Lady Sneer. Snake has juſt been rallying[1] me on our mutual attachment; but I have informed him of our real views. You know how useful he has been to us, and, believe me, the confidence is not ill placed.

Joseph S. Madam, it is impossible for me to suspeᴄt a man of Mr. Snake's sensibility and discernment.

Lady Sneer. Well, well, no compliments now; but tell me when you saw your miſtress, Maria—or, what is more material to me, your brother.

Joseph S. I have not seen either since I left you; but I can inform you that they never meet. Some of your ſtories have taken a good effeᴄt on Maria.

Lady Sneer. Ah! my dear Snake! the merit of this belongs to you: but do your brother's diſtresses increase?

Joseph S. Every hour. I am told he has had another execution in the house yeſterday. In short, his dissipation and extravagance exceed anything I have ever heard of.

Lady Sneer. Poor Charles!

Joseph S. True, madam; notwithſtanding his vices, one cannot help feeling for him. Aye, Poor Charles, indeed! I'm sure I wish it were in my power to be of any essential service to him; for the man who does not share in the diſtresses of a brother, even though merited by his own misconduᴄt, deserves——

Lady Sneer. O Lud! you are going to be moral, and forget that you are among friends.

Joseph S. Egad, that's true!—I'll keep that sentiment till I see Sir Peter;—however, it is certainly a charity to rescue Maria from such a libertine, who, if he is to be reclaimed, can be so only by a person of[2] your ladyship's superior accomplishments and underſtanding.

Snake. I believe, Lady Sneerwell, here's company coming: I'll go and copy the letter I mentioned to you.—Mr. Surface, your moſt obedient.   [*Exit* SNAKE.

Joseph S. Sir, your very devoted.—Lady Sneerwell, I am very sorry you have put any farther confidence in that fellow.

Lady Sneer. Why so?

---

[1]arraigning—Rae. *Em.* Crewe: 1823: (1781)   [2]one of—1799:—Crewe: Rae: 1826

Joseph S. I have lately detected him in frequent conference with old Rowley, who was formerly my father's steward, and has never, you know, been a friend of mine.

Lady Sneer. And do you think he would betray us?

Joseph S. Nothing more likely:—take my word for't, Lady Sneerwell, that fellow hasn't virtue enough to be faithful even to his own villainy.——Ah! Maria!

Enter MARIA.

Lady Sneer. Maria, my dear, how do you do?—What's the matter?

Maria. O there's that disagreeable lover of mine, Sir Benjamin Backbite, has just called at my guardian's, with his odious uncle, Crabtree; so I slipt out, and ran hither to avoid them.

Lady Sneer. Is that all?

Joseph S. If my brother Charles had been of the party, madam, perhaps you would have not been so much alarmed.

Lady Sneer. Nay, now you are severe; for I dare swear the truth of the matter is, Maria heard *you* were here.—But, my dear, what has Sir Benjamin done, that you would avoid him?[1]

Maria. O, he has done nothing—but 'tis for what he has said: His conversation is a perpetual libel on all his acquaintance.

Joseph S. Aye, and the worst of it is, there is no advantage in not knowing him—for he'll abuse a stranger just as soon as his best friend; and his uncle is as bad.

Lady Sneer. Nay, but we should make allowance—Sir Benjamin is a wit and a poet.

Maria. For my part, I confess, madam, wit loses its respect with me, when I see it in company with malice.—What do you think, Mr. Surface?

Joseph S. Certainly, madam; to smile at the jest which plants a thorn in another's breast is to become a principal in the mischief.

Lady Sneer. Pshaw!—there's no possibility of being witty without a little ill nature: the malice of a good thing is the barb that makes it stick.—What's your opinion, Mr. Surface?

Joseph S. To be sure, madam; that conversation, where the spirit of raillery is suppressed, will ever appear tedious and insipid.

[1]him so?—1799: Rae: 1826: (1781). *Em.*—Crewe.

Maria. Well, I'll not debate how far scandal may be allowable; but in a man, I am sure, it is always contemptible. We have pride, envy, rivalship, and a thousand little motives to depreciate each other; but the male slanderer muſt have the cowardice of a woman before he can traduce one.

Enter SERVANT.

Servant. Madam, Mrs. Candour is below, and if your lady-ship's at leisure, will leave her carriage.

Lady Sneer. Beg her to walk in.—[*Exit* SERVANT.]—Now, Maria, here is a charaćter to your taſte; for though Mrs. Candour is a little talkative, everybody allows her to be the beſt natured and beſt sort of woman.

Maria. Yet[1] with a very gross affećtation of good nature and benevolence, she does more mischief than the direćt malice of old Crabtree.

Joseph S. I'faith 'tis true, Lady Sneerwell: whenever I hear the current running againſt the charaćters of my friends, I never think them in such danger as when Candour undertakes their defence.

Lady Sneer. Hush!—here she is!——

Enter MRS. CANDOUR.

Mrs. Can. My dear Lady Sneerwell, how have you been this century?—Mr. Surface, what news do you hear?—though indeed it is no matter, for I think one hears nothing else but scandal.

Joseph S. Juſt so, indeed, madam.

Mrs. Can. Ah! Maria, child,—what, is[2] the whole affair off between you and Charles?—His extravagance, I presume—the town talks of nothing else.

Maria. I am very sorry, ma'am, the town has[3] so little to do.[4]

Mrs. Can. True, true, child: but there's no ſtopping people's tongues. I own I was hurt to hear it, as I indeed was to learn, from the same quarter, that your guardian, Sir Peter, and Lady Teazle have not agreed lately as well as could be wished.

---

[1]Yes—Rae: 1823: 1826: (1781). *Em.*—Crewe.   [2]child,—is—1799. *Em.*—Crewe: Rae: 1826.   [3]have—1799. *Em.*—Crewe: Rae: 1826.   [4]town is not better employed—1823: (1781).

Maria. 'Tis strangely impertinent for people to busy themselves so.

Mrs. Can. Very true, child:—but what's to be done? People will talk—there's no preventing it. Why, it was but yesterday I was told that Miss Gadabout had eloped with Sir Filigree Flirt. —But, Lord! there is no minding what one hears; though, to be sure, I had this from very good authority.

Maria. Such reports are highly scandalous.

Mrs. Can. So they are, child—shameful! shameful! But the world is so censorious, no character escapes.—Lord now! who would have suspected your friend, Miss Prim, of an indiscretion? Yet such is the ill-nature of people, that they say her uncle stopt her last week, just as she was stepping into the York diligence with her dancing-master.

Maria. I'll answer for't there are no grounds for the report.

Mrs. Can. O, no foundation in the world, I dare swear; no more, probably, than for the story circulated last month, of Mrs. Festino's affair with Colonel Cassino;—though, to be sure, that matter was never rightly cleared up.

Joseph S. The licence of invention some people take is monstrous indeed.

Maria. 'Tis so—but, in my opinion, those who report such things are equally culpable.

Mrs. Can. To be sure they are; tale-bearers are as bad as the tale-makers—'tis an old observation, and a very true one: but what's to be done, as I said before? how will you prevent people from talking? To-day, Mrs. Clackit assured me, Mr. and Mrs. Honeymoon were at last become mere man and wife, like the rest of their acquaintance. She likewise hinted that a certain widow, in the next street, had got rid of her dropsy and recovered her shape in a most surprising manner. And at the same time, Miss Tattle, who was by, affirmed, that Lord Buffalo had discovered his lady at a house of no extraordinary fame; and that Sir Harry Boquet and Tom Saunter were to measure swords on a similar provocation.—But, Lord, do you think I would report these things?—No, no! tale-bearers, as I said before, are just as bad as the tale-makers.

Joseph S. Ah! Mrs. Candour, if everybody had your forbearance and good-nature!——

Mrs. Can. I confess, Mr. Surface, I cannot bear to hear people attacked behind their backs; and when ugly circumstances come out against our acquaintance, I own I always love to think the best.—By-the-by, I hope 'tis not true that your brother is absolutely ruined.

Joseph S. I am afraid his circumstances are very bad indeed, madam.

Mrs. Can. Ah! I heard so—but you must tell him to keep up his spirits; everybody almost is in the same way—Lord Spindle,[1] Sir Thomas Splint, Captain Quinze, and Mr. Nickit—all up, I hear, within this week; so if Charles is undone, he'll find half his acquaintance ruined too, and that, you know, is a consolation.

Joseph S. Doubtless, ma'am—a very great one.

Enter SERVANT.

Servant. Mr. Crabtree and Sir Benjamin Backbite.

[*Exit* SERVANT.

Lady Sneer. So, Maria, you see your lover pursues you; positively you shan't escape.

Enter CRABTREE *and* SIR BENJAMIN BACKBITE.

Crabtree. Lady Sneerwell, I kiss your hand—Mrs. Candour, I don't believe you are acquainted with my nephew, Sir Benjamin Backbite? Egad! ma'am, he has a pretty wit, and is a pretty poet too; isn't he, Lady Sneerwell?

Sir Benj. B. Oh, fie, uncle!

Crabtree. Nay, egad, it's true; I back him at a rebus or a charade against the best rhymer in the kingdom.—Has your ladyship heard the epigram he wrote last week on Lady Frizzle's feather catching fire?—Do, Benjamin, repeat it, or the charade you made last night extempore at Mrs. Drowzie's conversazione. Come now;—your first is the name of a fish, your second a great naval commander, and——

[1]Spirits—Lord Spindle—1799. Em.—Crewe: Rae: 1826

Sir Benj. B. Uncle, now—prythee——

Crabtree. I'faith, ma'am, 'twould surprise you to hear how ready he is at all these things.

Lady Sneer. I wonder, Sir Benjamin, you never publish anything.

Sir Benj. B. To say truth, ma'am, 'tis very vulgar to print; and as my little productions are mostly satires and lampoons on particular people, I find they circulate more by giving copies in confidence to the friends of the parties. However, I have some love elegies, which, when favoured with this lady's smiles, I mean to give the public.

Crabtree. 'Fore Heaven, ma'am, they'll immortalize you!—you will be handed down to posterity, like Petrarch's Laura, or Waller's Sacharissa.

Sir Benj. B. Yes, madam, I think you will like them, when you shall see them on a beautiful quarto page, where a neat rivulet of text shall murmur[1] through a meadow of margin. 'Foregad, they will be the most elegant things of their kind!

Crabtree. But, ladies, that's true—have you heard the news?

Mrs. Can. What, sir, do you mean the report of——

Crabtree. No, ma'am, that's not it—Miss Nicely is going to be married to her own footman.

Mrs. Can. Impossible!

Crabtree. Ask Sir Benjamin.

Sir Benj. B. 'Tis true very, ma'am; everything is fixed, and the wedding liveries bespoke.

Crabtree. Yes—and they do say there were pressing reasons for it.

Lady Sneer. Why, I have heard something of this before.

Mrs. Can. It can't be—and I wonder any one should believe such a story, of so prudent a lady as Miss Nicely.

Sir Benj. B. O Lud! ma'am, that's the very reason 'twas believed at once. She has always been so cautious and so reserved, that everybody was sure there was some reason for it at bottom.

Mrs. Can. Why, to be sure, a tale of scandal is as fatal to the credit of a prudent lady of her stamp, as a fever is generally to

[1][meander—Rae]. *Em.*—Crewe: 1826: (1781).

II. D

those of the strongest constitutions. But there is a sort of puny sickly reputation, that is always ailing, yet will outlive the robuster characters of a hundred prudes.

Sir Benj. B. True, madam,—there are valetudinarians in reputation as well as constitution; who, being conscious of their weak part, avoid the least breath of air, and supply their want of stamina by care and circumspection.

Mrs. Can. Well, but this may be all a mistake. You know, Sir Benjamin, very[1] trifling circumstances often give rise to the most injurious tales.

Crabtree. That they do, I'll be sworn, ma'am.—Did you ever hear how Miss Piper came to lose her lover and her character last summer at Tunbridge?—Sir Benjamin, you remember it?

Sir Benj. B. Oh, to be sure!—the most whimsical circumstance.

Lady Sneer. How was it, pray?

Crabtree. Why, one evening, at Mrs. Ponto's assembly, the conversation happened to turn on the difficulty of breeding Nova[1] Scotia sheep in this country. Says a young lady[2] in company, I have known instances of it—for Miss Letitia Piper, a first cousin of mine, had a Nova Scotia sheep that produced her twins.—What! cries the Lady Dowager Dundizzy (who you know is as deaf as a post), has Miss Piper had twins?—This mistake, as you may imagine, threw the whole company into a fit of laughing. However, 'twas the next day everywhere reported, and in a few days believed by the whole town, that Miss Letitia Piper had actually been brought to bed of a fine boy and a girl; and in less than a week there were some people who could name the father, and the farm-house where the babies were put out to[3] nurse.

Lady Sneer. Strange, indeed!

Crabtree. Matter of fact, I assure you.—O Lud! Mr. Surface, pray is it true that your uncle, Sir Oliver, is coming home?

Joseph S. Not that I know of, indeed, sir.

Crabtree. He has been in the East Indies a long time. You can scarcely remember him, I believe—Sad comfort whenever he returns, to hear how your brother has gone on!

[1][on the breeding Nova—1826].   [2][a lady].   [3][put to—1826].

Joseph S. Charles has been imprudent, sir, to be sure; but I hope no busy people have already prejudiced Sir Oliver againſt him—he may reform.

Sir Benj. B. To be sure he may: for my part, I never believed him to be so utterly void of principle as people say; and though he has loſt all his friends, I am told nobody is better spoken of by the Jews.

Crabtree. That's true, egad, nephew. If the Old Jewry was a ward, I believe Charles would be an alderman:—no man more popular there, 'foregad! I hear he pays as many annuities as the Irish tontine; and that whenever he is sick, they have prayers for the recovery of his health in all the synagogues.

Sir Benj. B. Yet no man lives in greater splendour. They tell me, when he entertains his friends he will[1] sit down to dinner with a dozen of his own securities; have a score of tradesmen waiting in[2] the antechamber, and an officer behind every gueſt's chair.

Joseph S. This may be entertainment to you, gentleman, but you pay very little regard to the feelings of a brother.

Maria. Their malice is intolerable.—Lady Sneerwell, I muſt wish you a good morning: I'm not very well.   [*Exit* MARIA.

Mrs. Can. O dear! she changes colour very much.

Lady Sneer. Do, Mrs. Candour, follow her: she may want assiſtance.

Mrs. Can. That I will, with all my soul, ma'am.—Poor dear creature, who knows what her situation may be!   [*Exit.*

Lady Sneer. 'Twas nothing but that she could not bear to hear Charles reflected on, notwithſtanding their difference.

Sir Benj. B. The young lady's *penchant* is obvious.

Crabtree. But, Benjamin, you muſt not give up the pursuit for that:—follow her, and put her into good humour. Repeat her some of your own verses. Come, I'll assiſt you.

Sir Benj. B. Mr. Surface, I did not mean to hurt you; but depend on't your brother is utterly undone.

Crabtree. O Lud, ay! undone as ever mah was. Can't raise a guinea!

Sir Benj. B. Everything sold, I am told, that was movable.

[1]can—Crewe: Rae. *Em.*—1823: 1826. [2]tradesmen in—1799. *Em*—Crewe: Rae: 1826,

Crabtree. I have seen one that was at his house. Not a thing left but some empty bottles that were overlooked, and the family pictures, which I believe are framed in the wainscot——

Sir Benj. B. And I'm very sorry, also, to hear some bad stories against him.   [*Going.*

Crabtree. O! he has done many mean things, that's certain.

Sir Benj. B. But, however, as he's your brother—— [*Going.*

Crabtree. We'll tell you all another opportunity.   [*Exeunt.*

Lady Sneer. Ha! ha! 'tis very hard for them to leave a subject they have not quite run down.

Joseph S. And I believe the[1] abuse was not more acceptable to your ladyship than to Maria.

Lady Sneer. I doubt her affections are farther engaged than we imagine. But the family are to be here this evening, so you may as well dine where you are, and we shall have an opportunity of observing farther; in the meantime, I'll go and plot mischief, and you shall study sentiment.   [*Exeunt.*

SCENE II

Sir Peter Teazle's *house.*

Enter Sir Peter.

Sir Peter T. When an old bachelor marries[2] a young wife, what is he to expect? 'Tis now six months since Lady Teazle made me the happiest of men—and I have been the most miserable[3] dog ever since that ever committed wedlock![4] We tift a little going to church, and came to a quarrel[5] before the bells had[6] done ringing. I was more than once nearly choked[7] with gall during the honeymoon, and had lost all comfort in life before my friends had done wishing me joy. Yet I chose with caution—a girl bred wholly in the country, who never knew luxury beyond one silk gown, nor dissipation beyond the annual gala of a race ball. Yet now she plays her part in all the extravagant fopperies of the

---

[1]their—1799. *Em.*—Crewe: Rae: 1826.   [2]takes—Crewe: Rae: *Em.*—1826: (1781).
[3]miserablest—Crewe. *Em.*—Rae: 1826: (1781).   [3]ever since. We—1799: 1826: (1781).
Em.—Crewe: Rae.   [5][fairly quarrelled—(1781).]   [6]were—Crewe. *Em.*—Rae:
(1826).   [7]once choked—Crewe. *Em.*—Rae: 1826: (1781).

fashion and the town, with as ready a grace as if she had never seen a bush or a grass-plot out of Grosvenor Square! I am sneered at by all my acquaintance, and paragraphed in the newspapers. She dissipates my fortune, and contradicts all my humours; yet, the worst of it is, I doubt I love her, or I should never bear all this. However, I'll never be weak enough to own it.

Enter ROWLEY.

Rowley. O Sir Peter, your servant: how is it with you, sir?

Sir Peter T. Very bad, Master Rowley, very bad. I meet with nothing but crosses and vexations.

Rowley. What can have happened to trouble you since yesterday?

Sir Peter T. A good question to a married man!

Rowley. Nay, I'm sure Sir Peter,[1] your lady can't be the cause of your uneasiness.

Sir Peter T. Why, has anyone told you she was dead?

Rowley. Come, come, Sir Peter, you love her, notwithstanding your tempers don't exactly agree.

Sir Peter T. But the fault is entirely hers, Master Rowley. I am, myself, the sweetest-tempered man alive, and hate a teasing temper; and so I tell her a hundred times a day.

Rowley. Indeed!

Sir Peter T. Aye; and what is very extraordinary, in all our disputes she is always in the wrong! But Lady Sneerwell, and the set she meets at her house, encourage the perverseness of her disposition.—Then, to complete my vexation, Maria, my ward, whom I ought to have the power of a father over,[2] is determined to turn rebel too, and absolutely refuses the man whom I have long resolved on for her husband; meaning, I suppose, to bestow herself on his profligate brother.

Rowley. You know, Sir Peter, I have always taken the liberty to differ with you on the subject of these two young gentlemen. I only wish you may not be deceived in your opinion of the elder. For Charles, my life on't! he will retrieve his errors yet. Their worthy father, once my honoured master, was at his years, nearly

---

[1][Peter, I'm sure], *Em.*—Crewe: 1826.   [2][power over], *Em.*—Crewe: Rae: 1826.

as wild a spark; yet,[1] when he died, he did not leave a more benevolent heart to lament his loss.

Sir Peter T. You are wrong, Master Rowley. On their father's death, you know, I acted as a kind of guardian to them both till their uncle Sir Oliver's eastern liberality[2] gave them an early independence. Of course, no person could have more opportunities of judging of their hearts, and I was never mistaken in my life. Joseph is indeed a model for the young men of the age. He is a man of sentiment, and acts up to the sentiments he professes, but for the other, take my word for't, if he had any grain of virtue by descent, he has dissipated it with the rest of his inheritance. Ah! my old friend, Sir Oliver, will be deeply mortified when he finds how part of his bounty has been misapplied.

Rowley. I am sorry to find you so violent against the young man, because this may be the most critical period of his fortune. I came hither with news that will surprise you.

Sir Peter T. What! let me hear.

Rowley. Sir Oliver *is* arrived, and at this moment in town.

Sir Peter T. How! you astonish me! I thought you did not expect him this month.

Rowley. I did not; but his passage has been remarkably quick.

Sir Peter T. Egad, I shall rejoice to see my old friend. 'Tis sixteen years since we met.—We have had many a day together: —but does he still enjoin us[3] not to inform his nephews of his arrival?

Rowley. Most strictly. He means, before it is known, to make some trial of their dispositions.

Sir Peter T. Ah! there needs no art to discover their merits— he shall have his way: but, pray, does he know I am married?

Rowley. Yes, and will soon wish you joy.

Sir Peter T. What, as we drink health to a friend in a consumption? Ah! Oliver will laugh at me. We used to rail at matrimony together, and he has been steady to his text.—Well, he must lie[4] at my house, though!—I'll instantly give orders for his

[1]but—1799. *Em.*—Crewe: 1826.   [2][Oliver's liberality], *Em.*—Crewe: 1826: (1781). [3]me—1799. *Em.*—Crewe: Rae: 1826.   [4][be soon at—1823] be at—Crewe: Rae: 1826: lie at—the obvious emendation (Cf. *qu'il logera chez moi*—Delille's trans., 1789).

reception.—But, Master Rowley, don't drop a word that Lady Teazle and I ever disagree.

Rowley. By no means.

Sir Peter T. For I should[1] never be able to stand Noll's jokes; so I'd have him think, Lord forgive me! that we are a very happy couple.

Rowley. I understand you:—but then you must be very careful not to differ while he is in the house with you.

Sir Peter T. Egad, and so we must—and that's impossible. Ah! Master Rowley, when an old bachelor marries a young wife, he deserves—no—the crime carries the[2] punishment along with it.   [*Exeunt.*

---

[1]shall—Crewe. *Em.*—Rae: 1823: 1826.   [2][its—1826]: *Em.*—Crewe: Rae: (1781).

END OF THE FIRST ACT

Act the Second

SCENE I

Sir Peter Teazle's *house*.

Enter Sir Peter *and* Lady Teazle.

Sir Peter
Teazle.
LADY Teazle, Lady Teazle, I'll not bear it!

Lady T. Sir Peter, Sir Peter, you may bear it or not, as you please; but I ought to have my own way in everything, and what's more, I will, too. What! though I was educated in the country, I know very well that women of fashion in London are accountable to nobody after they are married.

Sir Peter T. Very well, ma'am, very well;—so a husband is to have no influence, no authority?

Lady T. Authority! No, to be sure:—if you wanted authority over me, you should have adopted me, and not married me: I am sure you were[1] old enough.

Sir Peter T. Old enough!—aye—there it is. Well, well, Lady Teazle, though my life may be made unhappy by your temper, I'll not be ruined by your extravagance.

Lady T. My extravagance? I'm sure I'm not more extravagant than a woman of fashion ought to be.

Sir Peter T. No, no, madam, you shall throw away no more sums on such unmeaning luxury. 'Slife! to spend as much to furnish your dressing-room with flowers in winter as would suffice to turn the Pantheon into a greenhouse, and give a *fête champêtre* at Christmas.

Lady T. Lord, Sir Peter, am I to blame because flowers are dear in cold weather? You should find fault with the climate, and not with me. For my part, I'm sure, I wish it was spring all the year round, and that roses grew under one's[2] feet!

[1]are—1799. *Em.*—Crewe: Rae: 1826. [2]our—1799: 1823. *Em.*—Crewe: Rae.

Sir Peter T. Oons! madam—if you had been born to this, I shouldn't wonder at your talking thus; but you forget what your situation was when I married you.

Lady T. No, no, I don't; 'twas a very disagreeable one, or I never should[1] have married you.

Sir Peter T. Yes, yes, madam, you were then in somewhat an[2] humbler style:—the daughter of a plain country squire. Recollect, Lady Teazle, when I saw you first,[3] sitting at your tambour, in a pretty figured linen gown, with a bunch of keys by your side; your hair combed smooth[4] over a roll, and your apartment hung round with fruits in worsted, of your own working.

Lady T. Oh, yes! I remember it very well, and a curious life I led! my daily occupation to inspect the dairy, superintend the poultry, make extracts from the family receipt-book; and comb my aunt Deborah's lap-dog.

Sir Peter T. Yes, yes, Madam, 'twas so indeed.

Lady T. And then, you know, my evening amusements! To draw patterns for ruffles, which I had not materials to make up; to play Pope Joan with the curate; to read a sermon to my aunt; or to be stuck down to an old spinet to strum my father to sleep after a fox-chase.

Sir Peter T. I am glad you have so good a memory. Yes, madam, these were the recreations I took you from; but now you must have your coach,—*vis-à-vis*,—and three powdered footmen before your chair; and, in the summer,[5] a pair of white cats to draw you to Kensington Gardens. No recollection, I suppose, when you were content to ride double, behind the butler, or a dock'd coach-horse?

Lady T. No—I swear I never did that: I deny the butler and the coach-horse.

Sir Peter T. This, madam, was your situation; and what have I done for you? I have made you a woman of fashion, of fortune, of rank; in short, I have made you *my wife.*

Lady T. Well, then,— and there is but one thing more you can make me to add to the obligation, and that is——

[1]should never—1799: Rae. *Em.*—Crewe.   [2]then somewhat in—1799. *Em.*—Crewe: 1826.   [3]first saw you—Crewe. *Em.*—Rae: 1826.   [4]smoothly—Crewe. *Em.*—Rae: 1826: (1781).   [5]in summer—Crewe. *Em.*—Rae: 1826.

Sir Peter T. My widow, I suppose?

Lady T. Hem! hem!

Sir Peter T. I thank you, madam—but don't flatter yourself; for though your ill conduct may disturb my peace, it shall never break my heart, I promise you: however, I am equally obliged to you for the hint.

Lady T. Then why will you endeavour to make yourself so disagreeable to me, and thwart me in every little elegant expense?

Sir Peter T. 'Slife, madam, I say, had you any of these little elegant expenses when you married me?

Lady T. Lud, Sir Peter! would you have me be out of the fashion?

Sir Peter T. The fashion, indeed! what had you to do with the fashion when[1] you married me?

Lady T. For my part, I should think you would like to have your wife thought a woman of taste.

Sir Peter T. Aye—there again—taste—Zounds! madam, you had no taste when you married me!

Lady T. That's very true indeed, Sir Peter; and after having married you, I am sure I should[2] never pretend to taste again.[3] But now, Sir Peter, if we have finished our daily jangle, I presume I may go to my engagement at Lady Sneerwell's.

Sir Peter T. Aye, there's another precious circumstance—a charming set of acquaintance you have made there.

Lady T. Nay, Sir Peter, they are all people of rank and fortune, and remarkably tenacious of reputation.

Sir Peter T. Yes, egad, they are tenacious of reputation with a vengeance; for they don't choose anybody should have a character but themselves!—Such a crew! Ah! many a wretch has rid on a hurdle who has done less mischief than these utterers of forged tales, coiners of scandal, and clippers of reputation.

Lady T. What! would you restrain the freedom of speech?

Sir Peter T. Oh! they have made you just as bad as any one of the society.

[1]before—1799: Rae: 1823. *Em.*—Crewe.   [2]you. I should—1799: Rae. *Em.*—Crewe: 1823.   [3]again, I allow.—1799: Rae. *Em.*—Crewe: 1823. [2 and 3—Sheridan's MS. amendments in Crewe copy.]

Lady T. Why, I believe I do bear a part with a tolerable grace. But I vow I bear[1] no malice against the people I abuse. When I say an ill-natured thing, 'tis out of pure good humour; and I take it for granted, they[2] deal exactly in the same manner with me. But, Sir Peter, you know you promised to come to Lady Sneerwell's too.

Sir Peter T. Well, well, I'll call in just to look after my own character.

Lady T. Then indeed you must make haste after me, or you'll be too late. So, good-bye to you.   [*Exit* LADY TEAZLE.

Sir Peter T. Soh!—I have gained much by my intended expostulation: yet, with what a charming air she contradicts everything I say, and how pleasingly she shows her contempt for my authority! Well, though I can't make her love me, there is great satisfaction in quarrelling with her; and I think she never appears to such advantage as when she is doing everything in her power to plague me.   [*Exit.*

SCENE II

LADY SNEERWELL'S *house.*

LADY SNEERWELL, MRS. CANDOUR, CRABTREE, SIR BENJAMIN BACKBITE, *and* JOSEPH SURFACE *discovered, servants attending with tea.*

Lady Sneer. Nay, positively, we will hear[3] it.

Joseph S. Yes, yes, the epigram, by all means.

Sir Benj. B. Oh, plague on't, uncle! 'tis mere nonsense.

Crabtree. No, no; 'foregad, very clever for an extempore!

Sir Benj. B. But, ladies, you should be acquainted with the circumstance. You must know, that one day last week, as Lady Betty Curricle was taking the dust in Hyde Park, in a sort of a duodecimo phaeton, she desired me to write some verses on her ponies; upon which I took out my pocket-book, and in one moment produced the following:

[1]have—Crewe. *Em.*—Rae: 1826.   [2]they'll—Crewe. *Em.*—Rae: 1826.
[3]have—1799. *Em.*—Crewe: Rae: 1826.

Sure never were seen two such beautiful ponies;
Other horses are clowns, but these macaronies:
To give 'em this title I'm sure isn't wrong,
Their legs are so slim, and their tails are so long.

Crabtree. There, ladies, done in the smack of a whip, and on horseback too.

Joseph S. A very Phœbus, mounted—indeed, Sir Benjamin.

Sir Benj. B. O dear sir,—trifles—trifles.

Enter LADY TEAZLE *and* MARIA.

Mrs. Can. I muſt have a copy.

Lady Sneer. Lady Teazle, I hope we shall see Sir Peter?

Lady T. I believe he'll wait on your ladyship presently.

Lady Sneer. Maria, my love,[1] you look grave. Come, you shall sit down to cards[2] with Mr. Surface.

Maria. I take very little pleasure in cards—however, I'll do as your ladyship pleases.

Lady T. I am surprised Mr. Surface should sit down with her; I thought he would have embraced this opportunity of speaking to me, before Sir Peter came.   [*Aside.*

Mrs. Can. Now, I'll die, but you are so scandalous, I'll forswear your society.

Lady T. What's the matter, Mrs. Candour?

Mrs. Can. They'll not allow our friend Miss Vermillion to be handsome.

Lady Sneer. O, surely she's a pretty woman.

Crabtree. I am very glad you think so, madam.

Mrs. Can. She has a charming fresh colour.

Lady T. Yes, when it is fresh put on.

Mrs. Can. O, fie! I'll swear her colour is natural: I have seen it come and go.

Lady T. I dare swear you have, ma'am; it goes off at night, and comes again in the morning.

[*Sir Benj. B.* True, ma'am, it not only comes and goes, but, what's more—egad, her maid can fetch and carry it!][3]

---

[1]dear—1799: 1826. *Em.*—Crewe: Rae.   [2]picquet—1799: Rae: 1826. *Em.*—Crewe.   [3]*Om.*—Crewe: 1799. *Em.*—Rae: 1826: (1781).

Mrs. Can. Ha! ha! ha! how I hate to hear you talk so! But surely now,[1] her sister *is*, or *was*, very handsome.

Crabtree. Who? Mrs. Evergreen? O Lord! she's six and fifty if she's an hour!

Mrs. Can. Now positively you wrong her; fifty-two or fifty-three is the utmost—and I don't think she looks more.

Sir Benj. B. Ah! there's no judging by her looks, unless one could see her face.

Lady Sneer. Well, well, if Mrs. Evergreen *does* take some pains to repair the ravages of time, you must allow she effects it with great ingenuity; and surely that's better than the careless manner in which the widow Ochre caulks[2] her wrinkles.

Sir Benj. B. Nay now, Lady Sneerwell, you are severe upon the widow. Come, come, 'tis not that she[3] paints so ill—but when she has finished her face, she joins it so badly to her neck, that she looks like a mended statue, in which the connoisseur sees at once that the head's modern, though the trunk's antique.

Crabtree. Ha! ha! ha! Well said, nephew!

Mrs. Can. Ha! ha! ha! Well, you make me laugh; but I vow I hate you for it.—What do you think of Miss Simper?

Sir Benj. B. Why, she has very pretty teeth.

Lady T. Yes, and on that account, when she is neither speaking nor laughing (which very seldom happens), she never absolutely shuts her mouth, but leaves it always on a jar, as it were, [thus—   [*Shows her teeth.*][4a]

Mrs. Can. How can you be so ill-natured?

Lady T. Nay, I'll allow even[4] that's better than the pains Mrs. Prim takes to conceal her losses in front. She draws her mouth till it positively resembles the aperture of a poor's box, and all her words appear to slide out edgewise. [As it were thus *How do you do, madam. Yes madam.*][4b]

Lady Sneer. Very well, Lady Teazle; I see you can be a little severe.

Lady T. In defence of a friend it is but justice.—But here comes Sir Peter to spoil our pleasantry.

[1]surely—Crewe. *Em.*—1799: Rae: 1826.   [2]chaulks—Rae: chalks—1823: (1781): *Em.*—Crewe: 1826.   [3]the widow—1799. *Em.*—Crewe: Rae.   [4a], [4b]*Om.*—Crewe: Rae. *Em.*—1823: 1826: (1781).

Enter SIR PETER TEAZLE.

Sir Peter T. Ladies, your moſt obedient.—Mercy on me! here is the whole set! a chara&ter dead at every word, I suppose.
[*Aside.*

Mrs. Can. I am rejoiced you are come, Sir Peter. They have been so censorious—they will allow good qualities to nobody; not even good nature to our friend Mrs. Pursy.

Lady T. What, the fat dowager who was at Mrs. Codrille's[1] laſt night?

Mrs. Can. Nay, her bulk is her misfortune; and when she takes such pains to get rid of it, you ought not to refle&t on her.

Lady Sneer. That's very true, indeed.

Lady T. Yes, I know she almoſt lives on acids and small whey; laces herself by pulleys; and often in the hotteſt noon in summer, you may see her on a little squat pony, with her hair plaited up behind like a drummer's, and puffing round the Ring on a full trot.

Mrs. Can. I thank you, Lady Teazle, for defending her.

Sir Peter T. Yes, a good defence, truly!

Mrs. Can. But Sir Benjamin is as censorious as Miss Sallow.

Crabtree. Yes, and she is a curious being to pretend to be censorious—an awkward gawky, without any one good point under heaven.

Mrs. Can. Positively you shall not be so very severe. Miss Sallow is a relation[2] of mine by marriage, and as for her person, great allowance is to be made; for, let me tell you, a woman labours under many disadvantages who tries to pass for a girl at six and thirty.

Lady Sneer. Though, surely, she is handsome ſtill—and for the weakness in her eyes, considering how much she reads by candle-light, it is not to be wondered at.

Mrs. Can. True, and then as to her manner; upon my word I think it is particularly graceful, considering she never had the leaſt education: for you know her mother was a Welch milliner, and her father a sugar-baker at Briſtol.

Sir Benj. B. Ah! you are both of you too good-natured!

---

[1]Codille's—Crewe. *Em.*—Rae, Quadrilles—1823: (1781).   [2][a near relation—1826].

Sir Peter T. Yes, damned good-natured! This their own relation! mercy on me! [*Aside.*

[*Mrs. Can.* For my part, I own I cannot bear to hear a friend ill spoken of.

Sir Peter T. No, to be sure!]¹

Sir Benj. B. And Mrs. Candour is of so moral a turn, [she can sit for an hour and hear Lady Stucco talk sentiments.

Lady T. Nay, I vow Lady Stucco is very well with the dessert after dinner; for she's juſt like the French fruit one cracks for mottoes—made up of paint and proverb.]²

Mrs. Can. Well, I never will join in ridiculing a friend; and so I conſtantly tell my cousin Ogle, and you all³ know what pretensions she has to be critical on beauty.

Crabtree. Oh, to be sure! she has herself the oddeſt countenance that ever was seen; 'tis a colleƈtion of features from all the different countries of the globe.

Sir Benj. B. So she has, indeed—an Irish front—

Crabtree. Caledonian locks— —

Sir Benj. B. Dutch nose——

Crabtree. Auſtrian lips——

Sir Benj. B. Complexion of a Spaniard.——

Crabtree. And teeth *à la Chinois*——

Sir Benj. B. In short, her face resembles a *table d'hôte* at Spa—where no two gueſts are of a nation——

Crabtree. Or a congress at the close of a general war—wherein all the members, even to her eyes, appear to have a different intereſt, and her nose and chin are the only parties likely to join issue.

Mrs. Can. Ha! ha! ha!

Sir Peter T. Mercy on my life!—a person they dine with twice a week. [*Aside.*

[*Lady Sneer.* Go, go; you are a couple of provoking toads.]⁴

Mrs. Can. Nay, but I vow you shall not carry the laugh off so —for give me leave to say, that Mrs. Ogle——

Sir Peter T. Madam, madam, I beg your pardon—there's no

¹*Om.*—Crewe: 1799. *Em.*—Rae: 1826.   ²*Om.*—1826. *Em.*—Crewe: Rae: 1823.
³well—Crewe. *Em.*—Rae: 1823: 1826.   ⁴*Om.*—Crewe. *Em.*—Rae: 1823: (1781).

ſtopping these good gentlemen's tongues.—But when I tell you, Mrs. Candour, that the lady they are abusing is a particular friend of mine, I hope you'll not take her part.

Lady Sneer. Well said, Sir Peter! but you are a cruel creature, —too phlegmatic yourself for a jeſt, and too peevish to allow wit in others.

Sir Peter T. Ah! madam, true wit is more nearly allied to good-nature than your ladyship is aware of.

Lady T. True, Sir Peter: I believe they are so near akin that they can never be united.

Sir Benj. B. Or¹ rather, madam, suppose them to be man and wife, because one seldom sees them together.

Lady T. But Sir Peter is such an enemy to scandal, I believe he would have it put down by Parliament.²

Sir Peter T. 'Fore Heaven, madam, if they were to consider the sporting with reputation of as much importance as the poaching on manors, and pass an Act for the Preservation of Fame, I believe there are many would thank for them the bill.

Lady Sneer. O Lud! Sir Peter; would you deprive us of our privileges?

Sir Peter T. Aye, madam; and then no person should be permitted to kill characters and run down reputations, but qualified old maids and disappointed widows.

Lady Sneer. Go, you monſter.

Mrs. Can. But, surely, you would not be quite so severe on those who only report what they hear?

Sir Peter T. Yes, madam, I would have Law-Merchant for them too; and in all cases of slander currency, whenever the drawer of the lie was not to be found, the injured party³ should have a right to come on any of the indorsers.

Crabtree. Well, for my part, I believe there never was a scandalous tale without some foundation.

Lady Sneer. Come, ladies, shall we sit down to cards in the next room?

¹Oh—1799. O—Rae. *Em.*—Crewe: 1826: (1781).   ²by Act of—Crewe [*Act* probably caught up from below]. *Em.*—Rae: 1826: (1781).   ³[parties—1826.]

Enter a SERVANT, *who whispers* SIR PETER.

Sir Peter T. I'll be with them directly.—I'll get away unper-
ceived.   [*Apart.*

Lady Sneer. Sir Peter, you are not leaving us?[1]

Sir Peter T. Your ladyship must excuse me; I'm called away
by particular business. But I leave my character behind me.

[*Exit* SIR PETER.

Sir Benj. B. Well—certainly, Lady Teazle, that lord of yours
is a strange being: I could tell you some stories of him would
make you laugh heartily,—if he were not your husband.

Lady T. Oh, pray don't mind that;—come, do let's hear them.

[LADY T. *joins the rest of the company going into the next room.*

Joseph S. Maria, I see you have no satisfaction in this
society.

Maria. How is it possible I should? If to raise malicious
smiles at the infirmities or[2] misfortunes of those who have never
injured us be the province of wit or humour, Heaven grant me a
double portion of dullness![3]

Joseph S. Yet they appear more ill-natured than they are—
they have no malice at heart.

Maria. Then is their conduct still more contemptible; for, in
my opinion, nothing could excuse the intemperance of their
tongues, but a natural and ungovernable bitterness of mind.

Joseph S. But can you, Maria, feel thus for others, and
be unkind to me alone? Is hope to be denied[4] the tenderest
passion?

Maria. Why will you distress me by renewing the subject?

Joseph S. Ah! Maria! you would not treat me thus, and oppose your guardian, Sir Peter's will, but that I see that profligate
Charles is still a favoured rival.

Maria. Ungenerously urged!—But whatever my sentiments
are for[5] that unfortunate young man,[6] be assured I shall not feel
more bound to give him up, because his distresses have lost him
the regard even of a brother.

[1][going to leave us!—1826.]   [2]and—Crewe. *Em.*—Rae: 1826.   [3]dulness. Nothing but a depravity of heart could tempt them to such practices—1799: (1781).
Em.—Crewe: Rae.   [4]hope denied—Crewe. *Em.*—Rae: 1826: (1781).   [5]sentiments
of—Crewe: Rae. *Em.*—1823: 1826.   [6]man are—Crewe. *Em.*—1823: 1826.

II. E

[*Enter* LADY TEAZLE *and comes forward.*

Joseph S. Nay, but Maria, do not leave me with a frown: by all
that's honest, I swear—— Gad's life, here's Lady Teazle!—
[*Aside.*]—You must not—no, you shall not—for, though I have
the greatest regard for Lady Teazle——

Maria. Lady Teazle!

Joseph S. Yet were Sir Peter once to suspect——

Lady T. What is this, pray? Do you[1] take her for me?—Child,
you are wanted in the next room.—[*Exit* MARIA.]—What is all
this, pray?

Joseph S. O the most unlucky circumstance in nature! Maria
has somehow suspected the tender concern[2] I have for your happiness, and threatened to acquaint Sir Peter with her suspicions,
and I was just endeavouring to reason with her when you
came in.[3]

Lady T. Indeed! but you seemed to adopt a very tender mode
of reasoning—do you usually argue on your knees?

Joseph S. Oh, she's a child, and I thought a little bombast——
But, Lady Teazle, when are you to give me your judgment on
my library, as you promised?

Lady T. No, no; I begin to think it would be imprudent, and
you know I admit you as a lover no farther than fashion requires.

Joseph S. True—a mere platonic cicisbeo—what every
London wife[4] is entitled to.

Lady T. Certainly, one must not be out of the fashion. However, I have so much[5] of my country prejudices left, that, though
Sir Peter's ill-humour may vex me ever so, it never shall provoke
me to——

Joseph S. The only revenge in your power. Well—I applaud
your moderation.

Lady T. Go—you are an insinuating wretch.——But we shall
be missed—let us join the company.

Joseph S. But we had best not return together.

[1]Does he—1799: 1826. *Em.*—Crewe: Rae: 1823.   [2]concern which—Crewe. *Em.*—
Rae: 1826.   [3]came—Crewe: Rae. *Em.*—1823: 1826.   [4]every wife—Crewe. *Em.*—
1799: Rae: 1826.   [5]many—1799: 1826. *Em.*—Crewe: Rae.

Lady T. Well—don't stay; for Maria shan't come to hear any more of your reasoning, I promise you.   [*Exit* LADY TEAZLE.

Joseph S. A curious dilemma, truly, my[1] politics have run me into! I wanted, at first, only to ingratiate myself with Lady Teazle, that she might not be my enemy with Maria; and I have, I don't know how, become her serious lover. Sincerely I begin to wish I had never made such a point of gaining so very good a character, for it has led me into so many cursed rogueries[2] that I doubt I shall be exposed at last.   [*Exit.*

SCENE III

SIR PETER TEAZLE'S.

Enter ROWLEY *and* SIR OLIVER SURFACE.

Sir Oliver S. Ha! ha! ha! So my old friend is married, hey?—a young wife out of the country.—Ha! ha! ha! that he should have stood bluff to old bachelor so long, and sink into husband at last.

Rowley. But you must not rally him on the subject, Sir Oliver: 'tis a tender point, I assure you, though he has been married only seven months.

Sir Oliver S. Then he has been just half a year on the stool of repentance!—Poor Peter!——But you say he has entirely given up Charles,—never sees him, hey?

Rowley. His prejudice against him is astonishing, and I am sure, greatly increased by a jealousy of him with Lady Teazle, which he has been industriously[3] led into by a scandalous society in the neighbourhood, who have contributed not a little to Charles's ill name. Whereas the truth is, I believe, if the lady is partial to either of them, his brother is the favourite.

Sir Oliver S. Aye, I know there are a set of malicious, prating, prudent gossips, both male and female, who murder characters to kill time; and will rob a young fellow of his good name, before he has years to know the value of it.—But I am not to be preju-

---

[1] [dilemma my.]   [2] many rogueries—1799. *Em.*—Crewe: Rae.
[3] [industriously been.]

diced against my nephew by such, I promise you.—No, no,—if Charles has done nothing false or mean, I shall compound for his extravagance.

Rowley. Then, my life on't, you will reclaim him.—Ah, sir! it gives me new life to find that *your* heart is not turned against him; and that the son of my good old master has one friend, however, left.

Sir Oliver S. What, shall I forget, Master Rowley, when I was at his years myself? Egad, my brother and I were neither of us very[1] prudent youths; and yet, I believe, you have not seen many better men than your old master was.

Rowley. Sir, 'tis this reflection gives me assurance that Charles may yet be a credit to his family.—But here comes Sir Peter.

Sir Oliver S. Egad, so he does.—Mercy on me!—he's greatly altered—and seems to have a settled married look! One may read *husband* in his face at this distance!

Enter SIR PETER.

Sir Peter T. Hah! Sir Oliver—my old friend! Welcome to England a thousand times!

Sir Oliver S. Thank you—thank you, Sir Peter! and i'faith I am glad to find you well, believe me.

Sir Peter T. Oh! 'tis a long time since we met—sixteen[2] years, I doubt, Sir Oliver, and many a cross accident in the time.

Sir Oliver S. Aye, I have had my share.—But, what! I find you are married, hey my old boy? Well,[3] well—it can't be helped —and so—I wish you joy with all my heart.

Sir Peter T. Thank you, thank you, Sir Oliver.—Yes, I have entered into—the happy state;—but we'll not talk of that now.

Sir Oliver S. True, true, Sir Peter: old friends should not begin on grievances at first meeting—no, no, no.

Rowley. Take care, pray, sir.   [*to* SIR OLIVER.

Sir Oliver S. Well—so one of my nephews is a wild young rogue, hey?[4]

---

[1]neither very—Crewe. *Em.*—Rae: 1823: 1826.   [2][fifteen—1826.]   [3][hey? Well.]. *Em.*—Crewe: Rae: 1826.   [4]Wild extravagant young fellow—1799. *Em.*—Crewe: (1781).

Sir Peter T. Wild!—Ah! my old friend, I grieve for your disappointment there; he's a loſt young man, indeed. However, his brother will make you amends; Joseph is, indeed, what a youth should be. Everybody in the world speaks well of him.

Sir Oliver S. I am sorry to hear it; he has too good a charaꞔer to be an honeſt fellow. Everybody speaks well of him!—Pshaw! then he has bowed as low to knaves and fools as to the honeſt dignity of genius and virtue.

Sir Peter T. What, Sir Oliver! do you blame him for not making enemies?

Sir Oliver S. Yes, if he has merit enough to deserve them.

Sir Peter T. Well, well—you'll be convinced when you know him. 'Tis edification to hear him converse; he professes the nobleſt sentiments.

Sir Oliver S. Oh! plague of his sentiments! If he salutes me with a scrap of morality in his mouth, I shall be sick direꞔly.—But, however, don't miſtake me, Sir Peter; I don't mean to defend Charles's errors: but before I form my judgement of either of them, I intend to make a trial of their hearts; and my friend Rowley and I have planned something for the purpose.

Rowley. And Sir Peter shall own he has been for once mistaken.[1]

Sir Peter T. Oh! my life on Joseph's honour.

Sir Oliver S. Well—come, give us a bottle of good wine, and we'll drink your lady's health,[2] and tell you our[3] scheme.

Sir Peter T. Allons then!

Sir Oliver S. And don't, Sir Peter, be so severe againſt your old friend's son. Odds my life! I am not sorry that he has run out of the course a little: for my part, I hate to see prudence clinging to the green suckers of youth; 'tis like ivy round a sapling, and spoils the growth of the tree. *[Exeunt.*

[1][own for once he has been mistaken—1826.] [2]lady's good health—Crewe. *Em.*—(1781) the lads' health—Rae [?yr lady's *as* ye lads']. the lad's health—1823: 1826. [3]tell all our—Crewe. *Em.*—Rae: 1823: 1826.

END OF THE SECOND ACT

Act the Third

SCENE I

Enter Sir Peter, Sir Oliver *and* Rowley.

Sir Peter T. Well, then, we will see this fellow first, and have our wine afterwards:—but how is this, master Rowley? I don't see the jet[1] of your scheme.

Rowley. Why, sir, this Mr. Stanley, whom I was speaking of, is nearly related to them by their mother. He was a merchant in Dublin, but has been ruined by a series of undeserved misfortunes. He has applied, by letter, since his confinement, both to[2] Mr. Surface and Charles: from the former he has received nothing but evasive promises of future service, while Charles has done all that his extravagance has left him power to do; and he is, at this time, endeavouring to raise a sum of money, part of which, in the midst of his own distresses, I know he intends for the service of poor Stanley.

Sir Oliver S. Ah!—he is my brother's son.

Sir Peter T. Well, but how is Sir Oliver personally to——

Rowley. Why, sir, I will inform Charles and his brother, that Stanley has obtained permission to apply in person to his friends, and as they have neither of them ever seen him, let Sir Oliver assume his character, and he will have a fair opportunity of judging, at least, of the benevolence of their dispositions; and believe me, sir, you will find in the youngest brother one who, in the midst of folly and dissipation, has still, as our immortal bard expresses it.

A tear, for[3] pity, and a hand, Open as day, for melting charity.

Sir Peter T. Pshaw! What signifies his having an open hand or purse either, when he has nothing left to give? Well, well—

[1]jest—1799. *Em.*—Crewe.   [2][confinement to.]   [3][heart to—1826.]

54

make the trial, if you please. But where is the fellow whom you brought for Sir Oliver to examine, relative to Charles's affairs?

Rowley. Below, waiting his commands, and no one can give him better intelligence. This, Sir Oliver, is a friendly Jew, who, to do him justice, has done everything in his power to bring your nephew to a proper sense of his extravagance.

Sir Peter T. Pray let us have him in.

Rowley. Desire Mr. Moses to walk upstairs. [*Calls to* SERVANT.

Sir Peter T. But, pray, why should you suppose he will speak the truth ?

Rowley. Oh! I have convinced him that he has no chance of recovering certain sums advanced to Charles, but through the bounty of Sir Oliver, who he knows is arrived; so that you may depend on his fidelity to his own interests: I have also another evidence in my power, one Snake, whom I have detected in a matter little short of forgery, and shall shortly[1] produce him to remove some of your prejudices, Sir Peter, relative to Charles and Lady Teazle.

Sir Peter T. I have heard too much on that subject.

Rowley. Here comes the honest Israelite.—[*Enter* MOSES.] —This is Sir Oliver.

Sir Oliver S. Sir, I understand you have lately had great dealings with my nephew, Charles.

Moses. Yes, Sir Oliver, I have done all I could[2] for him; but he was ruined before he came to me for assistance.

Sir Oliver S. That was unlucky for, truly; you have had no opportunity of showing your talents.

Moses. None at all; I hadn't the pleasure of knowing his distresses till he was some thousands worse than nothing.

Sir Oliver S. Unfortunate, indeed!—But I suppose you have done all in your power for him, honest Moses?

Moses. Yes, he owns[3] that;—this very evening I was to have brought him a gentleman from the city, who does not know him, and will, I believe, advance him some money.

---

[1][speedily]. *Em.*—Crewe: Rae: 1826.   [2]all my power—1799. *Em.*—Crewe: Rae: 1826.   [3]knows—1799: Rae: (1781). *Em.*—Crewe.

Sir Peter T. What,—one Charles has never had money from before?

Moses. Yes,—Mr. Premium, of Crutched Friars, formerly a broker.

Sir Peter T. Egad, Sir Oliver, a thought strikes me!—— Charles, you say, does not know Mr. Premium?

Moses. Not at all.

Sir Peter T. Now then, Sir Oliver, you may have a better opportunity of satisfying yourself than by an old romancing tale of a poor relation: go with my friend Moses, and represent Premium, and then, I'll answer for it, you'll see your nephew in all his glory.

Sir Oliver S. Egad, I like this idea better than the other, and I may visit Joseph afterwards as Old Stanley.

Sir Peter T. True—so you may.

Rowley. Well, this is taking Charles rather[1] at a disadvantage, to be sure;—however, Moses, you understand Sir Peter, and will be faithful?

Moses. You may depend upon me;—this is near the time I was to have gone.

Sir Oliver S. I'll accompany you as soon as you please, Moses, ——But hold! I forgot one thing—how the plague shall I be able to pass for a Jew?

Moses. There is no need—the principal is Christian.

Sir Oliver S. Is he? I am very sorry[2] to hear it. But then again, a'n't I rather[3] too smartly dressed to look like a money-lender?

Sir Peter T. Not at all; 'twould not be out of character, if you went in your own carriage—would it, Moses?

Moses. Not in the least.

Sir Oliver S. Well—but how must I talk? —there's certainly some cant of usury and mode of treating that I ought to know.

Sir Peter T. Oh! there's not much to learn. The great point, as I take it, is to be exorbitant enough in your demands—hey, Moses?

Moses. Yes, that's a very great point.

[1]Charles—1799. *Em.*—Crewe: Rae: 1826. [2]am sorry—Crewe. *Em.*—Rae: 1826.
[3]I—1799. *Em.*—Crewe: Rae: 1826

Sir Oliver S. I'll answer for't I'll not be wanting in that. I'll ask him eight or ten per cent. on the loan, at leaſt.

Moses. If you ask him no more than that,[1] you'll be diſcovered immediately.

Sir Oliver S. Hey!—what the plague!—how much then?

Moses. That depends upon circumſtances. If he appears not very anxious for the supply, you should require only forty or fifty per cent.; but if you find him in great diſtress, and want the moneys very bad, you muſt ask double.

Sir Peter T. A good honeſt trade you're learning, Sir Oliver!

Sir Oliver S. Truly, I think so—and not unprofitable.

Moses. Then, you know, you haven't the moneys yourself, but are forced to borrow them for him of an old friend.

Sir Oliver S. Oh! I borrow it of a friend, do I?

Moses. And your friend is an unconscionable dog: but you can't help it!

Sir Oliver S. My friend an unconscionable dog, is he?

Moses. Yes, and he himself has not the moneys by him, but is forced to sell ſtock at a great loss.

Sir Oliver S. He is forced to sell ſtock at a great loss, is he? Well, that's very kind of him.

Sir Peter T. I'faith, Sir Oliver—Mr. Premium, I mean, you'll soon be maſter of the trade. [But, Moses! would not you have him run out a little againſt the Annuity Bill? That would be in character, I should think.

Moses. Very much.

Rowley. And lament that a young man now muſt be at years of discretion before he is suffered to ruin himself?

Moses. Aye, great pity!

Sir Peter T. And abuse the public for allowing merit to an Aĉt, whose only objeĉt is to snatch misfortune and imprudence from the rapacious relief[2] of usury, and give the minor a chance of inheriting his eſtate without being undone by coming into possession.][3]

Sir Oliver S. So—So—Moses shall give me further inſtructions as we go together.

[1]more as dat.—Crewe: (1781). *Em.*—Rae: 1826.   [2]gripe—1823: (1781). *Em.* Crewe: Rae.   [3]*Om.*—1799: 1826: *Em.*—Crewe: Rae: 1823: (1781).

Sir Peter T. You will not have much time, for your nephew lives hard by.

Sir Oliver S. Oh! never fear: my tutor appears so able, that though Charles lived in the next street, it must be my own fault if I am not a complete rogue before I turn the corner.

[*Exeunt* SIR OLIVER *and* MOSES.

Sir Peter T. So, now, I think Sir Oliver will be convinced:— you are partial, Rowley, and would have prepared Charles for the other plot.

Rowley. No, upon my word, Sir Peter.

Sir Peter T. Well, go bring me this Snake, and I'll hear what he has to say presently.—I see Maria, and want to speak with her. [*Exit* ROWLEY.] I should be glad to be convinced my suspicions of Lady Teazle and Charles were unjust. I have never yet opened my mind on this subject to my friend Joseph—I am determined I will do it—he will give me his opinion sincerely.

Enter MARIA.

So, child, has Mr. Surface returned with you?

Maria. No, sir; he was engaged.

Sir Peter T. Well, Maria, do you not reflect, the more you converse with that amiable young man, what return his partiality for you deserves?

Maria. Indeed, Sir Peter, your frequent importunity on this subject distresses me extremely—you compel me to declare, that I know no man who has ever paid me a particular attention, whom I would not prefer to Mr. Surface.

Sir Peter T. So—here's perverseness!—No, no, Maria, 'tis Charles only whom you would prefer. 'Tis evident his vices and follies have won your heart.

Maria. This is unkind, sir. You know I have obeyed you in neither seeing nor corresponding with him: I have heard enough to convince me that he is unworthy my regard. Yet I cannot think it culpable, if, while my understanding severely condemns his vices, my heart suggests some pity for his distresses.

Sir Peter T. Well, well, pity him as much as you please; but give your heart and hand to a worthier object.

Maria. Never to his brother!

Sir Peter T. Go—perverse and obstinate! but take care, madam; you have never yet known what the authority of a guardian is: don't compel me to inform you of it.

Maria. I can only say, you shall not have a just reason. 'Tis true, by my father's will, I am for a short period bound to regard you as his substitute; but must cease to think you so, when you would compel me to be miserable.   [*Exit* MARIA.

Sir Peter T. Was ever man so crossed as I am? everything conspiring to fret me! I had not been involved in matrimony a fortnight, before her father, a hale and hearty man, died, on purpose, I believe, for the pleasure of plaguing me with the care of his daughter. But here comes my helpmate—She appears in great good humour. How happy I should be if I could tease her into loving me, though but a little.   [*Enter* LADY TEAZLE.

Lady T. Lud! Sir Peter, I hope you haven't been quarrelling with Maria? It is not using me well to be ill-humoured when I am not by.

Sir Peter T. Ah! Lady Teazle, you might have the power to make me good-humoured at all times.

Lady T. I am sure I wish I had; for I want you to be in a charming sweet temper at this moment. Do be good-humoured now, and let me have two hundred pounds, will you?

Sir Peter T. Two hundred pounds! what, an't I to be in a good humour without paying for it? But speak to me thus, and i'faith there's nothing I could refuse you. You shall have it; but seal me a bond for the repayment.

Lady T. Oh, no—there—my note of hand will do as well.

[*Offering her hand.*

Sir Peter T. And you shall no longer reproach me with not giving you an independent settlement. I mean shortly to surprise you:—but shall we always live thus, hey?

Lady T. If you please. I'm sure I don't care how soon we leave off quarrelling, provided you'll own you were tired first.

Sir Peter T. Well—then let our future contest be, who shall be most obliging.

Lady T. I assure you, Sir Peter, good nature becomes you—you look now as you did before we were married, when you used to walk with me under the elms, and tell me stories of what a gallant you were in your youth, and chuck me under the chin, you would; and ask me if I thought I could love an old fellow, who would deny me nothing—didn't you?

Sir Peter T. Yes, yes, and you were as kind and attentive——

Lady T. Aye—so I was, and would always take your part, when my acquaintance used to abuse you, and turn you into ridicule.

Sir Peter T. Indeed!

Lady T. Aye, and when my cousin Sophy has[1] called you a stiff, peevish old bachelor, and laughed at me for thinking of marrying one who might be my father, I have always defended you, and said, I didn't think you so ugly by any means.

Sir Peter T. Thank you.

Lady T. And[2] I dared say you'd make a very good sort of a husband.

Sir Peter T. And you prophesied right; and we shall certainly now[3] be the happiest couple——

Lady T. And never differ again?

Sir Peter T. No, never!—though at the same time, indeed, my dear Lady Teazle, you must watch your temper very narrowly;[4] for in all our little quarrels, my dear, if you recollect, my love, you always began first.

Lady T. I beg your pardon, my dear Sir Peter: indeed, you always gave the provocation.

Sir Peter T. Now see, my angel! take care[5]—contradicting isn't the way to keep friends.

Lady T. Then don't you begin it, my love!

Sir Peter T. There, now! you—you are going on. You don't perceive, my life, that you are just doing the very thing which you know always makes me angry.

Lady T. Nay, you know if you will be angry without any reason——my dear—[6]

---

[1]Sophy—1799. *Em.*—Crewe: Rae.   [2]And that—Crewe. *Em.*—1823: 1826.
[3][shall now—1826.]   [4][seriously—1826.]   [5]angel—Crewe. *Em.* Rae: 1823: 1826.
[6]reason—Crewe. *Em.* Rae: 1826.

Sir Peter T. There! now you want to quarrel again.

Lady T. No, I am sure I don't. But if you will be so peevish—

Sir Peter T. There now, who begins first?

Lady T. Why you, to be sure. I said nothing—but there's no bearing your temper.

Sir Peter T. No, no, madam: the fault's in your own temper.

Lady T. Aye, you are just what my cousin Sophy said you would be.

Sir Peter T. Your cousin Sophy is a forward, impertinent gipsy.

Lady T. You are a great bear, to abuse my relations. [How dare you abuse my relations?][1]

Sir Peter T. Now may all the plagues of marriage be doubled on me, if ever I try to be friends with you any more!

Lady T. So much the better.

Sir Peter T. No, no, madam: 'tis evident you never cared a pin for me, and I was a madman to marry you—a pert, rural coquette, that had refused half the honest 'squires in the neighbourhood.

Lady T. And I[2] am sure I was a fool to marry you—an old dangling bachelor, who was single at fifty, only because he never could meet with any one who would have him.

Sir Peter T. Aye, aye, madam; but you were pleased enough to listen to me: you never had such an offer before.

Lady T. No! didn't I refuse Sir Tivy Terrier, who everybody said would have been a better match? for his estate is just as good as yours, and he has broke his neck since we have been married.

Sir Peter T. I[3] have done with you, madam! You are an unfeeling, ungrateful—but there's an end of everything. I believe you capable of anything that is bad.—Yes, madam, I now believe the reports relative to you and Charles, madam.—Yes, madam, *you* and Charles are—not without grounds——

Lady T. Take care, Sir Peter! you had better not insinuate any such thing! I'll not be suspected without cause, I promise you.

[1]*Om.*—Crewe: 1826. *Em.*—Rae [*Sheridan instructed Mrs. Abington on delivering this.* —Sichel, I, 579.]   [2]I—Crewe. *Em.*—Rae: 1826.   [3]Oh! Oh! Oh! I—1799. *Em.*— Crewe: Rae.

Sir Peter T. Very well, madam, very well! A separate maintenance as soon as you please. Yes, madam, or a divorce! I'll
make an example of myself for the benefit of all old bachelors.—
Let us separate, madam.

Lady T. Agreed! agreed!—And now, my dear Sir Peter, we
are of a mind once more, we may be the happiest couple—and
never differ again, you know—ha! ha! ha! Well, you are going
to be in a passion, I see, and I shall only interrupt you—so, bye-
bye.   [*Exit.*

Sir Peter T. Plagues and tortures! Can't I make her angry
either! Oh, I am the miserablest fellow! but I'll not bear her
presuming to keep her temper: no! she may break my heart, but
she shall not keep her temper.   [*Exit.*

SCENE II

At CHARLES'S *house, a chamber.*

Enter TRIP, MOSES, *and* SIR OLIVER.

Trip. Here, master Moses! if you'll stay a moment, I'll try
whether Mr. ——what's[1] the gentleman's name?

Sir Oliver S. Mr. ——[*Apart.*][2] Moses, what is my name?

Moses. Mr. Premium.

Trip. Premium—very well.   [*Exit taking snuff.*

Sir Oliver S. To judge by the servants, one wouldn't believe
the master was ruined. But what!—sure, this was my brother's
house?

Moses. Yes, sir; Mr. Charles bought it of Mr. Joseph, with
the furniture, pictures, &c., just as the old gentleman left it. Sir
Peter thought it a piece of extravagance in him.

Sir Oliver S. In my mind,[3] the other's œconomy in selling it
to him was more reprehensible by half.   [*Enter* TRIP.

Trip. My master says you must wait, gentlemen: he has company, and can't speak with you yet.

<hr />

[1]whether—what's—Crewe. *Em.*—Rae.   [2]Mr. Moses—Crewe: 1826. *Em.*—Mr.
—Moses—Rae: [*Apart.*] *now added.*   [3]opinion—Crewe. *Em.*—Rae: 1823: 1826
[1781].

Sir Oliver S. If he knew who it was wanted to see him, perhaps he would not have sent[1] such a message?

Trip. Yes, yes, sir; he knows you are here—I did not forget little Premium; no, no, no——.

Sir Oliver S. Very well; and I pray, sir, what may be your name?

Trip. Trip, sir; my name is Trip, at your service.

Sir Oliver S. Well then, Mr. Trip, you have a pleasant sort of place here, I guess?

Trip. Why, yes—here are three or four of us pass our time agreeably enough; but then our wages are sometimes a little in arrear—and not very great[2] either—but fifty pounds a year, and find our own bags and bouquets.

Sir Oliver S. Bags and bouquets! halters and bastinadoes!   [*Aside.*

Trip. And, à propos, Moses—have you been able to get me that little bill discounted?

Sir Oliver S. Wants to raise money too!—mercy on me! Has his distresses, I warrant, like a lord, and affects creditors and duns.   [*Aside.*

Moses. 'Twas not to be done, indeed, Mr. Trip.

Trip. Good lack, you surprise me! My friend Brush has endorsed it, and I thought when he put his name at the back of a bill 'twas as good as cash.

Moses. No! 'twouldn't do.

Trip. A small sum—but twenty pounds. Hark'ee, Moses, do you think you couldn't[3] get it me by way of annuity?

Sir Oliver S. An annuity! ha! ha! a footman raise money by way of annuity! Well done, luxury, egad!   [*Aside.*

Moses. But you must insure your place.

Trip. Oh, with all my heart! I'll insure my place, and my life too, if you please.

Sir Oliver S. It's more than I would your neck.   [*Aside.*

[*Trip.* But then, Moses, it must be done before this d—d Register takes place; one wouldn't like to have one's name made public, you know.][4]

[1][not send—1826.]   [2]good—1799. *Em.*—Crewe: Rae: 1826.   [3]Could—1799
Rae. *Em.*—Crewe: 1823.   [4]*Om.*—1823: 1826. *Em.*—Crewe (1781).

Moses. No, certainly. But is there nothing you could deposit?

Trip. Why, nothing capital of my master's wardrobe has dropped lately; but I could give you a mortgage on some of his winter clothes, with equity of redemption before November—or you shall have the reversion of the French velvet, or a post-obit on the blue and silver:—these, I should think, Moses, with a few pair of point ruffles, as a collateral security—hey, my little fellow.

Moses. Well, well.   [*Bell rings.*

Trip. Egad, I heard the bell! I believe, gentlemen, I can now introduce you. Don't forget the annuity, little Moses! This way, gentlemen: insure my place, you know.

Sir Oliver S. If the man be a shadow of his master,[1] this is the temple of dissipation indeed!   [*Exeunt.*

SCENE III

CHARLES SURFACE, CARELESS, SIR TOBY BUMPER, &c., *discovered at a table, drinking wine.*

Charles S. 'Fore Heaven, 'tis true!—there's the great degeneracy of the age. Many of our acquaintance have taste, spirit, and politeness; but, plague on't, they won't drink.

Careless. It is so indeed, Charles! they give in to all the substantial luxuries of the table, and abstain from nothing but wine and wit.

Charles S. Oh, certainly society suffers by it intolerably; for now, instead of the social spirit of raillery that used to mantle over a glass of bright Burgundy, their conversation is become just like the Spa water they drink, which has all the pertness and flatulence of Champaign, without its spirit or flavour.

First Gent. But what are[2] they to do who love play better than wine?

Careless. True: there's Harry diets himself for gaming, and is now under a hazard regimen.

Charles S. Then he'll have the worst of it. What! you wouldn't train a horse for the course by keeping him from corn? For my

[1]the shadow of a master—1799. *Em.*—Crewe: Rae.
[2]have—Crewe. *Em.*—1799: Rae: 1826.

part, egad, I am never so successful as when I am a little merry: let me throw on a bottle of Champaign, and I never lose—at least, I never feel my losses, which is exactly the same thing.

Sec. Gent. Aye, that I believe.

Charles S. And then, what man can pretend to be a believer in love, who is an abjurer of wine? 'Tis the test by which the lover knows his own heart. Fill a dozen bumpers to a dozen beauties, and she that floats a top is the maid that has bewitched you.

Careless. Now then, Charles, be honest, and give us your real favourite.

Charles S. Why, I have withheld her only in compassion to you. If I toast her, you must give a round of her peers, which is impossible—on earth.

Careless. Oh! then we'll find some canonized vestals or heathen goddesses that will do, I warrant!

Charles S. Here then, bumpers, you rogues! bumpers! Maria! Maria——

First Gent. Maria who?

Charles S. Oh, damn the surname—'tis too formal to be registered in Love's calendar; but now, Sir Toby Bumper,[1] beware, we must have beauty[2] superlative.

Careless. Nay, never study, Sir Toby: we'll stand to the toast, though your mistress should want an eye, and you know you have a song will excuse you.

Sir Toby B. Egad, so I have! and I'll give him the song instead of the lady.

SONG.

Here's to the maiden of bashful fifteen;
   Here's to the widow of fifty;
Here's to the flaunting extravagant quean,
   And here's to the housewife that's thrifty.

Chorus.

Let the toast pass,—
   Drink to the lass,
I'll warrant she'll prove an excuse for the glass.

[1]Toby, beware—1799. *Em.*—Crewe.   [2]beauty's—1799: Rae. *Em.*—Crewe: 1823.

Here's to the charmer whose dimples we prize;
Now to the maid who has none, sir:
Here's to the girl with a pair of blue eyes,
And here's to the nymph with but *one*, sir.
Chorus. Let the toaſt pass, &c.

Here's to the maid with a bosom of snow;
Now to her that's as brown as a berry:
Here's to the wife with her[1] face full of woe,
And now to the damsel that's merry.
Chorus. Let the toaſt pass, &c.

For let 'em be clumsy, or let 'em be slim,
Young or ancient, I care not a feather;
So fill a pint bumper quite up to the brim,
And let us e'en toaſt them together.
Chorus. Let the toaſt pass, &c.

All. Bravo! bravo!

Enter TRIP, *and whispers* CHARLES.

Charles S. Gentlemen, you muſt excuse me a little. Careless, take the chair, will you?

Careless. Nay, prithee, Charles, what now? This is one of your peerless beauties, I suppose, has dropt in by chance?

Charles S. No, faith! To tell you the truth, 'tis a Jew and a broker, who are come by appointment.

Careless. Oh, damn it! let's have the Jew in.

Firſt Gent. Aye, and the broker too, by all means.

Sec. Gent. Yes, yes, the Jew and the broker.

Charles S. Egad, with all my heart! Trip, bid the gentlemen walk in—[*Exit* TRIP.] Though there's one of them a ſtranger, I can tell[2] you.

Careless. Charles, let us give them some generous Burgundy, and perhaps they'll grow conscientious.

Charles S. Oh, hang 'em, no! wine does but draw forth a man's

---

[1] [a—1826]. *Em.*—Crewe: (1781).   [2] assure—1799: 1826. *Em.*—Crewe: Rae.

natural qualities;[1] and to make them drink would only be to whet their knavery.

Enter TRIP, SIR OLIVER, *and* MOSES.

Charles S. So, honest Moses, walk in: walk in, pray, Mr. Premium—that's the gentleman's name, isn't it, Moses?

Moses. Yes, sir.

Charles S. Set chairs, Trip—sit down, Mr. Premium glasses, Trip—sit down, Moses. Come, Mr. Premium, I'll give you a sentiment; here's *Success to usury*—Moses, fill the gentleman a bumper.

Moses. Success to usury!

Careless. Right, Moses—usury is prudence and industry, and deserves to succeed.

Sir Oliver S. Then[2]—*here's all the success it deserves!*

Careless. No, no, that won't do, Mr. Premium; you have demurred to[3] the toast, and must drink it in a pint bumper.

First Gent. A pint bumper, at least.

Moses. Oh, pray, sir, consider—Mr. Premium's a gentleman.

Careless. And therefore loves good wine.

Sec. Gent. Give Moses a quart glass—this is mutiny, and a high contempt for the chair.

Careless. Here, now for't! I'll see justice done, to the last drop of my bottle.

Sir Oliver S. Nay, pray, gentlemen—I did not expect this usage.

Charles S. No, hang it,[4] you shan't! Mr. Premium's a stranger.

Sir Oliver S. Odd! I wish I was well out of their company.
                                                              [*Aside.*

Careless. Plague on 'em, then!—if they won't[5] drink, we'll not sit down with them. Come, Harry, the dice are in the next room—Charles, you'll join us when you have finished[6] your business with these gentlemen?

Charles S. I will! I will! [*Exeunt Gentlemen.*] Careless!

Careless. [*Returning.*] Well!

[1]the natural qualities of a man—1799. *Em.*—Crewe: Rae: 1826.   [2]And—Crewe. *Em.*—Rae: 1826: (1781).   [3][at—1826]. *Em.* Crewe: (1781).   [4]it, Careless—Crewe. *Em.*—1823: 1826.   [5][don't]. *Em.*—1826: (1781).   [6]you finish—Crewe. *Em.*—1823: 1826.

Charles S. Perhaps I may want you.

Careless. Oh, you know I am always ready: word, note, or bond, 'tis all the same to me.   [*Exit.*

Moses. Sir, this is Mr. Premium, a gentleman of the strictest honour and secrecy; and always performs what he undertakes. Mr. Premium, this is——

Charles S. Pshaw! have done.—Sir, my friend Moses is a very honest fellow, but a little slow at expression: he'll be an hour giving us our titles. Mr. Premium, the plain state of the matter is this: I am an extravagant young fellow who want to borrow money—you I take to be a prudent old fellow, who have got money to lend. I am blockhead enough to give fifty per cent. sooner than not have it; and you, I presume, are rogue enough to take an hundred if you can[1] get it. Now, sir, you see we are acquainted at once, and may proceed to business without farther ceremony.

Sir Oliver S. Exceeding frank, upon my word.—I see, sir, you are not a man of many compliments.

Charles S. O, no, sir! plain dealing in business I always think best.

Sir Oliver S. Sir, I like you the better for it—however, you are mistaken in one thing; I have no money to lend, but I believe I could procure some of a friend; but then he's an unconscionable dog, isn't he, Moses? And must sell stock to accommodate you mustn't he, Moses?

Moses. Yes, indeed! You know I always speak the truth, and scorn to tell a lie!

Charles S. Right. People that speak truth generally do: but these are trifles, Mr. Premium. What! I know money isn't to be bought without paying for't!

Sir Oliver S. Well—but what security could you give? You have no land, I suppose?

Charles S. Not a mole-hill, nor a twig, but what's in beau-pots at[2] the window!

Sir Oliver S. Nor any stock, I presume?

Charles S. Nothing but live stock—and that's only a few

[1]could—Crewe. *Em.*—1823: 1826: (1781).
[2][in the bough-pots out of—1826: (1781).]

pointers and ponies. But pray, Mr. Premium, are you acquainted at all with any of my connexions?

Sir Oliver S. Why, to say truth, I am.

Charles S. Then you muſt know that I have a dev'lish rich uncle in the Eaſt Indies, Sir Oliver Surface, from whom I have the greateſt expectations.

Sir Oliver S. That you have a wealthy uncle I have heard; but how your expectations will turn out is more, I believe, than you can tell.

Charles S. O no!—there can be no doubt. They tell me I'm a prodigious favourite, and that he talks of leaving me everything.

Sir Oliver S. Indeed! this is the firſt I've heard of it.

Charles S. Yes, yes, 'tis juſt so. Moses knows 'tis true, don't you, Moses?

Moses. Oh, yes! I'll swear to it.

Sir Oliver S. Egad, they'll persuade me presently I'm at Bengal.   [*Aside.*

Charles S. Now I propose, Mr. Premium, if it's agreeable to you, a[1] poſt-obit on Sir Oliver's life; though at the same time the old fellow has been so liberal to me, that I give you my word I should be very sorry to hear anything had happened to him.

Sir Oliver S. Not more than I should, I assure you. But the bond you mention happens to be juſt the worſt security you could offer me—for I might live to an hundred, and never recover[2] the principal.

Charles S. Oh, yes, you would—the moment Sir Oliver dies, you know you would come on me for the money.

Sir Oliver S. Then I believe I should be the moſt unwelcome dun you ever had in your life.

Charles S. What! I suppose you are afraid now that Sir Oliver is too good a life?

Sir Oliver S. No, indeed, I am not; though I have heard he is as hale and healthy as any man of his years in Chriſtendom.

Charles S. There again now you are misinformed. No, no, the climate has hurt him considerably, poor uncle Oliver! Yes, he

[1]to grant a—Crewe. *Em.*—1823: 1826.   [2][see—1826.]

breaks apace, I am told—and is so much altered lately, that his nearest relations wouldn't[1] know him.

Sir Oliver S. No! ha! ha! ha! ha! so much altered lately that his nearest relations wouldn't[2] know him!—that's droll, egad—ha! ha! ha!

Charles S. Ha! ha!—you're glad to hear that, little Premium?

Sir Oliver S. No, no, I'm not.

Charles S. Yes, yes, you are—ha! ha! ha!—You know that mends your chance.

Sir Oliver S. But I'm told Sir Oliver is coming over?—nay, some say he is actually arrived?

Charles S. Pshaw! Sure I must know better than you whether he's come[3] or not. No, no, rely on't he's at this moment at Calcutta—isn't he, Moses?

Moses. Yes, certainly.

Sir Oliver S. Very true, as you say, you must know better than I, though I have it from pretty good authority—haven't I, Moses?

Moses. Yes, most undoubted!

Sir Oliver S. But, sir, as I understand you want a few hundreds immediately—is there nothing you would dispose of?

Charles S. How do you mean?

Sir Oliver S. For instance, now, I have heard that your father left behind him a great quantity of massy old plate?

Charles S. O Lud!—that's gone long ago.—Moses can tell you how better than I.

Sir Oliver S. Good lack! all the family race-cups and corporation bowls! [*Aside.*]—Then it was also supposed that his library was one of the most valuable and compleat——[4]

Charles S. Yes, yes, so it was—vastly too much so for a private gentleman. For my part, I was always of a communicative disposition, so I thought it a shame to keep so much knowledge to myself.

Sir Oliver S. Mercy upon me! Learning that had run in the family like an heirloom! [*Aside.*]—Pray, what are become of the books?

---

[1]don't—Crewe. *Em.*—1799: 1826.   [2]don't—Crewe. *Em.*—1799: 1826.   [3]coming—Crewe. *Em.* 1823: 1826.   [4]compact—1823.

Charles S. You muſt inquire of the auctioneer, master Premium, for I don't believe even Moses can direct you.

Moses. I never meddle with[1] books.

Sir Oliver S. So, so, nothing of the family property left, I suppose?

Charles S. Not much, indeed; unless you have a mind to the family pictures. I have got a room full of anceſtors above, and if you have a taſte for paintings, egad, you shall have them a bargain.

Sir Oliver S. Hey! what the[2] devil! sure, you would not sell your forefathers, would you?

Charles S. Every man of 'em to the beſt bidder.

Sir Oliver S. What! your great uncles and aunts?

Charles S. Aye, and my great grandfathers and grandmothers too.

Sir Oliver S. Now I give him up. [*Aside.*]—What the plague have you no bowels for your own kindred? Odds life,[3] do you take me for Shylock in the play, that you would raise money of me on your own flesh and blood?

Charles S. Nay, my little broker, don't be angry: what need you care if you have your money's worth?

Sir Oliver S. Well, I'll be the purchaser: I think I can dispose of the family canvas.—[*Aside.*] Oh, I'll never forgive him this! never!   [*Enter* CARELESS.

Careless. Come, Charles, what keeps you?

Charles S. I can't come yet: i'faith we are going to have a sale above ſtairs;[4] here's little Premium will buy all my anceſtors.

Careless. Oh, burn your anceſtors!

Charles S. No, he may do that afterwards, if he pleases. Stay, Careless, we want you: egad, you shall be auctioneer; so come along with us.

Careless. Oh, have with you, if that's the case. I can handle a hammer as well as a dice-box!—[a going—a-going.][5]

Sir Oliver S. Oh, the profligates!   [*Aside.*

---

[1] I know nothing of—1799: 1826. *Em.*—Crewe: (1781).   [2] Hey! the—Crewe. *Em.* —1823: 1826.   [3] Odd's my life—1799. *Em.*—Crewe: 1826.   [4] above—Crewe. *Em.*—1826: (1781).   [5] *Om.*—Crewe. *Em.*—1799: 1826— (1781).

Charles S. Come, Moses, you shall be appraiser, if we want one. Gad's life, little Premium, you don't seem to like the business?

Sir Oliver S. Oh, yes, I do, vastly. Ha! ha! ha! yes, yes, I think it a rare joke to sell one's family by auction—ha! ha!—Oh, the prodigal!   [*Aside.*

Charles S. To be sure! when a man wants money, where the plague should he get assistance if he can't make free with his own relations?   [*Exeunt.*

END OF THE THIRD ACT

Act the Fourth

SCENE I

Picture Room at CHARLES'S *House.*

Enter CHARLES, SIR OLIVER, MOSES, *and* CARELESS.

Charles S. Walk in, gentlemen, pray walk in;[1]—here they are, the family of the Surfaces, up to the Conquest.

Sir Oliver S. And, in my opinion, a goodly collection.

Charles S. Aye, aye, these[2] are done in the true spirit of portrait painting;—no *volunteer grace*[3] and expression, not like the works of your modern Raphael, who gives you the strongest resemblance, yet contrives to make your own portrait independent of you; so that you may sink the original and not hurt the picture. No, no; the merit of these is the inveterate likeness—all stiff and awkward as the originals, and like nothing in human nature besides.

Sir Oliver S. Ah! we shall never see such figures of men again.

Charles S. I hope not.——Well, you see, Master Premium, what a domestic character I am; here I sit of an evening surrounded by my family.——But, come, get[4] to your pulpit, Mr. Auctioneer; here's an old gouty chair of my grandfather's will answer the purpose.

Careless. Aye, aye, this will do.——But, Charles, I have ne'er[5] a hammer; and what's an auctioneer without his hammer?

Charles S. Egad, that's true;—what parchment have we here? —*Richard heir to Thomas.*—Oh, our genealogy in full. Here, Careless—you shall have no common bit of mahogany, here's the family tree for you, you rogue,—this shall be your hammer, and now you may knock down my ancestors with their own pedigree.

¹walk in, pray—Crewe. *Em.*—1823: 1826.　²they—Crewe. *Em.*—1823: 1826,
³[*volontier grace*—1826.]　⁴go—1799. *Em.*—Crewe: 1823.　⁵[haven't—1826.]

73

Sir Oliver S. What an unnatural rogue!—an *ex post facto* parricide! [*Aside.*

Careless. Yes, yes, here's a lift of your generation indeed;—faith, Charles, this is the moft convenient thing you could have found for the business, for 'twill serve not only as a hammer, but a catalogue into the bargain.——But come, begin——A-going, a-going, a-going!

Charles S. Bravo, Careless!—Well, here's my great uncle, Sir Richard Raveline, a marvellous good general in his day, I assure you. He served in all the Duke of Marlborough's wars, and got that cut over his eye at the battle of Malplaquet.—What say you, Mr. Premium?—look at him—there's a hero for you, not cut out of his feathers, as your modern clipt captains are, but enveloped in wig and regimentals, as a general should be.—What do you bid?

[*Sir Oliver S.* Bid him speak] [*Aside to* MOSES.][1]

Moses. Mr. Premium would have *you* speak.

Charles S. Why, then, he shall have him for ten pounds, and I'm sure that's not dear for a ftaff-officer.

Sir Oliver S. Heaven deliver me! his famous uncle Richard for ten pounds! [*Aside.*]—Very well, sir, I take him at that.

Charles S. Careless, knock him down my uncle Richard.—Here, now, is a maiden fifter of his, my great aunt Deborah, done by Kneller, thought to be in[2] his beft manner, and efteemed a very formidable likeness.—There she is, you see, a shepherdess feeding her flock.—You shall have her for five pounds ten—the sheep are worth the money.

Sir Oliver S. Ah! poor Deborah! a woman who set such a value on herself! [*Aside.*]—Five pounds ten—she's mine.

Charles S. Knock down my aunt Deborah!—Here, now, are two that were a sort of cousins of theirs. You see, Moses, these pictures were done some time ago, when beaux wore wigs,[3] and the ladies[4] their own hair.

Sir Oliver S. Yes, truly, head-dresses appear to have been a little lower in those days.

---

[1]*Om.*—Crewe. *Em.*—1823: 1826. [2]Kneller, in—1799: 1826. *Em.*—Crewe: 1823.
[3][perriwigs—(1781.)]   [4]ladies wore—Crewe. *Em.*—1823: (1781).

Charles S. Well, take this[1] couple for the same.

Moses. 'Tis a good[2] bargain.

Charles S. This, now, is a grandfather of my mother's, a learned judge, well known on the western circuit.—What do you rate him at, Moses?

Moses. Four guineas.

Charles S. Four guineas!—Gad's life, you don't bid me the price of his wig.—Mr. Premium, you have more respect for the woolsack; do let us knock his lordship down at fifteen.

Sir Oliver S. By all means.

Careless. Gone!

Charles S. And there are two brothers of his, William and Walter Blunt, Esquires, both members of Parliament, and noted speakers, and what's very extraordinary, I believe this is the first time they were ever bought or sold.

Sir Oliver S. That is very extraordinary, indeed! I'll take them at your own price, for the honour of Parliament.

Careless. Well said, little Premium!—I'll knock them down at forty.

Charles S. Here's a jolly fellow—I don't know what relation, but he was mayor of Norwich: take him at eight pounds.

Sir Oliver S. No, no; six will do for the mayor.

Charles S. Come, make it guineas, and I'll throw you the two aldermen there into[3] the bargain.

Sir Oliver S. They're mine.

Charles S. Careless, knock down the mayor and aldermen.— But plague on't, we shall be all day retailing in this manner; do let us deal wholesale: what say you, little Premium?[4] Give me[5] three hundred pounds for the rest of the family in the lump.

[*Careless.* Aye, aye, that will be the best way.][6]

Sir Oliver S. Well, well, anything to accommodate you;— they are mine. But there is one portrait which you have always passed over.

Careless. What, that ill-looking little fellow over the settee?

Sir Oliver S. Yes, sir, I mean that, though I don't think him so ill-looking a little fellow, by any means.

Charles S. What, that?—Oh! that's my uncle Oliver; 'twas done before he went to India.

Careless. Your uncle Oliver!—Gad, then you'll never be friends, Charles. That, now, to me, is as stern a looking rogue as ever I saw; an unforgiving eye, and a damned disinheriting countenance! an inveterate knave, depend on't. Don't you think so, little Premium?

Sir Oliver S. Upon my soul, sir, I do not; I think it is as honest a looking face as any in the room, dead or alive;—but I suppose uncle Oliver goes with the rest of the lumber?

Charles S. No, hang it; I'll not part with poor Noll. The old fellow has been very good to me, and, egad, I'll keep his picture while I've a room to put it in.

Sir Oliver S. The rogue's my nephew after all! [*Aside.*]—But, sir, I have somehow taken a fancy to that picture.

Charles S. I'm sorry for't, for you certainly will not have it. Oons, haven't you got enough of 'em?

Sir Oliver S. I forgive him everything! [*Aside.*]—But, sir, when I take a whim in my head I don't value money. I'll give you as much for that as for all the rest.

Charles S. Don't tease me, master broker; I tell you I'll not part with it, and there's an end of it.

Sir Oliver S. How like his father the dog is!—Well, well, I have done.——I did not[1] perceive it before, but I think I never saw such a striking resemblance[2]—[*Aside.*]——Here is a draught for your sum.

Charles S. Why, 'tis for eight hundred pounds.

Sir Oliver S. You will not let Sir Oliver[3] go?

Charles S. Zounds! no!—I tell you once more.

Sir Oliver S. Then never mind the difference, we'll balance that another time—but give me your hand on the bargain; you are an honest fellow, Charles—I beg pardon, sir, for being so free.—Come, Moses.

Charles S. Egad, this is a whimsical old fellow! But hark'ee, Premium, you'll prepare lodgings for these gentlemen.

Sir Oliver S. Yes, yes, I'll send for them in a day or two.

[1]did—1799. *Em.*—Crewe: 1823.   [2]a resemblance—Crewe. *Em.*—1823 1781).
[3]let Oliver—Crewe. *Em.*—1823: 1826: (1781).

Charles S. But, hold; do now send a genteel conveyance for them, for, I assure you, they were moſt of them used to ride in their own carriages.

Sir Oliver S. I will, I will—for all but Oliver.

Charles A. Aye, all but the little honest nabob.[1]

Sir Oliver S. You're fixed on that?[2]

Charles S. Peremptorily.

Sir Oliver S. A dear extravagant rogue! [*Aside.*]—Good-day! —Come, Moses.——Let me hear now who dares call him pro-fligate!   [*Exeunt* SIR OLIVER SURFACE *and* MOSES.

Careless. Why, this is the oddeſt genius of the sort I ever saw!

Charles S. Egad, he's the prince of brokers, I think. I wonder how the devil Moses[3] got acquainted with so honeſt a fel-low.—Hah! here's Rowley; do, Careless, say I'll join the company in a moment.

Careless. I will—but don't let that old blockhead persuade you to squander any of that money on old muſty debts, or any such nonsense; for tradesmen, Charles, are the moſt exorbitant fellows.

Charles S. Very true, and paying them is only encouraging them.

Careless. Nothing else.

Charles S. Aye, aye, never fear. [*Exit* CARELESS.]—Soh! this was an odd old fellow, indeed.——Let me see—two-thirds of this is mine by right[4],—five hundred and thirty odd pounds.[5] 'Fore Heaven! I find one's anceſtors are more valuable rela-tions than I took them for!—Ladies and gentlemen, your moſt obedient and very grateful humble servant.——

Enter ROWLEY.

Hah! old Rowley! egad, you are juſt come in time to take leave of your old acquaintance.

Rowley. Yes, I heard they were a-going. But I wonder you can have such spirits under so many diſtresses.

Charles S. Why, there's the point! my diſtresses are so many,

[1][little nabob—1826.].   [2]fixed—1799. *Em.* Crewe: 1823.   [3][how Moses.]
[4][mine.] *Em.*—Crewe: (1781).   [5][pounds. Aye, right.]

that I can't afford to part with my spirits; but I shall be rich and splenetic, all in good time. However, I suppose you are surprised that I am not more sorrowful at parting with so many near relations; 'to be sure, 'tis very affecting: but rot 'em you[1] see they never move a muscle, so why should I?

Rowley. There's no making you serious a moment.

Charles S. Yes, faith, I am so now. Here, my honest Rowley, here, get me this changed directly, and[2] take a hundred pounds of it immediately, to old Stanley.

Rowley. A hundred pounds! Consider only——

Charles S. Gad's life, don't talk about it: poor Stanley's wants are pressing, and if you don't make haste, we shall have some one call that has a better right to the money.

Rowley. Ah! there's the point! I never will cease dunning you with the old proverb——

Charles S. "Be just before you're generous."—Why,[3] so I would if I could; but Justice is an old lame hobbling beldame, and I can't get her to keep pace with Generosity for the soul of me.

Rowley. Yet, Charles, believe me, one hour's reflection——

Charles S. Aye, aye, it's all very true; but, hark'ee, Rowley, while I have, by Heaven I'll give; so damn your œconomy, and now for hazard.   [*Exeunt.*

SCENE II

The Parlour.

Enter SIR OLIVER *and* MOSES.

Moses. Well, sir, I think, as Sir Peter said, you have seen Mr. Charles in high glory; 'tis great pity he's so extravagant.

Sir Oliver S. True, but he would not sell my picture.

Moses. And loves wine and women so much.

Sir Oliver S. But he would not sell my picture.

Moses. And games so deep.

Sir Oliver S. But he would not sell my picture.——Oh, here's Rowley.

[1][but you—1826.] [2][changed and.] [3]Hey, why—Crewe. *Em.*—1826: (1781).

Enter ROWLEY.

Rowley. So,[1] Sir Oliver, I find you have made a purchase——

Sir Oliver S. Yes, yes, our young rake has parted with his ancestors like old tapeſtry.

Rowley. And here has he commissioned me to re-deliver you part of the purchase-money—I mean, though, in your necessitous charaćter of old Stanley.

Moses. Ah! there is the pity of all; he is so damned charitable.

Rowley. And I left a hosier and two tailors in the hall, who, I'm sure, won't be paid, and this hundred would satisfy them.

Sir Oliver S. Well, well, I'll pay his debts, and his benevolences too.—But now I am no more a broker, and you shall introduce me to the elder brother[2] as old Stanley.

Rowley. Not yet awhile; Sir Peter, I know, means to call there about this time.

Enter TRIP.

Trip. Oh, gentlemen, I beg pardon for not showing you out; this way.——Moses, a word—— [*Exeunt* TRIP *and* MOSES.

Sir Oliver S. There's a fellow for you—would you believe it, that puppy intercepted the Jew on our coming, and wanted to raise money before he got to his maſter.

Rowley. Indeed!

Sir Oliver S. Yes, they are now planning an annuity business. —Ah! maſter Rowley, in my days servants were content with the follies of their maſters, when they were worn a little threadbare; but now, they have their vices, like their birthday cloaths, with the gloss on. [*Exeunt.*

SCENE III

A Library.

JOSEPH SURFACE *and a* SERVANT.

Joseph S. No letter from Lady Teazle?

Servant. No, sir.

Joseph S. I am surprised she has not sent, if she is prevented

[1]O—1799. *Em.*—Crewe: 1823.   [2]the brother—1799. *Em.*—Crewe: Rae.

from coming. Sir Peter certainly does not suspect me. Yet, I wish I may not lose the heiress, through the scrape I have drawn myself into[1] with the wife; however, Charles's imprudence and bad character are great points in my favour. [*Knock without.*]

Servant. Sir, I believe that must be Lady Teazle.

Joseph S. Hold!—See whether it is or not before you go to the door: I have a particular message for you, if it should be my brother.

Servant. 'Tis her ladyship, sir; she always leaves her chair at the milliner's in the next street.

Joseph S. Stay, stay; draw that screen before the window—that will do;—my opposite neighbour is a maiden lady of so curious a[2] temper.—[SERVANT *draws the screen, and exit.*]—I have a difficult hand to play in this affair. Lady Teazle has lately suspected my views on Maria; but she must by no means be let into that secret,—at least, till I have her more in my power.

Enter LADY TEAZLE.

Lady T. What, sentiment in soliloquy?[3] Have you been very impatient now?[4]—O Lud! don't pretend to look grave.—I vow I couldn't come before.

Joseph S. Oh, Madam, punctuality is a species of constancy, a very unfashionable quality in a lady.

Lady T. Upon my word you ought to pity me. Do you know Sir Peter is grown so ill-tempered to me of[5] late, and so jealous of Charles, too; that's the best of the story, isn't it?

Joseph S. I am glad my scandalous friends keep that up. [*Aside.*

Lady T. I'm sure I wish he would let Maria marry him, and then perhaps he would be convinced; don't you, Mr. Surface?

Joseph S. Indeed I do not. [*Aside.*]—Oh, certainly I do! for then my dear Lady Teazle would also be convinced, how wrong her suspicions were of my having any design on the silly girl.

Lady T. Well, well, I'm inclined to believe you. But isn't it provoking, to have the most ill-natured things said of one?—And there's my friend Lady Sneerwell has circulated I dont'

---

[1]in—1799: Rae. *Em.*—Crewe: 1823.   [2]of a curious—Crewe. *Em.*—Rae: 1823.
[3][soliloquy, now—1826.]   [4][impatient—1826.]   [5]ill-natured of—1799. *Em.*—Crewe.

know how many scandalous tales of me, and all without any foundation too—that's what vexes me.

Joseph S. Aye, madam, to be sure, that is the provoking circumstance—without foundation; yes, yes, there's the mortification, indeed; for when a scandalous story is believed against one, there certainly is no comfort like the consciousness of having deserved it.

Lady T. No, to be sure, then I'd forgive their malice; but to attack me, who am really so innocent, and who never say an ill-natured thing of anybody—that is, of my friends; and then Sir Peter too, to have him so peevish, and so suspicious, when I know the integrity of my own heart——indeed 'tis monstrous!

Joseph S. But, my dear Lady Teazle, 'tis your own fault if you suffer it. When a husband entertains a groundless suspicion of his wife, and withdraws his confidence from her, the original compact is broke,[1] and she owes it to the honour of her sex to endeavour to outwit[2] him.

Lady T. Indeed!—so that if he suspects me without cause, it follows, that the best way of curing his jealousy is to give him reason for't.

Joseph S. Undoubtedly—for your husband should never be deceived in you,—and in that case it becomes you to be frail in compliment to his discernment.

Lady T. To be sure, what you say is very reasonable, and when the consciousness of my innocence——

Joseph S. Ah! my dear madam, there is the great mistake: 'tis this very conscious innocence that is of the greatest prejudice to you. What is it makes you negligent of forms, and careless of the world's opinion?—why, the consciousness of your own innocence. What makes you thoughtless in your conduct, and apt to run into a thousand little imprudences?—why, the consciousness of your own innocence. What makes you impatient of Sir Peter's temper, and outrageous at his suspicions?—why, the consciousness of your innocence.

Lady T. 'Tis very true!

Joseph S. Now, my dear Lady Teazle, if you would but once

[1][broken—1826.]   [2][sex to outwit.] *Em.*—Crewe: Rae: 1826: (1781).

make a trifling *faux pas*, you can't conceive how cautious you would grow, and how ready to humour and agree with your husband.

Lady T. Do you think so?

Joseph S. Oh! I am sure on't; and then you would[1] find all scandal would cease at once, for, in short, your character at present is a like a person in a plethora, absolutely dying from too much health.

[*Lady T.* So, so; then I perceive your prescription is, that I must sin in my own defence, and part with my virtue to preserve my reputation?

Joseph S. Exactly so, upon my credit, ma'am.

Lady T. Well, certainly this is the oddest doctrine, and the newest receipt for avoiding calumny!

Joseph S. An infallible one, believe me. Prudence, like experience, must be paid for.][2]

Lady T. Why, if my understanding were once convinced——

Joseph S. Oh, certainly, your understanding madam, should be convinced.—Yes, yes—Heaven forbid I should persuade you to do anything you thought wrong. No, no, I have too much honour to desire it.

Lady T. Don't you think we may as well leave *honour* out of the question?

Joseph S. Ah! the ill effects of your country education, I see, still remain with you.

Lady T. I doubt they do indeed; and I will fairly own to you, that if I could be persuaded to do wrong, it would be by Sir Peter's ill usage sooner than your *honourable logic*, after all.

Joseph S. Then, by this hand, which he is unworthy of——
[*Taking her hand.*   [*Enter* SERVANT.
'Sdeath, you blockhead—what do you want?

Serv. I beg your pardon,[3] sir, but I thought you would not choose Sir Peter to come up[4] without announcing him.

Joseph S. Sir Peter!—Oons and the devil![5]

[1]you'd—Crewe: Rae. *Em.*—1823: 1826.   [2]*Om.*—1799. *Em.*—Crewe: Rae.
[3]beg pardon—Crewe. *Em.*—Rae: 1826.   [4]upstairs—Crewe. *Em.*—Rae: 1823: 1826.
[5][Oons! the Devil.—Rae: 1826.]

Lady T. Sir Peter! O Lud—I'm ruined—I'm ruined!

Servant. Sir, 'twasn't I let him in.

Lady T. Oh! I'm quite undone! What will become of me now, Mr. Logic?[1] Oh! he's on the ftairs—I'll get behind here —and if ever I'm so imprudent again—[*Goes behind the screen.*

Joseph S. Give me that book. [*Sits down,* SERVANT *pretends to adjust his hair.* [*Enter* SIR PETER.

Sir Peter T. Aye, ever improving himself—Mr. Surface, Mr. Surface——

Joseph S. Oh! my dear Sir Peter, I beg your pardon—[*Gaping —throws away the book.*]—I have been dozing over a ftupid book.—Well, I am much obliged to you for this call. You haven't been here, I believe, since I fitted up this room.—Books, you know, are the only things I am a coxcomb in.

Sir Peter T. 'Tis very neat indeed.—Well, well, that's proper; and you make[2] even your screen a source of knowledge—hung, I perceive, with maps.

Joseph S. Oh, yes, I find great use in that screen.

Sir Peter T. I dare you you muft, certainly, when you want to find anything in a hurry.

Joseph S. Aye, or to hide anything in a hurry either.
[*Aside.*

Sir Peter T. Well, I have a little private business——

Joseph S. You need not ftay [*to the* SERVANT].

Servant. No, sir. [*Exit.*

Joseph S. Here's a chair, Sir Peter—I beg——

Sir Peter T. Well, now we are alone, there is a subject, my dear friend, on which I wish to unburthen my mind to you—a point of the greateft moment to my peace; in short, my dear friend, Lady Teazle's conduct of late has made me extremely unhappy.

Joseph S. Indeed! I am very sorry[3] to hear it.

Sir Peter T. Aye, 'tis but too[4] plain she has not the leaft regard for me; but, what's worse, I have a pretty good authority to suspect[5] she has formed an attachment to another.

[1][me? Now, Mr. Logic—1826.]   [2][can make.]   [3]I'm sorry—Crewe. *Em.—* Rae: 1826   [4]['tis too.]   [5]suppose—1799. *Em.—*Crewe: Rae.

Joseph S. You[1] aſtonish me!

Sir Peter T. Yes; and, between ourselves, I think I've dis-covered the person.

Joseph S. How! you alarm me exceedingly.

Sir Peter T. Ah[2], my dear friend, I knew you would sym-pathize with me!

Joseph S. Yes—believe me, Sir Peter, such a discovery would hurt[3] me juſt as much as it would you.

Sir Peter T. I am convinced of it.—Ah! it is a happiness to have a friend whom one[4] can truſt even with one's family secrets. But have you no guess who I mean?

Joseph S. I haven't the moſt diſtant idea. It can't be Sir Benjamin Backbite!

Sir Peter T. O, no! What say you to Charles?

Joseph S. My brother! impossible! [O no, Sir Peter, you muſt not credit the scandalous insinuations you may hear. No, No, Charles to be sure has been charged with many things of this kind, but I can never think he would meditate so gross an injury.][5]

Sir Peter T. Ah, my dear friend, the goodness of your own heart misleads you. You judge of others by yourself.

Joseph S. Certainly, Sir Peter, the heart that is conscious of its own integrity is ever slow to credit another's treachery.[6]

Sir Peter T. True—but your brother has no sentiment—you never hear him talk so.

Joseph S. Yet, I can't but think[7] Lady Teazle herself has too much principle.

Sir Peter T. Aye,—but what is[8] principle againſt the flattery of a handsome, lively young fellow?

Joseph S. That's very true.

Sir Peter T. And then[9], you know, the difference of our ages makes it very improbable that she should have a great affection for me; and if she were to be frail, and I were to make it public, why the town would only laugh at me—the foolish old bachelor, who had married a girl.

[1]Indeed you—1799: Rae. *Em.*—Crewe.   [2][aye—1826.]   [3]distress—1799. *Em.* —Crewe: Rae.   [4][we—1826.]   [5]*Om.*—Crewe. *Em.*—Rae.   [6]baseness—1799. *Em.*—Crewe: Rae.   [7]think that—Crewe. *Em.*—Rae: 1826.   [8]what's her—Crewe. *Em.*—Rae: 1826.   [9][there's.]

Joseph S. That's true, to be sure—they *would* laugh.

Sir Peter T. Laugh—aye, and make ballads, and paragraphs, and the devil knows what of me.

Joseph S. No—you must never make it public.

Sir Peter T. But then again—that the nephew of my old friend, Sir Oliver, should be the person to attempt such a wrong, hurts me more nearly.

Joseph S. Aye, there's the point.—When ingratitude barbs the dart of injury, the wound has double danger in it.

Sir Peter T. Aye—I, that was, in a manner, left his guardian; in whose house he had been so often entertained; who never in my life denied him—my advice.

Joseph S. Oh, 'tis not to be credited. There may be a man capable of such baseness, to be sure; but, for my part, till you can give me positive proofs, I cannot but doubt it. However, if this[1] should be proved on him, he is no longer a brother of mine—I disclaim kindred with him: for the man who can break thro' the[2] laws of hospitality, and attempt[3] the wife of his friend, deserves to be branded as the pest of society.

Sir Peter T. What a difference there is between you! What noble sentiments!

Joseph S. Yet, I cannot suspect Lady Teazle's honour.

Sir Peter T. I am sure I wish to think well of her, and to remove all ground of quarrel between us. She has lately reproached me more than once with having made no settlement on her; and, in our last quarrel, she almost hinted that she should not break her heart if I was dead. Now, as we seem to differ in our ideas of expense, I have resolved she shall[4] be her own mistress in that respect for the future; and if I were to die, she shall find that I[5] have not been inattentive to her interests while living. Here, my friend, are the drafts of two deeds, which I wish to have your opinion on.—By one, she will enjoy eight hundred a year independent while I live; and, by the other, the bulk of my fortune after[6] my death.

---

[1][it—1826.]   [2][break the.]   [3][tempt—1826.]   [4][shall have her own way and—1826.]   [5][she will find I—1826.]   [6][at.]

Joseph S. This conduct, Sir Peter, is indeed truly generous.
——I wish it may not corrupt my pupil.   [*Aside.*

Sir Peter T. Yes, I am determined she shall have no cause to complain, though I would not have her acquainted with the latter instance of my affection yet awhile.

Joseph S. Nor I, if I could help it.   [*Aside.*

Sir Peter T. And now, my dear friend, if you please, we will talk over the situation of your hopes[1] with Maria.

Joseph S. [*Softly*]. No, no, Sir Peter; another time, if you please.

Sir Peter T. I am sensibly chagrined at the little progress you seem to make in her affections.

Joseph S. I beg you will not mention it.[2] What are my disappointments when your happiness is in debate! [*Softly.*]—'Sdeath I shall be ruined every way.   [*Aside.*

Sir Peter T. And though you are so averse to my acquainting Lady Teazle with *your* passion I am[3] sure she's not your enemy in the affair.

Joseph S. Pray, Sir Peter, now, oblige[4] me. I am really too much affected by the subject we have been speaking of,[5] to bestow a thought on my own concerns. The man who is entrusted with his friend's distresses can never——[*Enter* SERVANT.] Well, sir?

Servant. Your brother, sir, is speaking to a gentleman in the street, and says he knows you are within.

Joseph S. 'Sdeath, blockhead, I'm not within—I'm out for the day.

Sir Peter T. Stay—hold—a thought has struck me:—you shall be at home.

Joseph S. Well, well, let him up. [*Exit* SERVANT.] He'll interrupt Sir Peter, however.   [*Aside.*

Sir Peter T. Now, my good friend, oblige me, I entreat you. Before Charles comes, let me conceal myself somewhere—then do you tax him on the point we have been talking on, and[6] his answers[7] may satisfy me at once.

---

[1][affairs].   [2]it, sir—Crewe: 1826. *Em.*—Rae: 1823.   [3][passion for Maria. I'm.]
[4]Peter, oblige—Crewe. *Em.*—Rae: 1826.   [5]been talking—Crewe. *Em.*—Rae: 1826.
[6][talking and.]   [7][answer—1826.]

Joseph S. Oh, fie, Sir Peter! would you have me join in so mean a trick?—to trepan my brother too?

Sir Peter T. Nay, you tell me you are *sure* he is innocent; if so, you do him the greateſt service by giving him an opportunity to clear himself, and you will set my heart at reſt. Come, you shall not refuse me: here, behind this screen will be—Hey! what the devil! there seems to be one liſtener there already—I'll swear I saw a petticoat!

Joseph S. Ha, Ha! ha! Well, this is ridiculous enough. I'll tell you, Sir Peter, though I hold a man of intrigue to be a moſt despicable charaƈter, yet, you know, it does not follow that one is to be an absolute Joseph either! Hark'ee, 'tis a little French milliner—a silly rogue that plagues me,—and having some charaƈter to lose, on your coming, sir, she ran behind the screen.

Sir Peter T. Ah! you rogue! But, egad, she has overheard all I have been saying of my wife.

Joseph S. Oh, 'twill never go any farther, you may depend upon it.

Sir Peter T. No! then, ifaith, let her hear it out.—Here's a closet will do as well.

Joseph S. Well, go in there.

Sir Peter T. Sly rogue! sly rogue!   [*Going into the closet.*

Joseph S. A narrow escape, indeed! and a curious situation I'm in, to part man and wife in this manner.

Lady T. [*peeping*]. Couldn't I ſteal off?

Joseph S. Keep close, my angel!

Sir Peter T. [*peeping*]. Joseph, tax him home.

Joseph S. Back, my dear friend!

Lady T. Couldn't you lock Sir Peter in?

Joseph S. Be ſtill,[1] my life!

Sir Peter T. [*peeping*]. You're sure the little milliner won't blab?

Joseph S. In, in, my good[2] Sir Peter.—'Foregad, I wish I had a key to the door.

Enter CHARLES SURFACE.

Charles S. Holla! brother, what has been the matter? Your fellow would not let me up at firſt. What! have you had a Jew or a wench with you?

[1]Lie still—1799. *Em.*—Crewe: Rae.   [2]dear—1799. *Em.*—Crewe: Rae.

Joseph S. Neither, brother, I assure you.

Charles S. But what has made Sir Peter ſteal off? I thought he had been with you.

Joseph S. He *was*, brother; but hearing you were coming, he did not choose to ſtay.

Charles S. What! was the old gentleman afraid I wanted to borrow money of him?

Joseph S. No, sir: but I am sorry to find, Charles, you have lately given that worthy man grounds for great uneasiness.

Charles S. Yes, yes, yes!—[1] they tell me I do that to a great many worthy men.—But how so, pray? . . .

Joseph S. To be plain with you, brother—he thinks you are endeavouring to gain Lady Teazle's affeꝏctions from him.

Charles S. Who, I? O lud! not I, upon my word. Ha! ha! ha! ha! so the old fellow has found out that he has got a young wife, has he?—[or, what's worse, has her ladyship discovered she has an old husband?[2]]

Joseph S. This is no subjeꝏct to jeſt upon,[3] brother. He who can laugh——

Charles S. True, true, as you were going to say—then, seriously, I never had the leaſt idea of what you charge me with, upon my honour.

Joseph S. Well, it will give Sir Peter great satisfaꝏction to hear this.   [*Aloud.*

Charles S. To be sure, I once thought the lady seemed to have taken a fancy to me; but, upon my soul, I never gave her[4] the leaſt encouragement:—besides, you know my attachment to Maria.

Joseph S. But sure, brother, even if[4] Lady Teazle had betrayed the fondeſt partiality for you——

Charles S. Why, look ye, Joseph, I hope I shall never deliberately do a dishonourable aꝏction: but if a pretty woman was purposely to throw herself in my way—and that pretty woman married to a man old enough to be her father——

Joseph S. Well——

[1][Yes, they—Rae.]   [2]*Om.*—1799: 1826. *Em.*—Crewe: Rae [has Lady Teazle found—1823.]   [3][on—Rae.]   [4]brother, if—Crewe. *Em.*—Rae: 1826.

Charles S. Why, I believe I should be obliged to borrow a little of your morality, that's all.—But, brother, do you know now that you surprise me exceedingly, by naming *me* with Lady Teazle; for, 'faith, I always understood *you* were her favourite.

Joseph S. For shame, Charles! This retort is foolish.

Charles S. Nay, I swear I have seen you exchange such significant glances——

Joseph S. Nay, nay, sir, this is no jest.

Charles S. Egad, I'm serious. Don't you remember one day when I called here——

Joseph S. Nay, prithee, Charles——

Charles S. And found you together——

Joseph S. Zounds, sir! I insist——

Charles S. And another time when your servant——

Joseph S. Brother, brother, a word with you!—Gad, I must stop him.   [*Aside.*

Charles S. Informed, I say, that——

Joseph S. Hush! I beg your pardon, but Sir Peter has overheard all we have been saying. I knew you could clear yourself or I should not have consented.

Charles S. How, Sir Peter! where is he?

Joseph S. Softly; there!   [*Points to the closet.*

Charles S. Oh, 'fore Heaven, I'll have him out. Sir Peter, come forth!

Joseph S. No, no——

Charles S. I say, Sir Peter, come into court.—[*Pulls in* SIR PETER.]—What, my old guardian!—What! turn[1] inquisitor, and take[2] evidence incog?

Sir Peter T. Give me your hand, Charles—I believe I have suspected you wrongfully; but you mustn't be angry with Joseph—'twas my plan!

Charles S. Indeed!

Sir Peter T. But I acquit you. I promise you I don't think near so ill of you as I did: what I have heard has given me great satisfaction.

[1]urned—1799. *Em.*—Crewe.   [2]taking the—1799; take the—Crewe. *Em.*—Rae: 1823.

Charles S. Egad, then, 'twas lucky you didn't hear any more—wasn't it, Joseph?

Sir Peter T. Ah! you would have retorted on him.

Charles S. Aye, aye, that was a joke.

Sir Peter T. Yes, yes, I know his honour too well.

Charles S. But you might as well have suspected *him* as *me* in this matter, for all that—mightn't he, Joseph?

Sir Peter T. Well, well, I believe you.

Joseph S. Would[1] they were both out[2] of the room!   [*Aside.*

Enter SERVANT, *and whispers* JOSEPH SURFACE.

Sir Peter T. And in future perhaps we may not be such strangers.

[*Servant.* Lady Sneerwell is below, and says she will come up.][3]

Joseph S. [*to the* SERVANT]. Lady Sneerwell! [Gad's life, she mustn't come here].[4] Gentlemen, I beg pardon,—I must wait on you downstairs: here is a person come on particular business.

Charles S. Well,[5] you can see him in another room. Sir Peter and I have not met a long time, and I have something to say to him.

Joseph S. [*aside*]. They must not be left together. [*To* CHARLES] I'll send this man[6] away, and return directly.—Sir Peter, not a word of the French milliner.

Sir Peter. Oh,[7] not for the world!—[*Exit* JOSEPH.]—Ah! Charles, if you associated more with your brother, one might indeed hope for your reformation. He is a man of sentiment.—Well, there is nothing in the world so noble as a man of sentiment!

Charles S. Pshaw! he is too moral by half—and so apprehensive of his good name, as he calls it, that I suppose he would as soon let a priest into his house as a girl.

Sir Peter T. No, no,—come, come,—you may wrong him.—No, no! Joseph is no rake, but he is no such saint in that respect

---

[1]I wish—1799. *Em.*—Rae: Crewe.   [2][well out.]   [3]*Om.*—Crewe: Rae: 1823. *Em.*—1826: (1781).   [4]Sneerwell! Stop him by all means—Crewe. *Em.*—1826. [5]send Lady Sneerwell—1826.   [6]met for—Crewe. *Em.*—Rae: 1823.   [7][I—1826.] [8]Well, well—Crewe. *Em.*—Rae: 1823.

either.——I have a great mind to tell him—we should have a
laugh.[1]   [*Aside.*

Charles S. Oh, hang him! He's a very anchorite, a young
hermit.

Sir Peter T. Hark'ee—you muſt not abuse him: he may chance
to hear of it again, I promise you.

Charles S. Why, you won't tell him?

Sir Peter T. No—but—this way. Egad, I'll tell him.—[*Aside.*
Hark'ee, have you a mind to have a good laugh against[2] Joseph?

Charles S. I should like it of all things.

Sir Peter T. Then, i'faith, we will—I'll be quit with him for
discovering me.—[*Whispers.*]—He had a girl[3] with him when I
called.

Charles S. What! Joseph? you jeſt.

Sir Peter T. Hush!—a little French milliner—and the beſt of
the jeſt is—she's in the room now.

Charles S. The devil she is! [*Looking at the closet.*]

Sir Peter T. Hush! I tell you!   [*Points to the screen.*

Charles S. Behind the screen! 'Slife, let's unveil her!

Sir Peter T. No, no—he's coming—you shan't, indeed!

Charles S. Egad,[4] we'll have a peep at the little milliner!

Sir Peter T. Not[5] for the world—Joseph will never forgive
me——

Charles S. I'll ſtand by you——

Sir Peter T. Odds, here he is—[JOSEPH SURFACE *enters juſt as*
CHARLES SURFACE *throws down the screen.*]

Charles S. Lady Teazle, by all that's wonderful!

Sir Peter T. Lady Teazle, by all that's damnable![6]

Charles S. Sir Peter, this is one of the smarteſt French milliners I ever saw. Egad, you seem all to have been diverting
yourselves here at hide and seek, and I don't see who is out of
the secret.—Shall I beg your ladyship to inform me? Not a
word!—Brother, will you be pleased to explain this matter?
What! is Morality dumb too?—Sir Peter, though I found you

---

[1][laugh at Joseph—1826.]   [2][at—1826.]   [3]wench—1799. *Em.*—Crewe: Rae:
1826.   [4]O egad—1799: Rae. *Em.*—Crewe.   [5]No, not—1799. *Em.*—Crewe: Rae:
1826.   [6]horrible—Rae: (1781).

in the dark, perhaps you are not so now! All mute!—Well—though I can make nothing of the affair, I suppose you perfectly understand one another—so I'll leave you to yourselves—[*Going.*] Brother, I'm sorry to find you have given that worthy man grounds[1] for so much uneasiness.—Sir Peter! there's nothing in the world so noble as a man of sentiment!

[*Exit* CHARLES. *They stand for some time looking at each other.*]

Joseph S. Sir Peter—notwithstanding—I confess—that appearances are against me—if you will afford me your patience—I make no doubt—but I shall explain everything to your satisfaction.

Sir Peter T. If you please, sir.

Joseph S. The fact is, sir—that Lady Teazle, knowing my pretensions to your ward, Maria—I say, sir,—Lady Teazle, being apprehensive of the jealousy of your temper—and knowing my friendship to the family—she, sir, I say—called here—in order that—I might explain those pretensions—but on your coming—being apprehensive—as I said—of your jealousy—she withdrew—and this, you may depend on it, is the whole truth of the matter.

Sir Peter T. A very clear account, upon my word; and I dare swear the lady will vouch for every article of it.

Lady T. For not one word of it, Sir Peter!

Sir Peter T. How! don't you think[2] it worth while to agree in the lie?

Lady T. There is not one syllable of truth in what that gentleman has told you.

Sir Peter T. I believe you, upon my soul, ma'am!

Joseph S. [*aside*].'Sdeath, madam, will you betray me?

Lady T. Good Mr. Hypocrite, by your leave, I will speak for myself.

Sir Peter T. Aye, let her alone, sir; you'll find she'll make out a[3] better story than you, without prompting.

Lady T. Hear me, Sir Peter!—I came hither on no matter relating to your ward, and even ignorant of this gentleman's

---

[1][cause.]   [2]ever think—Crewe. *Em.*—Rae: 1826.
[3]make a—Crewe. *Em.*—Rae: 1826.

pretensions to her. But I came seduced by his insidious argu-
ments, at least to listen to his pretended passion, if not to sacrifice
your honour to his baseness.

Sir Peter T. Now, I believe, the truth is coming out indeed![1]

Joseph S. The woman's mad!

Lady T. No, sir—she has recovered her senses, and your own
arts have furnished her with the means.—Sir Peter, I do not expect you to credit me—but the tenderness you expressed for me,
when I am sure you could not think I was a witness to it, has
penetrated so to my heart,[2] that had I left the place without the
shame of this[3] discovery, my future life should have spoken the
sincerity of my gratitude. As for that smooth-tongued hypocrite,
who would have seduced the wife of his too credulous friend,
while he affected honourable addresses to his ward—I behold
him now in a light so truly despicable, that I shall never again[4]
respect myself for having listened to him.   [*Exit.*

Joseph S. Notwithstanding all this, Sir Peter, Heaven knows

———

Sir Peter T. That you are a villain! and so I leave you to your
conscience.

Joseph S. You are too rash, Sir Peter; you *shall* hear me. The
man who shuts out conviction by refusing to——

[*Sir Peter.* O damn your sentiments.][5]

[*Exeunt,* SURFACE *following and speaking.*[6]

———

[1]coming indeed—Rae: 1826. *Em.*—Crewe.   [2]penetrated—O to my heart—Crewe.
Em.—Rae: 1823.   [3]without this shame and full—Crewe. *Em.*—Rae: 1826.   [4]never
again shall—Crewe. *Em.*—Rae: 1826.   [5]*Om.*—Crewe: Rae. *Em.*—1799: 1823: 1826.
[6]*Om.*—Crewe. *Em.*—Rae.

END OF THE FOURTH ACT

Act the Fifth

SCENE I

THE *Library.*

Enter JOSEPH SURFACE *and* SERVANT.

Joseph S. Mr. Stanley!—and why should you think I would see him? you must know he comes to ask something.

Servant. Sir, I should not have let him in, but that Mr. Rowley came to the door with him.

Joseph S. Pshaw! blockhead! to suppose that I should now be in a temper to receive visits from poor relations!——Well, why don't you show the fellow up?

Servant. I will, sir.——Why, sir, it was not my fault that Sir Peter discovered my lady——

Joseph S. Go, fool! [*Exit* SERVANT.]—Sure Fortune never played a man of my policy such a trick before. My character with Sir Peter, my hopes with Maria, destroyed in a moment! I'm in a rare humour to listen to other people's distresses! I shan't be able to bestow even a benevolent sentiment on Stanley.—So![1] here he comes, and Rowley with him. I must try to recover myself, and put a little charity into my face, however.   [*Exit.*

Enter SIR OLIVER *and* ROWLEY.

Sir Oliver S. What! does he avoid us!—That was he, was it not?

Rowley. It was, sir. But I doubt you are come a little too abruptly. His nerves are so weak, that the sight of a poor relation may be too much for him. I should have gone first to break you to him.

Sir Oliver S. Oh, plague of his nerves! Yet this is he whom Sir Peter extols as a man of the most benevolent way of thinking!

[1]Oh—Crewe. *Em.*—Rae: 1826.

Rowley. As to his way of thinking, I cannot pretend to decide for, to do him juſtice, he appears to have as much speculative benevolence as any private gentleman in the kingdom, though he is seldom so sensual as to indulge himself in the exercise of it.

Sir Oliver S. Yet has a ſtring of charitable sentiments, I suppose, at[1] his fingers' ends.

Rowley. Or rather, at his tongue's end, Sir Oliver; for I believe there is no sentiment he has more faith in than[2] that "Charity begins at home."

Sir Oliver S. And his, I presume, is of that domeſtic sort; it never ſtirs abroad at all.

Rowley. I doubt you'll find it so;—but he's coming. I muſtn't seem to interrupt you; and you know immediately as you leave him, I come in to announce your arrival in your real charaƈter.

Sir Oliver S. True; and afterwards you'll meet me at Sir Peter's.

Rowley. Without losing a moment.   [*Exit*.

Sir Oliver S. So! I don't like the complaisance of his features.

Enter JOSEPH SURFACE.

Joseph S. Sir, I beg you ten thousand pardons for keeping you a moment waiting.——Mr. Stanley, I presume.

Sir Oliver S. At your service.[3]

Joseph S. Sir, I beg you will do me the honour to sit down— I entreat you, sir!

Sir Oliver S. Dear sir—there's no occasion——too civil by half!   [*Aside*.

Joseph S. I have not the pleasure of knowing you, Mr. Stanley; but I am extremely happy to see you look so well. You were nearly related to my mother, I think, Mr. Stanley?[4]

Sir Oliver S. I was, sir;—so nearly that my present poverty, I fear, may do discredit to her wealthy children, else I should not have presumed to trouble you.

Joseph S. Dear sir, there needs no apology:—He that is in diſtress, though a ſtranger, has a right to claim kindred with the wealthy. I am sure I wish I was of that class, and had it in my power to offer you even a small relief.

---

[1][sentiments at.]   [2][such faith in as—1826.]   [3]service, sir—Crewe. *Em*.—Rae 1826.   [4]mother, Mr. Stanley, I think—Crewe. *Em*. Rae: 1823.

Sir Oliver S. If your uncle, Sir Oliver, were[1] here, I should have a friend.

Joseph S. I wish he was, sir, with all my heart; you should not want an advocate with him, believe me, sir.

Sir Oliver S. I should not need one—my diſtresses would recommend me. But I imagined his bounty had enabled[2] you to become the agent of his charity.

Joseph S. My dear sir, you were ſtrangely misinformed. Sir Oliver is a worthy man, a very worthy sort of man;[3] but avarice, Mr. Stanley, is the vice of age. I will tell you, my good sir, in confidence, what he has done for me has been a mere nothing; though people, I know, have thought otherwise, and, for my part I never chose to contradiſt the report.

Sir Oliver S. What! has he never transmitted you bullion—rupees—pagodas?

Joseph S. O, dear sir, nothing of the kind!—No, no—a few presents now and then—china, shawls, congou tea, avadavats, and Indian crackers—little more, believe me.[4]

Sir Oliver S. Here's gratitude for twelve thousand pounds!—Avadavats and Indian crackers!   [*Aside.*

Joseph S. Then, my dear sir, you have heard, I doubt not, of the extravagance of my brother: there are very few would credit what I have done for that unfortunate young man.

Sir Oliver S. Not I, for one!   [*Aside.*

Joseph S. The sums I have lent him!—Indeed I have been exceedingly to blame; it was an amiable weakness—however—I don't pretend to defend it,—and now I feel it doubly culpable, since it has deprived me of the power[5] of serving *you*, Mr. Stanley, as my heart direſts.[6]

Sir Oliver S. Dissembler! [*Aside.*]—Then, sir, you can't assiſt me?

Joseph S. At present, it grieves me to say, I cannot; but, whenever I have the ability, you may depend upon hearing from me.

Sir Oliver S. I am extremely sorry——

Joseph S. Not more than I, believe me;—to pity without the

¹was—Crewe. *Em.*—Rae: 1823.   ²[would enable—1826.]   ³[worthy man—1826.]   ⁴crackers—Crewe. *Em.* 1799: Rae: 1826: (1781).   ⁵[pleasure—1826.] ⁶[dictates—1826.]

power to relieve, is still more painful than to ask and be denied.

Sir Oliver S. Kind sir, your most obedient humble servant.

Joseph S. You leave me deeply affected, Mr. Stanley.—
William, be ready to open the door.

Sir Oliver S. Oh, dear sir, no ceremony.

Joseph S. Your very obedient.

Sir Oliver S. Sir, your most obsequious.

Joseph S. You may depend upon hearing from me, whenever
I can be of service.

Sir Oliver S. Sweet sir, you are too good!

Joseph S. In the meantime I wish you health and spirits.

Sir Oliver S. Your ever grateful and perpetual humble
servant.

Joseph S. Sir, yours as sincerely.

Sir Oliver S. Charles, you are my heir![1]   [*Aside. Exit.*

Joseph S. This is one bad effect[2] of a good character; it invites
application from the unfortunate, and there needs no small degree of address to gain the reputation of benevolence without
incurring the expense. The silver ore of pure charity is an expensive article in the catalogue of a man's good qualities; whereas the sentimental French plate I use instead of it makes just as
good a show, and pays no tax.

Enter ROWLEY.

Rowley. Mr. Surface, your servant: I was apprehensive of
interrupting you, though my business demands immediate attention, as this note will inform you.

Joseph S. Always happy to see Mr. Rowley—
                                                  [*Reads the letter.*

How! Oliver—Surface![3]—My uncle, arrived!

Rowley. He is, indeed: we have just parted—quite well, after
a speedy voyage, and impatient to embrace his worthy nephew.

Joseph S. I am astonished!—William! stop Mr. Stanley, if
he's not gone.

Rowley. Oh! he's out of reach, I believe.

[1]Now, I'm satisfied—Crewe: 1826. *Em.*—1799: Rae: 1823.   [2]one of the bad effects
—Crewe. *Em.*—Rae: 1826.   [3]How, Sir Oliver Surface?—Crewe: 1823. *Em.* Rae (*i.e.*,
he reads the signature.)

II. H

Joseph S. Why did not you[1] let me know this when you came in together?

Rowley. I thought you had particular business;—but I must be gone to inform your brother, and appoint him here to meet his[2] uncle. He will be with you in a quarter of an hour.

Joseph S. So he says. Well, I am strangely overjoyed at his coming.——Never, to be sure, was anything so damned unlucky.   [*Aside.*

Rowley. You will be delighted to see how well he looks.

Joseph S. Ah! I'm rejoiced to hear it.——Just at this time!
                                                           [*Aside.*

Rowley. I'll tell him how impatiently you expect him.[3]

Joseph S. Do, do; pray give my best duty and affection. Indeed, I cannot express the sensations I feel at the thought of seeing him.—[*Exit* Rowley.]—Certainly his coming just at this
time is the cruellest piece of ill-fortune!

                                                           [*Exit.*

SCENE II

Sir Peter Teazle's.

Enter Mrs. Candour *and* Maid.

Maid. Indeed, ma'am, my lady will see nobody at present.

Mrs. Can. Did you tell her it was her friend Mrs. Candour?

Maid. Yes, ma'am; but she begs you will excuse her.

Mrs. Can. Do go again,—I shall be glad to see her, if it be
only[4] for a moment, for I am sure she must be in great distress.
[*Exit* Maid.] Dear heart, how provoking! I'm not mistress of
half the circumstances! We shall have the whole affair in the
newspapers, with the names of the parties at full length,[5] before I
have dropped the story at a dozen houses.

Enter Sir Benjamin Backbite.

Oh, Sir Benjamin! you have heard, I suppose——

Sir Benj. B. Of Lady Teazle and Mr. Surface——

Mrs. Can. And Sir Peter's discovery——

Sir Benj. B. Oh! the strangest piece of business, to be sure!

¹[you not—1826.]   ²[your—1826.]   ³him. *Exit* Rowley. Joseph *solus*—Crewe.
Em.—1823: (1781).   ⁴her only—Crewe. Em.—Rae: 1826.   ⁵[at length—Rae: 1826].

Mrs. Can. Well, I never was so surprised in my life. I am so sorry for all parties, indeed.

Sir Benj. B. Now, I don't pity Sir Peter at all: he was so extravagantly partial to Mr. Surface.

Mrs. Can. Mr. Surface! Why, 'twas with Charles Lady Teazle was detected!

Sir Benj. B. No such thing![1]—Mr. Surface is the gallant.

Mrs. Can. No, No![2] Charles is the man. 'Twas Mr. Surface brought Sir Peter on purpose to discover them.

Sir Benj. B. I tell you I had it from one——

Mrs. Can. And I have it from one——

Sir Benj. B. Who had it from one, who had it——

Mrs. Can. From one immediately——but here comes[3] Lady Sneerwell; perhaps she knows the whole affair.

Enter LADY SNEERWELL.

Lady Sneer. So, my dear Mrs. Candour, here's a sad affair of our friend Teazle.[4]

Mrs. Can. Aye, my dear friend, who could have thought it?

Lady Sneer. Well, there is no trusting appearances; though, indeed, she was always too lively for me.

Mrs. Can. To be sure, her manners were a little too free: but she was very young!

Lady Sneer. And had, indeed, some good qualities.

Mrs. Can. So she had, indeed. But have you heard the particulars?

Lady Sneer. No; but everybody says that Mr. Surface——

Sir Benj. B. Aye, there; I told you Mr. Surface was the man.

Mrs. Can. No, no, indeed; the assignation was with Charles.

Lady Sneer. With Charles! You alarm me, Mrs. Candour!

Mrs. Can. Yes, yes, he was the lover. Mr. Surface—do[5] him justice—was only the informer

Sir Benj B. Well, I'll not dispute with you, Mrs. Candour; but, be it which it may, I hope that Sir Peter's wound will not——

Mrs. Can. Sir Peter's wound! O mercy! I didn't hear a word of their fighting.

---

[1] [No, no, I tell you.] [2] [No such thing.] [3] here's—Crewe. *Em.*—Rae: 1823.
[4] friend Lady Teazle—Crewe. *Em.*—Rae: 1799. [5] to do—1799. *Em.*—Crewe: Rae.

Lady Sneer. Nor I, a syllable.

Sir Benj. B. No! what, no mention of the duel?

Mrs. Can. Not a word.

Sir Benj. B. Oh Lord, yes, yes:[1] they fought before they left the room.

Lady Sneer. Pray, let us hear.

Mrs. Can. Aye, do oblige us with the duel.

Sir Benj. B. "Sir," says Sir Peter, immediately after the discovery, "you are a most ungrateful fellow."

Mrs. Can. Aye, to Charles——

Sir Benj. B. No, no—to Mr. Surface—"a most ungrateful fellow; and old as I am, sir," says he, "I insist on immediate satisfaction."

Mrs. Can. Aye, that must have been to Charles; for 'tis very unlikely Mr. Surface should go fight[2] in his own house.

Sir Benj. B. Gad's life, ma'am, not at all—"Giving me immediate satisfaction." On this, ma'am, Lady Teazle, seeing Sir Peter in such danger, ran out of the room in strong hysterics, and Charles after her, calling out for hartshorn and water; then, madam, they began to fight with swords——

Enter CRABTREE.

Crabtree. With pistols, nephew—pistols:[3] I have it from undoubted authority.

Mrs. Can. Oh, Mr. Crabtree, then it is all true!

Crabtree. Too true, indeed, madam, and Sir Peter[4] dangerously wounded——

Sir Benj. B. By a thrust in *segoon*[5] quite through his left side

Crabtree. By a bullet lodged in the thorax.

Mrs. Can. Mercy on me! Poor Sir Peter!

Crabtree. Yes, madam; though Charles would have avoided the matter, if he could.

Mrs. Can. I knew Charles was the person.

Sir Benj. B. My uncle, I see, knows nothing of the matter.

Crabtree. But Sir Peter taxed him with the basest ingratitude.

[1][Oh yes—1826.]   [2][should fight—1826] should go to—Rae.   [3]pistols, nephew—Crewe: Rae. Em.—1826: (1781).   [4][Peter is.].   [5]seconde—1823. Em.—Crewe: 1826.

Sir Benj. B. That I told you, you know——

Crabtree. Do, nephew, let me speak! and insisted on im-mediate——[1]

Sir Benj. B. Just as I said——

Crabtree. Odds life, nephew, allow others to know something too. A pair of pistols lay on the bureau (for Mr. Surface, it seems, had come home the night before late from Salthill, where he had been to see the Montem with a friend, who has a son at Eton), so, unluckily, the pistols were left charged.

Sir Benj. B. I heard nothing of this.

Crabtree. Sir Peter forced Charles to take one, and they fire, it seems, pretty nearly together. Charles's shot took place,[2] as I tell you, and Sir Peter's missed; but what is very extraordinary, the ball struck against a little bronze Pliny[3] that stood over the fire-place,[4] grazed out of the window at a right angle, and wounded the postman, who was just coming to the door with a double letter from Northamptonshire.

Sir Benj. B. My uncle's account is more circumstantial, I must confess;[5] but I believe mine is the true one, for all that.

Lady Sneer. I am more interested in this affair than they imagine, and must have better information.   [*Aside. Exit.*

Sir Benj. B. [*After a pause, looking at each other*]. Ah! Lady Sneerwell's alarm is very easily accounted for.

Crabtree. Yes, yes, they certainly *do* say—but that's neither here nor there.

Mrs. Can. But, pray, where is Sir Peter at present?

Crabtree. Oh! they brought him home, and he is now in the house, though the servants are ordered to deny him.

Mrs. Can. I believe so, and Lady Teazle, I suppose, attending him.

Crabtree. Yes, yes; and I saw one of the faculty enter just be-fore me.

Sir Benj. B. Hey! who comes here?

Crabtree. Oh, this is he: the physician, depend on't.

---

[1]immediate satisfaction—Crewe. *Em.*—Rae: 1823.   [2][effect—1826.].   [3]Shake-speare—1799: 1826: (1781). *Em.*—Crewe: Rae. [*Possibly* Shakespeare *was Sheridan's amendment.*]   [4]chimney-place—Crewe. *Em.* Rae: 1826 [chimney-piece—Sichel, I, 571.]   [5][I confess—1826.]

Mrs. Can. Oh, certainly: it must be the physician; and now we shall know.

Enter SIR OLIVER.

Crabtree. Well, doctor, what hopes?

Mrs. Can. Aye, doctor, how's your patient?

Sir Benj. B. Now, doctor, isn't it a wound with a small sword?

Crabtree. A bullet lodged in the thorax, for a hundred.

Sir Oliver S. Doctor! a wound with a small sword! and a bullet in the thorax! What! are you mad, good people?

Sir Benj. B. Perhaps, sir, you are not a doctor?

Sir Oliver S. Truly, I am to thank you for my degree if I am.

Crabtree. Only a friend of Sir Peter's, then, I presume. But, sir, you must have heard of his accident?

Sir Oliver S. Not a word!

Crabtree. Not of his being dangerously wounded?

Sir Oliver S. The devil he is!

Sir Benj. B. Run through the body——

Crabtree. Shot in the breast——

Sir Benj. B. By one Mr. Surface——

Crabtree. Aye, the[1] younger.

Sir Oliver S. Hey! what the plague! you seem to differ strangely in your accounts: however, you agree that Sir Peter is dangerously wounded.

Sir Benj. B. Oh, yes, we agree there.[2]

Crabtree. Yes, yes, I believe there can be no doubt of that.

Sir Oliver S. Then, upon my word, for a person in that situation, he is the most imprudent man alive; for here he comes, walking as if nothing at all was the matter.

Enter SIR PETER.

Odds heart, Sir Peter, you are come in good time, I promise you for we had just given you over.

Sir Benj. B. Egad, uncle, this is the most sudden recovery!

Sir Oliver S. Why, man, what do you out of bed[3] with a small sword through your body, and a bullet lodged in your thorax?

Sir Peter T. A small sword, and a bullet!

Sir Oliver S. Aye, these gentlemen would have killed you

[1]Ay, by the—1799. *Em.*—Rae: 1826. [2]agree in that—1799: Rae. *Em.*—Crewe. [3]your bed—Crewe. *Em.*—Rae: 1823.

without law, or physic, and wanted to dub me a doctor, to make me an accomplice.

Sir Peter T. Why, what is all this?

Sir Benj. B. We rejoice, Sir Peter, that the story of the duel is not true, and are sincerely sorry for your other misfortune.

Sir Peter T. So, so; all over the town already.   [*Aside.*

Crabtree. Though, Sir Peter, you were certainly vastly to blame to marry at all at[1] your years.

Sir Peter T. Sir, what[2] business is that of yours?[3]

Mrs. Can. Though, indeed, as Sir Peter made so good a husband, he's very much to be pitied.

Sir Peter T. Plague on your pity, ma'am! I desire none of it.

Sir Benj. B. However, Sir Peter, you must not mind the laughing and jests you will meet with on the occasion.

Sir Peter T. Sir, sir,[4] I desire to be master in my own house.

Crabtree. 'Tis no uncommon case, that's one comfort.

Sir Peter T. I insist on being left to myself: without ceremony —I insist on your leaving my house directly.

Mrs. Can. Well, well, we are going, and depend on't we'll make the best report of you[5] we can.   [*Exit.*

Sir Peter T. Leave my house!

Crabtree. And tell how hardly[6] you've been treated.   [*Exit.*

Sir Peter T. Leave my house!

Sir Benj. B. And how patiently you bear it.   [*Exit.*

Sir Peter T. Fiends![7] vipers! furies! Oh! that their own venom would choke them!

Sir Oliver S. They are very provoking, indeed, Sir Peter.

Enter ROWLEY.

Rowley. I heard high words: what has ruffled you, Sir Peter?[8]

Sir Peter T. Pshaw! what signifies asking? Do I ever pass a day without my vexations?

Sir Oliver S. Well, I'm not inquisitive. I come only to tell you, that I have seen both my nephews in the manner we proposed.

Sir Peter T. A precious couple they are!

¹[marry at—1826.]   ²[What.]   ³[Yours, sir.]   ⁴Sir—Crewe. *Em.*—1826: 1823.   ⁵[it—1826.]   ⁶hard—Crewe. *Em.*—Rae: 1826.   ⁷Leave my house [*Exeunt.*] Fiends!—Crewe. *Em.*—Rae: 1823.   ⁸[Sir—1826.]

Rowley. Yes, and Sir Oliver is convinced that your judgment was right, Sir Peter.

Sir Oliver S. Yes, I find Joseph is indeed the man, after all.

Rowley. Aye, as Sir Peter says, he is a man of sentiment.

Sir Oliver S. And acts up to the sentiments he professes.

Rowley. It certainly is edification to hear him talk.

Sir Oliver S. Oh, he's a model for the young men of the age! ——But how's this, Sir Peter? you don't join us in[1] your friend Joseph's praise, as I expected.

Sir Peter T. Sir Oliver, we live in a damned wicked world, and the fewer we praise the better.

Rowley. What! do you say so, Sir Peter, who were never mistaken in your life?

Sir Peter T. Pshaw! Plague on you both! I see by your sneering you have heard the whole affair. I shall go mad among you!

Rowley. Then, to fret you no longer, Sir Peter, we are indeed acquainted with it all. I met Lady Teazle coming from Mr. Surface's so humbled, that she deigned to request me to be her advocate with you.

Sir Peter T. And does Sir Oliver know all, too?[2]

Sir Oliver S. Every circumstance.

Sir Peter T. What, of the closet—and the screen, hey?

Sir Oliver S. Yes, yes, and the little French milliner. Oh, I have been vastly diverted with the story! Ha! ha! ha!

Sir Peter T. 'Twas very pleasant.

Sir Oliver S. I never laughed more in my life, I assure you: ha! ha! ha!

Sir Peter T. Oh, vastly diverting! Ha! ha! ha!

Rowley. To be sure, Joseph with his sentiments: ha! ha! ha!

Sir Peter T. Yes, yes, his sentiments! Ha! ha! ha! A hypocritical villain!

Sir Oliver S. Aye, and that rogue Charles to pull Sir Peter out of the closet: ha! ha! ha!

Sir Peter T. Ha! ha! 'twas devilish entertaining, to be sure!

Sir Oliver S. Ha! ha! ha! Egad, Sir Peter, I should like to have seen your face when the screen was thrown down: ha! ha!

Sir Peter T. Yes, yes, my face when the screen was thrown down: ha! ha! ha! Oh, I muſt never show my head again!

Sir Oliver S. But come, come, it isn't fair to laugh at you neither, my old friend; though, upon my soul, I can't help it.

Sir Peter T. Oh, pray don't reſtrain your mirth on my account; it does not hurt me at all! I laugh at the whole affair myself. Yes, yes, I think being a ſtanding jeſt for all one's acquaintance a very happy situation. Oh, yes, and then of a morning to read the paragraphs about Mr. S——, Lady T——,[1] and Sir P——, will be so diverting! I shall certainly leave town tomorrow and never look mankind in the face again.[2]

Rowley. Without affeſtation, Sir Peter, you may despise the ridicule of fools: but I see Lady Teazle going towards the next room; I am sure you muſt desire a reconciliation as earneſtly as she does.

Sir Oliver S. Perhaps my being here prevents her coming to you. Well, I'll leave honeſt Rowley to mediate between you; but he muſt bring you all presently to Mr. Surface's, where I am now returning, if not to reclaim a libertine, at leaſt to expose hypocrisy.

Sir Peter T. Ah, I'll be present at your discovering yourself there with all my heart; though 'tis a vile unlucky place for discoveries.

Rowley. We'll follow.   *[Exit* SIR OLIVER.

Sir Peter T. She is not coming here, you see, Rowley.

Rowley. No, but she has left the door of that room open, you perceive. See, she's in tears.

Sir Peter T. Certainly a little mortification appears very becoming in a wife. Don't you think it will do her good to let her pine a little?

Rowley. Oh, this is ungenerous in you!

Sir Peter T. Well, I know not what to think. You remember[3] the letter I found of hers evidently intended for Charles?

Rowley. A mere forgery, Sir Peter, laid in your way on purpose. This is one of the points which I intend Snake shall give you conviſtion on.

[1]About Lady T.—Crewe. *Em.*—Rae: 1826.   [2]diverting—Crewe. *Em.*—Rae: 1823: 1826.   [3]remember, Rowley—Crewe. *Em.*—1823, 1826.

Sir Peter T. I wish I were[1] once satisfied of that. She looks this way. What a remarkably elegant turn of the head she has! Rowley, I'll go to her.

Rowley. Certainly.

Sir Peter T. Though when it is known that we[2] are reconciled people will laugh at me ten times more.

Rowley. Let them laugh, and retort their malice only by showing them you are happy in spite of it.

Sir Peter T. I'faith, so I will! and if I'm not miſtaken, we may yet be the happieſt couple in the country.

Rowley. Nay, Sir Peter, he who once lays aside suspicion——

Sir Peter T. Hold, my dear Rowley![3] if you have any regard for me, never let me hear you utter anything like a sentiment: I have had enough of them to serve me the reſt of my life. [*Exeunt.*

SCENE III

The Library.

Enter JOSEPH SURFACE *and* LADY SNEERWELL.

Lady Sneer. Impossible! Will not Sir Peter immediately be reconciled to Charles, and of consequence[4] no longer oppose his union with Maria? The thought is diſtraction to me.

Joseph S. Can passion furnish a remedy?

Lady Sneer. No, nor cunning either.[5] Oh! I was a fool, an idiot, to league with such a blunderer!

Joseph S. Sure, Lady Sneerwell, I am the greateſt sufferer; yet you see I bear the accident with calmness.

Lady Sneer. Because the disappointment doesn't reach your heart; your intereſt only attached you to Maria. Had you felt for her what I have for that ungrateful libertine, neither your temper nor hypocrisy, could prevent your showing the sharpness of your vexation.

Joseph S. But why should your reproaches fall on me for this disappointment?

---

[1]Was—Crewe. *Em.*—Rae: 1823.   [2]known we—Crewe. *Em.*—Rae: 1823.
[3]Hold, Master Rowley—1799: Rae: 1823. *Em.*—Crewe: (1781).   [4][course.]
[5][neither—1826.]

Lady Sneer. Are you not the cause of it? What had you to bate[1] in your pursuit of Maria to pervert Lady Teazle by the way? Had you not a sufficient field for your roguery in blinding[2] Sir Peter, and supplanting your brother, but you must endeavour to seduce his wife? I hate[3] such an avarice of crimes; 'tis an unfair monopoly, and never prospers.

Joseph S. Well, I admit I have been to blame. I confess I deviated[4] from the direct road of wrong, but I don't think we're so totally defeated neither.[5]

Lady Sneer. No!

Joseph S. You tell me you have made a trial of Snake since we met, and that you still believe him faithful to us.

Lady Sneer. I do believe so.

Joseph S. And that he has undertaken, should it be necessary, to swear and prove, that Charles is at this time contracted by vows and honour to your ladyship, which some of his former letters to you will serve to support.

Lady Sneer. This, indeed, might have assisted.

Joseph S. Come, come; it is not too late yet. [*Knocking at the door.*] But hark! this is probably my uncle, Sir Oliver: retire to that room; we'll consult farther when he is gone.

Lady Sneer. Well, but if *he* should find you out too?

Joseph S. Oh, I have no fear of that. Sir Peter will hold his tongue for his own credit's sake—and you may depend on it I shall soon discover Sir Oliver's weak side!

Lady S. I have no diffidence of your abilities! only be constant to one roguery at a time.   [*Exit* LADY SNEERWELL.

Joseph S. I will, I will. So! 'tis confounded hard, after such bad fortune, to be baited by one's confederate in evil. Well, at all events my character is so much better than Charles's, that I certainly——hey!—what!—this is not Sir Oliver, but old Stanley again. Plague on't that he should return to tease me just now—I shall have Sir Oliver come and find him here—and——

---

[1] [do.]   [2] [imposing upon—(1781).]   [3] brother. I hate—Crewe: Rae. *Em.*— 1799: 1823: (1781).   [4] I have deviated—Crewe. *Em.* Rae: 1826.   [5] either— Crewe. *Em.*—Rae: 1823.

Enter SIR OLIVER.

Gad's life, Mr. Stanley, why have you come back to plague me
at this time? You must not stay now, upon my word.

Sir Oliver S. Sir, I hear your uncle Oliver is expected here, and
though he has been so penurious to you, I'll try what he'll do for
me.

Joseph S. Sir, 'tis impossible for you to stay now, so[1] I must
beg——[2]Come any other time, and I promise you, you shall be
assisted.

Sir Oliver S. No: Sir Oliver and I must be acquainted.

Joseph S. Zounds, sir! then I insist on your quitting the room
directly.

Sir Oliver S. Nay, sir——

Joseph S. Sir, I insist on't: —here, William! show this gentleman out. Since you compel me, sir, not one moment—this is
such insolence!

Enter CHARLES.

Charles S. Hey day! what's the matter now![3] What the devil
have you got hold of my little broker here? Zounds, brother,
don't[4] hurt little Premium. What's the matter, my little fellow?

Joseph S. So! he has been with you too, has he?

Charles S. To be sure he has. Why, he's as honest a little——
But sure, Joseph, you have not been borrowing money too, have
you?

Joseph S. Borrowing! no! But, brother, you know we expect
Sir Oliver here every——[5]

Charles S. O Gad, that's true! Noll mustn't find the little
broker here, to be sure.

Joseph S. Yet Mr. Stanley insists——

Charles S. Stanley! why his name's Premium.

Joseph S. No, no,[6] Stanley.

Charles S. No, no, Premium.

Joseph S. Well, no matter which—but——

Charles S. Aye, aye, Stanley or Premium, 'tis the same thing
as you say; for I suppose he goes by half a hundred names, be-

[1]stay, so—Crewe. *Em.*—Rae: 1826.   [2]beg you—Crewe. *Em.*—Rae: 1826
[3]matter—Crewe. *Em.*—Rae: 1826.   [4]Zounds, don't—Crewe. *Em.*—Rae: 1826.
[5]Oliver every—Crewe: Rae. *Em.*—1826 (1781).   [6][No, sir—1826.]

sides A. B. at the coffee-houses.   [*Knocking.*

Joseph S. 'Sdeath! here's Sir Oliver at the door. Now I beg, Mr. Stanley——

 Charles S. Aye, aye, and I beg, Mr. Premium——

 Sir Oliver S. Gentlemen——

 Joseph S. Sir, by Heaven you shall go!

 Charles S. Aye, out with him, certainly!

 Sir Oliver S. This violence——

 Joseph S. 'Tis[1] your own fault.

 Charles S. Out with him, to be sure.

      [*Both forcing* SIR OLIVER *out.*

Enter SIR PETER *and* LADY TEAZLE, MARIA, *and* ROWLEY.

 Sir Peter T. My old friend, Sir Oliver—hey! What in the name of wonder—here are dutiful nephews—assault their uncle at a firſt visit!

 Lady T. Indeed, Sir Oliver, 'twas well we came in to release[2] you.

 Rowley. Truly, it was; for I perceive, Sir Oliver, the character of old Stanley was not a protection to you.

 Sir Oliver S. Nor of Premium either: the necessities of the former could not extort a shilling from that benevolent gentleman; and now, egad,[3] I ſtood a chance of faring worse than my anceſtors, and being knocked down without being bid for.

 Joseph S. Charles!

 Charles S. Joseph!

 Joseph S. 'Tis now complete!

 Charles S. Very!

 Sir Oliver S. Sir Peter, my friend, and Rowley, too, look on that elder nephew of mine. You know what he has already received from my bounty; and you also know how gladly I would have regarded half my fortune as held in truſt for him: judge then my disappointment in discovering him to be deſtitute of truth,[4] charity, and gratitude.

 Sir Peter T. Sir Oliver, I should be more surprised at this declaration, if I had not myself found him to be selfish, treacherous, and hypocitical.

[1][Sir, 'tis—1826.] [2]rescue—1799: Rae. *Em.*—Crewe. [3]and with the other—1799: Rae: 1826. *Em.*—Crewe. [4][faith.]

Lady T. And if the gentleman pleads not guilty to these, pray let him call *me* to his character.

Sir Peter T. Then, I believe, we need add no more: if he knows himself, he will consider it as the most perfect punishment, that he is known to the world.

Charles S. If they talk this way to Honesty, what will they say to me, by and by? [*Aside.*

Sir Oliver S. As for that prodigal, his brother, there——

Charles S. Aye, now comes my turn: the damned family pictures will ruin me. [*Aside.*

Joseph S. Sir Oliver—uncle, will you honour me with a hearing?

Charles S. Now if Joseph would make one of his long speeches I might recollect myself a little. [*Aside.*

Sir Peter T. I suppose you would undertake to justify yourself entirely? [*To* JOSEPH.

Joseph S. I trust I could.

Sir Oliver. Pshaw!—[nay if you desert your roguery in this distress and try to be justified, you have even less principle than I thought you had.]¹ [*Turns from him in contempt.*] Well. Sir [*to* CHARLES.] and you could justify yourself too, I suppose?

Charles S. Not that I know of, Sir Oliver.

Sir Oliver S. What!—Little Premium has been let too much into the secret, I presume?²

Charles S. True, sir; but they were *family* secrets, and should not³ be mentioned again, you know.

Rowley. Come, Sir Oliver, I know you cannot speak of Charles's follies with anger.

Sir Oliver S. Odds heart, no more I can: nor with gravity either.——Sir Peter, do you know, the rogue bargained with me for all his ancestors; sold me judges and generals by the foot and maiden aunts as cheap as broken china.

Charles S. To be sure, Sir Oliver, I did make a little free with the family canvas, that's the truth on't. My ancestors may certainly rise⁴ in judgment against me, there's no denying it;⁵ but

¹*Om.*—Crewe: 1826. *Em.*—Rae: 1799. ²[suppose—1826.] ³never—Crewe. *Em.*—Rae: 1826. ⁴[may rise.] ⁵denying—Crewe. *Em.*—Rae: 1826.

believe me sincere when I tell you—and upon my soul I would not say so[1] if I was not—that if I do not appear mortified at the exposure of my follies, it is because I feel at this moment the warmest satisfaction in seeing you, my liberal benefactor.

Sir Oliver S. Charles, I believe you; give me your hand again:[2] the ill-looking little fellow over the settee has made your peace.

Charles S. Then, sir, my gratitude to the original is still increased.

Lady T. Yet, I believe, Sir Oliver, here[3] is one whom Charles is still more anxious to be reconciled to.

Sir Oliver S. Oh, I have heard of his attachment there; and with the young lady's pardon, if I construe right—that blush

———

Sir Peter T. Well, child, speak your sentiments!

Maria. Sir, I have little to say, but that I shall rejoice to hear that he is happy; for me—whatever claim I had to his affection,[4] I willingly resign to one who has a better title.

Charles S. How, Maria!

Sir Peter T. Hey day! what's the mystery now?—While he appeared an incorrigible rake, you would give your hand to no one else; and now that he is likely to reform, I'll warrant you won't have him.

Maria. His own heart and Lady Sneerwell know the cause.

Charles S. Lady Sneerwell!

Joseph S. Brother, it is with great concern I am obliged to speak on this point, but my regard to justice compels me, and Lady Sneerwell's injuries can no longer be concealed.

[*Goes to door.*

Enter LADY SNEERWELL.

All. Lady Sneerwell!

Sir Peter T. So! another French milliner! Egad, he has one in every room in the house, I suppose.

Lady Sneer. Ungrateful Charles! Well may you be surprised, and feel for the indelicate situation your perfidy has forced me into.

[1]say it—Crewe. *Em.*—Rae: 1826.   [2]hand—Crewe. *Em.*—Rae: 1826.   [3]there—Crewe. *Em.*—Rae: 1826.   [4]attention—Crewe: 1826. *Em.*—Rae: 1823.

Charles S. Pray, uncle, is this another plot of yours? For, as I have life, I don't understand it.

Joseph S. I believe, sir, there is but the evidence of one person more necessity to make it extremely clear.

Sir Peter T. And that person, I imagine, is Mr. Snake.—Rowley, you were perfectly right to bring him with us, and pray let him appear.

Rowley. Walk in, Mr. Snake.

Enter SNAKE.

I thought his testimony might be wanted: however, it happens unluckily, that he comes to confront Lady Sneerwell, and not[1] to support her.

Lady Sneer. A villain! Treacherous to me at last!—Speak, fellow; have you too conspired[2] against me?

Sneer. I beg your ladyship ten thousand pardons: you paid me extremely liberally for the lie in question; but I unfortunately have[3] been offered double to speak the truth.

Sir Peter T. Plot and counterplot, egad! I wish your ladyship joy of the success of your negociation.

Lady Sneer. The torments of shame and disappointment on you all!

Lady T. Hold, Lady Sneerwell—before you go, let me thank you for the trouble you and that gentleman have taken, in writing letters from me to Charles, and answering them yourself; and let me also request you to make my respects to the Scandalous College, of which you are president, and inform them, that Lady Teazle, licentiate, begs leave to return the diploma they granted[4] her, as she leaves off practice, and kills characters no longer.

Lady Sneer. You too, madam—provoking—insolent—May your husband live these fifty years!   [*Exit.*

[*Sir Peter T.* Oons! what a fury![5]]

Lady T. What a malicious creature it is![6]

Sir Peter T. Hey! Not for her last wish?

Lady T. Oh, no!

[1][Sneerwell, not—1826.]   [2]you conspired—Crewe. *Em.*—Rae: 1826.   [3]have unfortunately—Crewe. *Em.*—Rae: 1826.   [4][gave.]   [5]*Om.*—Crewe. *Em.*—1799: Rae: 1826.   [6][A malicious creature, indeed—Rae: 1826]. *Em.*—Crewe: (1781).

Sir Oliver S. Well, sir, and what have you to say now?

Joseph S. Sir, I am so confounded, to find[1] that Lady Sneerwell could be guilty of suborning Mr. Snake in this manner, to impose on us all, that I know not what to say: however, left her revengeful spirit should prompt her to injure my brother, I had certainly better follow her directly.   [*Exit.*

Sir Peter T. Moral to the laſt drop!

Sir Oliver S. Aye, and marry her, Joseph, if you can.—Oil and Vinegar, egad! you'll do very well together.

Rowley. I believe we have no more occasion for Mr. Snake at present?

Snake. Before I go, I beg pardon once for all, for whatever uneasiness I have been the humble inſtrument of causing to the parties present.

Sir Peter T. Well, well, you have made atonement by a good deed at laſt.

Snake. But I muſt requeſt of the company that it shall never be known.

Sir Peter T. Hey!—What the plague!—Are you ashamed of having done a right thing once in your life?

Snake. Ah, sir! consider,—I live by the badness of my character; I have nothing but my infamy to depend on! and if it were once known that I had been betrayed into an honeſt action, I should lose every friend I have in the world.

Sir Peter T. Here's a precious rogue!

Sir Oliver S. Well, well,—we'll not traduce you by saying anything to[2] your praise, never fear.   [*Exit* SNAKE.

Lady T. See, Sir Oliver, there needs no persuasion now to reconcile your nephew and Maria.

Sir Oliver S. Aye, aye, that's as it should be, and egad, we'll have the wedding to-morrow morning.

Charles S. Thank you, my dear[3] uncle!

Sir Peter T. What, you rogue! don't you ask the girl's consent firſt?

Charles S. Oh, I have done that a long time—above a[4] minute ago—and she has looked *yes.*

[1]confounded—1799. *Em.*—Crewe: Rae.   [2][in].   [3][you, dear—1826.]
[4][time, a—1826.]

Maria. For shame, Charles!—I protest, Sir Peter, there has not been a word.

Sir Oliver S. Well, then, the fewer the better;—may your love for each other never know abatement!

Sir Peter T. And may you live as happily together as Lady Teazle and I—intend to do.

Charles S. Rowley, my old friend, I am sure you congratulate me; and I suspect that I owe you much.

Sir Oliver S. You do indeed, Charles.

Rowley. If my efforts to serve you had not succeeded, you would have been in my debt for the attempt; but deserve to be happy, and you overpay me.

Sir Peter T. Aye, honest Rowley always said you would reform.

Charles S. Why, as to reforming, Sir Peter, I'll make no promises, and that I take to be a proof that I intend to set about it but here shall be my monitor—my gentle guide—ah! can I leave the virtuous path those eyes illumine?

Tho' thou, dear maid, shouldst waive thy beauty's sway,
Thou still must rule, because I will obey:
A humble fugitive from Folly view,
No sanctuary near but Love—
      [*To the audience*]—and you;
You can, indeed, each anxious fear remove,
For even Scandal dies if you approve.

END OF THE FIFTH ACT

Epilogue[1]

Written by GEORGE COLMAN, *Esq.*

Spoken by Mrs. ABINGTON *in the character of* LADY TEAZLE

I, who was late so volatile and gay,
Like a trade wind muſt now blow all one way,
Bend all my cares, my ſtudies, and my vows,
To one dull ruſty weathercock—my spouse!
So wills our virtuous bard—the pye-ball'd[2] Bayes
Of crying epilogues and laughing plays!
Old batchelors, who marry smart young wives,
Learn from our play to regulate your lives.
Each bring his dear to town, all faults upon her—
London will prove the very source of honour.
Plung'd fairly in, like a cold bath it serves,
When principles relax,—to brace the nerves:
Such is my case—and yet I muſt deplore
That the gay dream of dissipation's o'er:
And say, ye fair, was ever lively wife,
Born with a genius for the higheſt life,
Like me, untimely blaſted in her bloom,
Like me, condemned to such a dismal doom?
Save money—when I juſt knew how to *waſte* it!
Leave London—juſt as I began to taſte it!
　　Muſt I then watch the early crowing cock,
The melancholy ticking of a clock;
In the lone ruſtic hall for ever pounded,
With dogs, cats, rats, and squalling brats surrounded?
With humble curates can I now retire,
(While good Sir Peter boozes with the squire),
And at backgammon mortify my soul,

[1]From *The Town and Country Magazine*, for June, 1777.　　[2]motley—1823.

115

That pants for loo, or flutters at a vole?
Seven's the main! Dear sound! that muſt expire,
Loſt at hot cockles round a Chriſtmas fire!
The transient hour of fashion too soon spent,
"Farewell the tranquil mind, farewell content!
"Farewell the *plumèd* head, the cushion'd *tête*,
"That takes the cushion from its proper seat!
"The spirit-ſtirring drum—card drums I mean,
"Spadille—odd trick—pam—baſto—king and queen!
"And you, ye knockers, that, with brazen throat,
"The welcome visitors' approach denote;
"Farewell!—all quality of high renown,
"Pride, pomp, and circumſtance of glorious Town!
"Farewell! your revels I partake no more,
"And Lady Teazle's occupation's o'er!"
All this I told our bard; he smil'd, and said 'twas clear,
I ought to play deep tragedy next year.
Meanwhile he drew wise morals from his play,
And in these solemn periods ſtalk'd away:
"Bleſt were the fair like you; her faults who ſtopt,
"And clos'd her follies when the curtain dropt!
"No more in vice or error to engage,
"Or play the fool at large on life's great ſtage."

The Evolution of
The School for Scandal

IT happens that *The School for Scandal* is one of the few dramatic masterpieces whose earlier phases of development can be studied. Sheridan preserved, or neglected to destroy, a mass of early drafts, from which it is to be learned that in its final form *The School for Scandal* was a combination of two earlier comedies, distinguished usually as "the Teazle-play," or *The Teazles*, and "the Clerimont-play." The latter, however, is more significantly called "the Sneerwell-play," although quite possibly Sheridan intended to call it, as in some early jottings, *The Slanderers*. Both of these exist at various stages of evolution in fragments, and there is also a penultimate version, the last discarded draft of the full piece, commonly called "the Rae text."

It is not certain when either *The Teazles* or *The Slanderers* was commenced. Mr. Sichel contends that the sheet of jottings bearing the latter title was written in 1772; he asserts that "the first phase" of *The School for Scandal* had been "thought out and only required to be written while yet he was at Bath." Unfortunately, he cites no authority, beyond an allusion to "Sheridan's sister," from which his statement appears to be a liberal interpretation of Alicia Lefanu's comment upon the stupid old charge that Sheridan stole the play from one sent to him, as manager of Drury Lane (that is, after September, 1776), by "a young lady of Thames Street." Her exact words, in her *Life of Mrs. Frances Sheridan* are: "The whole story of the supposed manner in which the play of *The School for Scandal* came into Mr. Sheridan's hands is perfectly groundless, the writer of these lines having frequently heard him speak on the subject long before the play appeared; many of the characters and incidents related to persons known to them both, and were laughingly talked over with his family."

As "the characters and incidents" may have been those of the Teazle-play or the Sneerwell-play, the statement is of no great assistance; it certainly does not warrant Mr. Sichel's conclusion. There is, indeed, as Moore said explicitly, "No date on the MSS. nor any other certain clue to decide the precedency of time" between the two comedies. But it is convenient to consider *The Teazles*, which contains no hint of the theme of scandal, before the other comedy.

THE TEAZLES

The Teazles is fairly straightforward. Moore gives from MS. this list of *Dramatis Personae*:—

>Sir Rowland Harpur.
>—— Plausible.
>Capt. Harry Plausible.
>Freeman.
>Old Teazle. (*Left off trade.*)
>Mrs. Teazle.
>Maria.

It appears to have been originally conceived as an afterpiece in two acts of the same type as Murphy's *Three Weeks After Marriage*. Moore adds that, "From this list of the personages we may conclude that the quarrels of Old Teazle and his wife, the attachment between Maria and one of the Plausibles, and the intrigue of Mrs. Teazle with the other, formed the sole materials of the piece, as then constructed." Only the first few lines, however, preserve the names of the personages as thus given, and they obviously survive from an earlier draft. In the rest of the scene, "Old Solomon" Teazle, the old widower "retired from trade" and married for the third time, had become Sir Peter, the old bachelor newly married. If one must "date" it, this is to be fixed by the allusion to the *Fête Champêtre*, a word not popularized till the rural festivities at the Oaks in the summer of 1774, after which the revision must therefore have been made. ("Old Solomon's" firſt speech is an attempt to convey an earlier date, perhaps 1772 or 1773.)

Act I.—Scene I.

Old Teazle, *alone*.

In the year 44, I married my firſt wife; the wedding was at the end of the year—aye, 'twas in December; yet, before Ann. Dom. 45, I repented. A month before, we swore we preferred each other to the whole world—perhaps we spoke truth; but, when we came to promise to love each other till death, there I am sure we lied. Well, Fortune owed me a good turn; in 48 she died. Ah, silly Solomon, in 52 I find thee married again! Here, too, is a catalogue of ills—Thomas, born February 12; Jane, born Jan. 6; so they go on to the number of five. However, by death I ſtand credited but by one. Well, Margery, reſt her soul! was a queer creature; when she was gone, I felt awkward at firſt, and being sensible that wishes availed nothing, I often wished for her return. For ten years more I kept my senses and lived single. Oh, blockhead, dolt Solomon! Within this twelvemonth thou art married again—married to a woman thirty years younger than thyself; a fashionable woman. Yet I took her with caution; she had been educated in the country; but now she has more extravagance than the daughter of an Earl, more levity than a Countess. What a defeɛt it is in our laws, that a man who has once been branded in the forehead should be hanged for the second offence.

Enter Jarvis.

Teazle. Who's there? Well, Jarvis?

Jarvis. Sir, there are a number of my miſtress's tradesmen without, clamorous for their money.

Teazle. Are those their bills in your hand?

Jarvis. Something about a twentieth part, sir.

Teazle. What! have you expended the hundred pounds I gave you for her use.

Jarvis. Long ago, sir, as you may judge by some of the

items:—"Paid the coach-maker for lowering the front seat of the coach."

Teazle. What the deuce was the matter with the seat?

Jarvis. Oh Lord, the carriage was too low for her by a foot when she was dressed—so that it muſt have been so, or have had a tub at top like a hat-case on a travelling trunk. Well, sir, (*reads*) "Paid her two footmen half a year's wages, 50*l.*"

Teazle. 'Sdeath and fury! does she give her footmen a hundred a year?

Jarvis. Yes, sir, and I think, indeed, she has rather made a good bargain, for they find their own bags and bouquets.

Teazle. Bags and bouquets for footmen!—halters and bastinadoes![1]

Jarvis. "Paid for my lady's own nosegays, 50*l.*"

Teazle. Fifty pounds for flowers! enough to turn the Pantheon into a green-house, and give a Fête Champêtre at Christmas.

Lady Teazle.[2] Lord, Sir Peter, I wonder you should grudge me the moſt innocent articles in dress—and then, for the expense—flowers cannot be cheaper in winter—you should find fault with the climate, and not with me. I am sure I wish with all my heart, that it was Spring all the year round, and that roses grew under one's feet.

Sir Peter. Nay, but, madam, then you would not wear them; but try snow-balls, and icicles. But tell me, madam, how can you feel any satisfaction in wearing these, when you might re-

[1]Transferred afterwards to Trip and Sir Oliver.—Moore.

[2]We observe here a change in his plan, with respect both to the titles of Old Teazle and his wife, and the presence of the latter during this scene, which was evidently not at first intended.

From the following skeleton of the scenes of this piece, it would appear that he had an idea of extending the plot through five acts.

Act 1st, Sir Peter and Steward—2d, Sir P. and Lady—then Young Pliable.

Act 2d, Sir P. and Lady—Young Harrier—Sir P. and Sir Rowland, and Old Jeremy—Sir R. and Daughter—Y. P. and Y. H.

Act 3d, Sir R., Sir P. and O. J.—2d, Y. P. and Company, Y. R. O. R.—3d, Y. H. and Maria—Y. H., O. R. and Young Harrier, to borrow.

Act 4th, Y. P. and Maria, to borrow his money; gets away what he had received from his uncle—Y. P. Old Jer. and tradesmen—P. and Lady T., &c. &c.—Moore.

[Apparently, the brothers Plausible or Pliable were here to become two friends Pliant and Harrier. But the scenario is very hazy.]

flect that one of the rose-buds would have furnished a poor family with a dinner?

Lady Teazle. Upon my word, Sir Peter, begging your pardon, that is a very absurd way of arguing. By that rule, why do you indulge in the least superfluity? I dare swear a beggar might dine tolerably on your great-coat, or sup off your laced waistcoat—nay, I dare say, he wouldn't eat your gold-headed cane in a week. Indeed, if you would reserve nothing but necessaries, you should give the first poor man you meet your wig, and walk the streets in your night-cap, which, you know, becomes you very much.

Sir Peter. Well, go on to the articles.

Jarvis [*reading*]. "Fruit for my lady's monkey, 5*l.* per week."

Sir Peter. "Five pounds" for the monkey!—why 'tis a dessert for an alderman!

Lady Teazle. Why, Sir Peter, would you starve the poor animal? I dare swear he lives as reasonably as other monkeys do.

Sir Peter. Well, well, go on.

Jarvis. "China for ditto"—

Sir Peter. What, does he eat out of china?

Lady Teazle. Repairing china that he breaks—and I am sure no monkey breaks less.

Jarvis. "Paid Mr. Warren for perfumes—milk of roses, 30*l.*"

Lady Teazle. Very reasonable.

Sir Peter. 'Sdeath, madam, if you had been born to these expenses I should not have been so much amazed; but I took you, madam, an honest country squire's daughter—

Lady Teazle. Oh, filthy; don't name it. Well, heaven forgive my mother, but I do believe my father must have been a man of quality.

Sir Peter. Yes, madam, when first I saw you, you were drest in a pretty figured linen gown, with a bunch of keys by your side; your occupations, madam, to superintend the poultry; your accomplishments, a complete knowledge of the family receipt-book—then you sat in a room hung round with fruit in worsted of your own working; your amusements were to play country-dances on an old spinet to your father while he went asleep after a fox-chase—to read Tillotson's sermons to your aunt Deborah. These, madam, were your recreations, and there the accomplishments that captivated me. Now, forsooth, you must have two footmen to your chair, and a pair of white dogs in a phaeton; you forget when you used to ride double behind the butler on a docked bay coach-horse. . . . Now you must have a French hair-dresser; do you think you did not look as well when you had your hair combed smooth over a roller?'. . . Then you could be content to sit with me, or walk by the side of the Ha! Ha!

Lady Teazle. True, I did; and, when you asked me if I could love an old fellow, who would deny me nothing, I simpered and said "'Till death."

Sir Peter. Why did you say so?

Lady Teazle. Shall I tell you the truth?

Sir Peter. If it is not too great a favour.

Lady Teazle. Why, then, the truth is I was heartily tired of all these agreeable recreations you have so well remembered, and having a spirit to spend and enjoy fortune, I was determined to marry the first fool I should meet with . . . you made me a wife, for which I am much obliged to you, and if you have a wish to make me more grateful still, make me a widow.[1]

    *   *   *   *   *

Sir Peter. Then, you never had a desire to please me, or add to my happiness?

Lady Teazle. Sincerely, I never thought about you; did you imagine that age was catching? I think you have been overpaid for all you could bestow on me. Here am I surrounded by half a hundred lovers, not one of whom but would buy a single smile by a thousand such baubles as you grudge me.

Sir Peter. Then you wish me dead?

---

[1] The speeches which I have omitted consist merely of repetitions of the same thoughts, with but very little variation of the language.—Moore.

Lady Teazle. You know I do not, for you have made no settlement on me.

*   *   *   *   *

Sir Peter. I am but middle-aged.

Lady Teazle. There's the misfortune; put yourself on, or back, twenty years, and either way I should like you the better.

*   *   *   *   *

Yes, sir, and then your behaviour too was different; you would dress, and smile, and bow; fly to fetch me any thing I wanted; praise every thing I did or said; fatigue your stiff face with an eternal grin; nay, you even committed poetry, and muffled your harsh tones into a lover's whisper to sing it yourself, so that even my mother said you were the smartest old bachelor she ever saw—a billet-doux engrossed on buckram ! ! ! ! ! ![1]

*   *   *   *   *

Let girls take my advice and never marry an old bachelor. He must be so either because he could find nothing to love in women, or because women could find nothing to love in him.

"The greater part of this dialogue," says Moore, "is evidently *experimental*, and the play of repartee protracted with no other view, than to take the chance of a trump of wit or humour turning up.

"In comparing the two characters in this sketch with what they became at last, it is impossible not to be struck by the signal change that they have undergone. The transformation of Sir Peter into a gentleman has refined, without weakening, the ridicule of his situation; . . . The improvement in the character of Lady Teazle is still more marked and successful. Instead of an ill-bred shrew, whose readiness to do wrong leaves the mind in but little uncertainty as to her fate, we have a lively and innocent, though imprudent country girl, transplanted into the midst of all that can bewilder and endanger her, but with still enough of the purity of rural life about her heart, to keep the blight of the world from settling upon it permanently.

[1] These notes of admiration are in the original, and seem meant to express the surprise of the author at the extravagance of his own joke.—Moore.

"There is, indeed, in the original draught a degree of glare and coarseness, which proves the eye of the artist to have been fresh from the study of Wycherly and Vanbrugh; and this want of delicacy is particularly observable in the subsequent scene between Lady Teazle and Surface—the chastening down of which to its present tone is not the least of those triumphs of taste and skill which every step in the elaboration of this fine comedy exhibits."

This subsequent scene (the final Act IV, scene iii) survives from a later stage of evolution, when "Young Plausible" had become Young Pliant. According to Moore, this scene "underwent many changes afterwards, and was oftener put back into the crucible than any other part of the play." It appeared in *The Teazles* thus:

Scene—YOUNG PLIANT'S *Room*.

Young Pliant. I wonder her ladyship is not here: she promised me to call this morning. I have a hard game to play here, to pursue my designs on Maria. I have brought myself into a scrape with the mother-in-law. However, I think we have taken care to ruin my brother's character with my uncle, should he come to-morrow. Frank has not an ill quality in his nature; yet, a neglect of forms, and of the opinion of the world, has hurt him in the estimation of all his graver friends. I have profited by his errors, and contrived to gain a character, which now serves me as a mask to lie under.

Enter LADY TEAZLE.

Lady Teazle. What, musing, or thinking of me?

Young Pliant. I was thinking unkindly of you; do you know now that you must repay me for this delay, or I must be coaxed into good humour?

Lady Teazle. Nay, in faith you should pity me—this old curmudgeon of late is grown so jealous, that I dare go scarce out, till I know he is secure for some time.

Young Pliant. I am afraid the insinuations we have had spread about Frank have operated too strongly on him— we meant only to direct his suspicions to a wrong object.

Lady Teazle. Oh, hang him! I have told him plainly that if he continues to be so suspicious, I'll leave him entirely, and make him allow me a separate maintenance.

Young Pliant. But, my charmer, if ever that should be the case, you see before you the man who will ever be attached to you. But you must not let matters come to extremities; you can never be revenged so well by leaving him, as by living with him, and let my sincere affection make amends for his brutality.

Lady Teazle. But how shall I be sure now that you are sincere? I have sometimes suspected, that you loved my niece.[1]

Young Pliant. Oh, hang her, a puling idiot, without sense or spirit.

Lady Teazle. But what proofs have I of your love to me, for I have still so much of my country prejudices left, that if I were to do a foolish thing (and I think I can't promise) it shall be for a man who would risk every thing for me alone. How shall I be sure you love me?

Young Pliant. I have dreamed of you every night this week past.

Lady Teazle. That's a sign you have slept every night for this week past; for my part, I would not give a pin for a lover who could not wake for a month in absence.

Young Pliant. I have written verses on you out of number.

Lady Teazle. I never saw any.

Young Pliant. No—they did not please me, and so I tore them.

Lady Teazle. Then it seems you wrote them only to divert yourself.

Young Pliant. Am I doomed for ever to suspense?

Lady Teazle. I don't know—if I was convinced——

Young Pliant. Then let me on my knees——

Lady Teazle. Nay, nay, I will have no raptures either. This much I can tell you, that if I am to be seduced to do wrong, I am not to be taken by storm, but by deliberate capitulation, and that only where my reason or my heart is convinced.

---

[1] He had not yet decided whether to make Maria the daughter-in-law or niece of Lady Teazle.—Moore.

Young Pliant. Then, to say it at once—the world gives itself liberties——

Lady Teazle. Nay, I am sure without cause; for I am as yet unconscious of any ill, though I know not what I may be forced to.

Young Pliant. The fact is, my dear Lady Teazle, that your extreme innocence is the very cause of your danger; it is the integrity of your heart that makes you run into a thousand imprudences which a full consciousness of error would make you guard against. Now, in that case, you can't conceive how much more circumspect you would be.

Lady Teazle. Do you think so?

Young Pliant. Most certainly. Your character is like a person in a plethora, absolutely dying of too much health.

Lady Teazle. So then you would have me sin in my own defence, and part with my virtue to preserve my reputation.[1]

Young Pliant. Exactly so, upon my credit ma'am."

*   *   *   *   *

"It will be observed," Moore comments, "from all I have cited, that much of the original material is still preserved throughout; but that, like the ivory melting in the hands of Pygmalion, it has lost all its first rigidity and roughness, and, assuming at every touch some variety of aspect, seems to have gained new grace by every change."

THE SLANDERERS AND THE SNEERWELL-PLAY

The history of the scandal-play is rather more complicated than that of *The Teazles*. It was never intended to be more than a "farce" or comedy in two acts, and it is most likely to have been the piece which Sheridan told Linley on the last day of 1775 would be in rehearsal in a week at Covent Garden. The main plot of the Sneerwell-play (or "the Clerimont-play" as Mr.

[1] This sentence seems to have haunted him—I find it written in every direction, and without any material change in its form, over the pages of his different memorandum books.—Moore.

Sichel calls it) was the attempt of Lady Sneerwell to separate her ward from the hero, Florival or Clerimont, by forged letters and newspaper scandal. At some time or other Sheridan jotted down certain "hints for dialogue," as Moore termed them, under the title of *The Slanderers*. From his note "A Pump-Room Scene," he intended it as a satire upon the gossips of Bath:—

Friendly caution to the newspapers.

It is whispered——

She is a constant attendant at church, and very frequently takes Dr. M'Brawn home with her.

Mr. Worthy is very good to the girl;—for my part, I dare swear he has no ill intention.

What! Major Wesley's Miss Montague?

Lud, ma'am, the match is certainly broke—no creature knows the cause;—some say a flaw in the lady's character, and others, in the gentleman's fortune.

To be sure they do say——

I hate to repeat what I hear.

She was inclined to be a little too plump before she went.

The most intrepid blush;—I've known her complexion stand fire for an hour together.

She had twins,—How ill-natured! as I hope to be saved, ma'am, she had but one! and that a little starved brat not worth mentioning.

Certain ideas in this fragment may be traced in *The School for Scandal*, through the Sneerwell-play, whose opening line ("the paragraphs, you say, were all inserted") is forecasted by the first words, "friendly caution to the newspapers." Moore guessed (from the style of the handwriting, perhaps) that *The Slanderers* was written "before *The Rivals* or very soon after": Mr. Sichel guessed that it was written (with *The Ode to Scandal*) during Sheridan's convalescence after his second duel with Matthews in July, 1772. Moore's date seems to me much more likely. Indeed, while mine also is a guess, I am inclined to trace the germ of the scandal-plot to a short story in *The Town and Country*

Magazine for October, 1774. This effusion, "The Printed Lie:
a Moral Tale," must have caused a deal of ironical amusement to
to the readers of its scandalous chronicle, "the Histories of the
Têtes-à-Têtes." It is, significantly enough, a story about people at
Bath, and much too dull to recount, except for this passage:—

Charlotte Tyson had met with so many mortifications from
the negligence or contempt of the men, that she pined with
envy, she glowed with resentment, when any of her sex were
about to enjoy a felicity from which she was perpetually ex-
cluding herself by the folly of her behaviour and the badness
of her disposition. The approaching nuptials of Mr. Mendip
and Miss Derwent gave her particular disquiet, and she put
her ingenuity to the full stretch in order to prevent the celebration of them. Charlotte did as much mischief as she possibly could with her tongue; she often had recourse to pen for
the more extensive circulation of her ill-nature, and frequently
rejoiced at the disquiet she occasioned in deserving families
by printed lies. In news-papers innumerable were her lies
inserted, and too hastily believed. The lie which she despatched to one of these fugitive pieces with regard to Louisa Derwent and her lover was so plausibly related, and so artfully
timed, that it put a stop to hymenial proceedings... To the infinite satisfaction of Louisa, the letter which made her so unhappy proved to be false from the beginning to the end of it,
by the detection of Charlotte Tyson, who wrote it, she could
never appear again at Bath.

I take the liberty of guessing that after reading "The Printed
Lie: A Moral Tale," Sheridan's mind was impregnated with
the germ of the dramatic action, the germ of the character of
Lady Sneerwell. Then, or soon afterwards, he jotted down on a
sheet of notepaper the outline of a conversation at Bath with the
title of "*The Slanderers: A Pump Room Scene.*"

The Slanderers in its later developments survives in some
fragments commonly called *Clerimont* or "the Clerimont-play."
But there are other scraps, including a scenario in Sheridan's
summary manner, in which the hero and heroine are called
Florival and Emma and not Clerimont and Maria. The former

names appear to me to be the earlier, but in both phases the action is that of "the Sneerwell-play," as it is more significantly to be called. These parts developed into the present Act I, Scene i.

LADY SNEERWELL *and* SPATTER.

Lady Sneerwell. The paragraphs, you say, were all inserted.

Spatter. They were, madam.

Lady Sneerwell. Did you circulate the report of Lady Brittle's intrigue with Captain Boastall?

Spatter. Madam, by this Lady Brittle is the talk of half the town; and in a week will be treated as a demirep.

Lady Sneerwell. What have you done as to the innuendo of Miss Niceley's fondness for her own footman?

Spatter. 'Tis in a fair train, ma'am. I told it to my hair-dresser,—he courts a milliner's girl in Pall Mall, whose mistress has a first cousin who is waiting-woman to Lady Clackit. I think, in about fourteen hours it must reach Lady Clackit, and then you know the business is done.

Lady Sneerwell. But is that sufficient, do you think?

Spatter. O Lud, ma'am, I'll undertake to ruin the character of the primmest prude in London with half as much. Ha! ha! Did your ladyship never hear how poor Miss Shepherd lost her lover and her character last summer at Scarborough? this was the whole of it. One evening at Lady ——'s, the conversation happened to turn on the difficulty of breeding Nova Scotia sheep in England. "I have known instances," says Miss ——, "for last spring, a friend of mine, Miss Shepherd of Ramsgate, had a Nova Scotia sheep that produced her twins." —"What!" cries the old deaf dowager Lady Bowlwell, "has Miss Shepherd of Ramsgate been brought to bed of twins?" This mistake, as you may suppose, set the company a laughing. However, the next day, Miss Verjuice Amarilla Lonely, who had been of the party, talking of Lady Bowlwell's deafness, began to tell what had happened; but, unluckily, forgetting to say a word of the sheep, it was understood by the company, and, in every circle, many believed, that Miss Shepherd of Ramsgate had actually been brought to bed of a fine boy and a girl; and, in less than a fortnight, there were people who could name the father, and the farm-house where the babies were put out to nurse.

Lady Sneerwell. Ha! ha! well, for a stroke of luck, it was a very good one. I suppose you find no difficulty in spreading the report on the censorious Miss ——.

Spatter. None in the world,—she has always been so prudent and reserved, that every body was sure there was some reason for it at bottom.

Lady Sneerwell. Yes, a tale of scandal is as fatal to the credit of a prude as a fever to those of the strongest constitutions; but there is a sort of sickly reputation that outlives hundreds of the robuster character of a prude.

Spatter. True, ma'am, there are valetudinarians in reputation as in constitution; and both are cautious from their appreciation and consciousness of their weak side, and avoid the least breath of air.[1]

Lady Sneerwell. But, Spatter, I have something of greater confidence now to entrust you with. I think I have some claim to your gratitude.

Spatter. Have I ever shown myself one moment unconscious of what I owe you?

Lady Sneerwell. I do not charge you with it, but this is an affair of importance. You are acquainted with my situation, but not all my weaknesses. I was hurt, in the early part of my life, by the envenomed tongue of scandal, and ever since, I own, have no joy but in sullying the fame of others. In this I have found you an apt tool: you have often been the instrument of my revenge, but you must now assist me in a softer passion. A young widow with a little beauty and easy fortune is seldom driven to sue,—yet is that my case. Of the many you have seen here, have you ever observed me, secretly, to favour one?

---

[1] This is one of the many instances, where the improving effect of revision may be traced. The passage at present stands thus:—"There are valetudinarians in reputation as well as constitution; who, being conscious of their weak part, avoid the least breath of air, and supply the want of stamina by care and circumspection."—Moore. [The revised speeches are given to Sir Benjamin and Mrs. Candour, a still further improvement.]

Spatter. Egad! I never was more posed: I'm sure you cannot mean that ridiculous old knight, Sir Christopher Crab?

Lady Sneerwell. A wretch! his assiduities are my torment.

Spatter. Perhaps his nephew, the baronet, Sir Benjamin Backbite, is the happy man?

Lady Sneerwell. No, though he has ill-nature and a good person on his side, he is not to my taste. What think you of Clerimont?

Spatter. How! the professed lover of your ward, Maria; between whom, too, there is a mutual affection.

Lady Sneerwell. Yes, that insensible, that doater on an idiot, is the man.

Spatter. But how can you hope to succeed?

Lady Sneerwell. By poisoning both with jealousy of the other, till the credulous fool, in a pique, shall be entangled in my snare.

Spatter. Have you taken any measure for it?

Lady Sneerwell. I have. Maria has made me the confidante of Clerimont's love for her: In return, I pretended to entrust her with my affection for Sir Benjamin, who is her warm admirer. By strong representation of my passion, I prevailed on her not to refuse to see Sir Benjamin, which she once promised Clerimont to do. I entreated her to plead my cause, and even drew her in to answer Sir Benjamin's letters with the same intent. Of this I have made Clerimont suspicious; but 'tis you must inflame him to the pitch I want.

Spatter. But will not Maria, on the least unkindness of Clerimont, instantly come to an explanation?

Lady Sneerwell. This is what we must prevent by blinding.

A little later comes a scene between Lady Sneerwell and Maria which gives, as Moore says, some insight into the use that was to be made of this intricate groundwork.[1]

[1] The following is his own arrangement of the Scenes of the Second Act [as planned in the Florival phase]

"Act II. Scene 1st. All.—2nd. Lady S. and Mrs. C.—3d. Lady S. and * * Em. and Mrs. C. listening.—4th. L. S. and Flor. shows him into the room,—bids him return the other way.—L. S. and Emma.—Emma and Florival;—fits,—maid.—Emma fainting and sobbing:—'Death, don't expose me!'—enter maid,—will call out—all come on with cards and smelling-bottles."—Moore.

Lady Sneerwell. Well, my love, have you seen Clerimont to-day?

Maria. I have not, nor does he come as often as he used. Indeed, madam, I fear what I have done to serve you has by some means come to his knowledge, and injured me in his opinion. I promised him faithfully never to see Sir Benjamin. What confidence can he ever have in me, if he once finds I have broken my word to him.

Lady Sneerwell. Nay, you are too grave. If he should suspect any thing, it will always be in my power to undeceive him.

Maria. Well, you have involved me in deceit, and I must trust to you to extricate me.

Lady Sneerwell. Have you answered Sir Benjamin's last letter in the manner I wished?

Maria. I have written exactly as you desired me; but I wish you would give me leave to tell the whole truth to Clerimont at once. There is a coldness in his manner of later, which I can no ways account for.

Lady Sneerwell [*aside*]. I'm glad to find I have worked on him so far;—fie, Maria, have you so little regard for me? would you put me to the shame of being known to love a man who disregards me? Had you entrusted me with such a secret, not a husband's power should have forced it from me. But, do as you please. Go, forget the affection I have shown you: forget that I have been as a mother to you, whom I found an orphan. Go, break through all ties of gratitude, and expose me to the world's derision, to avoid one sullen hour from a moody lover.

Maria. Indeed, madam, you wrong me; and you who know the apprehension of love should make allowance for its weakness. My love for Clerimont is so great—

Lady Sneerwell. Peace; it cannot exceed mine.

Maria. For Sir Benjamin, perhaps not, ma'am——and, I am sure, Clerimont has as sincere an affection for me.

Lady Sneerwell. Would to heaven I could say the same!

Maria. Of Sir Benjamin:—I wish so too, ma'am. But I am

sure you would be extremely hurt, if, in gaining your wishes, you were to injure me in the opinion of Clerimont.

Lady Sneerwell. Undoubtedly; I would not for the world— Simple fool! [*Aside.*] But my wishes, my happiness depend on you—for, I doat so on the insensible, that it kills me to see him so attached to you. Give me but Clerimont, and——

Maria. Clerimont!

Lady Sneerwell. Sir Benjamin, you know, I mean. Is he not attached to you? am I not slighted for you? Yet, do I bear any enmity to you, as my rival? I only request your friendly inter-cession, and you are so ungrateful, you would deny me that.

Maria. Nay, madam, have I not done every thing you wished? For you, I have departed from truth, and contamin-ated my mind with falsehood—what could I do more to serve you?

Lady Sneerwell. Well, forgive me, I was too warm, I know you would not betray me. I expect Sir Benjamin and his uncle this morning—why, Maria, do you always leave our little parties?

Maria. I own, madam, I have no pleasure in their conversa-tion. I have myself no gratification in uttering detraction, and therefore none in hearing it.

Lady Sneerwell. Oh fie! you are serious—'tis only a little harmless raillery.

Maria. I never can think that harmless which hurts the peace of youth, draws tears from beauty, and gives many a pang to the innocent.

Lady Sneerwell. Nay, you must allow that many people of sense and wit have this foible—Sir Benjamin Backbite, for instance.

Maria. He may, but I confess I never can perceive wit where I see malice.

Lady Sneerwell. Fie, Maria, you have the most unpolished way of thinking! It is absolutely impossible to be witty without being a little ill-natured. The malice of a good thing is the barb that makes it stick. I protest now when I say an ill-natured thing, I have not the least malice against the person; and, indeed, it may be of one whom I never saw in my life; for I hate to abuse a friend—but I take it for granted, they all speak as ill-naturedly of me.

Maria. Then you are, very probably, conscious you deserve it—for my part, I shall only suppose myself ill-spoken of, when I am conscious I deserve it.

Enter SERVANT.

Servant. Mrs. Candour.

Maria. Well, I 'll leave you.

Lady Sneerwell. No, no, you have no reason to avoid her, she is good nature itself.

Maria. Yes with an artful affectation of candour, she does more injury than the worst backbiter of them all.

Enter MRS. CANDOUR.

Mrs. Candour. So, Lady Sneerwell, how d'ye do? Maria, child, how dost? Well, who is't you are to marry at last? Sir Benjamin or Clerimont. The town talks of nothing else."

"Through the remainder of this scene," says Moore, "the only difference in the speeches of Mrs. Candour is, that they abound more than at present in ludicrous names and anecdotes, and occasionally straggle into that loose wordiness, which, knowing how much it weakens the sap of wit, the good taste of Sheridan was always sure to lop away. The same may be said of the greater part of that scene of scandal, which at present occurs in the second Act, and in which all that is now spoken by Lady Teazle was originally put into the mouths of Sir Christopher Crab and others—the caustic remarks of Sir Peter Teazle being, as well as himself, an after creation."

"It is chiefly," he continues, "however, in Clerimont, the embryo of Charles Surface, that we perceive how imperfect may be the first lineaments, that Time and Taste contrive to mould gradually into beauty. The following is the scene that introduces him to the audience, and no one ought to be disheartened by the failure of a first attempt after reading it. The spiritless language —the awkward introduction of the sister into the plot—the antiquated expedient[1] of dropping the letter—all, in short, is of the most undramatic and most unpromising description, and as little like what it afterwards turned to as the block is to the statue, or the grub to the butterfly."

It must be objected, however, that Clerimont is not "the embryo of Charles Surface." This highly moral young man, the Florival of the earlier scheme, is the sentimental and romantic hero whom Sheridan discarded in favour of another person altogether, the young spendthrift from *The Teazles*. Of the scene which introduced Clerimont to the audience, not a single trace survives in *The School for Scandal:*—

Sir Christopher. This Clerimont is, to be sure, the drollest mortal! he is one of your moral fellows, who does unto others as he would they should do unto him.

Lady Sneerwell. Yet he is sometimes entertaining.

Sir Christopher. Oh hang him, no—he has too much good nature to say a witty thing himself, and is too ill-natured to praise wit in others.

Enter CLERIMONT.

Sir Benjamin. So, Clerimont—we were just wishing for you to enliven us with your wit and agreeable vein.

Clerimont. No, Sir Benjamin, I cannot join you.

Sir Benjamin. Why, man, you look as grave as a young lover the first time he is jilted.

Clerimont. I have some cause to be grave, Sir Benjamin. A word with you all. I have just received a letter from the country in which I understand that my sister has suddenly left my uncle's house, and has not since been heard of.

Lady Sneerwell. Indeed! and on what provocation?

Clerimont. It seems they were urging her a little too hastily to marry some country squire that was not to her taste.

---

*This objection seems to have occurred to himself; for one of his memorandums is— "Not to drop the letter, but take it from the maid."—Moore.

Sir Benjamin. Positively I love her for her spirit.

Lady Sneerwell. And so do I, and would protect her, if I knew where she was.

Clerimont. Sir Benjamin, a word with you—[*Takes him apart.*] I think, sir, we have lived for some years on what the world calls the footing of friends.

Sir Benjamin. To my great honour, sir.—Well, my dear friend?

Clerimont. You know that you once paid your addresses to my sister. My uncle disliked you; but I have reason to think you were not indifferent to her.

Sir Benjamin. I believe you are pretty right there; but what follows?

Clerimont. Then I think I have a right to expect an implicit answer from you, whether you are in any respect privy to her elopement?

Sir Benjamin. Why, you certainly have a right to ask the question, and I will answer you as sincerely—which is, that though I make no doubt but that she would have gone with me to the world's end, I am at present entirely ignorant of the whole affair. This I declare to you upon my honour—and, what is more, I assure you my devotions are at present paid to another lady—one of your acquaintance, too.

Clerimont [*aside*]. Now, who can this other be to whom he alludes?—I have sometimes thought I perceived a kind of mystery between him and Maria—but I rely on her promise, though, of late her conduct to me has been strangely reserved.

Lady Sneerwell. Why, Clerimont, you seem quite thoughtful. Come with us; we are going to kill an hour at ombre—your mistress will join us?

Clerimont. Madam, I attend you.

Lady Sneerwell [*taking* SIR BENJAMIN *aside*]. Sir Benjamin, I see Maria is now coming to join us—do you detain her awhile, and I will contrive that Clerimont should see you, and then drop this letter.

[*Exeunt all but* SIR BENJAMIN.

Enter MARIA.

Maria. I thought the company were here, and Clerimont—

Sir Benjamin. One, more your slave than Clerimont, is here.

Maria. Dear Sir Benjamin, I thought you promised me to drop this subject. If I have really any power over you, you will oblige me—

Sir Benjamin. Power over me! What is there you could not command me in? Have you not wrought on me to proffer my love to Lady Sneerwell? Yet though you gain this from me, you will not give me the smallest token of gratitude.

Enter CLERIMONT *behind.*

Maria. How can I believe your love sincere, when you continue still to importune me?

Sir Benjamin. I ask but for your friendship, your esteem.

Maria. That you shall ever be entitled to—then I may depend upon your honour?

Sir Benjamin. Eternally—dispose of my heart as you please.

Maria. Depend upon it I shall study nothing but its happiness. I need not repeat my caution as to Clerimont?

Sir Benjamin. No, no, he suspects nothing as yet.

Maria. For, within these few days, I almost believed that he suspects me.

Sir Benjamin. Never fear, he does not love well enough to be quick sighted; for just now he taxed me with eloping with his sister.

Maria. Well, we had now best join the company. [*Exeunt.*

Clerimont. So, now—who can ever have faith in woman? D—d deceitful wanton! why did she not fairly tell me that she was weary of my addresses? that woman, like her mind, was changed, and another fool succeeded.

Enter LADY SNEERWELL.

Lady Sneerwell. Clerimont, why do you leave us? Think of my losing this hand. (*Clerimont.* She has no heart!)—Five mate—(*Clerimont.* Deceitful wanton!)—spadille.

Clerimont. Oh, yes, ma'am—'twas very hard.

Lady Sneerwell. But you seem disturbed ; and where are Maria and Sir Benjamin? I vow I shall be jealous of Sir Benjamin.

Clerimont. I dare swear they are together very happy,—but, Lady Sneerwell—you may perhaps often have perceived that I am discontented with Maria. I ask you to tell me sincerely— have you ever perceived it?

Lady Sneerwell. I wish you would excuse me.

Clerimont. Nay, you have perceived it—I know you hate deceit.

It would be interesting to know what brought the Sneerwell play to a standstill. The habit of calling it *Clerimont* has obscured certain factors which have (to the best of my knowledge) been entirely overlooked. It is true that most writers of Sheridan have been ignorant of the drama of the previous decade, with the solitary and almost irrelevant exception of the two plays of Goldsmith. Nevertheless, the Sneerwell-plot (which was, to reiterate, "the attempt of Lady Sneerwell to separate her ward from the hero, Florival or Clerimont, by forged letters and newspaper scandal") had been used at least twice previously :—

(i) By George Colman in *The English Merchant* (1767). In this play (adapted from Voltaire) Lady Alton, in order to break off a match between Lord Falbridge and Amelia Douglas, employs a hackney-writer named Spatter to vilify the girl's character. "The writings of authors," says Spatter's "patroness," in a *sentiment*, "are public advertisements of their qualifications; and when they profess to live upon scandal, it is as much as to say that they are ready for any other dirty work in which we chuse to employ them." Actually the "dirty work" of Spatter is not concerned with newspapers, but in Garrick's Epilogue to the comedy this is forecasted as a sequel :—

Lady Alton. Attack Amelia, both in verse and prose,
Your wits can make a nettle of a rose.

Spatter. A stinging nettle for his lordship's breast:

And to my stars and dashes leave the rest . . .
I know my genius, and can trust my plan—
I'll break a woman's heart with any man.

(ii) By Samuel Foote in *The Bankrupt* (1773) which was an
attack on the licentiousness of newspapers. In this Lady
Rescounter, in order to break off a match between her step-
daughter Lydia and a baronet (whom she desires for the husband of her own daughter) employs a clerk named James to
concoct a scurrilous paragraph which is duly printed in a
newspaper.

It seems to me that Sheridan, working upon the Sneerwell-plot,
the plot of "A Printed Lie," would (when he once knew of them)
avoid repeating either of these developments. A journalist was a
natural person to introduce into the plot, and Spatter a natural
name for one type of journalist as Puff was for another. Charlotte Tyson in "The Printed Lie" (or whoever the germ of this
character was), developed in Lady Sneerwell, who especially in
the early drafts, was a vindictive and jealous termagant with a
close resemblance to Colman's Lady Alton. It was therefore (I
suggest) to avoid any appearance of being a plagiary that Sheridan at a later stage divided Spatter into two characters, Miss
Verjuice the sour spinster who concocted the paragraphs, and
Snake the hackney-journalist who was also an adept at forgery.
So they stood in the last discarded draft of *The School for Scandal*
where Sir Peter's last words about Snake are, "There's a precious
rogue. Yet that fellow's a writer and a Critic." But this double
characterization so weakened the continuity of the plot, that
Sheridan eventually restored to Snake the part given to Miss
Verjuice. This argument, however, has anticipated the union of
the two plays.

Of course, we shall never know when or where Sheridan derived the idea of combining the Sneerwell-play with *The Teazles*. But the *flux*, to borrow a term from metallurgy, which caused
this amalgamation can have been only one thing—the specific
invention of the Scandalous College, as distinct from the general
theme of scandal, gossip, and slander. The creation of this Col-

lege caused Sheridan to look about for probationers. It entirely transformed the characters, only Mrs Candour, and (with certain reservations) Lady Sneerwell, remaining untouched, Sir Benjamin Backbite turned from a villain, a clockwork villain, all springs and wheels, into a macaroni; and Sir Christopher Crab preserved a few of his lineaments in the person of Crabtree. But the need for the typical figure of a smart young wife brought in Lady Teazle; and, with her, all her train. In the transit she acquired a grace and good breeding which effaced all the coarseness and vulgarity that had been the legacy of her existence as "Mrs. Teazle, the third wife of old Solomon Teazle, retired from trade." She was enriched with spoils of pleasantry from Sir Christopher Crab. Sir Peter, too, was given a new strength as a caustic commentator on the Scandalous College: at one time the story of Miss Piper's twins, afterwards allotted to Crabtree, was taken from Spatter to give to him. Young Pliant, the hypocritical moralist, became Joseph Surface, and his brother or friend, the Captain Plausible, the Frank Pliant, the Young Harrier of previous incarnations, settled into his genial spendthrift character as Charles Surface, summarily ejecting that solemn priggish gentleman, Sir Charles Clerimont *alias* Florival, after borrowing his Christian name. With the new scheme came the development of the two best scenes in the comedy, the auction of pictures from his spendthrift habits, the screen-scene from some clumsy expedient of locking a woman in a cupboard. The transformation weakened the dramatic force, though not the histrionic effectiveness, of Mrs. Candour, Sir Benjamin Backbite, and others, by removing them from any direct association in the Sneerwell-plot. Nevertheless this charge of dramatic irrelevance has been grossly exaggerated: their malice has a joyousness of invention which lightens the melodramatic and termagant intensity of Lady Sneerwell, and it reaches its height of comic effectiveness in their story of the duel and the mockery of Sir Peter. Indeed, almost all the best situations came after the amalgamation of the two plots. The idea of the Scandalous College was indeed the flux which amalgamated two bad plays into one great comedy.

It may be urged that the idea was latent in the comedy which began with the gossip of *The Slanderers*. Nevertheless, greatly daring, I am about to suggest that this flux, the conception of the College, came from *The Silent Woman*, by Ben Jonson. This theory may seem to be the spoils of a plagiary-hunt through the comedies of an era that was then considered antiquated. But it is not. This is the essential passage (Act I, Scene i):—

> *Truewit.* When were you at the College?
> *Clerimont.* What College?
> *Truewit.* A new foundation, sir, here in the Town, of ladies who call themselves the Collegiates, an order between courtiers and country-madams, that live from their husbands, and give entertainment to all the wits and braveries of the time, as they call them; cry down, or up, what they like, or dislike, in a brain or a fashion, with most masculine, or rather hermaphroditical authority; and every day gain to their College some new probationer.
> *Clerimont.* Who is the President?
> *Truewit.* The grave and youthful matron, Lady Haughty.

This source is by no means "literary" nor an attempt to show that Sheridan was an earnest student of Ben Jonson. For *The Silent Woman*, altered by George Colman was acted at Drury Lane for the first time on January 13th, 1776. His prologue said:

> " On fair Collegiates let no critics frown;
> A ladies club still holds its rank in town."

which, in the paraphrase of *The Town and Country Magazine* "compared the College Ladies in the days of Ben Jonson to the Coterie of the present *ton*."

This club, held at "the Thatcht House in St. James's," embraced the fashionable women of the period and was notorious for its dancing, quadrille-playing and scandalous gossip. Lady Teazle, Lady Sneerwell, and Mrs. Candour would have been at home in its portals.

The characters of *The School for Scandal* were again modified by another factor, the special talents of the company at the Theatre-Royal, Drury Lane. They became, as it were, acting-parts written for them. It may be, of course, that Moses would have been the same Moses if the part had been intended for Wewitzer of Covent Garden instead of Baddeley of Drury Lane. But without Mrs. Abington, Lady Teazle would have been another personality: without Palmer and Smith, Joseph and Charles would have been different. Such at least was the testimony of all who knew the circumstances of the original casting.

THE PENULTIMATE VERSION

(COMMONLY CALLED "THE RAE TEXT")

The Sheridan MSS. at Frampton Court includes a draft of *The School for Scandal,* which was first printed by Fraser Rae in *Sheridan's Plays as He Wrote Them.* It is incomplete, omitting the latter part of Act III, Scene iii, and all Act IV, Scene i. This was certainly not the version acted at the first representation of May 8th, 1777, for there was no Miss Verjuice in the original cast. It had been merged into that of Snake. Nevertheless, the allusion to the Annuity Bill cannot have been written before April 25th of that year, when it was discussed in the House of Commons.

The amendments of consequence were made chiefly in two scenes: Act I, Scene i and Act II, Scene i.

ACT I, SCENE I

[In the final version the character of Miss Verjuice was merged into that of Snake, an admirable example of dramatic economy. Many sentences, here enclosed in square brackets, were deleted, with a great increase in conciseness. No attempt is made to indicate minor changes, but each of them deserves attention.]

LADY SNEERWELL's *House.*

LADY SNEERWELL *at her dressing-table with* LAPPET; MISS VERJUICE *drinking chocolate.*

Lady Sneerwell. The Paragraphs you say were all inserted:
Verjuice. They were Madam—and as I copied them my-

self in a feigned Hand there can be no suspicion whence they came.

Lady Sneerwell. Did you circulate the Report of Lady Brittle's Intrigue with Captain Boaſtall?

[*Verjuice.* Madam by this Time Lady Brittle is the Talk of half the Town—and I doubt not in a week the Men will toaſt her as a Demirep.

Lady Sneerwell. What have you done as to the insinuations as to a certain Baronet's Lady and a certain Cook.]

Verjuice. That is in as fine a Train as your Ladyship could wish. [I told the ſtory yeſterday to my own maid with directions to communicate it direʄtly to my Hairdresser. He I am informed has a Brother who courts a Milliners' Prentice in Pallmall whose miſtress has a firſt cousin whose siſter is Feme de Chambre to Mrs. Clackit—so that] in the common course of Things it muſt reach Mrs. Clackit's Ears within four-and-twenty hours and then you know the Business is as good as done.

Lady Sneerwell. Why truly Mrs. Clackit has a very pretty Talent—a great deal of induſtry[1]—yet she has been tolerably successful in her way—To my knowledge she has been the cause of breaking off six matches, of three sons being disinherited and four Daughters being turned out of Doors. Of three several Elopements, as many close confinements—nine separate maintenances and two Divorces.—nay I have more than once traced her causing a *Tête-à-Tête* in the Town and Country Magazine—when the Parties perhaps had never seen each other's Faces before in the course of their Lives.

Verjuice. She certainly has Talents.

Lady Sneerwell. But her manner is gross.

Verjuice. 'Tis very true. She generally designs well, has a free tongue and a bold invention—but her colouring is too dark and her outline often extravagant—She wants that delicacy of Tint—and mellowness of sneer—which diſtinguish your Ladyship's Scandal.

Lady Sneerwell. Ah you are Partial Verjuice.

[1]Transferred to Snake.

Verjuice. Not in the least—everybody allows that Lady Sneerwell can do more with a word or a Look than many can with the most laboured Detail even when they happen to have a little truth on their side to support it.

Lady Sneerwell. Yes my dear Verjuice. I am no Hypocrite to deny the satisfaction I reap from the Success of my Efforts. Wounded myself, in the early part of my Life by the envenomed Tongue of Slander I confess I have since known no Pleasure equal to the reducing others to the Level of my own injured Reputation.

Verjuice. Nothing can be more natural—But my dear Lady Sneerwell There is one affair in which you have lately employed me, wherein, I confess I am at a Loss to guess your motives.

Lady Sneerwell. I conceive you mean with respect to my neighbour, Sir Peter Teazle, and his Family—[Lappet.— And has my conduct in this matter really appeared to you so mysterious? [*Exit* MAID.

Verjuice. Entirely so.]

Lady Sneerwell. [An old Batchelor as Sir Peter was having taken a young wife from out of the Country—as Lady Teazle is—are certainly fair subjects for a little mischievous raillery.

Verjuice. But]¹ here are two young men—to whom Sir Peter has acted as a kind of Guardian since their Father's death, the eldest possessing the most amiable Character and universally well spoken of[,] the youngest the most dissipated and extravagant young Fellow in the Kingdom, without Friends or character—the former one an avowed admirer of yours and apparently your Favourite[,] the latter attached to Maria Sir Peter's ward—and confessedly beloved by her. Now on the face of these circumstances it is utterly unaccountable to me why you a [young] Widow with [no great] jointure —should not close with the passion of a man of such character and expectations as Mr. Surface—and more so why you should

¹The rest of this speech clearly belongs to Verjuice though given to Lady Sneerwell in the MS.

be so uncommonly earneſt to deſtroy the mutual Attachment subsiſting between his Brother Charles and Maria.

Lady Sneerwell. Then at once to unravel this miſtery—I muſt inform you that Love has no share whatever in the intercourse between Mr. Surface and me.

Verjuice. No!

Lady Sneerwell. His real attachment is to Maria or her Fortune—but finding in his Brother a favoured Rival, He has been obliged to mask his Pretensions—and profit by my Assiſtance.

Verjuice. Yet ſtill I am more puzzled why you should intereſt yourself in his success.

Lady Sneerwell. Heavens! how dull you are! cannot you surmise the weakness which I hitherto, thro' shame have concealed even from you—muſt I confess that Charles—that Libertine, that extravagant, that Bankrupt in Fortune and Reputation—that He it is for whom I am thus anxious and malicious and to gain whom I would sacrifice—everything—

Verjuice. Now indeed—your conduct appears consiſtent and I no longer wonder at your enmity to Maria, but how came you and Surface so confidential?

Lady Sneerwell. For our mutual intereſt—but I have found out him a long time since, altho' He has contrived to deceive everybody beside—I know him to be artful, selfish and malicious—[while with Sir Peter, and indeed with all his acquaintance, He passes for a youthful Miracle of Prudence—good sense and Benevolence.]

Verjuice. Yes yes—I know Sir Peter vows He has not his equal in England; and, above all, He praises him as a *man of sentiment.*

Lady Sneerwell. True and with the assiſtance of his sentiments and hypocrisy he has brought Sir Peter entirely in his intereſts with respect to Maria [and is now I believe attempting to flatter Lady Teazle into the same good opinion towards him]—[while poor Charles has no Friend in the House—though I fear he has a powerful one in Maria's Heart, againſt whom we muſt direct our schemes.]

Servant. Mr. Surface.

Lady Sneerwell. Show him up. [He generally calls about this Time. I don't wonder at People's giving him to me for a Lover.]

Enter SURFACE.

Surface. My dear Lady Sneerwell, how do you do to-day—your moſt obedient.

Lady Sneerwell. Miss Verjuice has juſt been arraigning me on our mutual attachment now; but I have informed her of our real views [and the Purposes for which our Geniuses at present co-operate.] You know how useful she has been to us —and believe me the confidence is not ill-placed.

Surface. Madam, it is impossible for me to suspect that a Lady of Miss Verjuice's sensibility and discernment——

Lady Sneerwell. Well—well—no compliments now—but tell me when you saw your miſtress, or what is more material to me, your Brother.

Surface. I have not seen either since I saw you—but I can inform you that they are at present at Variance—some of your ſtories have taken good effect on Maria.

Lady Sneerwell. Ah! my dear Verjuice the merit of this belongs to you. But do your Brother's Diſtresses encrease?

Surface. Every hour. I am told He had another execution in his house yeſterday—in short his Dissipation and extravagance exceed anything I have ever heard of

Lady Sneerwell. Poor Charles!

Surface. True, Madam—notwithſtanding his Vices one can't help feeling for him—ah poor Charles! I'm sure I wish it was in my Power to be of any essential Service to him—for the man who does not share in the Diſtresses of a Brother—even though merited by his own misconduct—deserves——

Lady Sneerwell. O Lud you are going to be moral, and forget that you are among Friends.

Surface. Egad, that's true—I'll keep that sentiment till I see Sir Peter. However it is certainly a charity to rescue Maria from such a Libertine who—if He is to be reclaim'd, can be

so only by a Person of your Ladyship's superior accomplishments and understanding.

[*Verjuice.* 'Twould be a Hazardous experiment.]

Surface. But—Madam—let me caution you to place no
more confidence in our Friend Snake the Libeller—I have
lately detected him in frequent conference with old Rowland
who was formerly my Father's Steward and has never been a
friend of mine.

Lady Sneerwell. I'm not disappointed in Snake, I never suspected the fellow to have virtue enough to be faithful even to
his own Villany.[1]

Enter MARIA.

Maria my dear—how do you do—what's the matter?

Maria. O here is that disagreeable lover of mine, Sir Benjamin Backbite, has just call'd at my guardian's with his odious
Uncle Crabtree—so I slipt out and ran hither to avoid them.

Lady Sneerwell. Is that all?

[*Verjuice.* Lady Sneerwell—I'll go and write the Letter I
mention'd to you.]

Surface. If my Brother Charles had been of the Party,
madam, perhaps you would not have been so much alarmed.

Lady Sneerwell. Nay now—you are severe for I dare swear
the Truth of the matter is Maria heard *you* were here—but my
dear—what has Sir Benjamin done that you should avoid him
so——

Maria. Oh He has done nothing—but his conversation is a
perpetual Libel on all his Acquaintance.

Surface. Aye and the worst of it is there is no advantage in
not knowing Them, for He'll abuse a stranger just as soon as
his best Friend—and Crabtree is as bad.

Lady Sneerwell. Nay but we should make allowance—Sir
Benjamin is a wit and a poet.

Maria. For my Part—I own madam—wit loses its respect
with me, when I see it in company with malice.—What do
you think, Mr. Surface?

Surface. Certainly, Madam, to smile at the jest which plants

[1]Partly transferred to Joseph.

a Thorn on another's Breaſt is to become a principal in the mischief.

Lady Sneerwell. Pshaw—there's no possibility of being witty without a little [ill] nature—the malice of a good thing is the Barb that makes it ſtick.—What's your opinion, Mr. Surface?

Surface. Certainly madam—that conversation where the Spirit of Raillery is suppressed will ever appear tedious and insipid—

Maria. Well I'll not debate how far Scandal may be allowable—but in a man I am sure it is always contemptible.—We have Pride, envy, Rivalship, and a Thousand motives to depreciate each other—but the male-slanderer muſt have the cowardice of a woman before He can traduce one.

[*Lady Sneerwell.* I wish my Cousin Verjuice hadn't left us —she should embrace you.

Surface. Ah! she's an old maid and is privileged of course.]

Enter SERVANT.

Madam Mrs. Candour is below and if your Ladyship's at leisure will leave her carriage.

Lady Sneerwell. Beg her to walk in. Now, Maria[,] however here is a Character to your Taſte, for tho' Mrs. Candour is a little talkative everybody allows her to be the beſt-natured and beſt sort of woman.

Maria. Yes with a very gross affeΓation of good Nature and Benevolence—she does more mischief than the DireΓt malice of old Crabtree.

Surface. Efaith 'tis very true Lady Sneerwell—Whenever I hear the current running again the charaΓters of my Friends, I never think them in such Danger as when Candour undertakes their Defence.

Lady Sneerwell. Hush here she is——

Enter MRS. CANDOUR.

Mrs. Candour. My dear Lady Sneerwell how have you been this Century. I have never seen you tho' I have heard of you very often.—Mr. Surface—[the World says scandalous things of you]—but indeed it is no matter [what the world says] for I think one hears nothing else but scandal.

Surface. Juſt so, indeed, Ma'am.

ACT II, SCENE 1

[In the final version, the speeches between Sir Peter and Lady Teazle were rediſtributed with consummate effeĉtiveness. In *The Teazles*, Sir Peter had delivered a monologue upon his wife's occupations before her marriage, which in the penultimate version is made more dramatic by her interruptions; in these, however, there is no great charaĉter. In the final version the whole passage becomes alive by letting Lady Teazle join in the account with a mocking glee, until she "denies the butler and the coach-horse" with great spirit and annoyance. In *The Teazles* she bluntly asserts she was glad to marry the firſt fool she met with, and hoped he would complete her gratitude at making her a wife by making her a widow. This was rediſtributed in the penultimate version, but the perfeĉtion of comedy was only achieved when in the final version her "plain-dealing" about marrying the firſt rich man was eliminated entirely, and her desire to be made a widow was conveyed to Sir Peter by a pause of well-bred malice. The numerous verbal improvements, too, merit a close ſtudy.]

SIR PETER *and* LADY TEAZLE.

Sir Peter. Lady Teazle—Lady Teazle I'll not bear it.

Lady Teazle. Sir Peter—Sir Peter you—may scold or smile according to your Humour[,] but I ought to have my own way in everything, and what's more I will too—what! tho'I was educated in the country I know very well that women of Fashion in London are accountable to nobody after they are married.

Sir Peter. Very well! ma'am very well! so a husband is to have no influence, no authority?

Lady Teazle. Authority! no, to be sure—if you wanted

authority over me, you should have adopted me and not married me[:] I am sure you were old enough.

Sir Peter. Old enough—aye there it is—well—well—Lady Teazle, tho' my life may be made unhappy by your Temper—I'll not be ruined by your extravagance—

Lady Teazle. My extravagance! I'm sure I'm not more extravagant than a woman of Fashion ought to be.

Sir Peter. No no Madam, you shall throw away no more sums on such unmeaning Luxury—'Slife to spend as much to furnish your Dressing Room with Flowers in winter as would suffice to turn the Pantheon into a Greenhouse, and give a *Fête Champêtre* at Christmas.

Lady Teazle. Lord! Sir Peter am I to blame because Flowers are dear in cold weather? You should find fault with the Climate, and not with me. For my Part I 'm sure I wish it was spring all the year round—and that Roses grew under one's Feet!

Sir Peter. Oons! Madam—if you had been born to those Fopperies I shouldn't wonder at your talking thus;—but you forget what your situation was when I married you—

... *Lady Teazle.* No, no, I don't—'twas a very disagreeable one or I should never have married you.

Sir Peter. Yes, yes, madam, you were then in somewhat a humbler Style—the daughter of a plain country Squire. Recollect Lady Teazle when I saw you first—sitting at your tambour in a pretty figured linen gown—with a Bunch of Keys at your side, and your apartment hung round with Fruits in worsted of your own working—

Lady Teazle. O horrible!—horrible!—don't put me in mind of it!

Sir Peter. Yes, yes Madam and your daily occupation to inspect the Dairy, superintend the Poultry, make extracts from the Family Receipt-book, and comb your aunt Deborah's Lap Dog.

Lady Teazle. Abominable!

Sir Peter. Yes Madam—and what were your evening amusements? to draw Patterns for Ruffles, which you hadn't

the materials to make—play Pope Joan with the Curate—to
read a sermon to your Aunt— or be stuckdown to an old Spinet
to strum your father to sleep after a Fox Chase.

Lady Teazle. Scandalous— Sir Peter not a word of it true—

Sir Peter. Yes, Madam—These were the recreations I took
you from—and now—no one more extravagantly in the Fashion—Every Fopery adopted—a head-dress to o'er top Lady
Pagoda with feathers pendant horizontal and perpendicular
—you forget, Lady Teazle—when a little wired gauze with a
few beads made you a fly Cap not much Bigger than a blew-
bottle, and your Hair was comb'd smooth over a Roll—

Lady Teazle. Shocking! horrible Roll!!

Sir Peter. But now—you must have your coach,—*Vis-à-vis*,
—and three powder'd Footmen before your Chair—and in
the summer a pair of white cats[1] to draw you to Kensington
Gardens—no recollection when you were content to ride
double, behind the Butler, on a docked Coach-Horse?

Lady Teazle. Horrid!—I swear I never did.

Sir Peter. This, madam, was your situation—and what
have I not done for you? I have made you woman of Fashion
of Fortune of Rank—in short I have made you my wife.

Lady Teazle. Well then and there is but one thing more you
can make me to add to the obligation.

Sir Peter. What's that pray?

Lady Teazle. Your widow.—

Sir Peter. Thank you Madam—but don't flatter yourself
for though your ill-conduct may disturb my Peace it shall
never break my Heart I promise you—however I am equally
obliged to you for the Hint.

Lady Teazle. Then why will you endeavour to make yourself so disagreeable to me—and thwart me in every little elegant expense.

Sir Peter. 'Slife—Madam I pray, had you any of these
elegant expenses when you married me?

Lady Teazle. Lud Sir Peter would you have me be out of
the Fashion?

[1]Rae reads "cobs," an obvious error. [Cf. "dogs" in *The Teazles*.]

Sir Peter. The Fashion indeed!—what had you to do with the Fashion before you married me?

Lady Teazle. For my Part—I should think you would like to have your wife thought a woman of taste—

Sir Peter. Aye there again—Taste—Zounds Madam you had no Taste when you married me—

Lady Teazle. That's very true indeed Sir Peter! after having married you I should never pretend to Taste again I allow.

[*Sir Peter.* So—so then—Madam—if these are your Sentiments pray how came I to be honour'd with your Hand?

Lady Teazle. Shall I tell you the Truth?

Sir Peter. If it's not too great a Favour.

Lady Teazle. Why the Fact is I was tired of all those agreeable Recreations which you have so good naturally Described—and having a Spirit to spend and enjoy a Fortune—I determined to marry the first rich man that would have me.

Sir Peter. A very honest confession—truly—but pray madam there was no one else you might have tried to ensnare but me.

Lady Teazle. O Lud—I drew my net at several but you were the only one I could catch.

Sir Peter. This is plain dealing indeed—][1]

Lady Teazle. But now Sir Peter if we have finish'd our daily Jangle I presume I may go to my engagement at Lady Sneerwell's?

Sir Peter. Aye—there's another Precious circumstance—a charming set of acquaintance—you have made there!

Lady Teazle. Nay Sir Peter they are People of Rank and Fortune—and remarkably tenacious of reputation . . . . .

Sir Peter. Yes egad they are tenacious of Reputation with a vengeance, for they don't chuse anybody should have a Character but themselves! Such a crew! Ah! many a wretch has rid on hurdles who has done less mischief than these utterers of forged Tales, coiners of Scandal, and clippers of Reputation.

Lady Teazle. What would you restrain the freedom of speech?

[1] This passage was omitted in the final version.

Sir Peter. Aye they have made you juſt as bad [as] any one of the Society.

Lady Teazle. Why—I believe I do bear a Part with a tolerable Grace—But I vow I bear no malice againſt the People I abuse, when I say an ill-natured thing, 'tis out of pure Good Humour—and I take it for granted they deal exaĉtly in the same manner with me, but Sir Peter you know you promised to come to Lady Sneerwell's too.

Sir Peter. Well well I'll call in, juſt to look after my own charaĉter.

Lady Teazle. Then, indeed, you muſt make Haſte after me, or you'll be too late—so good bye to ye.

Sir Peter. So—I have gain'd much by my intended expoſtulation—yet with what a charming air she contradiĉts every thing I say—and how pleasingly she shows her contempt of my authority—Well tho' I can't make her love me, there is certainly a great satisfaĉtion in quarrelling with her; and I think she never appears to such advantage as when she is doing everything in her Power to plague me.   [*Exit.*

The Genuine and Piratical Texts:

WITH A BIBLIOGRAPHY

OF all the problems in theatrical bibliography, those of *The School for Scandal* are the prettiest. While Sheridan lived, numerous editions were published, chiefly in Dublin, but none of them was authorized, and the greater number of them—indeed (I think) all but one issued between 1781 and 1823—followed the same corrupt and piratical text. Since this fact is not recorded by Sheridan's three bibliographers, Anderson, Sichel, and Williams, my task has been one of considerable difficulty. The editions fall into three divisions, (i) the piratical text, (ii) the genuine text, (iii) the political parodies issued under the same title,[1] beginning with *The School for Scandal*: London (Bladon and Thresher) 1779. Sichel recorded only eight Dublin editions of this comedy printed in Sheridan's lifetime; but in a list he compiled for me from the various Irish libraries, Mr. E. R. McC. Dix added seven more, to which I have made further additions. It seems to me possible, therefore, that this bibliography is not yet exhaustive, since so many small and surreptitious editions were printed in Dublin.

Thomas Moore in his *Life of Sheridan* gave the essentials in a summary which, though perfectly correct, seems never to have been correctly interpreted. It has given rise to misunderstanding after misunderstanding. He wrote:—

"It appears singular that, during the life of Mr. Sheridan, no authorized or correct edition of this play should have been published in England. He had, at one time, disposed of the copyright to Mr. Ridgway of Piccadilly, but, after repeated applications from the latter for the manuscript, he was told by Mr. Sheridan, as an excuse for keeping it back, that he had

[1] These are considered among the Sheridan Apocrypha of the present Edition.

been nineteen years endeavouring to satisfy himself with the style of *The School for Scandal*, but had not yet succeeded. Mr. Ridgway, upon this, ceased to give him any further trouble on the subject.

"The edition printed in Dublin is, with the exception of a few unimportant omissions and verbal differences, perfectly correct. It appears that, after the success of the comedy in London, he presented a copy of it to his eldest sister, Mrs. Lefanu, to be disposed of, for her own advantage, to the manager of the Dublin Theatre. The sum of a hundred guineas, and free admissions for her family, were the terms upon which Ryder, the manager at that period, purchased from this lady the right of acting the play; and it was from this copy thus procured that the edition afterwards published in Dublin was printed. I have collated this edition with the copy given by Mr. Sheridan to Lady Crewe (the last, I believe, ever revised by himself) and find it, with the few exceptions already mentioned, correct throughout."

It happens that there were numerous editions printed in Dublin. The earliest of them is considered (but erroneously) to be an undated issue with the imprint of J. Ewling. The reason for considering this edition as the first was that it contains a page of errata, often interpreted as "author's corrections." As the author never sanctioned any issue, much less corrected the proofs, this argument is flagrantly untenable. Nevertheless, a verbal collation of several Dublin editions of *The School for Scandal* demonstrates that they all agreed (some three or four misprints excepted) with the Ewling edition, which might therefore be assumed as having the authority of the Lefanu MS. However, having a peculiar and intimate knowledge of the ways of dramatic pirates, I had my doubts, for there were innumerable curious divergencies from the accepted text. Then came my discovery (with the aid of Mr. W. J. Lawrence, to whom my doubts were confided) of the very copy which Thomas Moore had used in his collation with the Crewe MS. This edition, with the imprint "Dublin, Printed and sold by the Booksellers. 1799," was described on the title-page as "taken from a correct copy, performed at the Theatres, London and Dublin," and Moore's MS. corrections brought it into consonance with the Crewe MS. Here, then, at last was the text which Moore described as "the last ever revised by Sheridan himself." It disposed at once of the authority of the other "Dublin editions."

My enquiry, however, began long before this discovery, when the first London collection edition—*The Dramatic Works of R. B. Sheridan, Esq.*," London: Printed for A. Millar, W. Law and R. Cater" [1797] was perplexing me with its corrupt texts of *The Duenna* and *The School for Scandal*. Three early editions of *The School for Scandal* came into my hands with these imprints:—

    (i) Dublin. Printed in the year MDCCLXXXI.

    (ii) Dublin. Printed in the year MDCCLXXXII.

    (iii). Dublin. Printed for the Booksellers. 1802.

Since the names of printers and publishers were suppressed, it was to be deduced that the issues were piratical. A collation of the copies showed that they all followed the same incorrect version which was printed in Millar's Edition of *Sheridan's Works*. This I compared with John Murray's Edition of *The School for Scandal* (1823), the accepted text of the Oxford Edition (1906). Two extracts from Act III, Scene iii, will show the difference:—

THE MILLAR TEXT

CHARLES, CARELESS, SIR TOBY, AND GENTLEMEN, *Discovered Drinking.*

Char.—Ha, ha, ha—'Fore heaven you are in the right—the degeneracy of the age is astonishing; there are many of our acquaintance who are men of wit, genius, and spirit, but then they won't drink.

Care.—True, Charles; they sink into the more substantial luxuries of the table, and quite neglect the bottle.

Char.—Right—besides, society suffers by it; for instead of the mirth and humour that used to mantle over a bottle of Burgundy, their conversation has become as insipid as the Spa water they drink, which has all the pertness of Champagne, without its spirit and flavour.

THE MURRAY TEXT

CHARLES SURFACE, CARELESS, &c., *at a table with* WINE, &c.

Charles S.—Fore Heaven. 'Tis true!—there's the great degeneracy of the age. Many of our acquaintance have taste, spirit, and politeness, but, plague on't, they won't drink.

Careless.—It is so indeed, Charles! they get in to all the substantial luxuries of the table and abstain from nothing but wine and wit.

[*Charles S.*].—Oh, certainly society suffers by it intolerably: for now, instead of the social spirit of raillery that used to mantle over a glass of bright Burgundy, their conversation is become just like the Spa water they drink, which has all the pertness and flatulence of Champagne, without the spirit or flavour.

   .   .   .   .   .

Trip enters and whispers Charles.

Char.—Gentlemen, I must beg your pardon: (*rising*) I must leave you upon business—Careless, take the chair.

Care.—What, this is some wench—but we won't lose you for her.

Char.—No, upon my honour. It is only a Jew and a broker come by appointment.

Care.—A Jew and a broker! We'll have 'em in.

Char.—Then desire Mr. Moses to walk in.

Trip.—And little Premium too, Sir?

Care.—Aye, Moses and Premium (*Exit Trip.*) Charles, we'll give the rascals some generous Burgundy.

Enter Trip and whispers Charles Surface.

Charles S.—Gentlemen, you must excuse me a little. Careless, take the chair, will you?

Care.—Nay, prithee Charles, what now? This is one of your peerless beauties, I suppose, has dropt in by chance.

Charles S.—No, faith! To tell the truth, 'tis a Jew and a broker who are come by appointment.

Care.—O, damn it! Let's have the Jew in.

Sir H.—Ay, and the broker, too, by all means.

Care.—Yes, yes, the Jew and the broker.

Charles.—Egad, with all my heart. Trip bid the gentlemen walk in. (*Exit Trip.*) Though there's one of them a stranger, I can tell you.

Care.—Charles, let us give them some generous Burgundy, and perhaps they'll grow conscientious.

These variations are found in almost every scene in the piracies. The two most famous lines in the comedy are both altered— "Here's to the maiden of *bashful* fifteen" becomes "blushing," and "Lady Teazle by all that's *damnable*" becomes "horrible." A casual reader would scarcely notice the differences without a word for word comparison, yet there are dozens of passages as incorrect as this, while there are others in absolute accordance with the authentic copy. It is quite clear that somebody who was well acquainted with the comedy wrote many of the speeches from memory—an unusual, trained memory, like an actor's, but by no means, as is clear, perfect.

Sheridan would not permit copies of *The School for Scandal* to be taken for performances by other companies. He did, however, make two exceptions. After six months had elapsed, he allowed it to be acted at Bath, where, indeed, he conducted the rehearsals. For this he had his price—the services of Henderson the actor, "buying up" said James Boaden in his *Life of Mrs. Siddons*, "the forfeiture of his articles with Palmer, the Bath manager, by a privilege to act there the unpublished *School for Scandal.*" A few months later, the Bath company acted it at

Richmond, but Sheridan had stipulated that no copies of the prompt-book should be made for other companies.

Another exception was made for Dublin, where it was acted for the first time on January 8th, 1778, "by command of His Excellency the Lord Lieutenant" at the Theatre Royal, Crow-Street, whose manager was Ryder, the pirate of *The Governess.* Moore's account of this permission is confirmed by *The Public Advertiser* of January 31st, 1778, which says in a Dublin letter: "Miss Sheridan, sister of the manager of Drury Lane, being presented by her brother with a copy of *The School for Scandal,* that lady lately sold the copy to Mr. Ryder, our manager, for 100 guineas, in consequence of which he brought it out last week." It can hardly be doubted that Ryder would guard his prompt-book very carefully, and it was twenty-one years before it got into print, being then the first edition of the genuine text ever to be published. Subsequently, three other authentic versions, each with minor differences were printed at long intervals. Their textual importance, except for John Murray's Edition of 1823, has been consistently overlooked. Before passing to the piratical text, therefore, it is convenient to deal with these authentic editions and to suggest, with considerable diffidence, their relation to the original prompt-book of the Theatre Royal, Drury Lane.

THE GENUINE TEXT: PROMPT-BOOKS AND EDITIONS

The mainspring of the whole complicated machinery which is called a theatrical production is the prompt-book. As soon as it is prepared, the author's manuscript has (from the aspect of the theatre) no value but sentimental: if it were sufficiently legible, it might indeed have been used as the prompt-book, but as a rule in Sheridan's time the prompter preferred to make his own copy. From the prompt-book were transcribed the actors' parts, and any other prompt-books or authorized transcripts which were made.

Before the firſt prompt-book of *The School for Scandal* was prepared there was, therefore, what is properly described as "the author's MS."—not necessarily holograph, as Sheridan's rough drafts were often fair-copied by his wife. Moore saw the author's MS. which he described in these terms:—

"Notwithſtanding the labour which he beſtowed upon this comedy (or, perhaps, in consequence of that labour) the firſt representation of the piece was announced before the whole of the copy was in the hands of the actors. The manuscript, indeed, of the five laſt scenes bears evident marks of this haſte in finishing—there being but one rough draught of them, scribbled upon detached pieces of paper; while, of all the preceding acts, there are numerous transcripts, scattered promiscuously through six or seven books, with new interlineations and memorandums to each. On the laſt leaf of all, which exiſts juſt as we may suppose it to have been despatched by him to the copyiſt, there is the following curious specimen of doxology, written haſtily, in the hand-writing of the respective parties, at the bottom:—

Finished at laſt, thank God!

R. B. *Sheridan.*

Amen!

W. *Hopkins.*"

The obvious interpretation of this "doxology" is that Sheridan wrote his comment when he had made the laſt corrections in his foul copy. This *brouillon* was duly transcribed in the beſt theatrical copper-plate in the prompter's room, and at the completion of this transcript Hopkins the prompter subscribed his "Amen" before returning it to the author.

What eventually became of the MS. thus endorsed is unknown. Mr. Sichel presumes some remarks in Percy Fitzgerald's *Lives of the Sheridans* (1886) to mean that it had passed into the possession of Sir George Chetwynd, but there is little to go upon. The MS. at Frampton Court, the seat of the Sheridans, is earlier and incomplete; it is printed in Fraser Rae's

Sheridan's Plays as he Wrote Them, and reprinted in Nettleton's *Sheridan's Major Dramas.* However (as is shown in my discussion of "The Evolution of *The School for Scandal*") this was certainly not the copy from which Hopkins prepared his prompt-book. Accordingly, this attempt is made to trace the prompt-book and its authorized transcripts :—

1. *The prompt-book of Drury Lane Theatre* (1777)

According to an unnoticed remark under "Richard Brinsley Sheridan," in *The Thespian Dictionary* (1802):—

"The copy of this play was lost after the first night's representation, and all the performers in it were summoned, early the next day, in order, by the assistance of their parts, to prepare another prompter's copy." Whether this is or is not true, the prompt-book remained in the theatre for many years, and I am not satisfied as to whether it was or was not destroyed in the fire of 1809.[1] If so, the new prompt-book was most probably derived from the MS. copy belonging to Covent Garden Theatre. However, from the Drury Lane prompt-book of 1826 I suppose this Edition to have been copied.

The School for Scandal. A Comedy . . . Printed from the Acting Copy. With Remarks by D——— G. London. John Cumberland, 19 Ludgate Hill [1826].

12mo, pp. 88.

2. *The copy sent to the Lord Chamberlain* (1777).

What happened to this is unknown. Many MS. plays of this period were sold after the death of John Larpent, Examiner of Plays from 1778 to 1824, by his executors, although he had no claim to the MSS. Eventually many of these were

[1]On this point another MS. should be noticed:
"*The School for Scandal.* A Comedy in Five Acts. Copied from the Prompter's Book of the Theatre Royal, Drury Lane, which was preserved from the late fire."
This MS. was purchased at the sale of the Royal Dramatic College in February, 1881, by Clement Scott, who mentioned it in *The Theatre* for October, 1881. Mr. W. J. Lawrence tells me it is now in the theatrical library at Harvard University. It was a transcript made obviously after 1809. But elsewhere I have seen it stated that the prompt-book was destroyed, with others, in the fire.

purchased by Mr. Henry E. Huntington of California, but among them there is no copy of *The School for Scandal*.

3. *The prompt-book of the Theatre-Royal, Bath* (1777).

This copy was authorized by Sheridan, who conducted the rehearsals of *The School for Scandal* at Bath in November, 1777:—
"A MS. of this comedy—said to be the original, but more probably a copy of that—was destroyed when the Bath Theatre was burnt in the spring of 1862."—Clement Scott in *The Theatre*, October, 1881.

4. *The prompt-book of the Theatre Royal, Dublin* (1778).

This copy was authorized by Sheridan, who gave it to his sister Alicia (Mrs. Lefanu). It was eventually printed as the Dublin Edition of 1799, "taken from a Correct Copy," which is therefore the *Editio princeps* of the authentic text.

The School for Scandal, A Comedy; In Five Acts. By Richard Brinsley Sheridan, Esq. Taken from a Correct Copy. Performed at the Theatres, London and Dublin. Dublin. Printed and Sold by the Booksellers. 1799.

8vo, pp. [ii] + 84.

Mr. George W. Panter's copy, presented to Charles Harcourt the actor in 1878, has written on the title page :
"The gift of Richard Brinsley Sheridan to my grandfather, Gustavus Hume Rochfort, M.P. when on a visit at Rochfort. County Westmeath. Letitia C. R. Brooke."

5. *The Copy sent to Mrs. Crewe.*

This was sent, "finely bound," with the poem called *A Portrait*, and was collated by Moore about 1823 with a copy of the edition of 1799, now in the Library of the Royal Irish Academy, Dublin. It is the source of the present text. The Crewe MS. has always been assumed, but erroneously, to have been used for John Murray's edition of 1823 (*q.v.*). No doubt the MS. transcript was made by one of the theatrical copyists, with corrections by Sheridan.

In *Book-Prices Current*, 1923 a MS. "To Mrs. Crewe from the Author" is recorded as being sold in New York for $275. But for various reasons fuller particulars are required to establish its authenticity.

6. *The prompt-book of the Theatre Royal, Covent Garden.*

The School for Scandal was acted for the first time at Covent Garden by permission of the author on March 31st, 1798. for the Benefit of Lewis. It was probably the copy then used which was destroyed with the rest of the dramatic library in the fire at Covent Garden in March, 1856; being mentioned specifically in the contemporary *Illustrated Times* as (of course) "the original MS." (see Saxe Wyndham, *Annals of Covent Garden Theatre*, vol. II, p. 211).

I suppose this to have been transcribed for:—

(i) The School for Scandal: London, John Murray, 1823. 8vo, pp. 158.

> This eventually became the text of the Oxford Edition (1906). It reads, however, "Mayor of Manchester" where all other copies read "Mayor of Norwich" and may have been obtained from some other source. Murray bought the copyright from Ridgway. The first English Edition of the authentic text.

(ii) The School for Scandal ["Carefully Collated from the Author's Own Copy"] London. Thomas Hailes Lacy [1840?]. 8vo.

> This contains a Covent Garden cast of 1836-1839. Anderson (*Shakespeare Bibliography*, p. vi) dates it as 1858, which may be correct, although I believe the transcript must have been made some twenty years earlier. There are differences between the two texts, Murray's and Lacy's, chiefly of minor importance, but both preserve the same errors in general, e.g.:—
> Act ii, scene iii [*Sir Oliver*] "We'll drink *the lad's* health" for *your lady's* (i.e. *yr. lady's* was mistaken for *ye lads*.)
> Act iii ; scene iii [*Sir Oliver*] "His library ... was valuable and *compact*" for *compleat*.

The Library of the Theatre Royal, Birmingham, contains contemporary copies of these two editions, used as prompt-books with MS. notes.

THE PIRATICAL TEXT

[It has already been noted that Sheridan permitted transcripts of his prompt-book to be made for Bath and Dublin at the end of 1777, yet he continued to refuse his permission for performances by other companies. Nevertheless, another Tate Wilkinson was at hand in the person of John Bernard, the original Backbite of the Bath company. It was not until forty years later, writing from memory, that Barnard told how he "vamped" a version for performance at Exeter in 1779. In his *Retrospections of the Stage* (1832), he wrote:

"Hughes, the manager, wanted a powerful novelty, and proposed *The School for Scandal*, then new and greatly discussed. Its success at Bath had dispersed its fame about the West of England, and it was highly probable that, if the play were produced at Exeter, it would run a number of nights to full houses. But the Comedy was not yet published and the managers who had copies of it, had obtained them on condition that they did not permit the same to become the parents of others. . . . Under these circumstances I offered to attempt a compilation of the comedy, if Mr. Hughes would give me his word that the manuscript should be destroyed at the end of the season. This was agreed to, and I set about my task in the following manner. I had played Sir Benjamin at Bath and Charles at Richmond, and went on for Sir Peter one or two evenings when Edwin was indisposed; thus I had three parts in my possession. Dimond and Blissit (Joseph and Sir Oliver) transmitted theirs by post, on conveying the assurance to them which Mr. Hughes had to me. Old Rowley was in the Company, and my wife had played both Lady Teazle and Mrs. Candour. With these materials for a groundwork, my general knowledge of the play collected in rehearsing and performing in it above forty times, enabled me in a week to construct a comedy in five acts, called, in imitation of the original *The School for Scandal*.

"Result, the public not being let into the secret the play drew crowded houses twice a week to the end of the season.

While his details may not have been exact—his own part, for instance, of Sir Peter may have been written from memory—the method is one which was frequently used, and, indeed, is sometimes used to this day by players in small companies "vamping" a play. From the limited number of actors who had appeared in it before 1780, and the absence of incentive in most cases, it seems to me most likely that Bernard's Exeter version of 1779 was surreptitiously copied by some other actor, who sold it to an Irish printer. It is very unlikely, from the immense difficulties of the undertaking, that this piratical text was obtained by shorthand from the auditorium. Dramatic piracies were quite frequent, but the pirates were usually actors whose primary motive was not publication, but performance. With these preliminary explanations, the bibliography of the piratical texts may be set out formally.

1780

[The School for Scandal. A Comedy. As it is performed at the Theatres Royal in London and Dublin. Dublin. Printed in the Year MDCCLXXX.]

12mo.

Incomplete copy in National Library, Dublin, apparently of this Edition.
Text only, pp. 1-78, sigs. B-G6 in sixes, H in three.
Copy wants Sig. A and pp. 17-20 (Sig. C3-4).
At the end on separate leaf (verso blank) is an advertisement.
"This day is published (Price 1s. 7d h.) Pranceriana Poetica or Prancer's Garland. Being a Collection of Fugitive Poems Written since the publication of Pranceriana and the Appendix. The Second Edition [&c., &c.]. The type and text are identical with "the Fourth Edition" (1782).—E.R.McC.D.
[Three copies are recorded in Book-Prices Current as sold in 1920-21. The title page is taken from this, for which also it appears that the Edition (with the advertisement of Pranceriana Poetica) has no Prologue or Epilogue: the title-page prints "Dublin" with the b upside down. Not having examined a copy, for none is to be traced in England, these notes are submitted with all diffidence. While, however, some of the early political parodies have been confused with Editions of the play, Mr. Dix's collation of the incomplete copy seems to allay any doubts.]

1781

(i)

The School for Scandal: A Comedy; as it is performed at the Theatres Royal in London and Dublin. Dublin. Printed in the year M.DCC.LXXXI.

Pagination. P. [i] half-title, *The School for Scandal, A Comedy;* p. [ii] blank; p. [iii] title; p. [iv] *Dramatis Personæ*; pp. [1] + 2–82 text; pp. [83–84] blank. Signatures, B–H in sixes [no sig. A].

This Edition, like that of 1780, has no Prologue or Epilogue, which were added in subsequent Editions. It appears, therefore, from the wording of the title-page, to be reprinted from the First Edition. Against the characters in *Dramatis Personæ* there are no names of players, though subsequent Editions give either a London or Dublin cast. This seems therefore to be the Second Edition.

(ii)

The School for Scandal, A Comedy; As it is performed at the Theatre-Royal in Crowe-Street, Dublin: Printed in the Year M.DCC.LXXXI.

12mo.

Pagination. P. [i] title; p. [ii] blank; pp. [iii–iv] *Prologue* and *Dramatis Personæ*; pp. [1, sig. B] & 2–78 Text; pp. [79–80] *Epilogue.*

This Edition has the Irish Cast; Teazle, Mr. Ryder ; Sir Toby Bumper, Mr. Owenson, etc. The parts of Careless and Snake are not followed by the names of their players. Mr. Percival F. Hinton's copy.

(iii)

The School for Scandal. A Comedy: as it is performed at the Theatre Royal in Drury Lane. Dublin. M.DCC.LXXXI.

Small 4to.

Pp. [ii] + 64 + [2].

Copy in the Bradshaw Collection, Cambridge University Library. Mr. Dix, who called my attention to this edition, has traced no other copy in the Dublin Libraries. I have had no opportunity of examining it.

1782

(i)

The School for Scandal, A Comedy; As it is performed at the Theatre-Royal in Drury-Lane. Dublin: Printed in the Year M.DCC.LXXXII.

12mo.

Pagination. P. [1] title; p. [2] *Dramatis Personæ*; pp. [3] + 4–70 text; pp. [71–72] *Prologue* and *Epilogue.*

(ii)

The School for Scandal, A Comedy; As it is performed at the Theatre-Royal in Crow-Street. The Fourth Edition. Dublin. Printed in the Year M.DCC.LXXXII.

12mo.

Pagination. P. [1] title; p. [2] blank; pp. [3–4] *Prologue* and *Dramatis Personæ*; pp. [5] & 6–76 text; pp. [77–78] *Epilogue*, p. 79 *New Books*; p. 80 blank. Signatures A–G3.

Copy belonging to R. Crompton Rhodes. Mr. E. R. McC. Dix had collated a copy in the National Library, Dublin, which agrees with the above, except that it lacks the last leaf of advertisements. In the *Dramatis Personæ*, by the accidental omission of Bumper, the name of Owenson is placed against Careless.

1783

(i)

The Real and Genuine School for Scandal, A Comedy; Acted with bursts of Applause, at the Theatres in London and Dublin. Written by Brinsley Sheridan, Esquire. Hold the Mirror up to Nature, and shew Vice in its own Image. London. Printed for T. Cadell, In The Strand. M.DCC.LXXXIII.

12mo.

Pagination. P. [1] title; p. [2] *Dramatis Personæ*; pp. [3] & [4] *Prologue*; pp. [5] & 6–86 text; pp. 86 & 87 *Epilogue*; p. 88 blank.

Mr. Sichel records this among the parodies of *The School for Scandal*, no doubt (as Mr. Williams suggests) by confusion with some other book. The terms "real and genuine" were obviously intended to distinguish it from the catchpenny political pamphlets which had borrowed the title. Cadell's Edition was the first printed in London, and it cannot be doubted that it was suppressed, though on this point I have no positive evidence.

(ii)

The School for Scandal. Dublin. Printed in the Year M.DCC.LXXXIII.

12mo, pp.72.

1784

L'Ecole de la Médisance, comédie en 5 actes, en prose; traduite de l'anglais par Mad. de Passe. 1784.

From Querard *La France Littéraire* (1838), where it is described as "sans nom de ville ni d'imprimeur." Delille in his preface to *L'Ecole du Scandale* (London, 1789)

mentions that "on l'a déjà traduite en Français: elle a paru sur le théâtre à Géneve."
Perhaps, therefore, this translation was printed at Geneva. The first Paris Edition of the
English text appeared five years later.

1785

The School for Scandal. Dublin. 1785. 12mo.

In "A Volume of Plays as performed at the Theatre, Smoke-Alley, Dublin. Containing *The Duenna, The Poor Soldier, The Agreeable Surprise, Love a la Mode,* and the
School for Scandal. Printed for the Booksellers. M.DCC.LXXXV." Since there is
separate pagination, and signatures, to each play, copies were apparently sold singly.
Copy of volume in Cambridge University Library, Bradshaw Collection.

1786

(i)

The School for Scandal. New York: Printed by Hugh Gaine at the Bible in Hanover Square. 1786. 8vo.

From *Book-Prices Current,* 1914, as having been sold at Sotheby's on December 10th.
No other copy recorded. Apparently the first American Edition. Nettleton's bibliography to *Sheridan's Major Dramas* (Boston, 1906) records no American Edition of
the play before 1821.

(ii)

The School for Scandal, A Comedy: As it is Acted at the Theatre, Smoke-Alley. Dublin. Printed for the Booksellers. M.DCC.LXXXVI.

12mo, pp. 74.

Pagination. P. [1] title; p. [2] blank; p. [3] *Prologue;* p. [4]
Dramatis Personæ; pp. 5–73 & [74] text with *Epilogue.*

Two Engravings, Screen Scene, and Sir Oliver Viewing the Pictures. Copy in Dublin Municipal Library.—E. R. McC. D.
[Apparently issued as one of the five plays (with separate pagination) in "A Volume
of Plays as they are acted at Smoke Alley." 12mo. Copy in Bradshaw Collection,
Cambridge University Library.]

(iii)

The School for Scandal. Dublin. M.DCC.LXXXVI. 8vo.

In an 8vo Edition of "A Volume of Plays" with the same title and contents as the
preceding, also printed with separate pagination. Copy in Bradshaw Collection,
Cambridge University Library.
Sichel records only one "Dublin 1786" Edition, described as 16mo, but apparently
one of the two here noted.

1787

The School for Scandal; A Comedy. As it is performed at the Theatre Royal in Drury Lane. Dublin. Printed in the Year M.DCC.LXXXVII.

12mo.

Pagination. P. [1] title; p. [2] *Dramatis Personæ*; pp. [3]+ 4–70 text; [71–72] *Prologue* and *Epilogue*.

1788

(i)

The School for Scandal, A Comedy; as it is performed at the Theatre-Royal in Crow-Street. The Fifth Edition. Dublin. Printed in the Year M.DCC.LXXXVIII.

12mo, pp. 78.

This edition corresponds with the Fourth Edition, line by line and word for word, except a few printer's errors [e.g., p. 13, "Old Jewery" for "Old Jewry", p. iv "Dramatic Personæ" for "Dramatis Personæ"]. No names of players appear against the parts. This edition is uniform with *The Governess* (as performed at Crow-Street). 1788. Mr. Percy F. Hinton's copy.

(ii)

The School for Scandal. The Fifth Edition. London. 1788. 12mo.

This is recorded by Anderson, Sichel, and Nettleton. Despite the imprint, it was probably printed in Dublin.

1789

(i)

The School for Scandal. Printed for Theophilus Barrois. Rue Haute feuille, Paris. 1789.

12mo.

From Sichel, *Sheridan*, vol. II, p. 451.

This Edition, which I have never seen, must be exceedingly rare. It is not recorded in the standard bibliography *La France Littéraire* by Querard (1838) who mentions no earlier edition than Barrois, quay Voltaire, 1804, which is, however, described on the title page as "A New Edition." Delille's preface to his translation *L'Ecole du Scandale* (London, 1789) mentions that "*The School for Scandal* a été imprimée [furtivement] à Dublin, et réimprimée à Paris." Apparently this is the Paris reprint that he had in mind.

(ii)

L'Ecole du Scandale, ou Les Mœurs du Jour, Comedie par Monsieur Sheridan: traduite en françois par Mr. Bunel Delille, Avocat au Parlement de Paris. *Contre la médisance il n'est point de rampert.* Tartuffe, *Acte premier, scene premiere.* A Londres; Imprimé par Galabin, Ingram Court. Et se trouve chez Mr. Debrett, Libraire, Piccadilly; chez Mr. Hookham, New Bond-Street; chez Mr. Southern, St. James's Street; chez Bossiere, St. James's Street; chez Balcetti. Pall-Mall; chez Mr. Egerton, Whitehall ; chez Mr. Richardson, Royal-Exchange. M.DCC.LXXXIX.

Pagination. P. [i] title; p. [ii] blank; pp. [iii–ix] *Epitre Dedicatoire a Milord Macdonald*; pp. [x–xv] *Souscripteurs* [with Errata on lower-half of xv]; p. [xvi] *Personages*; pp. [1] & 2–159 text; p. 160 blank.

Although often described as such, this is not the *first* French translation, but it is a very interesting Edition. A copy of it "a handsome, thin, octavo volume, bound in whole red morocco, with gilt edges, looking more like a psalm-book from a Royal Chapel than a book containing a play" (a copy which appeared "never to have been opened since it left the binder's hands") was described in *The Theatre* for August, 1880, by Sir Frederick Pollock: it had probably belonged to the Prince of Wales (King George IV) who headed the list of subscribers. Although in this article the dialogue is spoken of as "well-rendered," it is in fact translated from the piratical text.

The translator explained that no edition of *The School for Scandal* had been printed except surreptitiously (at Dublin and Paris), but that one day in the previous summer the piece *en manuscrit in-folio* had appeared in a mysterious manner on his table, and when he asked Sheridan's permission to "transplant to my climate his precious plant which should fructify in every soil, and do honour to the gardener." Sheridan therefore "abandoned the plant" to Delille : his horticultural simile, which he developed with amazing assiduity, is rather confusing, but among his subscribers, Delille proudly placed the name of Sheridan. Despite this permission Delille used the piratical version, which he translated literally.

There are a few phrases and a single passage which show that the MS. used by Delille was not precisely that of the text printed in all the Dublin piratical editions. For instance, all the printed books (genuine or piratical) speak of the portrait of "the Mayor of Norwich" in the auction-scene, with the exception of John Murray's 1823 Edition which calls him "the Mayor of Manchester." Delille writes *le Maire de Bristol.* Similarly, "the little bronze Shakespeare" of every other edition appears as "*un petit Pline de bronze* "—the little bronze Pliny of the Crewe MS. With these trivial exceptions, and the half-Frenchified names—Sir Peter Teazle becomes Sir John Pandolphe; Mrs. Sneerwell, Lady Mordante ; and so on—the text is that of the piratical versions.

1792

(i)

The School for Scandal, A Comedy. By R. B. Sheridan, Esq. Adapted for Theatrical Representation. As performed at the Theatre Royal in Drury Lane. Regulated from the prompt-book. Dublin. Printed by William Porter for William Jones, No. 86 Dame-Street. MDCCXCII.

No reliance is to be placed on the statement "Regulated from the prompt-book" which appeared on all Jones's plays. This Edition is usually found with separate title page in (the continuously paged) Volume V of the British Theatre, Dublin; printed by John Chambers for William Jones, 1795.

(ii)

The School for Scandal. A Comedy. As it is acted at the Theatre, Smoke-Alley. Dublin. Printed for the Booksellers. M.DCC.XCII.

Small 8vo. pp. 128.

The text of this Edition differs slightly from the previous issues. For example on p. 6 it corrects "she wants that delicacy of *hint* and mellowness of sneer *which distinguishes your ladyship's scandal*" into "tint" and "for which your ladyship is so eminently distinguished." It may have been set up from MS. but more likely from a previous printed edition with MS. alterations by an actor.

1793

The School for Scandal, A Comedy. As it is acted at the Theatre, Smoke-Alley, Dublin, Printed for the Booksellers. M.DCC.XCIII.

Pagination. P. [1] title-page; p. [2] *Dramatis Personæ* [with Drury Lane company, giving Vernon as "Sir Harry Bumber" (*sic*)]; pp. [3 & 4] *Prologue*; pp. 5–123 text; p. 124 blank; pp. 125–7 *Epilogue*; p. 128 blank; Engravings at pp. 73 & 93.

N.B.—No place of printing.—E.R.McC.D.

1798

The School for Scandal. London. E. Powell. 1798. 12mo.

From Sichel, *Sheridan*, vol. II, p. 451.
The Booklover's Leaflet, Pickering & Chatto, gives this as 16mo.

Ewling's Edition [1799?]

The School for Scandal. A Comedy.

> Satire has always shone among the rest
> And is the boldest way, if not the best,
> To tell men freely of their foulest faults,
> To laugh at their vain deeds, and vainer thoughts.
> In satire, too, the wise took different ways
> To each deserving its peculiar praise.—DRYDEN.

Dublin: Printed for J. Ewling.

8vo, pp. 104. [vi—96—2 blank.]

Mr. E. R. McC. Dix first informed me that there was no Dublin printer or book-seller named Ewling at this period, nor during the century. Several, however, were named Ewing (Mr. Sichel by some curious chance consistently used the named Ewing instead of Ewling). It seems to me that it was a fictitious imprint used by some London printer or bookseller to deceive the owners of the English copyright. It is octavo and not the usual duodecimo of Dublin play-books.

Ewling's Edition is accepted as the first by Anderson, Sichel and Williams. There is nothing to support the supposition. Anderson assumed (it must be supposed), that the "Errata" were author's corrections, but Sheridan certainly had nothing to do with it. He dated it as 1777, but Sichel described it as (?1778-9) because he concluded that it was printed from the copy acted at Dublin in 1778—which, is of course, erroneous. *The date is proved as about* 1799 *by the use (though intermittent) of the short "s" instead of long.* (Cf. Mr. M. J. Ryan in *Times Lit. Supp.*, March 22, &c., 1928.)

1800

The School for Scandal, A Comedy in Five Acts. Dublin. Printed for the Booksellers. 1800.

12mo. pp. 72.

Portrait of Mr. Farren as Sir Peter Teazle. Issued in plain wrappers. Copy belonging to R. Crompton Rhodes. Apparently the same Edition as the copy in the Bradshaw Collection, Cambridge University Library.

1804

The School for Scandal. A New Edition, Paris, Printed for Theophilus Barrois, junior. 1804.

12mo.

Later French editions of the English text were :

Paris, Baudry, 1822, in-18.

Paris, Baudry, 1827, in-8.

Paris, Baudry, 1827, in-32.

From Querard, *La France Littéraire*, Paris, 1838, none of these editions being known to Sichel. I surmise they followed the piratical text, but that the genuine text was used for three editions by J. W. Lake, with explanatory French notes, etc.

Paris, Truchy, 1829.

The Second Edition. Much improved. Paris, Truchy, 1833.

The Third Edition. Paris, Truchy, 1838.

These are recorded by Querard, but are not mentioned by any English bibliographers of Sheridan.

1818

The School for Scandal. Dublin. P. Byrne, 1818, 8vo.

The Cambridge University Library, Bradshaw Collection, has a copy "in yellow wrappers." Whether this is the genuine or piratical text I do not know.

Since this piratical text found its way into the early collected Editions (Dublin, Jones, 1795; London, Millar, 1797; Greenock, Columbian Press, 1828) and in numerous later collections of plays, it is a matter of some interest to determine whether all of them were derived ultimately from the same printed copy. The French translation by Bunel Delille (London, 1789) was professedly made from MS. and with this version I compared eleven early editions of various dates and places. A single tell-tale word seems to me to show clearly that none of them was printed from MS. In Act III, Scene 1, Lady Teazle describes Sir Peter as "a dangling old batchelor," having previously called him "a stiff, peevish old batchelor." In the piratical editions there is a meaningless phrase, "a stiff, crop, dangling old batchelor," but there is no doubt that the compiler wrote "cross"; Delille renders it, crudely but unmistakably, "*vieux penard, villain bourru.*" So, again, all the piracies read a woman who "strives to pass for a *flirt* at six and thirty," which is a printer's error for "girl," which Delille translates "*une agnes.*" Another curious instance is that all the piracies pervert Sir Oliver's "that he *should have stood bluff to old batchelor* so long and sink into husband at last," into "that he should buff to old batchelor." Delille was obviously puzzled, writing "*après avoir été si long-tems la perle de vieux garçons.*" "To stand bluff" was a frequent idiom.

There were, however, some attempts in the various editions at the correction of printer's errors. Sheridan wrote (Act II, Scene 1) "to spend as much to furnish your dressing room in winter to turn the Pantheon into a green-house and give a Fête Champêtre at Christmas." Delille reads "*à Noël,*" and the compiler of the piracy obviously wrote "at Xmas." All the printed editions, with one exception read "a mas——," obviously understanding it as "a masquerade," the word being interrupted. The Dublin edition of 1802 reads very strangely, "a Mass," but the Smoke Alley edition of 1793 reads correctly "at Christmas."

Sheridan wrote (Act II, Scene 2), her face resembles "a table d'hôte at Spa." The readings are:—

table drote. 1781 ("London and Dublin"); 1781 ("Crowe-Street"); 1782 (Crow-Street); 1788.

table droit. 1782 (1782 "Drury Lane").

table d'hôte. 1793 ("Smoke Alley"); 1795 (Jones); 1797 (Miller); 1804 Paris; 1828 Greenock.

Similarly (Act II, Scene 3) Sheridan wrote "Allons then," or rather "Alons then." This the compiler altered to "Alons—done," rendered by Delille "Allons-tope" understanding it to mean "Come, agreed." The readings are:—

Alons-done. 1781 ("London and Dublin"); 1781 ("Crowe-Street)"; 1782 ("Crow-Street"); 1788; 1795 (Jones).

Allons, done. 1804 (Paris).

Alons, donc, 1872 ("Drury Lane"); 1787.

Alons, donc. 1797 (Millar); 1828 (Greenock).

Alons, dons. 1793 ("Smoke-Alley").

Again, Sheridan wrote (Act III, Scene 3) "an unnatural rogue, an ex post facto parricide."

The readings are:—

Expert faȼto paracide. 1781 ("London and Dublin"); 1781 (Crowe Street); 1782 ("Crow Street").

Expert faȼto parricide. 1782 ("Drury Lane"); 1787; 1793 ("Smoke-Alley"); 1804 (Paris).

Expoſt faȼto parricide. 1795 (Jones).

Expert de faȼto parricide. Miller. 1797; Greenock. 1828.

These notes indicate a line of inquiry rather than a definite conclusion, as to the relation of the several editions.

While the spurious text is devoid of independent authority, it has a collaborative value in collation. For inſtance, in Aȼt I, scene i, a speech of Lady Sneerwell's is omitted not only from the Edition of 1823 (the basis of the "accepted text" of former editions) but also from the Crewe MS.; the Rae text shows, however, that it was in Sheridan's draft, and the 1826 edition that it was in the contemporary prompt-book of Drury Lane. Its presence in the spurious text indicates, with the other evidence, that it was spoken on the ſtage *circa* 1779. In only one inſtance, however, have I accepted a trivial emendation from it, without other absolute authority, while also another necessary change, "he muſt lie at my house" for "be at," is supported not by the English text, but by Delille's translation.

The Critic,
or A Tragedy Rehearsed

Note

"THE CRITIC or a Tragedy Rehearsed ... by RICHARD BRINSLEY SHERIDAN, ESQ," was printed in 1781 with a Dedication "To MRS. GREVILLE" signed by the Author. All other early Editions followed this text, which is here reprinted.
The relation of this text to SHERIDAN's late MS. draft printed in FRASER RAE's *Sheridan's Plays as he Wrote Them* is discussed in the note on the Text.

R.C.R.

CONTENTS

II N

Introduction

SO long as tragedy is written and acted or read, so long as playwrights are playwrights, and the theatre is the theatre, the satire of *The Critic* will keep its gaiety and point and freshness. *The Rehearsal*, its avowed precursor, was of an age ; *The Critic* is for all time. Mr. Bayes perished with the plays of his era:

> In those gay days of wickedness and wit
> When Villiers criticised what Dryden writ,
> The Tragic Queen, to please a tasteless crowd,
> Had learned to bellow, rant, and roar, so loud,
> That frighten'd Nature, her best friend before,
> The blust'ring beldam's company forswore.[1]

Sheridan's playwrights, Mr. Puff and Sir Fretful Plagiary are perennial. Even though Mr. Puff, "dwindled" as his contemporaries said, "into a mere Bayes" at the rehearsal of his tragedy, he still survives as the forefather of a great tribe, the prince of publicity-agents. Even though Sir Fretful Plagiary came into being as a caricature of one single dramatist, he still survives as the mirror of many, the incarnation of the Vanity of Authors. Indeed, though Sir Fretful was recognized as "one of the most harsh and severe caricatures since the days of Aristophanes" [2] it is tempting to forget all about Richard Cumberland, and apply to Sir Fretful Dryden's words on Sir Fopling Flutter:—

> Yet none Sir Fretful him, or him, can call
> He's Knight o' the Shire, and represents ye all,
> From each he meets, he culls whate'er he can,
> Legion's his name, a People in a Man.

[1] Prologue to *The Critic*. By Richard Fitzpatrick.
[2] *The Lady's Magazine* for October, 1779.

And this in despite of the fact that Sheridan did undoubtedly caricature Cumberland in Sir Fretful Plagiary, perhaps because of his conduct during the rehearsals of *The Battles of Hastings* (1778) his tragedy at Drury Lane.[1] Cumberland is dead: Sir Fretful lives. Yet *The Critic* abounds in ancient topicalities, in allusions, recognized or unsuspected, to contemporary theatrical conditions and contemporary political events. Whoever, delighting in its gaiety and wit, remembers that *The Critic* was written in one of the darkest hours of English history? It was produced in October, 1779, in a year which (as *The Annual Register* reflected) "presented the most aweful appearance of public affairs which this country has perhaps beheld for many ages. Friends and allies were no more with respect to us. On the contrary, whether it proceeded from our fault, or whether it was merely our misfortune, mankind seemed to wait, with an aspect which at best spoke indifference, for the event of that ruin which was expected to burst upon us." In the June of 1779, the Spanish Ambassador delivered a declaration of war at the Court of St. James. In the October of 1779 Sheridan made fun of the situation by bringing on the stage of Drury Lane Mr. Puff's historical tragedy, *The Spanish Armada*. *The Critic* is not only the perdurable masterpiece of a great wit and playwright, it is a topical skit written by the manager of Drury Lane. Beneath its surface there are numerous allusions to the topics of 1779, theatrical and political.

Its ultimate origin, however, belongs to nearly ten years before. Its embryo is to be discovered in the burletta of *Ixion*, which Sheridan had adapted from *Jupiter*, a mythological travesty by his old schoolfellow Halhed. It was the future author of *The Critic* who planned to turn it into a "rehearsal." His example at the time was not, however, the Duke of Buckingham's play, but one of its more recent imitations, a piece overlooked by Sheridan's Editors, *A Peep Behind the Curtain; or, The New Rehearsal* (1767) by David Garrick, which showed Mr. Glib the author rehearsing his burletta of Orpheus. It was from Ixion that *The Critic* was to germinate and fructify.[2]

[1] See "Cumberland as Sir Fretful Plagiary" in this edition.
[2] See "The Burletta of Ixion" in the present edition.

The Critic is essentially a piece of the theatre. From one aspect, it has, like *A Peep Behind the Curtain*, the air of a family charade. The manager of Drury Lane Theatre was making fun of himself, his actors and actresses, and his stage staff. Mr. Fosbrook, the treasurer, was mentioned by name: Mr. Hopkins, the prompter, appeared in his own person. On the first night the audience saw also in their own persons such important domestic functionaries as "Mr. Butler the head carpenter" and "Mr. Langley the master lamplighter,"[1] Mr. Puff's example of the Puff Direct was a Puff Direct of the most humorously unabashed sort: King, as Puff said, quoting an imaginary critique, to Dodd as Dangle and Palmer as Sneer, "Mr. Dodd was astonishingly great as Sir Harry: that universal and judicious actor, Mr. Palmer, never appeared to greater advantage than as the Colonel; but it is not in the power of language to do justice to Mr. King—indeed, he merited those repeated bursts of applause which he drew from a brilliant and judicious audience."[2] These examples may be deduced from the text: but other "domestic" jokes are not so apparent. In *The Rehearsal* it was the custom for the players to "take off", as they called it, other players. It has always escaped notice that in the original production of *The Critic* there were similar imitations. Bannister as Don Whiskerandos "very happily copied Mr. Smith's harlequin-like death in Richard (Crookback, of course); Miss Pope, as Tilburina was very exact in her imitations of Mrs. Crawford in her mad scenes, and of Mrs. Yates in her laying against the scenes in *Jane Shore*"—the last a favourite pictorial subject for theatrical prints. Smith, "the airy, the genteel, the smart," was the original Charles Surface; Mrs. Yates, the original Berinthia in *A Trip to Scarborough*. This aspect of the first representation, the jocular domesticity of it, perished with the original performers.

It has always seemed to me that in the beginning Sheridan in-

---

[1] Their scene is the single passage that was afterwards deleted from the printed edition.

[2] This characteristic was exhibited by *A Peep Behind the Curtain*. In this Jonston, the House-Keeper, appeared in his own person; Hopkins, the prompter, was impersonated by Bannister; and Saunders, the Carpenter, by Moody. Mrs. Clive as Lady Fuz says to the House-Keeper—"Remember my box the first night—and don't forget Clive's benefit." King, as the Author, wants somebody to speak the Epilogue: Patent the manager replies—"Smart, degagee and not want assurance—King is the very man!" And so on.

tended Sir Fretful Plagiary and not Mr. Puff to be the writer of the tragedy. But he drew Puff for King and Plagiary for Parsons. Now, I have recently discovered a new and telling circumstance. *The Gazetteer*, a newspaper, advertised on August 16th, 1779, as "produced last week" at Sadler's Wells, "A new favourite Musical Piece consisting of Airs serious and comic, Recitatives, Choruses, &c., called *The Prophecy; or, Queen Elizabeth at Tilbury*. In the course of which will be introduced variety of Machinery and Decorations, particularly an emblematical Frontispiece, at the top of which, in a small Transparency, will be represented the Destruction of the famous Spanish Armada, and the view through the said Frontispiece will be closed by a Moving Perspective, representing the present Grand Fleet. The Recitatives and Choruses by Mr. Olive, the Airs selected from the best Masters, and the Paintings by Mr. Greenwood. Rope-dancing by Signora Mariana and Mr. Ferzi."[1]

The theatre at Sadler's Wells was managed by Thomas King, the original Puff, who accordingly was the "producer," and most likely also the inventor, of *The Prophecy; or Queen Elizabeth at Tilbury*. This settles, to my mind, why Sheridan represented Mr. Puff and not Sir Fretful Plagiary as the author of *The Spanish Armada*. It was another of his domestic jokes. Of course, *The Prophecy* was a pageant rather than a play, a "pantomime" in the old sense, with songs.

It would be easy to stress unduly the political background of *The Critic*, forgetting that the chief point of Mr. Puff's tragedy is made by those immortal lines:

> The Spanish Fleet thou canst not see—Because
> It is not yet in sight.

The air was full of rumours of invasion, but no enemy fleet came. The combined fleet of France and Spain had, indeed, been seen

[1]This piece is unknown even to Mr. Allardyce Nicoll, who does not mention it in his *XVIII Century Drama* (1750-1800). It was, however, acted at the Theatre in New Street, Birmingham, on August 10th, 1781, as "a favourite Musical Entertainment (never acted here) called *The Prophecy; or, Queen Elizabeth at Tilbury Fort*... To conclude with a view of the ocean and a sea-fight between the British Fleet and the Spanish Armada." *Aris's Gazette:* "A Dialogue Song" from this piece was printed in *The London Magazine* for October, 1779.

outside Plymouth Harbour in the previous Auguſt, but had sailed away without doing any great damage to the shipping. A new musical farce called *Plymouth in an Uproar* was performed at Covent Garden on October 19th, to which there were numerous objections.[1] Unlike the author of this farce, Sheridan touched very lightly upon the political situation; he handled his theme with incomparable tact and dexterity. Although the more formal explanation of his topical allusions[2] demands a curious knowledge of theatrical and political by-ways, their purpose is obvious to any intelligent person. So it is unnecessary to bury *The Critic* beneath a mass of commentary. The research into his "sources" has occupied many Editors, who seem entirely to misunderſtand the problem, or indeed to create one where there is none. Since the name of *The Rehearsal* is invoked in the Prologue there is no queſtion that Sheridan, like so many other playwrights, had a general indebtedness to the plan of the earlier play. But as for any particular debts of situation and idea, the evidence is disputable. Moore, for inſtance, offered these parallels:

"Now then for my magnificence! my battle! my noises! and my procession!"—Puff in *The Critic*.

"Now, gentlemen, I will be bold to say, I'll show you the greateſt scene that England ever saw; I mean not for words, for those I don't value, but for ſtate, shew, and magnificence."—Bayes in *The Rehearsal*.

[1] "The business of the French and Spanish fleets appearing off Plymouth was a matter of too serious and alarming a nature to be the subject of wit or humour. The formidable strength of our enemies naturally excites resolutions of opposing them with determined courage, but a truly brave people feel the impropriety of treating them with contempt and ridicule."—*Lloyd's Evening-Post*, October 22, 1779.

[2] One instance is in Dangle's comment: "Ay, that antithesis of persons is a most established figure," upon the Governor's phrase "The father softens; but the Governor is fixed." This is primarily a reference to parliamentary procedure. When intervening in the quarrel between Lord George Germaine and Temple Luttrell in the Saratoga debate (November, 1777) Charles Fox distinguished between general attacks upon a public character, and personal attacks upon a private character, and the mutual apologies of Germaine and Luttrell took the form of establishing the "antithesis of persons. . . ." Similarly, and more obviously, Fox apologized to Germaine, on another occasion, saying that it was "the inability of the minister he attacked, not that of the man, whom he had the highest opinion of." The joke is there, however, without the explanation.

"Now, Mr. Sneerwell, we shall begin my third and laſt aĉt; and I believe I may defy all the poets who have ever writ, or ever will write to produce its equal: it is, Sir, so cramm'd with drums and trumpets, thunder and lightning, battles and ghoſts, that I believe the audience will want no entertainment after it."

—Trapwit in *Pasquin* (by Fielding).

Such "parallels" could be increased without difficulty, and without significance. They are inevitable coincidences; it would be impossible to write a burlesque of a theatrical rehearsal of any play of this type without repeating some point or other that had been made by Buckingham or Fielding—more especially, indeed, if one had never read them. In the theatre, while authors are authors and aĉtors are aĉtors, the same things will recur and recur: playwrights will make their plays too long, managers will cut them, and playwrights will proteſt vehemently. This disposes of Moore's parallel between Puff's remonſtrances about the cutting of his tragedy and a passage in Fielding's *Pasquin*:

Sneerwell. Yes, faith, I think I would cut out a turn or two.
Trapwit. Sir, I'll sooner cut off an ear or two; Sir, that's the very beſt thing in the whole play.

The metaphor may be varied, but the thought behind it will be the same till the laſt producer offers to cut a line in the laſt author's laſt tragedy. The "parallels" prove only one thing—the theatre's essential unchangeableness.[1]

Mr. Sneer's ironical comment that "the theatre in proper hands might certainly be made the school of morality" is the echo of a commonplace. When Hugh Kelly's offered to "the goddess of the woeful countenance—the sentimental Muse."— his comedy of *The False Delicacy*—Garrick wrote a lively and disarming prologue saying:

Write *moral* plays—the blockhead!—why, good people,
You'll soon expeĉt this house to wear a ſteeple!

[1]Moore suggested that the joke about Sheridan "writing himself" was borrowed from Marplay in Fielding's *The Author's Farce*. In "rehearsals" it seems inevitable that playwrights should joke about themselves. Shaw does so in *Fanny's First Play* and Pirandello in *Six Characters in Search of an Author*.

For our fine piece, to let you into facts,
Is quite a *Sermon*, only preached in Acts.

Kelly's play ended with these speeches:—

> *Sir Harry*. If this story was to be represented upon the stage,
> the poet would think it his duty to punish me for life, because
> I was once culpable.
> *Winworth*. That wou'd be very wrong. The stage shou'd be
> a school of morality, and the noblest of all lessons is the for-
> giveness of injuries.

There is, however, no point in multiplying such instances, the
comment is still as pointed as ever it was: the theatre might be
made a school of morality, "but now, I am sorry to say, people
seem to go there principally for their entertainment."

There is one "plagiarism" of Sheridan's that cannot be passed
without comment. Dr. Nettleton says[1] "After arduous pursuit of
parallels in *The Critic* to little known and less read originals, it is a
relief to find one instance close enough to satisfy the most exact-
ing critic. Moore has drawn attention to Sir Fretful Plagiary's
speech, 'Steal!—to be sure they may; and, egad, serve your best
thoughts as gypsies do stolen children, disfigure them to make
'em pass for their own,' in connection with Churchill's lines (in
The Apology)

> Still pilfers wretched plans, and makes them worse,
> Like gipsies, lest the stolen brat be known,
> Defacing first, then claiming for his own.

So deadly, indeed, is this parallel, and so different from the in-
tangible borrowings usually ascribed to Sheridan, that one might
be tempted to run the gauntlet of critics with the perhaps over
subtle suggestion that Sheridan may have put these words, possibly familiar to Churchill's own contemporaries, into Sir Fretful's
mouth with malice aforethought, the better to show that Sir Fretful's own practice did not coincide with his preaching. Since,
however, Moore adds that 'this simile was again made use of by

[1] *Sheridan's Major Dramas*. Introduction to *The Critic*.

him in a speech upon Mr. Pitt's India Bill,' it is well to convict Sheridan, on this count, of high plagiarism." [1]

The verdict is astonishing. The "plagiarism" is deliberate: it was Sheridan's way of showing how Sir Fretful, accused of having a Commonplace Book where stray jokes and pilfered witticisms are kept with as much method as the ledger of a Lost and Stolen Office, lived up to his reputation.

In *The Critic* Sheridan was writing a treatise on dramatic art in the form of a satirical drama. He was burlesquing the eternal faults of bad tragedy as they were then exhibited in contemporary representations. But he was not directly parodying any particular plays of the period. Indeed, it was complained that he had parodied Shakespeare, Massinger and even Milton rather than the new tragedies like *The Law of Lombardy*, *Albina*, *The Fatal Falsehood*, &c., &c. It was, of course, deliberate, for how could he ridicule Hannah More's tragedy, when he had blessed it with a Prologue? Moreover, as Fitzpatrick enquired, [2] "Can he, undaunted, in civil broils with brother bards engage?" It makes it all the stranger that he should have caricatured Cumberland, even though he refrained from parodying his plays; the provocation must have been great.

The Monthly Review of 1781, discussing the printed play, complained that "this *Tragedy Rehears'd* proceeds too closely in the beaten track of the Duke of Buckingham's *Rehearsal*. The mode and objects of ridicule are generally the same; except that the Author of *The Critic* has too indiscriminately attacked Tragedy in general, and levelled some of his severest traits against the very best modern tragedy in our language, we mean the tragedy

[1] The House of Commons relished a theatrical joke, like the comparison of Lord Sandwich to Jemmy Twitcher in *The Beggar's Opera*. There was nothing very heinous in Sheridan slyly comparing Pitt to Sir Fretful Plagiary by quoting his most characteristic plagiarism. In 1783 he had amused the House by likening Pitt to "one of Ben Jonson's best characters, the Angry Boy in *The Alchemist*." Edmund Burke, too, quoted *The Critic*. Boaden in his *Memoirs of Mrs. Siddons* (vol. I, p. 199). "The greatest honour that it received was in a sportive allusion by Burke, in his masterly speech upon œconomical reform in February, 1780. He just touches the conscience of the Governor of Tilbury Fort. *Rebellion*, says the orator, *may not now indeed be so critical an event to those who engage in it since its price is so correctly ascertained at just a THOUSAND POUND*. (*Tilburina*. "A thousand pounds!"; *Governor*. "Hah! thou hast touch'd me nearly.")."

[2] In the Prologue to *The Critic*.

of *Douglas*! The theatrical rage, however, for *situation, attitude, discoveries, processions,* etc., is properly and humourously exposed." The burlesque of *Douglas* was generally perceived; for although it is a general satire on all dramatic recognitions from the days of Æschylus to our own, the likeness is particular. In Home's tragedy Lady Randolph, welcoming the "young stranger" who has saved her husband's life, is instinctively reminded of the lost son of her first husband, Douglas. To her confidante, Anna, she laments:

> I thought, that had the son of Douglas liv'd,
> He might have been like this young gallant stranger,
> And pair'd with him in features and in shape.

So the Justice's Lady, on seeing the youthful prisoner, says:

> Strange bodings seized
> My flutt'ring heart—and to myself I said,
> An' if our Jack had lived he'd surely been
> This stripling's height.

In both cases the unknown turns out to be the long-lost son to whom "some powerful sympathy" has directed the mother's heart.

The parody is clinched by the response of the prisoner in Puff's tragedy to the Justice, "My name's John Wilkins—*Alias* have I none"—of young Norval's most famous speech, long a favourite declamation, "My name is Norval."

The only other instance that has occurred to me during a prolonged acquaintance with eighteenth-century plays comes from Brooke's *Gustavus Vasa*. Sivard, narrating the death of Stenon says:

> "Soldier," he cried, "if it e'er be thy lot
> To see my cousin, great Gustavus,
> Tell him—for once, that I have fought like him,
> And wou'd like him have——"
> Conquer'd—he shou'd have said—but there, O there,
> Death stopt him short.

This surely was the origin of the Beefeater's

> -nity—he would have added, but stern Death
> Cut short his being and the noun at once.

Beyond these, nobodyhasyetproducedanyspecificparodiesof contemporary drama. *The Public Advertiser* of November 2nd, 1779, in its account of the first performance, applauded it as a general travesty of theatrical absurdities: "The tedious and unartificial Commencements of modern Tragedies, the inflated Diction, the figurative Tautology, the *Jeu de Théâtre* of Embraces and Groans, Vows and Prayers, florid Pathos, whining Heroism, and, above all, the Trick of Stage Situation, are ridiculed with a Burlesque which may be thought rather too refined for the Multitude, but certainly is perfect in its Stile."

A last word on Mr. Puff. Watkins, Sheridan's first stupid biographer, saw in him only a poor copy of Shift in Foote's comedy, *The Minor*. They are both types of the adventurer of the period. So was Figaro, whose story of his own career in that long engaging monologue in *The Marriage of Figaro* is the history of another Mr. Puff. There were other such adventurers before them, like those in Foote's plays—Papillon in *The Lyar*,[1] Dactyl in *The Patron*, Shift in *The Minor*. Puff is the adventurer as journalist, the society paragrapher, the compiler of auctioneers' catalogues, the dramatic critic—the "puff to the playhouses" as Dactyl is called. Though he is reduced to undeserved futility at his rehearsal, he struts with undiminished splendour at Mr. Dangle's theatrical levee. He is, like Figaro, a great personality for all time.

---

[1]Papillon's literary reviewing (Act I, scene i) is like Puff's dramatic criticism. But neither Sheridan nor Foote invented their methods—nor killed them.

Dramatis Personae

Dangle	Mr. Dodd
Sneer	Mr. Palmer
Sir Fretful Plagiary	Mr. Parsons
Signor Pasticcio Retornello	Mr. Delpini
Interpreter	Mr. Baddeley
Under Prompter and	Mr. Phillimore
Puff	Mr. King
Mrs. Dangle	Mrs. Hopkins
Italian Girls	{Miss Field and the {Miss Abrams

Characters of the TRAGEDY

Lord Burleigh	Mr. Moody
Governor of Tilbury Fort	Mr. Wrighten
Earl of Leicester	Mr. Farren
Sir Walter Raleigh	Mr. Burton
Sir Christopher Hatton	Mr. Waldron
Master of the Horse	Mr. Kenny
Beefeater	Mr. Wright
Justice	Mr. Packer
Son	Mr. Lamash
Constable	Mr. Fawcett
Thames and	Mr. Gawdry
Don Ferolo Wiskerandos	Mr. Bannister, jun.
1st Niece	Miss Collet
2nd Niece	Miss Kirby
Justice's Lady	Mrs. Johnston
Confidant and	Mrs. Bradshaw
Tilburina	Miss Pope

Guards, Constables, Servants, Chorus, Rivers, Attendants, &c., &c.

Dedication

MADAM,

*I*N *requesting your permission to address the following pages to you, which as they aim themselves to be critical, require every protection and allowance that approving taste or friendly prejudice can give them, I yet ventured to mention no other motive than the gratification of private friendship and esteem. Had I suggested a hope that your implied approbation would give a sanction to their defects, your particular reserve, and dislike to the reputation of critical taste, as well as of poetical talent, would have made you refuse the protection of your name to such a purpose. However, I am not so ungrateful as now to attempt to combat this disposition in you. I shall not here presume to argue that the present state of poetry claims and expects every assistance that taste and example can afford it: nor endeavour to prove that a fastidious concealment of the most elegant productions of judgment and fancy is an ill return for the possession of those endowments.—Continue to deceive yourself in the idea that you are known only to be eminently admired and regarded for the valuable qualities that attach private friendships, and the graceful talents that adorn conversation. Enough of what you have written, has stolen into full public notice to answer my purpose; and you will, perhaps, be the only person, conversant in elegant literature, who shall read this address and not perceive that by publishing your particular approbation of the following drama, I have a more interested object than to boast the true respect and regard with which*

I have the honour to be,

MADAM,

Your very sincere,

And obedient humble servant,

R. B. SHERIDAN.

Prologue

Written by the Honorable RICHARD FITZPATRICK.

THE Sister Muses, whom these realms obey,
    Who o'er the Drama hold divided sway,
    Sometimes, by evil counsellors, 'tis said
Like earth-born potentates have been misled:
In those gay days of wickedness and wit,
When Villiers criticiz'd what Dryden writ,
The Tragick Queen, to please a tasteless crow'd,
Had learn'd to bellow, rant, and roar so loud,
That frighten'd Nature, her best friend before,
The blust'ring beldam's company forswore.
Her comic Sister, who had wit 'tis true,
With all her merits, had her failings too;
And would sometimes in mirthful moments use
A style too flippant for a well-bred Muse.
Then female modesty abash'd began
To seek the friendly refuge of the fan,
Awhile behind that slight intrenchment stood,
'Till driv'n from thence, she left the stage for good.
In our more pious, and far chaster times!
These sure no longer are the Muse's crimes!
But some complain that, former faults to shun,
The reformation to extremes has run.
The frantick hero's wild delirium past,
Now insipidity succeeds bombast;
So slow Melpomene's cold numbers creep,
Here dullness seems her drowsy court to keep,
And we, are scarce awake, whilst you are fast asleep.
Thalia, once so ill behav'd and rude,
Reform'd; is now become an arrant prude,

Retailing nightly to the yawning pit,
The purest morals, undefil'd by wit!
Our Author offers in these motley scenes,
A slight remonstrance to the Drama's queens,
Nor let the goddesses be over nice;
Free spoken subjects give the best advice.
Although not quite a novice in his trade,
His cause to night requires no common aid.
To this, a friendly, just, and pow'rful court,
I come Ambassador to beg support.
Can he undaunted, brave the critick's rage?
In civil broils, with brother bards engage?
Hold forth their errors to the publick eye,
Nay more, e'en Newspapers themselves defy?
Say, must his single arm encounter all?
By numbers vanquish'd, e'en the brave may fall;
And though no leader should success distrust,
Whose troops are willing, and whose cause is just;
To bid such hosts of angry foes defiance,
His chief dependance must be, YOUR ALLIANCE.

THE CRITIC

Act the First

SCENE I

MR. *and* MRS. DANGLE *at Breakfast, and reading Newspapers.*

Dangle "BRUTUS to LORD NORTH."—"Letter the
(reading). second on the STATE OF THE ARMY"—Pshaw!
"To the first L—dash D of the A—dash Y."—
"Genuine Extract of a Letter from St. KITT'S"...."COXHEATH
INTELLIGENCE."..."It is now confidently asserted that SIR
CHARLES HARDY."...Pshaw!...Nothing but about the fleet,
and the nation!...and I hate all politics but theatrical politics....
Where's the MORNING CHRONICLE?

Mrs. Dangle. Yes, that's your gazette.

Dangle. So here we have it.———
"*Theatrical intelligence extraordinary.*———
We hear there is a new tragedy in rehearsal at Drury-Lane
Theatre, call'd the SPANISH ARMADA, said to be written by Mr.
PUFF, a gentleman well known in the theatrical world; if we may
allow ourselves to give credit to the report of the performers,
who, truth to say, are in general but indifferent judges, this piece
abounds with the most striking and received beauties of modern
composition"—So! I am very glad my friend PUFF's tragedy is
in such forwardness.—Mrs. Dangle, my dear, you will be very
glad to hear that PUFF's tragedy———

Mrs. Dangle. Lord, Mr. Dangle, why will you plague me
about such nonsense?—Now the plays are begun I shall have
no peace.—Isn't it sufficient to make yourself ridiculous by
your passion for the theatre, without continually teazing me to
join you? Why can't you ride your hobby-horse without desiring
to place me on a pillion behind you, Mr. Dangle?

Dangle. Nay, my dear, I was only going to read———

193

Mrs. Dangle. No, no; you never will read any thing that's worth listening to:—you hate to hear about your country; there are letters every day with Roman signatures, demonstrating the certainty of an invasion, and proving that the nation is utterly undone.—But you never will read any thing to entertain one.

Dangle. What has a woman to do with politics, Mrs. Dangle?

Mrs. Dangle. And what have you to do with the theatre, Mr. Dangle? Why should you affect the character of a Critic? I have no patience with you!—haven't you made yourself the jest of all your acquaintance by your interference in matters where you have no business? Are not you call'd a theatrical Quidnunc, and a mock Mæcenas to second-hand authors?

Dangle. True; my power with the Managers is pretty notorious; but is it no credit to have applications from all quarters for my interest?—From lords to recommend fidlers, from ladies to get boxes, from authors to get answers, and from actors to get engagements.

Mrs. Dangle. Yes, truly; you have contrived to get a share in all the plague and trouble of theatrical property, without the profit, or even the credit of the abuse that attends it.

Dangle. I am sure, Mrs. Dangle, you are no loser by it, however; YOU have all the advantages of it:—mightn't you, last winter, have had the reading of the new Pantomime a fortnight previous to its performance? And doesn't Mr. Fosbrook let you take places for a play before it is advertis'd, and set you down for a Box for every new piece through the season? And didn't my friend, Mr. Smatter, dedicate his last Farce to you at my particular request, Mrs. Dangle?

Mrs. Dangle. Yes; but wasn't the Farce damn'd, Mr. Dangle? And to be sure it is extremely pleasant to have one's house made the motley rendezvous of all the lackeys of literature:—The very high change of trading authors and jobbing critics!—Yes, my drawing-room is an absolute register-office for candidate actors, and poets without character; then to be continually alarmed with Misses and Ma'ams piping histeric changes on JULIETS and DORINDAS, POLLYS and OPHELIAS; and the very furniture trembling at the probationary ſtarts and unprovok'd rants of would-be RICHARDS and HAMLETS!—And what is worse than all, now that the Manager has monopoliz'd the Opera-House, haven't we the Signors and Signoras calling here, sliding their smooth semi-breves, and gargling glib divisions in their outlandish throats—with foreign emissaries and French spies, for ought I know, disguised like fidlers and figure dancers!

Dangle. Mercy! Mrs. Dangle!

Mrs. Dangle. And to employ yourself so idly at such an alarming crisis as this too—when, if you had the leaſt spirit, you would have been at the head of one of the Weſtminſter associations—or trailing a volunteer pike in the Artillery Ground?—But you —o' my conscience, I believe if the French were landed to-morrow your firſt enquiry would be, whether they had brought a theatrical troop with them.

Dangle. Mrs. Dangle, it does not signify—I say the ſtage is "the Mirror of Nature," and the actors are "the Abſtract, and brief Chronicles of the Time:"—and pray what can a man of sense ſtudy better?—Besides, you will not easily persuade me that there is no credit or importance in being at the head of a band of critics, who take upon them to decide for the whole town, whose opinion and patronage all writers solicit, and whose recommendation no manager dares refuse!

Mrs. Dangle. Ridiculous!—Both managers and authors of the leaſt merit, laugh at your pretensions.—The PUBLIC is their CRITIC—without whose fair approbation they know no play can reſt on the ſtage, and with whose applause they welcome such attacks as yours, and laugh at the malice of them, where they can't at the wit.

Dangle. Very well, Madam—very well.

Enter SERVANT.

Servant. Mr. Sneer, Sir, to wait on you.

Dangle. O, shew Mr. Sneer up. [*Exit* SERVANT.]—Plague on't, now we muſt appear loving and affectionate, or Sneer will hitch us into a ſtory.

Mrs. Dangle. With all my heart; you can't be more ridiculous than you are.

Dangle. You are enough to provoke——

Enter MR. SNEER.

——Hah! my dear Sneer, I am vastly glad to see you. My dear, here's Mr. Sneer.

Mrs. Dangle. Good morning to you, Sir.

Dangle. Mrs. Dangle and I have been diverting ourselves with the papers.—Pray, Sneer, won't you go to Drury-lane theatre the first night of Puff's tragedy?

Sneer. Yes; but I suppose one shan't be able to get in, for on the first night of a new piece they always fill the house with orders to support it. But here, Dangle, I have brought you two pieces, one of which you must exert yourself to make the managers accept, I can tell you that, for 'tis written by a person of consequence.

Dangle. So! now my plagues are beginning!

Sneer. Aye, I am glad of it, for now you'll be happy. Why, my dear Dangle, it is a pleasure to see how you enjoy your volunteer fatigue, and your solicited solicitations.

Dangle. It's a great trouble—yet, egad, it's pleasant too.— Why, sometimes of a morning, I have a dozen people call on me at breakfast time, whose faces I never saw before, nor ever desire to see again.

Sneer. That must be very pleasant indeed!

Dangle. And not a week but I receive fifty letters, and not a line in them about any business of my own.

Sneer. An amusing correspondence!

Dangle [*reading*]. "Bursts into tears, and exit." What, is this a tragedy!

Sneer. No, that's a genteel comedy, not a translation—only *taken from the French*; it is written in a stile which they have lately tried to run down; the true sentimental, and nothing ridiculous in it from the beginning to the end.

Mrs. Dangle. Well, if they had kept to that, I should not have been such an enemy to the stage, there was some edification to be got from those pieces, Mr. Sneer!

Sneer. I am quite of your opinion, Mrs. Dangle; the theatre, in proper hands, might certainly be made the school of morality; but now, I am sorry to say it, people seem to go there principally for their entertainment!

Mrs. Dangle. It would have been more to the credit of the Managers to have kept it in the other line.

Sneer. Undoubtedly, Madam, and hereafter perhaps to have had it recorded, that in the midst of a luxurious and dissipated age, they preserv'd *two* houses in the capital, where the conversation was always moral at least, if not entertaining!

Dangle. Now, egad, I think the worst alteration is in the nicety of the audience.—No double entendre, no smart inuendo admitted; even Vanburgh and Congreve oblig'd to undergo a bungling reformation!

Sneer. Yes, and our prudery in this respect is just on a par with the artificial bashfulness of a courtezan, who encreases the blush upon her cheek in an exact proportion to the diminution of her modesty.

Dangle. Sneer can't even give the Public a good word!—But what have we here?—This seems a very odd——

Sneer. O, that's a comedy, on a very new plan; replete with wit and mirth, yet of a most serious moral! You see it is call'd "THE REFORMED HOUSEBREAKER;" where by the mere force of humour, HOUSEBREAKING is put into so ridiculous a light, that if the piece has its proper run, I have no doubt but that bolts and bars will be entirely useless by the end of the season.

Dangle. Egad, this is new indeed!

Sneer. Yes; it is written by a particular friend of mine, who has discovered that the follies and foibles of society, are subjects unworthy the notice of the Comic Muse, who should be taught to stoop only at the greater vices and blacker crimes of humanity—gibbeting capital offences in five acts and pillorying petty larcenies in two.—In short, his idea is to dramatize the penal laws, and make the stage a court of ease to the Old Bailey.

Dangle. It is truly moral.

Enter SERVANT.

Servant. Sir Fretful Plagiary, Sir.

Dangle. Beg him to walk up.—[*Exit* SERVANT.]—Now, Mrs. Dangle, Sir Fretful Plagiary is an author to your own taste.

Mrs. Dangle. I confess he is a favourite of mine, because every body else abuses him.

Sneer.—Very much to the credit of your charity, Madam, if not of your judgment.

Dangle. But, egad, he allows no merit to any author but himself, that's the truth on't—tho' he's my friend.

Sneer. Never.—He is as envious as an old maid verging on the desperation of six-and-thirty: and then the insiduous humility with which he seduces you to give a free opinion on any of his works, can be exceeded only by the petulant arrogance with which he is sure to reject your observations.

Dangle. Very true, egad—tho' he's my friend.

Sneer. Then his affected contempt of all newspaper strictures; tho' at the same time, he is the sorest man alive, and shrinks like scorch'd parchment from the fiery ordeal of true criticism: yet is he so covetous of popularity, that he had rather be abused than not mentioned at all.

Dangle. There's no denying it—tho' he is my friend.

Sneer. You have read the tragedy he has just finished, haven't you?

Dangle. O yes; he sent it to me yesterday.

Sneer. Well, and you think it execrable, don't you?

Dangle. Why between ourselves, egad I must own—tho' he's my friend—that it is one of the most——He's here [*Aside.*]—finished and most admirable perform——

[SIR FRETFUL *without.*] Mr. Sneer with him, did you say?

Enter SIR FRETFUL.

Ah, my dear friend!—Egad, we were just speaking of your Tragedy.—Admirable, Sir Fretful, admirable!

Sneer. You never did any thing beyond it, Sir Fretful—never in your life.

Sir Fretful. You make me extremely happy; for without a

compliment, my dear Sneer, there isn't a man in the world whose judgment I value as I do yours.——And Mr. Dangle's.

Mrs. Dangle. They are only laughing at you, Sir Fretful; for it was but just now that——

Dangle. Mrs. Dangle!——Ah, Sir Fretful, you know Mrs. Dangle.——My friend Sneer was rallying just now——He knows how she admires you, and——

Sir Fretful. O Lord, I am sure Mr. Sneer has more taste and sincerity than to——A damn'd double-faced fellow! [*Aside.*

Dangle. Yes, yes,——Sneer will jest—but a better humour'd

Sir Fretful. O, I know——

Dangle. He has a ready turn for ridicule—his wit costs him nothing.——

Sir Fretful. No, egad,——or I should wonder how he came by it.   [*Aside.*

Mrs. Dangle. Because his jest is always at the expence of his friend.

Dangle. But, Sir Fretful, have you sent your play to the managers yet?——or can I be of any service to you?

Sir Fretful. No, no, I thank you; I believe the piece had sufficient recommendation with it.—I thank you tho'—I sent it to the manager of COVENT-GARDEN THEATRE this morning.

Sneer. I should have thought now, that it might have been cast (as the actors call it) better at DRURY-LANE.

Sir Fretful. O lud! no—never send a play there while I live— harkee! [*Whispers* SNEER.]

Sneer. Writes himself!—I know he does——

Sir Fretful. I say nothing—I take away from no man's merit —am hurt at no man's good fortune—I say nothing—But this I will say—through all my knowledge of life, I have observed— that there is not a passion so strongly rooted in the human heart as envy!

Sneer. I believe you have reason for what you say, indeed,

Sir Fretful. Besides—I can tell you it is not always so safe to leave a play in the hands of those who write themselves.

Sneer. What, they may steal from them, hey, my dear Plagiary?

Sir Fretful. Steal!—to be sure they may; and, egad, serve your best thoughts as gypsies do stolen children, disfigure them to make 'em pass for their own.

Sneer. But your present work is a sacrifice to Melpomene, and HE, you know, never——

Sir Fretful. That's no security.—A dext'rous plagiarist may do any thing.—Why, Sir, for ought I know, he might take out some of the best things in my tragedy, and put them into his own comedy.

Sneer. That might be done, I dare be sworn.

Sir Fretful. And then, if such a person gives you the least hint or assistance, he is devilish apt to take the merit of the whole—

Dangle. If it succeeds.

Sir Fretful. Aye,—but with regard to this piece, I think I can hit that gentleman, for I can safely swear he never read it.

Sneer. I'll tell you how you may hurt him more——

Sir Fretful. How?——

Sneer. Swear he wrote it.

Sir Fretful. Plague on't now, Sneer, I shall take it ill.—I believe you want to take away my character as an author!

Sneer. Then I am sure you ought to be very much oblig'd to me.

Sir Fretful. Hey!—Sir!——

Dangle. O you know, he never means what he says.

Sir Fretful. Sincerely then—you do like the piece?

Sneer. Wonderfully!

Sir Fretful. But come now, there must be something that you think might be mended, hey?—Mr. Dangle, has nothing struck you?

Dangle. Why faith, it is but an ungracious thing for the most part to——

Sir Fretful.—With most authors it is just so indeed; they are in general strangely tenacious!—But, for my part, I am never so well pleased as when a judicious critic points out any defect to me; for what is the purpose of shewing a work to a friend, if you don't mean to profit by his opinion?

Sneer. Very true.—Why then, tho' I seriously admire the piece upon the whole, yet there is one small objection; which, if you'll give me leave, I'll mention.

Sir Fretful. Sir, you can't oblige me more.

Sneer. I think it wants incident.

Sir Fretful. Good God!—you surprise me!—wants incident!——

Sneer. Yes; I own I think the incidents are too few.

Sir Fretful. Good God!—Believe me, Mr. Sneer, there is no person for whose judgment I have a more implicit deference.—But I protest to you, Mr. Sneer, I am only apprehensive that the incidents are too crowded.—My dear Dangle, how does it strike you?

Dangle. Really I can't agree with my friend Sneer.—I think the plot quite sufficient; and the four first acts by many degrees the best I ever read or saw in my life. If I might venture to suggest any thing, it is that the interest rather falls off in the fifth——

Sir Fretful.—Rises; I believe you mean, Sir.

Dangle. No; I don't upon my word.

Sir Fretful. Yes, yes, you do upon my soul—it certainly don't fall off, I assure you—No, no, it don't fall off.

Dangle. Now, Mrs. Dangle, didn't you say it struck you in the same light?

Mrs. Dangle. No, indeed, I did not—I did not see a fault in any part of the play from the beginning to the end.

Sir Fretful. Upon my soul the women are the best judges after all!

Mrs. Dangle. Or if I made any objection, I am sure it was to nothing in the piece; but that I was afraid it was, on the whole, a little too long.

Sir Fretful. Pray, Madam, do you speak as to duration of time; or do you mean that the story is tediously spun out?

Mrs. Dangle. O Lud! no.—I speak only with reference to the usual length of acting plays.

Sir Fretful. Then I am very happy—very happy indeed,—because the play is a short play, a remarkably short play:—I should not venture to differ with a lady on a point of taste; but, on these occasions, the watch, you know, is the critic.

Mrs. Dangle. Then, I suppose, it must have been Mr. Dangle's drawling manner of reading it to me.

Sir Fretful. O, if Mr. Dangle read it! that's quite another affair!—But I assure you, Mrs. Dangle, the first evening you can spare me three hours and an half, I'll undertake to read you the whole from beginning to end, with the Prologue and Epilogue, and allow time for the music between the acts.

Mrs. Dangle. I hope to see it on the stage next.

Dangle. Well, Sir Fretful, I wish you may be able to get rid as easily of the news-paper criticisms as you do of ours.——

Sir Fretful. The NEWS-PAPERS!—Sir, they are the most villainous—licentious—abominable—infernal—Not that I ever read them—No—I make it a rule never to look into a newspaper.

Dangle. You are quite right—for it certainly must hurt an author of delicate feelings to see the liberties they take

Sir Fretful. No!—quite the contrary;—their abuse is, in fact, the best panegyric—I like it of all things.—An author's reputation is only in danger from their support.

Mr. Sneer. Why that's true—and that attack now on you the other day——

Sir Fretful. What? where?

Dangle. Aye, you mean in a paper of Thursday; it was compleatly ill-natur'd to be sure.

Sir Fretful. O, so much the better—Ha! ha! ha! —I wou'dn't have it otherwise.

Dangle. Certainly it is only to be laugh'd at; for——

Sir Fretful.—You don't happen to recollect what the fellow said, do you?

Sneer. Pray, Dangle—Sir Fretful seems a little anxious——

Sir Fretful.—O Lud, no!—anxious,—not I,—not the least.— I—But one may as well hear you know.

Dangle. Sneer, do *you* recollect?—Make out something.

[*Aside.*

Sneer. I will, [*to* DANGLE.]—Yes, yes, I remember perfectly.

Sir Fretful. Well, and pray now—Not that it signifies—what might the gentleman say?

Sneer. Why, he roundly asserts that you have not the slightest invention, or original genius whatever; tho' you are the greatest traducer of all other authors living.

Sir Fretful. Ha! ha! ha!—very good!

Sneer. That as to COMEDY, you have not one idea of your own, he believes, even in your common place-book—where stray jokes, and pilfered witticisms are kept with as much method as the ledger of the LOST-AND-STOLEN-OFFICE.

Sir Fretful.—Ha! ha! ha!—very pleasant!

Sneer. Nay, that you are so unlucky as not to have the skill even to steal with taste:—But that you glean from the refuse of obscure volumes, where more judicious plagiarists have been before you; so that the body of your work is a composition of dregs and sediments—like a bad tavern's worst wine.

Sir Fretful. Ha! ha!

Sneer. In your more serious efforts, he says, your bombast would be less intolerable, if the thoughts were ever suited to the expression; but the homeliness of the sentiment stares thro' the fantastic encumbrance of its fine language, like a clown in one of the new uniforms!

Sir Fretful. Ha! ha!

Sneer. That your occasional tropes and flowers suit the general coarseness of your stile, as tambour sprigs would a ground of linsey-wolsey; while your imitations of Shakespeare resemble the mimicry of Falstaff's Page, and are about as near the standard of the original.

Sir Fretful. Ha!——

Sneer.—In short, that even the finest passages you steal are of no service to you; for the poverty of your own language prevents their assimilating; so that they lie on the surface like lumps of marl on a barren moor, encumbering what it is not in their power to fertilize!——

Sir Fretful [*after great agitation*].——Now another person would be vex'd at this.

Sneer. Oh! but I wou'dn't have told you, only to divert you.

Sir Fretful. I know it—I *am* diverted,—Ha! ha! ha!—not the least invention!—Ha! ha! ha! very good!—very good!

Sneer. Yes—no genius! Ha! ha! ha!

Dangle. A severe rogue! Ha! ha! ha! But you are quite right, Sir Fretful, never to read such nonsense.

Sir Fretful. To be sure—for if there is any thing to one's praise, it is a foolish vanity to be gratified at it, and if it is abuse, —why one is always sure to hear of it from one damn'd good natur'd friend or another!

Enter SERVANT.

Servant. Sir, there is an Italian gentleman with a French Interpreter, and three young ladies, and a dozen musicians, who say they are sent by LADY RONDEAU and MRS. FUGE.

Dangle. Gadso! they come by appointment. Dear Mrs. Dangle do let them know I'll see them directly.

Mrs. Dangle. You know, Mr. Dangle, I shan't understand a word they say.

Dangle. But you hear there's an interpreter.

Mrs. Dangle. Well, I'll try to endure their complaisance till you come. [*Exit.*

Servant. And Mr. PUFF, Sir, has sent word that the last rehearsal is to be this morning, and that he'll call on you presently.

Dangle. That's true—I shall certainly be at home. [*Exit* SERVANT.] Now, Sir Fretful, if you have a mind to have justice done you in the way of answer—Egad, Mr. PUFF's your man.

Sir Fretful. Pshaw! Sir, why should I wish to have it answered, when I tell you I am pleased at it?

Dangle. True, I had forgot that.—But I hope you are not fretted at what Mr. Sneer——

Sir Fretful.—Zounds! no, Mr. Dangle, don't I tell you these things never fret me in the least.

Dangle. Nay, I only thought——

Sir Fretful.—And let me tell you, Mr. Dangle, 'tis damn'd affronting in you to suppose that I am hurt, when I tell you I am not.

Sneer. But why so warm, Sir Fretful?

Sir Fretful. Gadslife! Mr. Sneer, you are as absurd as Dangle; how often mu&t I repeat it to you, that nothing can vex me but your supposing it possible for me to mind the damn'd nonsense you have been repeating to me!—and let me tell you, if you continue to believe this, you mu&t mean to insult me, gentlemen—and then your disrespe& will affe& me no more than the newspaper criticisms—and I shall treat it—with exa&ly the same calm indifference and philosophic contempt—and so your servant. [*Exit.*

Sneer. Ha! ha! ha! Poor Sir Fretful! Now will he go and vent his philosophy in anonymous abuse of all modern critics and authors—But, Dangle, you mu&t get your friend PUFF to take me to the rehearsal of his tragedy.

Dangle. I'll answer for't, he'll thank you for desiring it. But come and help me to judge of this musical family; they are recommended by people of consequence, I assure you.

Sneer. I am at your disposal the whole morning—but I thought you had been a decided critic in musick, as well as in literature.

Dangle. So I am—but I have a bad ear.—Efaith, Sneer, tho', I am afraid we were a little too severe on Sir Fretful—tho' he is my friend.

Sneer. Why, 'tis certain, that unnecessarily to mortify the vanity of any writer, is a cruelty which mere dulness never can deserve; but where a base and personal malignity usurps the place of literary emulation, the aggressor deserves neither quarter nor pity.

Dangle. That's true egad!—tho' he's my friend!

SCENE II

A Drawing Room, Harpsichord, etc. Italian Family, French Interpreter, MRS. DANGLE *and Servants discovered.*

Interpreter. Je dis madame, j'ai l'honneur to *introduce* & de vous demander votre prote&ion pour le Signor PASTICCIO RETORNELLO & pour sa charmante famille.

Signor Paſticcio. Ah! Vosignoria noi vi preghiamo di favori-tevi colla voſtra protezione.

1ſt Daughter. Vosignoria fatevi queſti grazzie.

2nd Daughter. Si Signora.

Interpreter. Madame—*me interpret.*—C'eſt à dire—in English—quils vous prient de leur faire l'honneur—

Mrs. Dangle.—I say again, gentlemen, I don't underſtand a word you say.

Signor Paſticcio. Queſto Signore spiegheró.

Interpreter. Oui—*me interpret.*—nous avons les lettres de recommendation pour Monsieur Dangle de ——

Mrs. Dangle.—Upon my word, Sir, I don't underſtand you.

Signor Paſticcio. La Contessa Rondeau e noſtra padrona.

3rd Daughter. Si, padre, et mi Ladi Fuge.

Interpreter. O!—*me interpret.*—Madame, ils disent—*in* English—Qu'ils ont l'honneur d'etre proteges de ces Demes.— *You understand?*

Mrs. Dangle. No, Sir,——no underſtand!

Enter Dangle *and* Sneer.

Interpreter. Ah voici Monsieur Dangle!

All Italians. A! Signor Dangle!

Mrs. Dangle. Mr. Dangle, here are two very civil gentlemen trying to make themselves underſtood, and I don't know which is the interpreter.

Dangle. Ebien!

Interpreter. Monsieur Dangle—le grand bruit de vos talents pour la critique & de votre intereſt avec Messieurs les Direĉteurs a tous les Theatres.

Signor Paſticcio. Vosignoria flete si famoso par la voſtra conoscensa e voſtra interessa colla le Direttore da—

speaking together

Dangle. Egad I think the Interpreter is the hardeſt to be underſtood of the two!

Sneer. Why I thought Dangle, you had been an admirable linguiſt!

Dangle. So I am, if they would not talk so damn'd faſt.

Sneer. Well I'll explain that—the less time we lose in hearing them the better,—for that I suppose is what they are brought here for.

[SNEER *speaks to* SIG. PAST.—*They sing trios, &c.*[1] DANGLE *beating out of time.* SERVANT *enters and whispers* DANGLE.]

Dangle. Shew him up.   [*Exit* SERVANT.]

Bravo! admirable! bravissimo! admirablissimo!—Ah! Sneer! where will you find such as these voices in England?

Sneer. Not easily.

Dangle. But PUFF is coming.—Signor and little Signora's—obligatissimo!—Sposa Signora Danglena—Mrs. Dangle, shall I beg you to offer them some refreshments, and take their address in the next room.

[*Exit* MRS. DANGLE *with the* ITALIANS *and* INTERPRETER *ceremoniously.*]

Re-enter SERVANT.

Servant. Mr. PUFF, Sir!

Dangle. My dear PUFF!

Enter PUFF.

Puff. My dear Dangle, how is it with you?

Dangle. Mr. Sneer, give me leave to introduce Mr. PUFF to you.

Puff. Mr. Sneer is this? Sir, he is a gentleman whom I have long panted for the honour of knowing—a gentleman whose critical talents and transcendant judgment——

Sneer.—Dear Sir——

Dangle. Nay, don't be modeſt, Sneer, my friend PUFF only talks to you in the ſtile of his profession.

Sneer. His profession!

Puff. Yes, Sir; I make no secret of the trade I follow—among friends and brother authors, Dangle knows I love to be frank on the subjeċt, and to advertise myself *vivâ voce.*—I am, Sir, a Praċtitioner in Panegyric, or to speak more plainly—a Professor of the Art of Puffing, at your service—or any body else's.

Sneer. Sir, you are very obliging!—I believe, Mr. Puff, I have often admired your talents in the daily prints.

[1]For "The favourite Duetto" in this scene, see Vol. III, Addenda.

Puff. Yes, Sir, I flatter myself I do as much business in that way as any six of the fraternity in town—Devilish hard work all the summer—Friend Dangle? never work'd harder!—But harkee,—the Winter Managers were a little sore I believe.

Dangle. No—I believe they took it all in good part.

Puff. Aye!—Then that must have been affectation in them; for egad, there were some of the attacks which there was no laughing at!

Sneer. Aye, the humourous ones—But I should think Mr. Puff, that Authors would in general be able to do this sort of work for themselves.

Puff. Why yes—but in a clumsy way.—Besides, we look on that as an encroachment, and so take the opposite side.—I dare say now you conceive half the very civil paragraphs and advertisements you see, to be written by the parties concerned, or their friends?—No such thing—Nine out of ten, manufactured by me in the way of business.

Sneer. Indeed!——

Puff. Even the Auctioneers now—the Auctioneers I say, tho' the rogues have lately got some credit for their language—not an article of the merit their's!—take them out of their Pulpits, and they are as dull as Catalogues!——No, Sir;—'twas I first enrich'd their style—'twas I first taught them to crowd their advertisements with panegyrical superlatives, each epithet rising above the other—like the Bidders in their own Auction-rooms! From ME they learn'd to enlay their phraseology with variegated chips of exotic metaphor: by ME too their inventive faculties were called forth.—Yes Sir, by ME they were instructed to clothe ideal walls with gratuitous fruits—to insinuate obsequious rivulets into visionary groves—to teach courteous shrubs to nod their approbation of the grateful soil! or on emergencies to raise upstart oaks, where there never had been an acorn; to create a delightful vicinage without the assistance of a neighbour; or fix the temple of Hygeia in the fens of Lincolnshire!

Dangle. I am sure you have done them infinite service; for now, when a gentleman is ruined, he parts with his house with some credit.

Sneer. Service! if they had any gratitude, they would erect a statue to him; they would figure him as a presiding Mercury, the god of traffic and fiction, with a hammer in his hand instead of a caduceus.—But pray, Mr. Puff, what first put you on exercising your talents in this way?

Puff. Egad, Sir—sheer necessity—the proper parent of an art so nearly allied to invention: you must know, Mr. Sneer, that from the first time I tried my hand at an advertisement, my success was such, that for some time after, I led a most extraordinary life indeed!

Sneer. How, pray?

Puff. Sir, I supported myself two years entirely by my misfortunes.

Sneer. By your misfortunes?

Puff. Yes, Sir, assisted by long sickness, and other occasional disorders; and a very comfortable living I had of it.

Sneer. From sickness and misfortunes!—You practised as a Doctor, and an Attorney at once?

Puff. No, egad; both maladies and miseries were my own.

Sneer. Hey! —what the plague!

Dangle. 'Tis true, efaith.

Puff. Harkee!—By advertisements——"To the charitable and humane!" and "to those whom Providence hath blessed with affluence!"

Sneer. Oh,—I understand you.

Puff. And, in truth, I deserved what I got; for I suppose never man went through such a series of calamities in the same space of time!—Sir, I was five times made a bankrupt, and reduced from a state of affluence, by a train of unavoidable misfortunes! then, Sir, though a very industrious tradesman, I was twice burnt out, and lost my little all, both times!—I lived upon those fires a month —I soon after was confined by a most excruciating disorder, and lost the use of my limbs!—That told very well; for I had the case strongly attested, and went about to collect the subscriptions myself.

Dangle. Egad, I believe that was when you first called on me—

Puff.——In November last?—O no!—I was at that time a

close prisoner in the Marshalsea, for a debt benevolently contracted to serve a friend!—I was afterwards, twice tapped for a dropsy, which declined into a very profitable consumption!—I was then reduced to—O no—then, I became a widow with six helpless children,—after having had eleven husbands pressed, and being left every time eight months gone with child, and without money to get me into an hospital!

Sneer. And you bore all with patience, I make no doubt?

Puff. Why, yes,—tho' I made some occasional attempts at felo de se; but as I did not find those *rash actions* answer, I left off killing myself very soon.—Well, Sir,—at last, what with bankruptcies, fires, gouts, dropsies, imprisonments, and other valuable calamities, having got together a pretty handsome sum, I determined to quit a business which had always gone rather against my conscience, and in a more liberal way still to indulge my talents for fiction and embellishment, thro' my favourite channels of diurnal communication—and so, Sir, you have my history.

Sneer. Most obligingly communicative indeed; and your confession if published, might certainly serve the cause of true charity, by rescuing the most useful channels of appeal to benevolence from the cant of imposition —But surely, Mr. Puff, there is no great *mystery* in your present profession?

Puff. Mystery! Sir, I will take upon me to say the matter was never scientifically treated, nor reduced to rule before.

Sneer. Reduced to rule?

Puff. O Lud, Sir! you are very ignorant, I am afraid.— Yes, Sir,— PUFFING is of various sorts—the principal are, The PUFF DIRECT— the PUFF PRELIMINARY— the PUFF COLLATERAL— the PUFF COLLUSIVE, and the PUFF OBLIQUE, or PUFF by IMPLICATION. —These all assume, as circumstances require, the various forms of LETTER TO THE EDITOR—OCCASIONAL ANECDOTE—IMPARTIAL CRITIQUE—OBSERVATION from CORRESPONDENT,—or ADVERTISEMENT FROM THE PARTY.

Sneer. The puff direct, I can conceive——

Puff. O yes, that's simple enough,— for instance—A new Comedy or Farce is to be produced at one of the Theatres (though by the bye they don't bring out half what they ought to do). The author, suppose Mr. Smatter, or Mr. Dapper—or any particular friend of mine—very well; the day before it is to be performed, I write an account of the manner in which it was received—I have the plot from the author,—and only add—Characters strongly drawn—highly coloured—hand of a master—fund of genuine humour—mine of invention—neat dialogue—attic salt! Then for the performance—Mr. Dodd was astonishingly great in the character of Sir Harry! That universal and judicious actor, Mr. Palmer, perhaps never appeared to more advantage than in the Colonel;—but it is not in the power of language to do justice to Mr. King!—Indeed he more than merited those repeated bursts of applause which he drew from a most brilliant and judicious audience! As to the scenery—The miraculous power of Mr. De Loutherbourg's pencil are universally acknowledged!—In short, we are at a loss which to admire most,—the unrivalled genius of the author, the great attention and liberality of the managers—the wonderful abilities of the painter, or the incredible exertions of all the performers!——

Sneer. That's pretty well indeed, Sir.

Puff. O cool—quite cool—to what I sometimes do.

Sneer. And do you think there are any who are influenced by this.

Puff. O, Lud! yes, Sir;—the number of those who undergo the fatigue of judging for themselves is very small indeed!

Sneer. Well, Sir,—the Puff Preliminary?

Puff. O that, Sir, does well in the form of a *Caution.*—In a matter of gallantry now—Sir Flimsy Gossimer, wishes to be well with Lady Fanny Fete—He applies to me——I open trenches for him with a paragraph in the Morning Post.——It is recommended to the beautiful and accomplished Lady F four stars F dash E to be on her guard against that dangerous character, Sir F dash G; who, however pleasing and insinuating his manners may be, is certainly not remarkable for the *constancy of his attachments!*—in Italics.—Here you see, Sir Flimsy Gossimer is introduced to the particular notice of Lady Fanny

```
212  SHERIDAN'S PLAYS AND POEMS
```

—who, perhaps never thought of him before—she finds herself publickly cautioned to avoid him, which naturally makes her desirous of seeing him;—the observation of their acquaintance causes a pretty kind of mutual embarrassment, this produces a sort of sympathy of interest—which, if Sir Flimsy is unable to improve effectually, he at least gains the credit of having their names mentioned together, by a particular set, and in a particular way,—which nine times out of ten is the full accomplishment of modern gallantry.

Dangle. Egad, Sneer, you will be quite an adept in the business.

Puff. Now, Sir, the PUFF COLLATERAL is much used as an appendage to advertisements, and may take the form of anecdote. —Yesterday as the celebrated GEORGE BON-MOT was sauntering down St. James's-street, he met the lively Lady MARY MYRTLE, coming out of the Park,—'Good God, LADY MARY, I'm surprised to meet you in a white jacket,—for I expected never to have seen you, but in a full trimmed uniform and a light-horseman's cap!'—'Heavens, GEORGE, where could you have learned that?'—'Why, replied the wit, I just saw a print of you, in a new publication called THE CAMP MAGAZINE, which, by the bye, is a devilish clever thing,—and is sold at No. 3, on the right hand of the way, two doors from the printing-office, the corner of Ivy-lane, Paternoster-row, price only one shilling!'

Sneer. Very ingenious indeed!

Puff. But the PUFF COLLUSIVE is the newest of any; for it acts in the disguise of determined hostility.—It is much used by bold booksellers and enterprising poets.—An indignant correspondent observes—that the new poem called BEELZEBUB's COTILLION, or PROSERPINE's FETE CHAMPETRE, is one of the most unjustifiable performances he ever read! The severity with which certain characters are handled is quite shocking! And as there are many descriptions in it too warmly coloured for female delicacy, the shameful avidity with which this piece is bought by all people of fashion, is a reproach on the taste of the times, and a disgrace to the delicacy of the age!—Here you see the two strongest inducements are held forth;—First, that nobody ought to read it;—secondly, that every body buys it; on the strength of which, the publisher boldly prints the tenth edition, before he had sold ten of the first; and then establishes it by threatening himself with the pillory, or absolutely indicting himself for Scan. Mag.!

Dangle. Ha! ha! ha!—'gad I know it is so.

Puff. As to the Puff Oblique, or Puff by Implication, it is too various and extensive to be illustrated by an instance; it attracts in titles and presumes in patents; it lurks in the *limitation* of a subscription, and invites in the assurance of croud and incommodation at public places; it delights to draw forth concealed merit, with a most disinterested assiduity; and sometimes wears a countenance of smiling censure and tender reproach.— It has a wonderful memory for Parliamentary Debates, and will often give the whole speech of a favoured member with the most flattering accuracy. But, above all, it is a great dealer in reports and suppositions.—It has the earliest intelligence of intended preferments that will reflect *honor* on the *patrons*; and embryo promotions of modest gentlemen—who know nothing of the matter themselves. It can hint a ribband for implied services, in the air of a common report; and with the carelessness of a casual paragraph, suggest officers into commands—to which they have no pretension but their wishes. This, Sir, is the last principal class in the Art of Puffing——An art which I hope you will now agree with me, is of the highest dignity—yielding a tablature of benevolence and public spirit; befriending equally trade, gallantry, criticism, and politics: the applause of genius! the register of charity! the triumph of heroism! the self-defence of contractors! the fame of orators!—and the gazette of ministers!

Sneer. Sir, I am compleatly a convert both to the importance and ingenuity of your profession; and now, Sir, there is but one thing which can possibly encrease my respect for you, and that is, your permitting me to be present this morning at the rehearsal of your new trage——

Puff.—Hush, for heaven's sake.—*My* tragedy!—Egad, Dangle, I take this very ill—you know how apprehensive I am of being known to be the author.

Dangle. 'Efaith I would not have told—but it's in the papers, and your name at length—in the Morning Chronicle.

Puff.——Ah! those damn'd editors never can keep a secret! Well, Mr. Sneer—no doubt you will do me great honour—I shall be infinitely happy—highly flattered——

Dangle. I believe it muſt be near the time—shall we go together.

Puff. No; It will not be yet this hour, for they are always late at that theatre: besides, I muſt meet you there, for I have some little matters·here to send to the papers, and a few paragraphs to scribble before I go.   [*Looking at memorandums.*

—Here is 'a CONSCIENTIOUS BAKER, on the Subjeʗt of the Army Bread;' and 'a DETESTER OF VISIBLE BRICK-WORK, in favor of the new invented Stucco;' both in the ſtyle of JUNIUS, and promised for to-morrow.—The Thames navigation too is at a ſtand.—MISO-MUD or ANTI-SHOAL muſt go to work again direʗtly.—Here too are some political memorandums I see; aye —To take PAUL JONES, and get the INDIAMEN out of the SHANNON—reinforce BYRON—compel the DUTCH to—so!—I muſt do that in the evening papers, or reserve it for the Morning Herald, for I know that I have undertaken to-morrow; besides, to eſtablish the unanimity of the fleet in the Public Advertiser, and to shoot CHARLES FOX in the Morning Poſt.—So, egad, I h'n't a moment to lose!

Dangle. Well!—we'll meet in the Green Room.

[*Exeunt severally.*

END OF ACT THE FIRST

Act the Second

SCENE I

The THEATRE.

Enter DANGLE, PUFF, *and* SNEER, *as before the Curtain.*

Puff. NO, no, Sir; what Shakespeare says of ACTORS may be better applied to the purpose of PLAYS; *they* ought to be 'the abstract and brief Chronicles of the times.' Therefore when history, and particularly the history of our own country, furnishes any thing like a case in point, to the time in which an author writes, if he knows his own interest, he will take advantage of it; so, Sir, I call my tragedy The SPANISH ARMADA; and have laid the scene before TILBURY FORT.

Sneer. A most happy thought certainly!

Dangle. Egad it was—I told you so.—But pray now I don't understand how you have contrived to introduce any love into it.

Puff. Love!—Oh nothing so easy: for it is a received point among poets, that where history gives you a good heroic outline for a play, you may fill up with a little love at your own discretion: in doing which, nine times out of ten, you only make up a deficiency in the private history of the times. Now I rather think I have done this with some success.

Sneer. No scandal about Queen ELIZABETH, I hope?

Puff. O Lud! no, no.—I only suppose the Governor of Tilbury Fort's daughter to be in love with the son of the Spanish Admiral.

Sneer. Oh, is that all?

Dangle. Excellent, Efaith! I see it at once.—But won't this appear rather improbable?

Puff. To be sure it will—but what the plague! a play is not to

215

shew occurrences that happen every day, but things juſt so ſtrange, that tho' they never *did*, they *might* happen.

Sneer. Certainly nothing is unnatural, that is not physically impossible.

Puff. Very true—and for that matter Don Ferolo Wisker-andos—for that's the lover's name, might have been over here in the train of the Spanish Ambassador; or Tilburina, for that is the lady's name, might have been in love with him, from having heard his charaćter, or seen his pićture; or from knowing that he was the laſt man in the world she ought to be in love with —or for any other good female reason.—However, Sir, the faćt is, that tho' she is but a Knight's daughter, egad! she is in love like any Princess!

Dangle. Poor young lady! I feel for her already! for I can conceive how great the conflićt muſt be between her passion and her duty; her love for her country, and her love for Don Ferolo Wiskerandos!

Puff. O amazing!—her poor susceptible heart is swayed to and fro, by contending passions like——

Enter Under Prompter.

Under Prompter. Sir, the scene is set, and every thing is ready to begin if you please——

Puff. 'Egad; then we'll lose no time.

U. Prompter. Tho' I believe, Sir, you will find it very short, for all the performers have profited by the kind permission you granted them.

Puff. Hey! what!

U. Prompter. You know, Sir, you gave them leave to cut out or omit whatever they found heavy or unnecessary to the plot, and I muſt own they have taken very liberal advantage of your indulgence.

Puff. Well, well.—They are in general very good judges; and I know I am luxuriant.—Now, Mr. Hopkins, as soon as you please.

U. Prompter [*to the Musick*]. Gentlemen, will you play a few bars of something, juſt to——

Puff. Aye, that's right,—for as we have the scenes, and dresses, egad, we'll go to't, as if it was the first night's performance;—but you need not mind stopping between the acts.

[*Exit* UNDER PROMPTER.

Orchestra play. Then the Bell rings.

Soh! stand clear gentlemen.—Now you know there will be a cry of down!—down!—hats off! silence!—Then up curtain,— and let us see what our painters have done for us.

SCENE II

The Curtain rises and discovers TILBURY FORT.

Two Centinels asleep.

Dangle. Tilbury Fort!—very fine indeed!

Puff. Now, what do you think I open with?

Sneer. Faith, I can't guess—

Puff. A clock—Hark!—[*Clock strikes.*] I open with a clock striking, to beget an aweful attention in the audience—it also marks the time, which is four o'clock in the morning, and saves a description of the rising sun, and a great deal about gilding the eastern hemisphere.

Dangle. But pray, are the centinels to be asleep?

Puff. Fast as watchmen.

Sneer. Isn't that odd tho' at such an alarming crisis?

Puff. To be sure it is,—but smaller things must give way to a striking scene at the opening; that's a rule.—And the case is, that two great men are coming to this very spot to begin the piece; now, it is not to be supposed they would open their lips, if these fellows were watching them, so, egad, I must either have sent them off their posts, or set them asleep.

Sneer. O that accounts for it!—But tell us, who are these coming?——

Puff. These are they—SIR WALTER RALEIGH, and SIR CHRISTOPHER HATTON.—You'll know Sir CHRISTOPHER, by his turning out his toes—famous you know for his dancing. I like to preserve all the little traits of character.—Now attend.

Enter SIR WALTER RALEIGH *and* SIR CHRISTOPHER HATTON.

Sir Christopher.   True, gallant Raleigh!——

Dangle. What, they had been talking before?

Puff. O, yes; all the way as they came along.—I beg pardon gentlemen [*to the Actors.*] but these are particular friends of mine, whose remarks may be of great service to us.—Don't mind interrupting them whenever any thing strikes you.

                      [*To* SNEER *and* DANGLE.

Sir Christopher.   True, gallant Raleigh!

    But O, thou champion of thy country's fame,
    There *is* a question which I yet must ask;
    A question, which I never ask'd before—
    What mean these mighty armaments?
    This general muster? and this throng of chiefs?

Sneer. Pray, Mr. Puff, how came Sir Christopher Hatton never to ask that question before?

Puff. What, before the Play began? how the plague could he?

Dangle. That's true efaith!

Puff. But you will hear what he thinks of the matter.

Sir Christopher. Alas, my noble friend, when I behold
    Yon tented plains in martial symmetry
    Array'd—When I count o'er yon glittering lines
    Of crested warriors, where the proud steeds neigh,
    And valor-breathing trumpet's shrill appeal,
    Responsive vibrate on my listning ear;
    When virgin majesty herself I view,
    Like her protecting Pallas veil'd in steel,
    With graceful confidence exhort to arms!
    When briefly all I hear or see bears stamp
    Of martial vigilance, and stern defence,
    I cannot but surmise.—Forgive, my friend,
    If the conjecture's rash——I cannot but
    Surmise.——The state some danger apprehends!

Sneer. A very cautious conjecture that.

Puff. Yes, that's his character; not to give an opinion, but on secure grounds—now then.

Sir Walter. O, most accomplished Christopher——

Puff. He calls him by his christian name, to show that they are on the most familiar terms.

Sir Walter. O, most accomplish'd Christopher, I find
    Thy staunch sagacity still tracks the future,
    In the fresh print of the o'ertaken past.

Puff. Figurative!

Sir Walter. Thy fears are just.

Sir Christopher.   But where? whence? when? and what
    The danger is——Methinks I fain would learn.

Sir Walter. You know, my friend, scarce two revolving suns,
    And three revolving moons, have closed their course,
    Since haughty PHILIP, in despight of peace,
    With hostile hand hath struck at ENGLAND's trade,

Sir Christopher.   ——I know it well.

Sir Walter. PHILIP you know is proud, IBERIA's king![1]

Sir Christopher. He is.

Sir Walter.   ——His subjects in base bigotry
    And Catholic oppression held,——while we
    You know, the protestant persuasion hold.

Sir Christopher. We do.

Sir Walter.   You know beside,——his boasted armament,
    The fam'd Armada,——by the Pope baptized,
    With purpose to invade these realms——

Sir Christopher.   ——Is failed,
    Our last advices so report.

Sir Walter. While the Iberian Admiral's chief hope,
    His darling son——

Sir Christopher.   ——Ferolo Wiskerandos hight——

Sir Walter. The same—by chance a pris'ner hath been ta'en,
    And in this fort of Tilbury——

Sir Christopher.   ——Is now
    Confin'd,—'tis true, and oft from yon tall turrets top
    I've mark'd the youthful Spaniard's haughty mien
    Unconquer'd, tho' in chains;

Sir Walter.   You also know——

Dangle.—Mr. Puff, as he *knows* all this, why does Sir Walter go on telling him?

[1] The punctuation may be intentional.

Puff. But the audience are not supposed to know any thing of the matter, are they?

Sneer. True, but I think you manage ill: for there certainly appears no reason why Sir Walter should be so communicative.

Puff. For, egad now, that is one of the most ungrateful observations I ever heard—for the less inducement he has to tell all this, the more I think, you ought to be oblig'd to him; for I am sure you'd know nothing of the matter without it.

Dangle. That's very true, upon my word.

Puff. But you will find he was *not* going on.

Sir Christopher. Enough, enough,—'tis plain—and I no more
  Am in amazement lost!——

Puff. Here, now you see, Sir Christopher did not in fact ask any one question for his own information.

Sneer. No indeed:—his has been a most disinterested curiosity!

Dangle. Really, I find, we are very much oblig'd to them both.

Puff. To be sure you are. Now then for the Commander in Chief, the EARL OF LEICESTER! who, you know, was no favourite but of the Queen's.—We left off—"in amazement lost!"——

Sir Christopher.   Am in amazement lost.——
  But, see where noble Leicester comes! supreme
  In honours and command.
Sir Walter.   And yet methinks,
  At such a time, so perilous, so fear'd
  That staff might well become an abler grasp.
Sir Christopher. And so by heav'n! think I; but soft, he's here!

Puff. Aye, they envy him.

Sneer. But who are these with him?

Puff. O! very valiant knights; one is the Governor of the fort, the other the master of the horse.—And now, I think you shall hear some better language: I was obliged to be plain and intelligible in the first scene, because there was so much matter of fact in it; but now, efaith, you have trope, figure, and metaphor, as plenty as noun-substantives.

Enter EARL OF LEICESTER, *the Governor, and others.*

Leicester. How's this my friends! is't thus your new fledg'd zeal
 And plumed valor moulds in roosted sloth?
 Why dimly glimmers that heroic flame,
 Whose red'ning blaze by patriot spirit fed,
 Should be the beacon of a kindling realm?
 Can the quick current of a patriot heart,
 Thus stagnate in a cold and weedy converse,
 Or freeze in tideless inactivity?
 No! rather let the fountain of your valor
 Spring thro' each stream of enterprise,
 Each petty channel of conducive daring,
 Till the full torrent of your foaming wrath
 O'erwhelm the flats of sunk hostility!

Puff. There it is,—follow'd up!

Sir Walter. No more! the fresh'ning breath of thy rebuke
 Hath fill'd the swelling canvas of our souls!
 And thus, tho' fate should cut the cable of   [*All take hands.*
 Our topmost hopes, in friendship's closing line
 We'll grapple with despair, and if we fall,
 We'll fall in Glory's wake!
Leicester. There spoke Old England's genius!
 Then, are we all resolv'd?
All. We are—all resolv'd.
Leicester. To conquer——or be free?
All. To conquer, or be free.
Leicester. All?
All. All.

Dangle. Nem. con. egad!
Puff. O yes, where they *do* agree on the stage, their unanimity
is wonderful!

Leicester. Then, let's embrace——and now——

Sneer. What the plague, is he going to pray?
Puff. Yes, hush!—in great emergencies, there is nothing like
a prayer!

Leicester. O mighty Mars!

Dangle. But why should he pray to *Mars?*
Puff. Hush!

Leicester.   If in thy homage bred,
Each point of discipline I've still observ'd;
Nor but by due promotion, and the right
Of service, to the rank of Major-General
Have ris'n; assist thy votary now!
Governor. Yet do not rise,——hear me!
Master of Horse. And me!
Knight. And me!
Sir Walter. And me!
Sir Christopher. And me!

Puff. Now, pray all together.

All. Behold thy votaries submissive beg,
That thou will deign to grant them all they ask;
Assist them to accomplish all their ends,
And sanctify whatever means they use
To gain them!

Sneer. A very orthodox quintetto!
Puff. Vastly well, gentlemen.—Is that well managed or not?
Have you such a prayer as that on the stage?
Sneer. Not exactly.
Leicester [*to Puff*] But, Sir, you havn't settled how we are to
get off here.
Puff. You could not go off kneeling, could you?
Sir Walter [*to Puff*]. O no, Sir! impossible!
Puff. It would have a good effect faith, if you could! exeunt
praying!—Yes, and would vary the established mode of spring-
ing off with a glance at the pit.
Sneer. O never mind, so as you get them off, I'll answer for it
the audience won't care how.
Puff. Well then, repeat the last line standing, and go off the
old way.

All. And sanctify whatever means we use to gain them.   [*Exeunt.*

Dangle. Bravo! a fine exit.

Sneer. Well, really Mr. Puff.——
Puff. Stay a moment.——

The CENTINELS *get up.*

1st *Centinel.* All this shall to Lord Burleigh's ear.
2d *Centinel.* 'Tis meet it should.   [*Exeunt* CENTINELS.

Dangle. Hey!—why, I thought those fellows had been asleep?
Puff. Only a pretence, there's the art of it; they were spies of Lord Burleigh's.
Sneer.—But isn't it odd, they were never taken notice of, not even by the commander in chief.
Puff. O lud, Sir, if people who want to listen, or overhear, were not always conniv'd at in a Tragedy, there would be no carrying on any plot in the world.
Dangle. That's certain!
Puff. But take care my dear Dangle the morning gun is going to fire.   [*Cannon fires.*
Dangle. Well, that will have a fine effect.
Puff. I think so, and helps to realize the scene.——   [*Cannon twice.*
What the plague!—*three* morning guns!—there never is but one!—aye, this is always the way at the Theatre—give these fellows a good thing, and they never know when to have done with it. You have no more cannon to fire?
Prompter [*from within*]. No Sir.
Puff. Now then, for soft musick.
Sneer. Pray what's that for?
Puff. It shows that TILBURINA is coming; nothing introduces you a heroine like soft musick.—Here she comes.
Dangle. And her confidant, I suppose?
Puff. To be sure: here they are—inconsolable to the minuet in Ariadne!   [*Soft musick.*

Enter TILBURINA *and* CONFIDANT.

Tilburina. Now has the whispering breath of gentle morn,
Bad Nature's voice, and Nature's beauty rise;
While orient Phœbus with unborrow'd hues,

Cloaths the wak'd loveliness which all night slept
In heav'nly drapery! Darkness is fled.
Now flowers unfold their beauties to the sun,
And blushing, kiss the beam he sends to wake them,
The strip'd carnation, and the guarded rose,
The vulgar wall flow'r, and smart gillyflower,
The polyanthus mean—the dapper daizy,
Sweet William, and sweet marjoram,——and all
The tribe of single and of double pinks!
Now too, the feather'd warblers tune their notes
Around, and charm the listning grove.—The lark!
The linnet! chafinch! bullfinch! goldfinch! greenfinch!
——But O to me, no joy can they afford!
Nor rose, nor wall flow'r, nor smart gillyflower,
Nor polyanthus mean, nor dapper daizy,
Nor William sweet, nor marjoram—nor lark,
Linnet, nor all the finches of the grove!

Puff. Your white handkerchief madam——
Tilburina. I thought, Sir, I wasn't to use that 'till, "heart rending woe."
Puff. O yes madam—at "the finches of the grove," if you please.

Tilburina.   Nor lark,
    Linnet, nor all the finches of the grove!   [*Weeps.*

Puff. Vastly well madam!
Dangle. Vastly well indeed!

Tilburina. For, O too sure, heart rending woe is now
    The lot of wretched Tilburina!

Dangle. O!—'tis too much.
Sneer. Oh!——it is indeed.

Confidant. Be comforted sweet lady——for who knows,
    But Heav'n has yet some milk-white day in store.
Tilburina. Alas, my gentle Nora,
    Thy tender youth, as yet hath never mourn'd
    Love's fatal dart.—Else wouldst thou know, that when
    The soul is sunk in comfortless despair,
    It cannot taste of merryment.

Dangle. That's certain.

Confidant. But see where your stern father comes;
    It is not meet that he should find you thus.

Puff. Hey, what the plague!—what a cut is here!—why, what is become of the description of her first meeting with Don Wiskerandos? his gallant behaviour in the sea fight, and the simile of the canary bird?
Tilburina. Indeed Sir, you'll find they will not be miss'd.
Puff. Very well.—Very well!
Tilburina. The cue ma'am if you please.

Confidant. It is not meet that he should find you thus.
Tilburina. Thou counsel'st right, but 'tis no easy task
    For barefaced grief to wear a mask of joy.

Enter GOVERNOR.

Governor. How's this—in tears?——O Tilburina, shame!
    Is this a time for maudling tenderness,
    And Cupid's baby woes?——hast thou not heard
    That haughty Spain's Pope-consecrated fleet
    Advances to our shores, while England's fate,
    Like a clipp'd guinea, trembles in the scale!
Tilburina. Then, is the crisis of *my* fate at hand!
    I see the fleet's approach——I see——

Puff. Now, pray gentlemen mind.—This is one of the most useful figures we tragedy writers have, by which a hero or heroine, in consideration of their being often obliged to overlook things that *are* on the stage, is allow'd to hear and see a number of things that are not.
Sneer. Yes—a kind of poetical second-sight!
Puff. Yes—now then madam.

Tilburina.   I see their decks
    Are clear'd!——I see the signal made!
    The line is form'd!——a cable's length asunder!
    I see the frigates station'd in the rear;
    And now, I hear the thunder of the guns!
    I hear the victor's shouts——I also hear

The vanquish'd groan!——and now 'tis smoke——and now
I see the loose sails shiver in the wind!
I see——I see——what soon you'll see——
Governor. Hold daughter! peace! this love hath turn'd thy brain:
The Spanish fleet thou *canst* not see—because
——It is not yet in sight!

Dangle. Egad tho', the governor seems to make no allowance
for this poetical figure you talk of.
Puff. No, a plain matter-of-fact man—that's his character.

Tilburina. But will you then refuse his offer?
Governor. I must—I will—I can—I ought—I do.
Tilburina. Think what a noble price.
Governor. No more——you urge in vain.
Tilburina. His liberty is all he asks.

Sneer. All *who* asks Mr. Puff? Who is——
Puff. Egad Sir, I can't tell.—Here has been such cutting and
slashing, I don't know where they have got to myself.
Tilburina. Indeed Sir, you will find it will connect very well.

——And your reward secure.

Puff. O,—if they hadn't been so devilish free with their
cutting here, you would have found that Don Wiskerandos has
been tampering for his liberty, and has persuaded Tilburina to
make this proposal to her father—and now pray observe the
conciseness with which the argument is conducted. Egad, the
pro and con goes as smart as hits in a fencing match. It is indeed a
sort of small-sword logic, which we have borrowed from the
French.

Tilburina. A retreat in Spain!
Governor. Outlawry here!
Tilburina. Your daughter's prayer!
Governor. Your father's oath!
Tilburina. My lover!
Governor. My country!
Tilburina. Tilburina!
Governor. England!
Tilburina. A title!

Governor. Honor!
Tilburina. A pension!
Governor. Conscience!
Tilburina. A thousand pounds!
Governor. Hah! thou hast touch'd me nearly!

Puff. There you see——she threw in *Tilburina*, Quick, parry cart with *England!*—Hah! thrust in teirce a title!—parried by honor.—Hah! a pension over the arm!—put by by conscience. —Then flankonade with a thousand pounds—and a palpable hit egad!

Tilburina. Canst thou——
    Reject the *suppliant*, and the *daughter* too?
Governor. No more; I wou'd not hear thee plead in vain,
    The *father* softens—but the *governor*
    Is fix'd!   [*Exit.*

Dangle. Aye, that antithesis of persons—is a most establish'd figure.

Tilburina. 'Tis well,——hence then fond hopes,—fond passion hence;
    Duty, behold I am all over thine——
Wiskerandos [*without*]. Where is my love—my——
Tilburina. Ha!
Wiskerandos [*entering*]. My beauteous enemy——

Puff. O dear ma'am, you must start a great deal more than that; consider you had just determined in favour of duty—when in a moment the sound of his voice revives your passion,— overthrows your resolution, destroys your obedience.—If you don't express all that in your start—you do nothing at all.

Tilburina. Well, we'll try again!
Dangle. Speaking from within, has always a fine effect.
Sneer. Very.

Wiskerandos. My conquering Tilburina! How! is't thus
    We meet? why are thy looks averse! what means
    That falling tear——that frown of boding woe?
    Hah! now indeed I am a prisoner!
    Yes, now I feel the galling weight of these
    Disgraceful chains——which, cruel Tilburina!

Thy doating captive gloried in before——
But thou art false, and Wiskerandos is undone!
Tilburina. O no; how little dost thou know thy Tilburina!
Wiskerandos. Art thou then true? Begone cares, doubts and fears,
I make you all a present to the winds;
And if the winds reject you——try the waves.

Puff. The wind you know, is the established receiver of all
stolen sighs and cast off griefs and apprehensions.

Tilburina. Yet must we part?——stern duty seals our doom:
Though here I call yon conscious clouds to witness,
Could I pursue the bias of my soul,
All friends, all right of parents, I'd disclaim,
And thou, my Wiskerandos, should'st be father
And mother, brother, cousin, uncle, aunt,
And friend to me!
Wiskerandos. O matchless excellence!——and must we part?
Well, if——we must——we must—and in that case
The less is said the better.

Puff. Hey day! here's a cut!—What, are all the mutual pro-
testations out?
Tilburina. Now, pray Sir, don't interrupt us just here, you
ruin our feelings.
Puff. Your feelings!——but zounds, *my* feelings, ma'am !
Sneer. No; pray don't interrupt them.

Wiskerandos. One last embrace.——
Tilburina. Now,——farewell, for ever.
Wiskerandos. For ever!
Tilburina. Aye, for ever. [*Going.*

Puff. S'death and fury!—Gadslife! Sir! Madam, if you go
out without the parting look, you might as well dance out—
Here, here!
Confidant. But pray Sir, how am *I* to get off here?
Puff. You, pshaw! what the devil signifies how *you* get off!
edge away at the top, or where you will—[*Pushes the* CONFIDANT
off.] Now ma'am you see——
Tilburina. We understand you Sir.

Aye for ever.

Both. Ohh !   [*Turning back and exeunt. Scene closes.*

Dangle. O charming!

Puff. Hey!—'tis pretty well I believe—you see I don't attempt to strike out any thing new—but I take it I improve on the established modes.

Sneer. You do indeed.—But pray is not Queen Elizabeth to appear?

Puff. No not once—but she is to be talked of for ever; so that egad you'll think a hundred times that she is on the point of coming in.

Sneer. Hang it, I think its a pity to keep *her* in the green room all the night.

Puff. O no, that always has a fine effect—it keeps up expectation.

Dangle. But are we not to have a battle?

Puff. Yes, yes, you will have a battle at last, but, egad, it's not to be by land—but by sea—and that is the only quite new thing in the piece.

Dangle. What, Drake at the Armada, hey?

Puff. Yes, efaith—fire ships and all—then we shall end with the procession.—Hey! that will do I think.

Sneer. No doubt on't.

Puff. Come, we must not lose time—so now for the UNDER PLOT.

Sneer. What the plague, have you another plot?

Puff. O lord, yes—ever while you live, have two plots to your tragedy.—The grand point in managing them, is only to let your under plot have as little connexion with your main plot as possible—I flatter myself nothing can be more distinct than mine, for as in my chief plot, the characters are all great people—I have laid my under plot in low life—and as the former is to end in deep distress, I make the other end as happy as a farce.—Now Mr. Hopkins, as soon as you please.

Enter UNDER PROMPTER.

U. Prompter. Sir, the carpenter says it is impossible you can go to the Park scene yet.

Puff. The Park scene! No—I mean the description scene here in the wood.

U. Prompter. Sir, the performers have cut it out.

Puff. Cut it out!

U. Prompter. Yes Sir.

Puff. What! the whole account of Queen Elizabeth?

U. Prompter. Yes Sir.

Puff. And the description of her horse and side-saddle?

U. Prompter. Yes Sir.

Puff. So, so, this is very fine indeed! Mr. Hopkins, how the plague could you suffer this?

Hopkins [*from within*]. Sir, indeed the pruning knife——

Puff. The pruning knife—zounds the axe! why, here has been such lopping and topping, I shan't have the bare trunk of my play left presently.—Very well, Sir—the performers must do as they please, but upon my soul, I'll print it every word.

Sneer. That I would indeed.

Puff. Very well—Sir—then we must go on—zounds! I would not have parted with the description of the horse!—Well, Sir, go on—Sir, it was one of the finest and most laboured things—Very well, Sir, let them go on—there you had him and his accoutrements from the bit to the crupper—very well, Sir, we must go to the Park scene.

U. Prompter. Sir, there is the point, the carpenters say, that unless there is some business put in here before the drop, they shan't have time to clear away the fort, or sink Gravesend, and the river.

Puff. So! this is a pretty dilemma truly!—Gentlemen—you must excuse me, these fellows will never be ready, unless I go and look after them myself.

Sneer. O dear Sir—these little things will happen—

Puff. To cut out this scene!—but I'll print it—egad, I'll print it every word! [*Exeunt.*

END OF THE SECOND ACT

Act the Third

SCENE I

Before the Curtain.

Enter PUFF, SNEER, *and* DANGLE.

Puff. WELL, we are ready—now then for the justices. [*Curtain rises; Justices, Constables, &c. discovered.*

Sneer. This, I suppose, is a sort of senate scene.

Puff. To be sure—there has not been one yet.

Dangle. It is the under plot, isn't it?

Puff. Yes. What, gentlemen, do you mean to go at once to the discovery scene?

Justice. If you please, Sir.

Puff. O very well—harkee, I don't chuse to say any thing more, but efaith, they have mangled my play in a most shocking manner!

Dangle. It's a great pity!

Puff. Now, then, Mr. Justice, if you please.

Justice. Are all the volunteers without?
Constable.   They are.
    Some ten in fetters, and some twenty drunk.

Justice. Attends the youth, whose most opprobrious fame
    And clear convicted crimes have stampt him soldier?

Constable. He waits your pleasure; eager to repay
    The blest reprieve that sends him to the fields
    Of glory, there to raise his branded hand
    In honor's cause.

Justice.   'Tis well——'tis Justice arms him!
    O! may he now defend his country's laws
    With half the spirit he has broke them all!
    If 'tis your worship's pleasure, bid him enter.

Constable. I fly, the herald of your will.   [*Exit* CONSTABLE.

Puff. Quick, Sir!

Sneer. But, Mr. Puff, I think not only the Justice, but the clown seems to talk in as high a style as the first hero among them.

Puff. Heaven forbid they should not in a free country!—Sir, I am not for making slavish distinctions, and giving all the fine language to the upper sort of people.

Dangle. That's very noble in you indeed.

Enter JUSTICE'S LADY.

Puff. Now pray mark this scene.

Lady. Forgive this interruption, good my love;
    But as I just now past, a pris'ner youth
    Whom rude hands hither lead, strange bodings seiz'd
    My fluttering heart, and to myself I said,
    An if our TOM had liv'd, he'd surely been
    This stripling's height!

Justice. Ha! sure some powerful sympathy directs
    Us both——

Enter SON *and* CONSTABLE.

Justice. What is thy name?

Son. My name's TOM JENKINS—*alias,* have I none—
    Tho' orphan'd, and without a friend!

Justice. Thy parents?

Son. My father dwelt in Rochester——and was,
    As I have heard——a fishmonger——no more.

Puff. What, Sir, do you leave out the account of your birth, parentage and education?

Son. They have settled it so, Sir, here.

Puff. Oh! oh!

Lady. How loudly nature whispers to my heart!
    Had he no other name?

Son.   I've seen a bill
    Of his, sign'd *Tomkins,* creditor.

Justice. This does indeed confirm each circumstance
    The gypsey told!——Prepare!

Son. I do.

Justice. No orphan, nor without a friend ar't thou——
　　I am thy father, *here's* thy mother, *there*
　　Thy uncle——this thy first cousin, and those
　　Are all your near relations!
Mother. O ecstasy of bliss!
Son. O most unlook'd for happiness!
Justice. O wonderful event!
　　　　　　[They faint alternately in each others arms.

Puff. There, you see relationship, like murder, will out.

Justice. Now let's revive——else were this joy too much!
　　But come——and we'll unfold the rest within,
　　And thou my boy must needs want rest and food.
　　Hence may each orphan hope, as chance directs,
　　To find a father—where he least expects!　　　*[Exeunt.*

Puff. What do you think of that?
Dangle. One of the finest discovery-scenes I ever saw.—Why this under-plot would have made a tragedy itself.
Sneer. Aye, or a comedy either.
Puff. And keeps quite clear you see of the other.

　　　　Enter SCENEMEN, *taking away the Seats.*
Puff. The scene remains, does it?
Sceneman. Yes, Sir.
Puff. You are to leave one chair you know—But it is always awkward in a tragedy, to have you fellows coming in in your playhouse liveries to remove things—I wish that could be managed better.—So now for my mysterious yeoman.

　　　　　　Enter a BEEFEATER.
Beefeater. Perdition catch my soul but *I* do love thee.

Sneer. Haven't I heard that line before?
Puff. No, I fancy not—Where pray?
Dangle. Yes, I think there is something like it in Othello.
Puff. Gad? now you put me in mind on't, I believe there is—but that's of no consequence—all that can be said is, that two people happened to hit on the same thought—And Shakespeare made use of it first, that's all.

Sneer. Very true.

Puff. Now, Sir, your soliloquy—but speak more to the pit, if you please—the soliloquy always to the pit—that's a rule.

Beefeater. Tho' hopeless love finds comfort in despair,
  It never can endure a rival's bliss!
  But soft——I am observ'd.   [*Exit* BEEFEATER.

Dangle. That's a very short soliloquy.

Puff. Yes—but it would have been a great deal longer if he had not been observed.

Sneer. A moſt sentimental Beefeater that, Mr. Puff.

Puff. Hearke—I would not have you be too sure that he *is* a Beefeater.

Sneer. What a hero in disguise?

Puff. No matter—I only give you a hint—But now for my principal charaƈter—Here he comes—LORD BURLEIGH in person! Pray, gentlemen, ſtep this way—softly—I only hope the Lord High Treasurer is perfeƈt—if he is but perfeƈt!

Enter BURLEIGH, *goes slowly to a chair and sits.*

Sneer. Mr. Puff !

Puff. Hush! vaſtly well, Sir! vaſtly well! a moſt intereſting gravity!

Dangle. What, isn't he to speak at all?

Puff. Egad, I thought you'd ask me that—yes, it is a very likely thing—that a Miniſter in his situation, with the whole affairs of the nation on his head, should have time to talk!—but hush! or you'll put him out.

Sneer. Put him out! how the plague can that be, if he's not going to say any thing?

Puff. There's a reason! why his part is to *think*, and how the plague! do you imagine he can *think* if you keep talking?

Dangle. That's very true upon my word!

[BURLEIGH *comes forward, shakes his head, and exit.*

Sneer. He is very perfeƈt indeed—Now, pray what did he mean by that?

Puff. You don't take it?

Sneer. No; I don't upon my soul.

Puff. Why, by that shake of the head, he gave you to understand that even tho' they had more justice in their cause and wis-
dom in their measures—yet, if there was not a greater spirit
shown on the part of the people—the country would at last fall a
sacrifice to the hostile ambition of the Spanish monarchy.

Sneer. The devil!—did he mean all that by shaking his head?

Puff. Every word of it—If he shook his head as I taught him.

Dangle. Ah! there certainly is a vast deal to be done on the
stage by dumb show, and expression of face, and a judicious
author knows how much he may trust to it.

Sneer. O, here are some of our old acquaintance.

Enter HATTON *and* RALEIGH.

Sir Christopher. My niece, and *your* niece too!
       By heav'n! there's witchcraft in't——He could not else
       Have gain'd their hearts——But see where they approach;
       Some horrid purpose low'ring on their brows!

Sir Walter. Let us withdraw and mark them.   [*They withdraw.*

Sneer. What is all this?

Puff. Ah! here has been more pruning!—but the fact is, these
two young ladies are also in love with Don Whiskerandos.—
Now, gentlemen, this scene goes entirely for what we call SITUA-
TION and STAGE EFFECT, by which the greatest applause may be
obtained, without the assistance of language, sentiment or character: pray mark!

Enter the TWO NIECES.

1*st Niece.* Ellena here!
       She is his scorn as much as I—that is
       Some comfort still!

Puff. O dear madam, you are not to say that to her face!—
aside, ma'am, *aside.*—The whole scene is to be *aside.*

1*st Niece.* She is his scorn as much as I—that is
       Some comfort still!   [*Aside.*
2*nd Niece.* I know he prizes not Pollina's love,
       But Tilburina lords it o'er his heart.   [*Aside.*

1st Niece. But see the proud destroyer of my peace
    Revenge is all the good I've left.   [*Aside.*
2nd Niece. He comes, the false disturber of my quiet.
    Now vengeance do thy worst——   [*Aside.*

                        Enter WISKERANDOS.
Wiskerandos. O hateful liberty—if thus in vain
    I seek my Tilburina!
Both Nieces. And ever shalt!
                    SIR CHRISTOPHER *and* SIR WALTER *come forward.*
Sir Christopher and Sir Walter. Hold! we will avenge you.
Wiskerandos. Hold *you*——or see your nieces bleed!
        [*The two* NIECES *draw their two daggers to strike* WISKERAN-
        DOS, *the two* UNCLES *at the instant with their two swords
        drawn, catch their two nieces' arms, and turn the points of their
        swords to* WISKERANDOS, *who immediately draws two daggers,
        and holds them to the two nieces' bosoms.*]

Puff. There's situation for you! there's an heroic group!—
You see the ladies can't ſtab Whiskerandos—he durſt not ſtrike
them for fear of their uncles—the uncles durſt not kill him, because of their nieces—I have them all at a dead lock!—for every
one of them is afraid to let go firſt.
    Sneer. Why, then they muſt ſtand there for ever.
    Puff. So they would, if I hadn't a very fine contrivance for't
—Now mind——

                Enter BEEFEATER *with his Halberd.*
Beefeater. In the Queen's name I charge you all to drop
    Your swords and daggers!   [*They drop their swords and daggers.*

Sneer. That is a contrivance indeed.
Puff. Aye—in the Queen's name.

Sir Christopher. Come niece!
Sir Walter. Come niece!   [*Exeunt with the two* NIECES.
Wiskerandos. What's he, who bids us thus renounce our guard?
Beefeater. Thou must do more, renounce thy love!
Whiskerandos. Thou liest——base Beefeater!
Beefeater.   Ha! Hell! the lie!

By heav'n thou'st rous'd the lion in my heart!
Off yeoman's habit!—base disguise! off! off!
[*Discovers himself, by throwing off his upper dress, and appearing
in a very fine waistcoat.*]
Am I a Beefeater now ?
Or beams my crest as terrible as when
In Biscay's Bay I took thy captive sloop.

Puff. There, egad! he comes out to be the very Captain of the
privateer who had taken Whiskerandos prisoner—and was himself an old lover of Tilburina's.
Dangle. Admirably manag'd indeed.
Puff. Now, ſtand out of their way.

Whiskerandos. I thank thee fortune! that hast thus bestow'd
   A weapon to chastise this insolent.   [*Takes up one of the swords.*]
Beefeater. I take thy challenge, Spaniard, and I thank
   Thee Fortune too!—   [*Takes up the other sword.*]

Dangle. That's excellently contrived!—it seems as if the two
uncles had left their swords on purpose for them.
Puff. No, egad, they could not help leaving them.

Whiskerandos. Vengeance and Tilburina!
Beefeater.   Exactly so——
   [*They fight—and after the usual number of wounds given,* WHIS-
     KERANDOS *falls.*]
Whiskerandos. O cursed parry!——that last thrust in tierce
   Was fatal——Captain, thou hast fenced well!
   And Whiskerandos quits this bustling scene
   For all eter——
Beefeater.   —nity—He would have added, but stern death
   Cut short his being, and the noun at once!

Puff. O, my dear Sir, you are too slow, now mind me.—Sir,
shall I trouble you to die again?

Whiskerandos. And Whiskerandos quits this bustling scene
   For all eter——
Beefeater.   ——nity—He would have added——

Puff. No, Sir—that's not it—once more if you please—
Whiskerandos. I wish, Sir—you would practise this without me—I can't stay dying here all night.
Puff. Very well, we'll go over it by and bye—I must humour these gentlemen!   [*Exit* WHISKERANDOS.

Beefeater. Farewell——brave Spaniard! and when next——

Puff. Dear Sir, you needn't speak that speech as the body has walked off.
Beefeater. That's true, Sir—then I'll join the fleet.
Puff. If you please.   [*Exit* BEEFEATER.
Now, who comes on?

Enter GOVERNOR, *with his hair properly disordered.*
Governor. A hemisphere of evil planets reign!
  And every planet sheds contagious phrensy!
  My Spanish prisoner is slain! my daughter,
  Meeting the dead corse borne along——has gone
  Distract!   [*A loud flourish of trumpets.*
    But hark! I am summon'd to the fort,
  Perhaps the fleets have met! amazing crisis!
  O Tilburina! from thy aged father's beard
  Thou'st pluck'd the few brown hairs which time had left!
                    [*Exit* GOVERNOR.

Sneer. Poor gentleman!
Puff. Yes—and no one to blame but his daughter!
Dangle. And the planets——
Puff. True.—Now enter Tilburina!
Sneer. Egad, the business comes on quick here.
Puff. Yes, Sir—now she comes in stark mad in white satin.
Sneer. Why in white satin?
Puff. O Lord, Sir—when a heroine goes mad, she always goes into white satin—don't she, Dangle?
Dangle. Always—it's a rule.
Puff. Yes—here it is—(*looking at the book.*) 'Enter Tilburina stark mad in white satin, and her confidant stark mad in white linen.'

Enter TILBURINA *and* CONFIDANT *mad, according to custom.*

Sneer. But what the deuce, is the confidant to be mad too?

Puff. To be sure she is, the confidant is always to do whatever her mistress does; weep when she weeps, smile when she smiles, go mad when she goes mad.—Now madam confidant—but keep your madness in the back ground, if you please.

Tilburina. The wind whistles——the moon rises——see
    They have kill'd my squirrel in his cage!
Is this a grasshopper!——Ha! no, it is my
    Whiskerandos——you shall not keep him——
I know you have him in your pocket——
An oyster may be cross'd in love!——Who says
A whale's a bird?—Ha! did you call, my love?
——He's here! He's there!——He's every where!
Ah me! He's no where!   [*Exit* TILBURINA.

Puff. There, do you ever desire to see any body madder than that?

Sneer. Never while I live!

Puff. You observed how she mangled the metre?

Dangle. Yes—egad, it was the first thing made me suspect she was out of her senses.

Sneer. And pray what becomes of her?

Puff. She is gone to throw herself into the sea to be sure—and that brings us at once to the scene of action, and so to my catastrophe—my sea-fight, I mean.

Sneer. What you bring that in at last?

Puff. Yes—yes—you know my play is *called* the *Spanish Armada*, otherwise, egad, I have no occasion for the battle at all.—Now then for my magnificence!—my battle!—my noise!—and my procession!—You are all ready?

PROMPTER *within.*

Yes, Sir.

Puff. Is the Thames drest?

Enter THAMES *with two Attendants.*

Thames. Here I am, Sir.

Puff. Very well indeed—See, gentlemen, there's a river for you!—This is blending a little of the masque with my tragedy—a new fancy you know—and very useful in my case; for as there *must be a procession*, I suppose Thames and all his tributary rivers to compliment Britannia with a fete in honor of the victory.

Sneer. But pray, who are these gentlemen in green with him.

Puff. Those?—those are his banks.

Sneer. His banks?

Puff. Yes, one crown'd with alders and the other with a villa! —you take the allusions?—but hey! what the plague! you have got both your banks on one side—Here Sir, come round—Ever while you live, Thames, go between your Banks. (*Bell rings.*)—There, soh! now for't!—Stand aside my dear friends!—away Thames!

[*Exit* THAMES *between his banks.*

[*Flourish of drums—trumpets—cannon, &c. &c. Scene changes to the sea——the fleets engage——the musick plays 'Britons strike home.'—Spanish fleet destroyed by fire-ships, &c.— English fleet advances—musick plays 'Rule Britannia.'—The procession of all the English rivers and their tributaries with their emblems, etc. begins with Handels water musick, ends with a chorus, to the march in Judas Maccabæus.—During this scene,* PUFF *directs and applauds every thing——then*]

Puff. Well, pretty well—but not quite perfect—so ladies and gentlemen, if you please, we'll rehearse this piece again to-morrow.

CURTAIN DROPS.

END OF THIRD ACT

On the Text of *The Critic*

THERE is no doubt, not only because of its dedicatory letter to Mrs. Grenville, that the edition of *The Critic* printed in 1781 was authorized by Sheridan: for so he expressly told his second wife.[1] An attempt was made by Fraser Rae in *Sheridan's Plays as he Wrote Them* (1902) to discredit this edition on the grounds that Sheridan sanctioned no issue of any play except *The Rivals* (and *Pizarro*)—"All the other copies were reproductions of those used on the stage. Many changes had been made in them for histrionic purposes." In the case of *The Critic*, the differences between the Rae text[2] and the edition of 1781, though generally trivial, do at least establish the superior definiteness of the printed copy. For instance, in Mr. Puff's account of the Puff Direct (Act I, scene iii) these are the changes:

"Mr. Dodd was astonishingly great in the character *of young Mr. Something*" is corrected in the printed copy to "of Sir Harry" (i.e. Sir Harry Bouquet in *The Camp*).

"Mr. Palmer perhaps never appeared to more advantage" is corrected to "more advantage as the Colonel" (i.e. Colonel Lambert in *The Hypocrite*, then in rehearsal).

"Mr. Smatter or *Mr. Flimsey*" is corrected to "or Mr. Dapper."

"Mr. Loutherbourg's" is corrected to "Mr. de Loutherbourg's."

In Act II, scene ii, there are similar changes: Mr. Puff's exclamation about "three morning guns" is an addition by the printed copy, where "inconsolable to the minuet in *Ariadne*" replaces the less pointed "to the tune of the minuet in *Ariadne*." Again, in Act III, scene i, to the MS. "Enter Tilburina stark mad in white satin," the edition of 1781 adds, "and her confidant

---

[1] Sichel, *Sheridan*, vol. I, p. 511.
[2] This omits Act I, scenes i–ii.

241

ſtark mad in white linen." It would be tedious to record all these verbal improvements, but they do at leaſt eſtablish a careful and ſyſtematic revision.

However, the MS. preserves one passage of a purely domeſtic and transient intereſt which was judiciously suppressed in preparing the play for the press. At the original performance, the piece called upon the greater part of "the under aĉtors and servants of the company."[1] Among them were the Head Carpenter and the Maſter Lamplighter, who from the nature of their duties are very unlikely to have appeared after the firſt night. But in the MS. they appeared at the end of Aĉt II. The printed copy reads:

Und. Promp. Sir, there is the point, the carpenters say, that unless there is some business put in here before the drop, they shan't have time to clear away the Fort, or sink Gravesend, and the river.

Puff. So this is a pretty dilemma, truly! Gentlemen—you muſt excuse me, these fellows will never be ready, unless I go and look after them myself.

Sneer. O dear sir—these little things will happen——

Puff. To cut out this scene!—but I'll print it.—Egad, I'll print every word.

Inſtead of this the MS. reads:—

Und. Prom. Sir—there'sthe point—the Carpenters ſay that unless there is some Business put in here before the Drop, they shan't have time to clear away the Fort——

Puff. So! this is a pretty Dilemma, indeed—Do call the Head Carpenter to me.

Und. Promp. Mr. Butler—[*enter* CARPENTER *dress'd*]. Here he is Sir.

Puff. Hey—this is the Head Carpenter!

Und. Promp. Yes—Sir—He was to have walked as one of

[1]*The Lady's Magazine* for November, 1779.

the Generals at the Review—For the truth is your Tragedy employs everybody in the company.

Puff. O—then pray, Mr. General-Carpenter what is all this?

Carp. Why Sir, you only consider what my men have to do —they have to remove Tilbury Fort with the Cannon and to sink Gravesend and the River and I only desire three minutes to do it in.

Puff. Hah! and they've cut the Scene.

Carp. Besides if I could manage in less, I question if the Lamplighter could clear away the Sun in the time.

Puff. Do call one of them here.

Carp. Master Lamplighter!

[*Without*] Mr. Langley! [Lamplighter *without.*] Here! [*Enter* Lamplighter *as a River God and a Page holding up his train*].

Puff. Sir—your most obedient servant—Who the Devil's this!

Und. Promp. The master Lamplighter, Sir. He does one of the River Gods in the Procession.

Puff. O, a River God is he—well Sir you won't have time I understand——

L. Three minutes at least Sir—unless you have a mind to burn the Fort.

Puff. Hah! and they've cut out the Scene!

Carp. Lord Sir, there only wants a little business to be put in here—just as long as while we have been speaking will do it—

Puff. What then are you all ready now?

[*From behind.*] Yes all clear.

Puff. O then I shall easily manage it——

Und. Promp. Clear the Stage.

Puff. And do General keep a sharp look out and beg the River God not to spare his Oyl in the last scene—it must be brilliant. Gentlemen I beg a thousand Pardons.

Sneer. O dear Sir—these little things will happen. [*Exeunt.*

Michael Kelly says (in his *Reminiscences*, vol. II, p. 244) that on the laſt day but two before the firſt performance, Sheridan had not written "the laſt scene." By a trick King locked him in a room in the theatre with two bottles of claret and a dish of anchovy sandwiches, and there they kept him till he had written it. Apparently, the "laſt scene" meant the passage about the Thames and his banks, only part of which is found in the MS. as printed by Rae. The final ſtage-direction is omitted, so it is intereſting to read a summary of this in *The Lady's Magazine* of the month. "This tragedy rehearsal is concluded with a grand, beautiful, and very piƈturesque view of the Spanish and English fleets engaged, in which there are some very striking improvements of the ſtage-speƈtacle. Several of the ships are seen to move; and the fire-ships, which had so memorable an effeƈt in that engagement, which was one of the moſt important in the annals of mankind, were represented in a very natural manner. After the viƈtory is obtained, a procession of river gods, representing the principal rivers of England, takes place, which terminates in a general chorus,[1] and a dance by the river deities."

[1] The chorus was "the March in *Judas Maccabæus*," that is, "See the Conquering Hero comes."

The Burletta of Ixion

ABOUT the end of August, 1770, Sheridan received from his old schoolfellow, Nathaniel Brassey Halhed, the manuscript of a burletta entitled *Jupiter*, written on the model of Kane O'Hara's *Midas* (1764). After some weeks Sheridan, who had been invited to revise it, suggested the idea of "a rehearsal" to which Halhed agreed. It was not until the end of May, 1771, however, that Sheridan completed his revision under the title of *Ixion*, having remodelled the piece, not so much as an imitation of *The Rehearsal*, by the Duke of Buckingham (as everybody has said, from Moore to Mr. Sichel) but after the more recent example of *A Peep Behind the Curtain; or, the New Rehearsal*, by David Garrick (1767), which had incorporated the burletta of *Orpheus*. *Ixion* was submitted to Foote for the Haymarket, and rejected, meeting with the same fate a little later when sent to Garrick for Drury Lane. So says Mr. Sichel, though Moore thought it unlikely that the piece was presented to any of the managers, and he mentions a letter expressing fears that the small success which attended the production of "*Dido*,[1] on the same mythological plan" might prove "an obstacle to the reception of theirs." *Ixion*, however, has no importance except that it was the precursor of *The Critic*. In its characters are to be discerned, in Moore's phrase, "a sort of dim and shadowy pre-existence" of those in the comedy which was, ten years later, to delight the town. Simile the author is the precursor of Puff; O'Cul[lin] of Dangle; and Monopoly the manager (according to Mr. Sichel) of Sir Fretful Plagiary. Moore gave a number of excerpts from *Ixion* (*Sheridan*, pp. 13-19) here reproduced with part of his commentary:

"Their first joint production was a farce, or rather play, in three acts, called *Jupiter*, written in imitation of the burletta of

[1]The new burlesque Opera of Queen Dido was performed at the Theatre Royal in the Hay Market on the 24th instant... The story of this piece, which is written by the author of Homer Travesty, is taken from Cotton's Travesty of Virgil's Æneid"—*The Town and Country Magazine* for July, 1772. The author was Thomas Bridges.

Midas, whose popularity seems to have tempted into its wake a number of these musical parodies upon heathen fable. The amour of Jupiter with *Major* Amphitryon's wife, and *Sir Richard* Ixion's courtship of Juno, who substitutes *Miss Peggy Nubilis* in her place, form the subject of this ludicrous little drama, of which Halhed furnished the burlesque scenes,—while the form of a rehearsal, into which the whole is thrown, and which, as an anticipation of *The Critic* is highly curious, was suggested and managed entirely by Sheridan. The following extracts will give some idea of the humour of this trifle; and in the character of Simile the reader will at once discover a sort of dim and shadowy preexistence of Puff":

Simile. Sir, you are very ignorant on the subject,—it is the method most in vogue.

O'Cul. What! to make the music first, and then make the sense to it afterwards!

Sim. Just so.

Monop. What Mr. Simile says is very true, gentlemen; and there is nothing surprising in it, if we consider now the general method of writing *plays* to *scenes*.

O'Cul. Writing *plays* to *scenes!*—oh, you are joking.

Monop. Not I, upon my word. Mr. Simile knows that I have frequently a complete set of scenes from Italy, and then I have nothing to do but to get some ingenious hand to write a play to them.

Sim. I am your witness, Sir. Gentlemen, you perceive you know nothing about these matters.

O'Cul. Why, Mr. Simile, I don't pretend to know much relating to these affairs, but what I think is this, that in this method, according to your principles, you must often commit blunders.

Sim. Blunders! to be sure I must, but I always could get myself out of them again. Why, I'll tell you an instance of it.—You must know I was once a journeyman sonnet-writer to Signor Squallini. Now, his method, when seized with the *furor harmonicus* was constantly to make me sit by his side, while he was thrumming on his harpsichord, in order to make extempore verses to whatever air he should beat out to his liking. I remember, one morning, as he was in this situation, *thrum, thrum, thrum,* (*moving his fingers as if beating on the harpsichord*), ſtriking out something prodigiously great, as he thought,—"Hah!" said he, —"hah! Mr. Simile, *thrum, thrum, thrum,* by gar here is vary fine,—*thrum, thrum, thrum,* write me some words directly."—I durſt not interrupt him to ask on what subject, so inſtantly began to describe a fine morning.

"Calm was the land and calm the seas,
    And calm the heaven's dome serene,
Hush'd was the gale and hush'd the breeze,
    And not a vapour to be seen."

I sang it to his notes.—"Hah!" upon my vord vary pritt,—*thrum, thrum, thrum,*—ſtay, ſtay,—*thrum, thrum.*—Hoa! upon my vord, here it muſt be an adagio,—*thrum, thrum,*—oh! let it be an *Ode to Melancholy.*

Monop. The Devil!—there you were puzzled sure.

Sim. Not in the leaſt,—I brought in a *cloud* in the next ſtanza, and matters, you see, came about at once.

Monop. An excellent transition.

O'Cul. Vaſtly ingenious indeed.

Sim. Was it not? hey! it required a little command,—a little presence of mind,—but I believe we had better proceed.

Monop. The sooner the better,—come, gentlemen, resume your seats.

Sim. Now for it. Draw up the curtain, and (*looking at his book*) enter Sir Richard Ixion,—but ſtay,—zounds, Sir Richard ought to over-hear Jupiter and his wife quarrelling,—but, never mind, —these accidents have spoilt the division of my piece.—So enter Sir Richard, and look as cunning as if you had overheard them. Now for it, gentlemen,—you can't be too attentive.

Enter Sir Richard Ixion, *completely dressed, with bag, sword, &c.*

Ix. 'Fore George, at logger-heads,—a lucky minute,
'Pon honour, I may make my market in it.
Dem it, my air, address, and mien muſt touch her,

Now out of sorts with him,—less God than butcher.
O rat the fellow,—where can all his sense lie,
To gallify the lady so immensely?
Ah! *le grand bête qu'il est!*—how rude the bear is!
The world to two-pence he was ne'er at *Paris.*
Perdition ſtap my vitals,—now or never
I'll niggle snugly into Juno's favour.
Let's see,—(*looking in a glass*) my face,—toll loll—'twill work
upon her.
My person—oh, immense, upon my honour.
My eyes,—oh fie,—the naughty glass it flatters,—
Courage,—Ixion flogs the world to tatters.   [*Exit Ixion.*

Sim. There is a fine gentleman for you,—in the very pink of
the mode, with not a single article about him his own,—his
words pilfered from Magazines, his address from French valets,
and his clothes not paid for.

Macd. But pray, Mr. Simile, how did Ixion get into heaven?

Sim. Why, Sir, what's that to any body?—perhaps by Sal-
moneus's Brazen Bridge, or the Giant's Mountain, or the Tower
of Babel, or on Theobald's bull-dogs, or—who the devil cares
how?—he is there and that's enough.

.　　　.　　　.　　　.　　　.　　　.

Sim. Now for a Phœnix of a song.

Song by JUPITER.

You dogs, I'm Jupiter Imperial,
King, Emperor, and Pope ætherial,
Maſter of th' Ordnance of the sky.—

Sim. Z——ds, where's the ordnance? Have you forgot the
piſtol? [*to the Orcheſtra*].

Orcheſtra [*to some one behind the scenes*]. Tom, are not you prepared?

Tom [*from behind the scenes*]. Yes, Sir, but I flash'd in the pan a
little out of time, and had I ſtaid to prime, I should have shot a
bar too late.

Sim. Oh then, Jupiter, begin the song again.—We muſt not
lose our ordnance.

You dogs, I'm Jupiter Imperial,
King, Emperor, and Pope ætherial,
Master of th' Ordnance of the sky; &c. &c.
[*Here a pistol or cracker is fired from behind the scenes.*

Sim. This hint I took from Handel.—Well, how do you think we go on?
O'Cul. With vast spirit,—the plot begins to thicken.
Sim. Thicken! aye,—'twill be as thick as the calf of your leg presently. Well, now for the real, original, patentee Amphitryon. What, ho, Amphitryon! Amphitryon!—'tis Simile calls.—Why, where the devil is he?

Enter SERVANT.
Monop. Tom, where is Amphitryon?
Sim. Zounds, he's not arrested too, is he?
Serv. No, Sir, but there was but one black eye in the house, and he is waiting to get it from Jupiter.
Sim. To get a black eye from Jupiter,—oh, this will never do. Why, when they meet, they ought to match like two beef-eaters.

"According to their original plan for the conclusion of this farce, all things were at last to be compromised between Jupiter and Juno; Amphitryon was to be comforted in the birth of so mighty a son; Ixion, for his presumption, instead of being fixed to a *torturing* wheel, was to have been fixed to a vagrant mono-troche, as knife-grinder, and a grand chorus of deities (inter-mixed with "knives, scissors, pen-knives to grind," set to music as nearly as possible to the natural cry,) would have concluded the whole."

JOHNNY M'CREE

Moore adds: "It does not appear, however, that Sheridan ever actually presented this piece to any of the managers; and indeed it is probable, from the following fragment of a scene found among his papers, that he soon abandoned the ground-work of Halhed altogether, and transferred his plan of a rehearsal to some other subject, of his own invention and, therefore, more worthy of his wit. It will be perceived that the puffing author was here intended to be a Scotchman."

M. Sir, I have read your comedy, and I think it has infinite merit, but, pray, don't you think it rather grave?

S. Sir, you say true; it *is* a grave comedy. I follow the opinion of Longinus, who says comedy ought always to be sentimental. Sir, I value a sentiment of six lines in my piece no more than a nabob does a rupee. I hate those dirty, paltry equivocations, which go by the name of puns, and pieces of wit. No, Sir, it ever was my opinion that the stage should be a place of rational entertainment; instead of which I am very sorry to say, most people go there for their diversion; accordingly, I have formed my comedy so that it is no laughing, giggling piece of work. He must be a very light man that shall discompose his muscles from the beginning to the end.[1]

M. But don't you think it may be too grave?

S. O never fear; and as for hissing, mon, they might as well hiss the common prayer-book; for there is the viciousness of vice and the virtuousness of virtue in every third line.

M. I confess there is a great deal of moral in it; but, Sir, I should imagine if you tried your hand at tragedy——

S. No, mon, there you are out, and I'll relate to you what put me first on writing a comedy. You must know I had composed a very fine tragedy about the valiant Bruce. I showed it my Laird of Mackintosh, and he was a very candid mon, and he said my genius did not lie in tragedy: I took the hint, and, as soon as I got home, began my comedy.

"We have here," says Moore, "some of the very thoughts and words, that afterwards contributed to the fortune of Puff; and it is amusing to observe how long this subject was played with by the current of Sheridan's fancy, till at last, like 'a stone of lustre from the brook' it came forth with all that smoothness and polish, which it wears in his inimitable farce, *The Critic*."

But Moore (and everybody else) has overlooked a curious

[1] In this sentence "clearly lurks *The Critic* in embryo."—Sichel, *Sheridan*, vol. I, p.29.

circumstance. Speaking in the House of Commons in 1805, concerning the appointment of Lord Melville as First Lord of the Admiralty, Sheridan said:—

"It may be said, that as the Noble Lord was so unfit for the military department, the naval was the proper place for him. Perhaps there were people who would adopt this whimsical reasoning. I remember a story told respecting Mr. Garrick, who was once applied to by an eccentric Scotchman, to introduce a production of his on the stage. This Scotchman was such a good-humoured fellow, that he was called 'Honest Johnny M'Cree.' Johnny wrote four acts of a tragedy, which he showed to Mr. Garrick, who dissuaded him from finishing it; telling him that his talent did not lie that way; so Johnny abandoned the tragedy, and set about writing a comedy. When this was finished, he showed it to Mr. Garrick, who found it to be still more exceptionable than the tragedy, and of course could not be persuaded to bring it forward on the stage. This surprised poor Johnny, and he remonstrated. 'Nay, now, David (said Johnny), did you not tell me that my talents did not lie in tragedy?'—'Yes (replied Garrick), but I did not tell you that they lay in comedy.'—'Then (exclaimed Johnny), gin they dinna lie there, where the de'il dittha lie, mon?' Unless the Noble Lord at the head of the Admiralty has the same reasoning in his mind as Johnny M'Cree, he cannot possibly suppose that his incapacity for the direction of the War-department necessarily qualifies him for the Presidency of the Naval. Perhaps, if the Noble Lord be told that he has no talents for the latter, His Lordship may exclaim with honest Johnny M'Cree, 'Gin they dinna lie there, where the de'il dittha lie, mon?' "[1]

This fragment is then, only the story of "Honest Johnny M'Cree" put into dialogue. If the anecdote is genuine—was there such a man?—it might be dated about 1776 or 1777, when Sheridan had become known to Garrick. Perhaps, therefore, this is the actual germ to *The Critic*, which reminded Sheridan of his forgotten burletta.

[1] Quoted by Moore, *Sheridan*, pp. 612-3.

Richard Cumberland as Sir Fretful Plagiary

SIR FRETFUL PLAGIARY, said *The Lady's Magazine* for October, 1779, "exhibits one of the most harsh and severe caricatures that have been attempted since the days of Aristophanes, of which a celebrated sentimental writer is evidently the object: a great part of what is said by his representative being literally taken from his usual conversation, but with pointed and keen additions." This leaves no doubt that his contemporaries generally understood that Plagiary was intended as a caricature of Richard Cumberland.[1] Of the numerous testimonies as to the vain and sensitive nature of this once-famous dramatist, none is more telling than his own unintentional evidence in *The Memoirs of Richard Cumberland*, "Written by Himself" (1807). While these reminiscences have often been cited, the most striking and direct instance seems never to have been noticed. Where Dangle recounts an imaginary critique upon Plagiary, Sheridan was just staging something "taken from life," a trick actually played upon Cumberland. As the joker was David Garrick, there can be no doubt that the story went the rounds of green-rooms and lobbies, clubs and drawing-rooms, so that it would instantly be recognized by the "first-nighters" at

---

[1] Of course, the identification was not always so pointed. For example: "These Characters are introduced at Dangle's Theatrical Levee, and are succeeded by Sir Fretful Plagiary, whose Name is a Definition of himself. Upon him the Author seems to have employed the whole Force and finest Powers of his Wit.—He is at once original and striking. With an affected Candour he importunes his Friends for Comments which his Vanity has predetermined him to reject. His false Humanity is at perpetual Variance with his real Arrogance; and while this wou'd-be Stoic of Parnassus affects to be above all petty Censure, and even to be diverted by it, he becomes doubly ridiculous by betraying the meanest Subservience to those very Passions which he most affects not to feel.— Whether Sir Fretful Plagiary is drawn from Nature, or is only the Coinage of Fancy, we will not determine; but if the former is the Case, this Original certainly bids as fair for an enduring Ridicule as Dryden in Bayes."—*The Public Advertiser*, November 1, 1779.

The Critic. After *The West Indian* was first performed at Drury Lane in 1771, Cumberland was eager to collect the verdicts upon his new comedy. His *Memoirs* record

I paid respectful attention to all the floating criticisms, that came within my reach, but I found no opportunities of profiting by their remarks, and very little cause to complain of their personalities; in short I had more praise than I merited, and less cavilling than I expected. One morning when I called upon Mr. Garrick I found him with the St. James's evening paper in his hand, which he began to read with a voice and action of surprise, most admirably counterfeited, as if he had discovered a mine under my feet, and a train to blow me up to destruction——"Here, here," he cried, "if your skin is less thick than a rhinoceros's hide, egad, here is that will cut you to the bone. This is a terrible fellow; I wonder who it can be."—— He began to sing out his libel in a high declamatory tone, with a most comic countenance, and pausing at the end of the first sentence, which seemed to favour his contrivance for a little ingenious tormenting, when he found he had hooked me, he laid down the paper, and began to comment upon the cruelty of newspapers, and moan over me with a great deal of malicious fun and good humour—'Confound these fellows, they spare nobody. I dare say this is Bickerstaff again;[1] but you don't mind him; a little galled, but not much hurt: you may stop his mouth with a golden gag, but we'll see how he goes on.'—He then resumed his reading, cheering me all the way as it began to soften, till winding up in the most profest panegyric, of which he was himself the writer, I found my friend had had his joke, and I had enjoyed his praise, seasoned and set off, in his inimitable manner, which to be comprehended must have been seen.

Cumberland's sensitiveness to criticism made Garrick call him "the man without a skin." Whoever ventured to speak any-

[1] Cumberland attributed the failure of his Comic Opera, *A Summer's Day* (Covent Garden, 1765) to the attacks directed by his "rival" Bickerstaff whom he tried to bribe into silence—though he puts it more self-righteously than that! (*Memoirs*, vol. I, pp. 250-253). There speaks the authentic voice of Sir Fretful.

thing of him but praise was actuated by envy, malice, ignorance, and all uncharitableness. He had written, a few years before, a comedy called *The Fashionable Lover* (1772),—"a genteel comedy in the style they have lately tried to run down, the true sentimental." His conversation must then have often expatiated upon its merits, for five-and-thirty years afterwards he was still resentful of its failure:—

I have been reading it over with attention, and so many years have passed since I wrote it, that I have very little of the feeling of the author when I speak of it. I rather think I was right in giving it the preference to *The West-Indian*, though I am far from sure I was unprejudiced in my judgment at that time. An author, who is conscious that his new work will not be equally popular with his preceding one, will be very apt to imitate the dealer, who, having a pair of horses to sell, will bestow all his praise upon the worst, and leave the best to recommend himself. I verily believe if *The Fashionable Lover* was not my composition, and I were called upon to give my opinion of it (speaking only of its merits, and reserving to myself my opinion of its faults) I should be inclined to say it was a drama of a moral, grave and tender cast, inasmuch as I discovered in it sentiments, laudably directed against national prejudice, breach of trust, seduction, gaming, and the general dissipation of the time then present. I could not deny it a preference to *The West-Indian* in a moral light, and perhaps, if I were in very good humour with its author, I might be tempted to say that in point of diction it approached very nearly to what I conceived to be the true style of comedy—*Joca non infra soccum, seria non usque cothurnum.*

At the time when this play came out, the demands of the stage for novelty were much limited, and of course the excluded many had full leisure to wreak their malice on the selected few. I was silly enough to be in earnest and make serious appeal against cavillers and slanderers below notice: this induced my friend Garrick to call me the man without a skin, and sure enough I should have been without a skin, if the newspaper beadles could have had their will of me, for I conſtantly ſtood out againſt them, and would never ask quarter. I have been long since convinced of my folly, but I am not at all ashamed of my principle, for I always made common cause with my contemporaries, and never separated my own particular interestſ from those of literature in general, as will in part appear by the following paragraph, extraᷓ ed from the advertisement, which I prefixed to this comedy on its publication—"*Whether the reception of this comedy,*" I therein say, "*may be such as shall encourage me to future efforts is of small consequence to the public, but if it should chance to obtain some little credit with the candid part of mankind, and its author for once escape without those personal and unworthy aspersions, which writers, who hide their own names, fling on them, who publish their's, my success, it may be hoped, will draw forth others to the undertaking with far superior requisites; and that there are numbers under this description, whose sensibility keeps them silent, I am well persuaded when I consider how general it is for men of the fineſt parts to be subjeᷓ to the fineſt feelings; and I would submit whether this unhandsome praᷓ ice of abuse is not calculated to create in the minds of men of genius not only a disinclination to engage in dramatic compositions, but a languid and unanimated manner of executing them, &c. &c.—*"

But it was not only that "filthy neſt of vipers," as Cumberland ſtyled the newspaper critics, who attacked Cumberland's comedy. Oliver Goldsmith[1] is said to have been the writer (though it is not clear whether Cumberland knew this) of "An Essay on the Theatre; or, a Comparison between the Laughing and sentimental Comedy," in *The Weſtminſter Magazine* for December, 1772. It was partly direᷓ ed againſt *The Fashionable Lover*. Dis-

[1]"At this time I did not know Oliver Goldsmith even by person; I think our first meeting chanced to be at the British-Coffee-House; when we came together, we very speedily coalesced, and I believe he forgave me for all the little fame I had got by the success of my *West-Indian*, which had put him to some trouble, for it was not his nature to be unkind, and I had soon an opportunity of convincing him how incapable I was of harbouring resentment, and how zealously I took my share in what concerned his interest and reputation. That he was fantastically and whimsically vain all the world knows, but there was no settled and inherent malice in his heart."—*Memoirs*, vol. I, p. 379.

cussing his own comedy, *The Choleric Man* (1774), Cumberland wrote:—

> Whilst I was at Bath the rehearsals were going on, and the play was brought upon the stage during my absence. It succeeded to the utmost of my wishes, but when I perceived that the malevolence of the public prints suffered no abatement, and saw myself charged with having vented contemptuous and illiberal speeches in the theatre, where I could not have been, against productions of my contemporaries, which I had neither heard nor seen, galled with such false and cruel aspersions, which, under the pressure of my recent losses and misfortunes, fell on me with accumulated asperity, I was induced to retort upon my defamers, and accordingly prefixed to the printed copy of my comedy *a Dedication to Detraction*, in which I observe that *Ill-health and other melancholy attentions, which I need not explain, kept me at a distance from the scene of its decision.*—The chief object of this dedication was directed to a certain tract then in some degree of circulation, entitled *An Essay on the Theatre*, in which the writer professes to draw *a comparison between laughing and sentimental Comedy*, and under the latter description particularly points his observations at *The Fashionable Lover.*—There is no occasion for me to speak further of this dedication, as it is attached to the comedy, which is yet in print, except to observe that I can still repeat with truth what I there assert to my imaginary patron, that *I can take my conscience to witness I have paid him no sacrifice, devoted no time or study to his service, nor am a man in any respect qualified to repay his favours—*.[1]

There is, therefore, no doubt that Sir Fretful Plagiary was a caricature of Cumberland.[2] But why did Sheridan give this "Aristophanic" portrait, so alien from his usual methods, though of course, in a manner made familiar by the numerous personal

---

[1] *Memoirs* (vol. I, pp. 379-380).

[2] His contemporaries "gave a name" to Dangle, who is supposed to have been a theatrical amateur named Vaughan. But to identify Sneer with William Woodfall, the dramatic critic, is merely silly.

"takings-off" of Foote? Tradition associates the origin with Cumberland's behaviour at a performance of *The School for Scandal*. In his *Memoirs*, Cumberland (though nowhere hinting that he knew of this tradition) positively and credibly denied that he saw Sheridan's comedy on the first night, or during its first season:—

I solemnly protest that I have never written, or caused to be written, a single line to puff and praise myself, or to decry a brother dramatist, since I had life; of all such anonymous and mean manoeuvres I am clearly innocent and proudly disdainful; I have stood firm for the corps, into which I enrolled myself, and never disgraced my colours by abandoning the cause of the *legitimate comedy*, to whose service I am sworn, and in whose defence I have kept the field for nearly half a century, till at last I have survived all true national taste, and lived to see buffoonery, spectacle, and puerility so effectually triumph, that now to be repulsed from the stage is to be recommended to the closet, and to be applauded by the theatre is little else than a passport to the puppet-show. I only say what every body knows to be true: I do not write from personal motives, for I have no more cause for complaint than is common to many of my brethren of the corps. It is not my single misfortune to have been accused of vanity, which I did not feel, of satires, which I did not write, and of invectives, which I disdained even to meditate. It stands recorded of me in a review to this hour, that on the first night of *The School for Scandal* I was overheard in the lobby endeavouring to decry and cavil at that excellent comedy: I gave my accuser proof positive, that I was at Bath during the time of its first run, never saw it during its first season, and exhibited my pocket-journal in confirmation of my alibi: the gentleman was convinced of my innocence, but as he had no opportunity of correcting his libel, every body that read it remains convinced of my guilt. Now as none, who ever heard my name, will fail to suppose I must have said what is imputed to me in bitterness of heart, not from defect in head, this false aspersion of my character was cruel and injurious in the extreme. I hold it right to explain that the reviewer I am speaking of has been long since dead.

Despite this carefully worded disclaimer, there must have been something behind the story about Cumberland and *The School for Scandal*, which, told with several variations, has always the same ending. In his book *The School for Wits* (1815), dedicated, by the way, to Sheridan, one version is given by Ralph Wewitzer[1] the Comedian:—

> When *The School for Scandal* was first performed, Mr. Cumberland sat in the front of the stage-box with the most complete apathy, its wit and humour never affecting his risible muscles. This being reported to Mr. Sheridan, he observed, "That was very ungrateful, for I am sure I laughed heartily at his tragedy of *The Battle of Hastings*."[2]

As the tragedy was *The Battle of Hastings*, the incident which gave rise to the story could not have happened on the first night of *The School for Scandal*, for Cumberland's piece was not performed till January 24th, 1778, at Drury Lane. It had been accepted by Sheridan either on Garrick's advice, or, perhaps, like Shirley's *The Roman Sacrifice*, as a legacy from Garrick's management. In *The Private Correspondence of David Garrick* (vol. I, pp. 281-5) there are four letters endorsed by Garrick "Mr. Cumberland's letters to me about *The Battle of Hastings*—a true pic-

---

[1]Wewitzer, the original Lopez in *The Duenna*, was not a member of the Drury Lane company till 1787, when he made a great success as Moses in *The School for Scandal*.
[2]Kelly's version has Sheridan's authority; according to *The Reminiscences of Michael Kelly* (1826), vol. II, p. 135, when *The School for Scandal* "came out" Cumberland's children persuaded him to take them to see it from the stage-box. Their father sat by them, and each time they laughed, he pinched them, saying, "What are you laughing at, my dear little folks? You should not laugh, my angels, there is nothing to laugh at!" Then he added in an undertone, "Keep still, you little dunces." When the incident was rehearsed to Sheridan, he replied: "It was ungrateful of Cumberland to have been displeased with his children for laughing at my comedy, for when I went to see his tragedy I laughed from beginning to end."
A third version is told in *Sheridan's Works* (Greenock, 1828) but this is clearly a picturesque elaboration. It declares that after "the first night," Sheridan enquired what Cumberland said about the play. "Not a syllable," was the answer. "But did he seem amused?" "Why, faith, he might have hung up beside Uncle Oliver's picture: he had the damned disinheriting countenance. Like the ladies and gentlemen on the walls, he never moved a muscle." "Devilish ungrateful that," said Sheridan, "for I sat out his tragedy last week, and laughed from beginning to end."

ture of the man." Between the lines they show that Cumberland, so continually protesting about his tact and good-humour, had some trouble with the players and with Sheridan—who, perhaps, had never read the play. Cumberland wrote to Garrick (? January 5, 1778)[1]

> I read the tragedy in the ears of the performers on Friday morning; I was highly flattered by my audience, but your successor in management is not a representative of your polite attention to authors on such occasions. He came in yawning at the fifth act, with no other apology than having sate up two nights running. It gave me not the least offence, as I put it all to habit of dissipation and indolence; but I fear his office will suffer for want of due attention, and the present drop upon the theatre justifies my apprehensions.

It seems likely that Cumberland annoyed Sheridan intolerably during the rehearsals of *The Battle of Hastings*; so much so that no other play of his was produced at Drury Lane for nearly seven years, although six of them were staged at Covent Garden. "Your imitations of Shakespeare resemble the mimicry of Falstaff's page, and are about as near the standard of the original" might have been a contemporary verdict upon *The Battle of Hastings*, for *The Town and Country Magazine* for January, 1778, said, "Mr. Cumberland's language seems above the common altitude of dramatic poetry; he aims too much at the sublime that the gods themselves were often incapable of understanding him. He has stuck so close to Shakespeare that he frequently forgets himself." It must be concluded therefore that the caricature was provoked by Cumberland's conduct over *The Battle of Hastings*.

[1] *The Battle of Hastings* had previously been rejected by Covent Garden. Peake, *Memoirs of the Colman Family* (vol. I, pp. 417-418), prints a letter of September, 1776, from Cumberland to the elder Colman concerning this rejection, which is pure Sir Fretful. While Cumberland disclaim "presumption enough in my own behalf to say that they are not warranted in what they have done," he insists, "At the same time I would in no period of my life desert what may prove to be for the interests of literature in general, what ridicule soever may fall upon me in the upshot. In this light I ask you, as a scholar and an author of genius, if you have any objection to read and judge my piece. . . . My tragedy cost me great pains and much attention; hath been many years in hand; is entirely original in plan, popular in its subject, and free of all imitation. The opinions of men exceedingly high in the republic of letters have been unanimous, and more than warmly, in its favour."

Bibliography of *The Critic*.

GENUINE editions of *The Critic* should not be confused with *The Critic, or Tragedy Rehearsed*. 1780. 8vo, a Literary Catchpenny (Allardyce Nicoll *XVIII Century Drama*, 1750–1800, p. 323) or *The Critic, or, a Tragedy Rehearsed*. By the Author of *The Duenna*. London. S. Bladon. 1780. 8vo, a political satire.

I.—EDITIONS BY BECKET

The Critic; or, A Tragedy Rehearsed. A Dramatic Piece in three Acts, As it is performed at the Theatre Royal in Drury Lane. By Richard Brinsley Sheridan Esqr. London: Printed for T. Becket. Adelphi, Strand, MDCCLXXXI.

Pagination. P. [1] half-title. *The Critic; or, a Tragedy Rehearsed. Price One Shilling and Sixpence.* p. [2] blank; p. [i] title; p. [ii] blank; pp. iii–iv, *Dedication to Mrs. Greville*; pp.[iv–v] *Prologue*; pp. [vi–vii] *Dramatis Personæ*; p. viii blank; pp. [1]–2–98 text.

Fraser Rae and others have disputed the authenticity of this edition, and denied its authority. They are quite wrong, as the Dedication to Mrs. Greville signed " R. B. Sheridan" should have proved. Moreover, Sheridan presented copies to his friends: "In the library of Mr. Henry Bohn there exists a presentation copy to one of the Duke of Marlborough's family, with the undoubted autograph of the author," says Sigmund in his preface (p. 87) to *Sheridan's Works* (1848). Another was inscribed "To Stella from the Author," this being the name by which he and Mrs. Sheridan called the Duchess of Rutland (see *The Booklover's Leaflet*, No. 239, Pickering and Chatto, 1927). Great caution must be exercised in dealing with editions of *The Critic*, as the same engraved title page was used by Becket for a long period: and in most cases the half-title has been removed from the copies. For instance, an edition of 96 pp. is printed on paper watermarked 1795. In this instance the title page has in small letters at the foot: *S. J. Neele, Sculpt., Strand.*

The Critic. The Second Edition. London: Becket 1781. 8vo.

Without the half-title, it is impossible to distinguish a first edition from a second of this play. Both have the same number of pages (98)—Sichel, *Sheridan*, vol. II, p. 452.

The Critic. The Third Edition. London: Becket. 1781. 8vo.

The Critic. The Fourth Edition. London: Becket. 1781. 8vo.

The Critic. The Fifth Edition. London: Becket. 1781. 8vo.

The Critic. The Sixth Edition. London: Becket. 1781. 8vo.

All the above editions are from Sichel, *Sheridan*, vol. II, p. 452. They are to be distinguished by the half-titles, and I have not examined copies with these, since they are usually removed. The whole question requires further investigation, as the dates (from the engraved title-pages) are undoubtedly incorrect in the later issues.

The Critic. A New Edition. London: Becket. 1781. 8vo. [1795].

[This edition has 96 pages. It is printed on paper watermarked 1795; the title-page bears the name of the engravers, S. J. Neele. "A New Edition" appears only on the half-title.]

The Critic. London: Becket. 1808. 8vo.

The Critic. London: Becket and Porter. 1811. 8vo.

[Apparently a copy of this edition supplied the text for the Oxford Edition (1906).]

2.—OTHER LONDON EDITIONS

The Critic. London: Cawthorne. 1807. 12mo.

[Issued in wrappers. Usually bound in Cawthorne's *Minor Theatre*, vol. VI.]

The Critic. London. 1814. 16mo.

[Issued in blue wrappers. Usually bound in Dibden's *The London Theatre*, Vol. VIII.]

The Critic. Marked with the stage-business. London: Simpkin and Marshall. 1820. 12mo.

[Issued in wrappers as a number of *Oxberry's New British Drama*. Usually bound in vol. IX.]

The Critic, or A Tragedy Rehearsed . . . Printed from the Acting Copy. London. John Cumberland [1827].

[Issued in wrappers as No. 99 of Cumberland's *British Theatre*. Frontispiece of Jones as Puff. Preface by D—— G. (George Daniel).]

The interest of this text lies in its abbreviations and additions. In order to reduce it to two acts, the operatic audition is omitted, as no doubt had long been the case, and the tragedy is considerably shortened. On the other hand, a large number of actor's "gags," most of which became traditional, are added. These are specimens:—

I

Puff. Well, well. They are in general very good judges; and I know I am luxuriant. Gentlemen, be seated. [SNEER *and* DANGLE *sit.*] Now, Mr. Wodarch [*To Leader of the Band*] *please to play a few bars of something soft, just to prepare the audience for the curtain's rising.*

[*The Band strike* 'Bobbing Joan,' *very forte.*

Puff. [*Having stopped them with much difficulty.*] Now, really, gentlemen, this is unkind. I ask you to play a soothing air and you strike up Bobbing Joan! [*To* SNEER, &c.] The gentlemen will have their joke at rehearsal, you see. [*To Orchestra.*] Come, gentlemen, oblige me. [*The Band play a few bars of soft music.*] Aye, that's right,—for we have the scenes, and dresses; egad, we'll go to it, as if it was the first night's performance; but you need not mind stopping between the acts.

II

Sir. W. O, most accomplish'd Christopher, I find Thy fears are just.
Sir C. But where, whence, when, what, *which, and whose,*
The danger is—methinks, I fain would learn.
Sir W. You know, my friend, scarce two revolving suns—
Puff. [*Stopping him*] *Suit the word to the action, and the action to the word.*
You know, my friend, scarce two revolving suns."
[*Passes his hands one over the other, with a circular motion.*
Sir W. [*using the same action*]. You know, my friend, scarce two revolving suns,
"And three revolving moons,"—
Puff. No, no: *send your moons the other way, or you'll bring about an eclipse!*
[*Repeats the same lines again the second time, turning his hands the contrary way.*
Sir W. [*using Puff's action*]. You know, my friend scarce two revolving suns,
And three revolving moons, have closed their course,
Since haughty Philip, in despite of peace,
With hostile hand hath struck at England's trade.

III

Til. 'Tis well,—hence then, fond hopes,—fond passion, hence;
Duty, behold I am all over thine—
Whis. [*without*]. *Where is my love—my—behind!*
Puff. My *what?*—What's that, Mr. Penson?

Enter WHISKERANDOS.

Puff. Have the goodness to let me hear that line again?
Whis. *Where is my love—my behind?*
Puff. No, no, sir—' *Where is my love—my—behind the scenes* '—spoken behind the scenes.
Whis. Oh, I beg pardon, sir, but I assure you it is written so in my part. [*Exit.*

Enter WHISKERANDOS.

Whis. Where is my love—my—beauteous enemy.
[The speeches and directions here printed in italics are interpolations].

3.—DUBLIN EDITIONS

The Critic; or, a Tragedy Rehearsed. A Dramatic Piece of Three Acts. As it is performed at the Theatre Royal, in Drury Lane. By Richard Brinsley Sheridan, Esq. Dublin: Printed for Messrs. Sheppard, Wilkinson, [and others]. MDCCXXXI.

12mo.

Pagination. P.[i] Half title. *The Critic; or, a Tragedy Rehearsed*; p. [ii] blank; p. [iii] title; p. [iv] blank; pp. [v] + vi Dedication; pp. [vi–vii] Prologue; p. [ix] *Dramatis Personæ*; p. [x] blank; pp. [1] + 2–61 text; p. 62 blank.

Not recorded by Sichel. Copy belonging to R. Crompton Rhodes. [Others in National Library, Dublin; Municipal Library, Dublin; Trinity College, Dublin.—E.R.McC.D.]

The Critic. Dublin: Sheppard. 1785. 12mo.

The Critic. Dublin: Printed for J. Rice. No. 5, College Green. M.DCCX.

12mo. pp. 60.

[Copies in Bradshaw Collection, Cambridge University Library and Municipal Library, Dublin.—E.R.McC.D. [Not recorded by Sichel.]

The Critic. Dublin: Printed by William Porter, for William Jones, No. 86, Dame-Street. MDCCXCIII.

12mo.

[Reprinted with same title-page in Jones's *British Theatre*, vol. V, Dublin, 1795. Not recorded by Sichel.]

The Camp, an Entertainment

Note

THE CAMP, "A Musical Entertainment. By R. B. Sheridan, Esq." was printed (piratically) in 1795. George Daniel edited the farce (1833?) for Cumberland's British Theatre, his copy being taken, it is likely, from the prompt-book of Drury Lane Theatre. His edition is used for the present text ; but from the Greenock edition of *Sheridan's Plays* (1827) are restored a few sentences in Act I, scene i, and a passage in Act II, scene iii—which contains, in essence, Sheridan's Epilogue to *The Fatal Falsehood*—here distinguished by square brackets. Since 1826, but perhaps not earlier than MOORE's *Life of Sheridan, The Camp* has often been attributed to RICHARD TICKELL. It is here suggested however, that SHERIDAN may have been assisted in this after-piece by LIEUTENANT-GENERAL JOHN BURGOYNE.

R.C.R.

CONTENTS

CONTENTS

Introduction

"AS to the scenery—the miraculous powers of Mr. de Loutherbourg's pencil are universally acknowledged." Thus spake Mr. Puff in *The Critic*, with a glance (I think) at *The Camp*. At least, it is an echo of what the periodical press had said so recently about this "musical entertainment": *The Town and Country Magazine* (for October, 1778) said, "The chief merit of this performance is due to M. de Loutherbourg, whose fine representation of Cox-heath Camp does great honour to him as an artist. Indeed the whole performance seems chiefly designed to introduce the happy effects of that great master's pencil, as the dialogue, tho' written by Mr. Sheridan, can only be considered as a temporary *jeu d'esprit*." It was first acted on October 15th, 1778, at Drury Lane, and was no doubt written[1] (and painted) in haste. In consequence of an expected French invasion, several large military encampments had been formed in the early part of June, the most notable of which was at Cox-heath in Kent, under command of Lord Amherst. At once "the Camp" became a fashionable resort. Said the same magazine in the previous month, "The giddy, the idle, and the frivolous part of the world, will incessantly pursue a phantom and grasp a shadow.... They fly from one imaginary pleasure to another, from the play to the opera, from the concert to the masquerade, from London to Bath, from Bath to Scarborough—or Cox-heath." It was the fashion for ladies to dress *à la militaire*—hence (in *The Critic*) the print "in *The Camp Magazine*" of Lady Mary Myrtle "in a full-trimmed uniform and a light horseman's cap"; hence (in *The Camp*) the names of the ladies, Gorget, Plume, and Sash. They pitched their pleasure-tents about the encampment and turned it into a show-place. As in 1769 they had journeyed

[1] It was licensed for performance by Larpent only two days previously. (See Allardyce Nicoll, XIII *Century Drama* 1750–1800.)

269

to Stratford-upon-Avon to see "the Jubilee in Honour of Shake-speare";—as in 1774 they had thronged to the Oaks in Kent, to see the Fête Champêtre in celebration of the marriage of Lord Stanley and Lady Betty Hamilton—so in 1779 they descended upon Cox-heath to see the military manœuvres. London went camp-mad. As Garrick had promptly echoed the Stratford diversions in his own piece *The Jubilee* and the Stanley enter-tainments in *The Maid of the Oaks; or, the Fête Champêtre*, so Sheridan staged the encampment at Cox-heath in *The Camp*. It was, in short, nothing more nor less than a revue, with songs, comic and patriotic, and characters who typified the current follies. It satirised not only the fashionable camp-followers, but also the suttlers and contractors who cheated the soldiers out of every penny they could. A great deal that was then striking on the stage is, of course, not reflected in "the book"—not merely the scenery of Loutherbourg, but also the military display, first of all by Miss Walpole in the person of a girl disguised as a re-cruit, and lastly in the manœuvres of a company of soldiers (foot-guards, it seems, from the barracks) which "afforded much en-tertainment as well on account of their novelty as the dexterity with which they were performed." The American War of Inde-pendence had never possessed the minds of the multitude as they were now possessed by the threatened French invasion: indeed, popular opinion, as reflected in the periodical press, was largely sympathetic to the Americans. At least one may say that, in 1778 Saratoga was very far, Brest was very near. It is a little startling, though not inexplicable, to find that no Yankee character ap-peared on the European stage till 1786, when a certain Johna-than, an impoverished loyalist, figured in a comic opera called *A Match for a Widow* at the Theatre-Royal, Dublin.

George Daniel in his edition of *The Camp* said: "To fall with dignity is the most difficult experiment genius can make. It is safer to soar than to descend. Johnson, in reference to the sonnets of Milton, remarks that 'he never learned the art of doing *little things* with grace.' It has not always been so with great poets. Homer wrote *The Battle of the Frogs and Mice*; and Cowper, *Johnny Gilpin*. The author of the Begum Speech and *The School for Scandal* produced *The Camp*, which, as a flash of humour, a *jeu d'esprit*, is not unworthy of him."

Despite this rather quaint argument, there are very few touches that are in Sheridan's best vein—indeed, the neatest is the story of the contractor who supplied a regiment with lime instead of hair-powder, which "answered charmingly in fine weather; but when they were all caught in a fine soaking shower, the smoke ran all along the lines: 'ecod their heads were all slaked in an instant, and by the time they returned to the camp, damme if all their heads were not as smooth as an old half-crown." Another neat topical hit was Sir Harry Bouquet's ridicule of the affectation of using military similes in common talk, so that "the Camp jargon is as current as bad silver."[1]

The Camp, though produced anonymously, was universally accepted as Sheridan's by the press of the time, and also in such accounts of his life as that in *The European Magazine* (1782), in *The Children of Thespis* by Anthony Pasquin (1787), and *The Thespian Dictionary* (1802). Tate Wilkinson denied Sheridan's authorship in *The Wandering Patentee*, and though it was included in John Murray's Collected Edition (1821), Moore declared that the author was not Sheridan, but Richard Tickell, the author of the prologue, in whose handwriting was a rough draft which he discovered.[2] Since then it has been commonly assigned to Tickell, but as having been "corrected" by Sheridan. The only correction cited by Mr. Sichel is where the Sergeant describes his recruit as having "an eye like the King of Prussia's," Sheridan has inserted "a blood-spill eye." This is not found in any printed copy that I have seen. As for Tickell's authorship, a rough draft in his writing is not conclusive evidence: nor are there any comparisons to be made with his dramatic style, for *The Carnival of Venice* (1781), his only play, survives only in the songs.

[1] See Act II, scene iii.

[2] Moore's words are (*Life*, p. 194): "One of the novelties of the year was a musical entertainment called The Camp, which was falsely attributed to Mr. Sheridan at the time, and has since been inconsiderately admitted into the Collection of his Works. This unworthy trifle (as appears from a rough copy of it in my possession) was the production of Tickell, and the patience with which his friend submitted to the imputation of having written it was a sort of 'martyrdom of fame' which few but himself could afford."

It seems to have escaped notice, although so plainly said, that O'Daub the painter is a character from *The Maid of the Oaks* (acted in both plays by Moody)"I got so much credit at the Fête Champêtre that little Roscius [Garrick, of course] recommended me to the managers of Drury Lane, and so now I am a sort of deputy-superintendant under Mr. Lanternberg." It may therefore be suspected that if Sheridan had a collaborator it was the author of *The Maid of the Oaks*. The piece had been performed and printed as anonymous, and the author had been at some pains to conceal his identity. It was, indeed, common knowledge that the Fête Champêtre at the Oaks was arranged for Lord Stanley by his brother-in-law, who had allowed it to be reproduced as the Masque in *The Maid of the Oaks*. But it was not known that he was the author of the entire piece. Lord Stanley's brother-in-law was, of course, Lieutentant-General John Burgoyne. For many reasons, but chiefly because he was awaiting a Court of Enquiry as to his surrender at Saratoga, it would have been most inadvisable for Burgoyne's assistance in a military satire, however lightly written, to have been revealed. It may therefore, have been to keep the secret that Tickell, who had some concern with the management of the theatre, transcribed Burgoyne's draft before handing it to the usual copyists, the prompter or an under-prompter. It must not be forgotten that the author of *The School for Scandal* was the author of another such *jeu d'esprit*, *The Glorious First of June*. As to his close friendship with Burgoyne there are many testimonies, besides his production at Drury Lane of *The Lord of the Manor*, *The Heiress*, and *Richard Cœur de Lion*,[1] in which Burgoyne collaborated with Mrs. Sheridan.[2]

Nevertheless, such things as the description of the camp-toilet—varied and expanded shortly afterwards as the Epilogue to *The Fatal Falsehood*—and the account of the camp-jargon are indubitably Sheridan's.[3]

[1] See "A Note on John Burgoyne " Vol. II, pp. 303–5.
[2] See the note on "Richard Cœur de Lion," Vol. III, pp. 325–6.
[3] See "Prologues and Epilogues," Vol. III, pp. 275–278.

Dramatis Personae[1]

As originally performed at Drury Lane Theatre on October 15th,
1778

O'DAUB, a Painter	Mr. Moody
GAGE, an Exciseman	Mr. Parsons
SIR HARRY BOUQUET	Mr. Dodd
SERJEANT	Mr. Bannister
CORPORAL WILLIAM	Mr. Webster
MONSIEUR BOULARD	Mr. Baddely[2]
FIRST COUNTRYMAN	Mr. Fawcett
SECOND COUNTRYMAN	Mr. Wright
OLD MAN	Mr. Chapman[3]
ROBIN	Mr. Suett[3]

Officers, Recruits, &c.

LADY PLUME	Mrs. Robinson[4]
MISS GORGET	Mrs. Cuyler[4]
LADY SASH	Miss Farren[4]
NELL, a Market Woman	Mrs. Wrighten
NANCY	Miss Walpole

Market Women, &c.

[1] From *The Town and Country Magazine* for October, 1778, with additions as below.
[2] From *The London Magazine* for October, 1778.
[3] From *Cumberland's Edition*. These names, however, are doubtful, and may refer to an early revival.
[4] *Cumberland's Edition* gives Miss Farren as Lady Plume; Mrs. Ward as Lady Sash; and Mrs. Ward as Lady Gorget.

II. T

Prologue[1]

Written by RICHARD TICKELL, *Esq.*

THE stage is still the mirror of the day,
 Where fashion's forms in bright succession play;
 True to its end, what image can it yield,
In times like these, but the embattl'd field?—
What juster semblance than the glitt'ring plains
Of village warriors and heroic swains?—
Invasions, battles, now fill Rumour's breath,
From camps to fleets, from Plymouth to Cox-heath.
Thro' every rank some panic terrors spreads
And each, in varied phrase, express their dreads.

At 'Change, no vulgar, patriot, passions fright
The firm and philosophic—Israelite!
Ask him his hopes,—'Tis all de same to me;
I fix my wishes by my *policy*.
I'll *do* you Keppel: or, increase de barters,
You will, I'll underwrite de Duke of Chartres."

Miss Tittup, gasping from her stiff French stays,
"Why, if these French should come, we'll have French plays
Upon my word, I wish these wars wou'd cease!"
Settling her tucker, while she sighs for peace.

With wilder throbs, the glutton's bosom beats,
Anxious and trembling, for West-India fleets.
Sir Gobble Greenfat felt, in pangs of death,
The ruling passion taint his parting breath:
Such is the latest, as all in the past:
"O! save my turtle, Keppel!"—was his last.

[1]From *The Town and Country Magazine* for November, 1778. Not in 1795 edition,
and Cumberland's, but reprinted in the Greenock Edition.

No pang like this, the macaroni racks,
Calmly he dates the downfall of Almack's
"As Gad's my judge, I shall be glad to see
Our Paris friends here, for variety.
The Clubs are poor; let them their Louis bring,
The invasion wou'd be rather a good thing."

Perish such fears! what can our arms oppose,
When female warriors join our martial beaus!
Fierce from the toilet, the plum'd bands appear;
Miss struts a major, Ma'am a brigadier;
A spruce Bonduca simpers in the rear.
Unusual watch her *femmes de chambre* keep;
Militia phantoms haunt her in her sleep:
She starts, she wakes, she quivers, kneels, and prays,
"Side-saddle my horse? ah! lace up my stays!
Soft, soft, 'twas but a dream; my fears are vain
And Lady Minikin's herself again!"

—Yet hold; nor let false ridicule profane
These fair associates of the embattl'd plain:
Victorious wreaths their efforts justly claim,
Whose praise is triumph, and whose smiles are fame.

THE CAMP

Act the First

SCENE I

The Road near the Camp[1].

Enter OLD MAN.

Old Man. COME along, neighbours, come along; we shall be too late for the suttlers' market.

Enter SECOND MAN.

Second Man. Put on, put on, neighbours. Here, Robin, where are you, boy?

Robin [*behind*]. I'm coming, feather, as soon as I can get the colt up, for the plaguy beast is down again, and mother and chickens are all in the slough.

Old Man. Why, is the colt down again? You graceless dog, help your mother up—Oh, neighbour Farrow has helped her up, I see.

Enter OLD WOMAN.

Old Woman. Husband, as sure as you are alive, that rogue of a boy drove the colt in the dirt for the purpose, and down we came with such a wang——

Old Man. What a mercy it is the chickens escaped!—Come, put on, neighbours.

Enter ROBIN *and Colt.*

Robin. Why, feather, how could I help it?—The colt has not had an eye in his head these eight years.

[1]The passages in square brackets in this scene are restored from the Greenock Edition of *Sheridan's Plays* (1828).

277

[*Old Woman.* O, here comes our kinswoman, and her daughter——

Enter MISS.

Bless me, child! you are in such a heat you'll quite spoil your complexion.

Miss. Lord, neighbours, you hurry one so.——

Second Woman. Put on, put on; make haste, we shall be too late]—O dear, here comes Nell; and she'll scold us all, for cheating the soldiers.

[*Third Woman.* Damn that wench, she won't cheat herself, nor let other honest people do it, if she can help it; and she says she likes a soldier so well she would sell them goods for nothing.

Second Man. Come, neighbours, now we shall see what bargains your daughter will make at the Camp.

Second Woman. Aye, aye, soldiers are testy customers—They won't buy of the ugly ones——O, here Nell comes.]

Enter NELL.

Nell. Why, how now, what you are consulting how you shall cheat the poor soldiers; for shame! for shame! how can you use the poor fellows so? [a parcel of unfeeling wretches! Poor fellows] that risk their lives to defend your property, and yet you make it your study to defraud them.

Old Woman. It's very hard, Nell, you won't let us have a little picking among 'em. What is it to you what we do?

Nell. Yes, it is to me; I never will bear to see a soldier cheated, with my eyes open. I love a soldier, and will always stand by them.

[*Miss.* Mind your own business, Nell.

Nell. What's that you say, Miss Minx? Here's a wench dressed out: the poor soldiers are forced to pay for all this finery, you impudent slut you!]

Second Man. Why, Nell, if you go on at this rate we'll tell his worship, Mr. Gage, of you: he's an exciseman, and a great friend to us poor folks.

Nell. What's that you say, master Grinder? Come forward, you sneaking snivelling sot you, I think your tricks are pretty well known. Wasn't you caught soaking eggs in lime and water to make them pass for new ones: and did you not sit in the stocks for robbing the 'squire's rookery to make your pigeon pies.

Second Woman. Well, well, we'll tell Mr. Gage, and then what will he say to you?

Nell. Tell Mr. Gage, will you? he's a pretty protector indeed; he's a disgrace to his Majesty's inkhorn—while he seizes with one hand, he smuggles with the other.——Why, no longer ago than last summer, he was a broken attorney at Rochester, and came down here, and bought this place with his vote, and now he is both a smuggler and contractor. O my conscience, if I had the management of affairs, I would severely punish all such fellows, who would be so base as to cheat a poor soldier.

Second Woman. If his worship was here, you dare not say so. Here he comes, here he comes. Now you'll change your note.

Nell. Will I? you shall see if I do. No, no; I'll tell him my mind; that's always my way.

Enter GAGE.

All. Ah! Mr. Gage.

Gage. Hey day! what's the matter? What the plague, is there a civil war broke out among you?

First Woman. Why, Mr. Gage, Nell here has been scolding us for cheating the soldiers.

[*Second Woman.* Yes,] and says you encourage us in it.

Gage. Encourage you! to be sure I do, in the way of trade.

All. Aye, in the way of trade.

[*First Woman.* Yes, and she has been rating the poor girl, and says I dress her up thus only to make the better bargains.

Gage. And e'cod you're in the right of it; your mother is a sensible old woman. Well said, dame, put plenty in your baskets, and sell your wares at the sign of your daughter's face.

First Woman. Aye, aye, so I say.

Gage. Right—Soldiers are testy customers, and this is the market where the prettiest will always make the best bargains.

All. Very true, very true.

Gage. To be sure, I hate to see an awkward gawkey come sneaking into the market, with her damned half-price countenance, and is never able to get scarce double the value of her best goods.]

Nell. I can hold no longer: you are not ashamed, you who are a contractor, and has the honour to carry his Majesty's inkhorn at your button-hole, to teach these poor wretches all your court tricks. I'll tell you what—if I was to sit on a court-martial against such a fellow as you, you should have had your deserts, from the pilfering suttler to the head contractor, you should have the cat o' nine tails, and be forced to run the gauntlet, from Coxheath to Warley Common, that you should.

[*First Man.* How durst you talk so saucily to his worship?

Nell. Hold your tongue, or I'll throttle you, you sheep-biter.

[*Collaring him.*

First Man. O Lord, your worship! if you don't put her under an arrest she'll choke me.]

Gage [*aside*]. Come, Nell, hold your tongue, and I'll give you a pound of smuggled hyson, and throw you a silk handkerchief into the bargain.

Nell. Here's a rogue! Bear witness, neighbours, he has offered me a bribe;—a pound of tea. No, sir, take your pitiful present, and know that I am not to be bribed to screen your villanies by influence and corruption. [*Throws it at him.*

Gage. Don't mind her, she's mad, she talks treason. Away with you! I'll put every body under an arrest that stays to listen to her.

All. Aye, aye, she's mad. Come along, we shall be too late for market. [GAGE *drives them all off.*

Gage. Here, Nell, will you take the tea? [*Offers it to her.*

Nell. No, Sir, I won't.

Gage. Well, then, I will. [*Puts it in his pocket.*

AIR.—NELL.

Now coaxing, caressing,
Now wheedling, distressing,
As fortune delights to exalt or confound,
Her smile or her frown
Sets them up, knocks them down,
Turning, turning, turning as the wheel goes round.

O fie, Mr. Gage!
Quit the tricks of the age;
Scorn the slaves that to fortune, false fortune are bound,
Their cringes and bows,
Protections and vows,
Turning, turning, &c. [*Exit* NELL.

Gage. Foolish girl, not to accept a bribe, and follow the example of her betters——But who have we here?

Enter O'DAUB.

O'Daub. Ah, my little Gage! to be sure I am not in luck; I will not want an interpreter to show me the views about here; and by my shoul, I'll force you to accept my offer.

Gage. Why, what's your errand?

O'Daub. Why, upon my conscience, a very dangerous one: Jack the Painter's job was a fool to it. I am come to take the Camp.

Gage. The devil you are.

O'Daub. Aye, and must bring it way with me in my pocket too.

Gage. Indeed!

O'Daub. Aye, here's my military chest; these are my colours, you know.

Gage. O, I guess your errand.

O'Daub. Then, faith, it's a very foolish one. You must know, I got so much credit at the Fête Champêtre there, that little Roscius recommended me to the Managers of Drury-Lane, and so now I am a sort of deputy superintendant under Mr. Lanternberg, the great painter; that as soon as he executes a thing, I always design it after him, my jewel; so I'm going to take a side front view of it.

Gage. What then, they are going to introduce the Camp on the stage, I suppose.

O'Daub. To be sure you have hit it—Coxheath by candlelight, my jewel.

Gage. And will that answer?

O'Daub. O, to be sure it will answer, when a jontleman can have a warm seat, and see the whole tote of it for two thirteens, and be comfortable into the bargain. Why it has cost me above three guineas already, and I came the cheapest way too; for three of us went halves in the Maidstone Dilly, my dear.

Gage. Well, and how do you like the prospect?

O'Daub. Upon my shoul, my jewel, I don't know what to make on't, so I am come to be a little farther off, that I may have a nearer view of it. I think it looks like my cousin O'Doiley's great bleach-yard in the county of Antrim. [BOULARD *sings without.*] Tunder and wounds! what outlandish creature is this coming here?

Gage. O, that is Monsieur Boulard, the suttler.

O'Daub. Then perhaps he can help me to a bit of something to eat, for I feel a sort of craving in my stomach after my journey.

Gage. Why, he's a very honest fellow, and will be happy in obliging you. Oh, here he comes.

Enter BOULARD.

Boulard. Ah! begar, Monsieur Gage, I am glad I have found you; begar, I have been through Berkshire, Suffolk, and Yorkshire, and could not find you.

O'Daub. Through Berkshire, Suffolk, and Yorkshire—what the devil does he mean?

Gage. Oh, he means through the regiments.

Boulard. By gar, Monsieur Gage, I must depend on you for supply. I have got one, two, tree brigade dinners bespoke, besides the fat alderman and his lady from London.

Gage. Then you must send out a party of cooks to forage at Maidstone.

Boulard. Parbleu, Monsieur Gage, I must look to you, for begar, I have got nothing in de house to eat.

O'Daub. Then the devil burn me if I come to dine with you, honey.

Boulard. O, sare, I have got every ting for you and Monsieur Gage. You shall have any ting you like in von moment!

O'Daub. Ah, ah, I thank you, honey: but pray now, Mr. Blaud, if your own countrymen were to come over here, would not you be a little puzzled to know which side to be on?

Boulard. Puzzled!—parbleu, Monsieur, I do assure you I love de English ver well, and vill never leave dem vile dey are victorious; and I do love mine own countrymen very well; but depend on it, Monsieur Gage, I vill always ſtay with de ſtrongeſt.

Gage. You see, Mr. O'Daub, my friend, Monsieur Boulard, is diveſted of all national prejudice, I assure you.

Boulard. Prejudice——by gar, I have too much honour ever to leave de English while dey do vin de battle. But, Monsieur Gage, vil you bring your friend and taſte my vine; I have got every ting for you and your friend. I assure you, M. Gage, I vill never forsake de English, so long as dey are viċtorious; but if mine own countrymen were to come, and made de English run, I would run a little way with dem; and if mine own countrymen were likely to overtake dem, I would ſtop short, bow to dem, and say, how do you do, my ver good countrymen. By gar, I shall be ver glad to see you both, so come along——but depend on mine honour, Monsieur Gage, I vill never leave de English vile dey do vin de battle—No, never, never. [*Exit singing.*

Gage. Well said, Monsieur Boulard.

O'Daub. Your sarvant, Mr. Blaud, though, faith, to do him juſtice, he has forgot the fashion of his country, for when he is determined to be a rogue he is honeſt enough to own it. But pray what connexion have you with the suttlers? You are no viċtualler here, are you?

Gage. Not absolutely a viċtualler, but I deal in various articles.

O'Daub. Indeed.

Gage. Yes, but no business is done here only by contraċt.

O'Daub. A contraċtor! Why, what the devil, you are not risen to such preferment as that sure? I never knew you was able to furnish any contraċt.

Gage. Nothing more easy; the circumſtance depends upon the quantity, not the quality. I got on very well lately, but at firſt it brought me into several confounded scrapes.

O'Daub. As how?

Gage. Why, I undertook to serve a regiment with hair powder.

O'Daub. Hair powder! What, and you sent them flour, I suppose.

Gage. Flour! no, no—I should have saved nothing by that: I went to the fountain head—the pit, and gave them a plentiful stock of lime.

O'Daub. Lime! brick and mortar lime?

Gage. Yes, brick and mortar lime.

O'Daub. And, what the plague, was not the cheat found out?

Gage. Why at first it answered the purpose very well; while the weather was fine it did charmingly; but one field day they were all caught in a fine soaking shower; the smoke ran along the lines, ecod, their heads were all slack'd in an instant and by the time they returned to the camp, damme if all their heads were not as smooth as an old half-crown.

O'Daub. A very cross accident indeed.

Gage. Yes, I stood a near chance of being tied up to the halberts; but I excused myself by saying, they looked only like raw recruits before; but now they appeared like old veterans of service.

O'Daub. But you lost your contract, I suppose.

Gage. Yes, but I soon got another; a shaving contract to a company of grenadiers.

O'Daub. 'Faith, I never knew you practised that business.

Gage. Never handled a razor in all my life: I shave by deputy; hired Sam Sickle down from London—an excellent hand! handles a razor like a scythe;—he'll mow you down a regiment of beards in the beating of revally.

O'Daub. Upon my conscience, a pretty way this of working at second-hand. I wish myself could do a little by proxy.

Gage. But come, what say you for something to eat, and a glass of my friend Boulard's wine, and drink his Majesty's health.

O'Daub. With all my heart, my dear, and to the two camps, if you will.

Gage. Two! —what two do you mean?

O'Daub. Why, the one at Coxheath, and the other at Drury-Lane.

[*Exeunt.*

SCENE II

A Grove near the Camp.

Enter TWO COUNTRYMEN.

First Countryman. I tell you I will certainly lift; I ha' made up my mind on't.

Second Countryman. Well, well, I'll say no more.

First Countryman. Besides, the camp lies so convenient, I mayn't have such another opportunity.

Second Countryman. Why, it's main jolly to be sure, and all that so fair. Now, if I were to lift, I should like hugely to belong to a regiment of horse, and here is one of the grandeft troop com'd lately. I see'd two of the officers, mighty delicate looking gentlemen; they were dreft quite different from the others; their jackets, indeed, are pretty much the same: but then they wear a sort of petticoat as 'twere, with a large hat and feather, and a mortal sight of hair. I suppose now they are some of your outlandish troops; your foreign Hessians, or such like.

First Countryman. Aye, like enough. Here comes the serjeant. Ecod, he can sing louder than his own drum. Zooks! see how brave they march. Well, walking is a mighty dull way of going, after all.

Enter SERJEANT, DRUMMER, RECRUITS, *&c.*

SONG.—SERJEANT.

Great Cæsar once renown'd in fame,
    For a mighty arm, and a laurel brow;
  With his VE-NI, VI-DI, VI-CI came,
And he conquer'd the world with his row, dow, dow.

Chorus.

Row, dow, dow; row, dow, dow,
    And he conquer'd the world, &c.

Then should our vaunting enemies come,
    And winds, and waves, their cause allow,

By freedom's flag we'll beat our drum,
And they'll fly from the sound of our row, dow, dow.
Row, dow, dow, &c.

Then come, my lads, our bounty share,
While honeſt hearts British valour avow;
In freedom's cause to camp repair,
And follow the beat of my row, dow, dow.
Row, dow, dow, &c.

Serjeant. Come, my lads, now is your time to serve the King, and make men of yourselves: well, my lad, what do you say?

Second Countryman. I canno' leave my farm.

Serjeant. Your farm!—what, would you plow and sow for the hungry Frenchmen to come and reap? Come my lads! let your fields lie fallow this year, and I'll insure you double crops ever after. Why, now, here's a fellow made for a soldier; there's a leg for a spatterdash, with an eye like the king of Prussia.

Firſt Countryman. Aye, but serjeant, I hanna' the air.

Serjeant. The air! O, we'll soon learn you that; why now, here's little Ralph; there's a fellow, for you; he has not been liſted a fortnight, and see what a presence—there's dignity! O, there is nothing like the drill for grace.

Firſt Countryman. Serjeant, I'm your man.

Second Countryman. And so am I.

Serjeant. That's right, my lads; this is much better than to be dragg'd away like a slave, or be scratch'd off the church-door for the militia. Now you have present pay, and the bounty-money into the bargain. But come, my lads, let me ask you a few questions, and then the business is done.

TRIO.—SERJEANT *and* COUNTRYMEN.

Serjeant. Yet ere you're permitted to liſt with me,
    Answer me ſtraight twice queſtions three.

Firſt C. No lies, maſter serjeant, we'll tell unto you,
    For tho' we be poor lads, we're honeſt and true.

Serjeant. Firſt, can you drink well?

First C.	Cheerly, cheerly.
Serjeant.	Each man a gallon?
Second C.	Nearly, nearly.
Serjeant.	Love a sweet wench too!
Both.	Dearly, dearly.
Serjeant.	The answer is honeſt, bold, and fair;
	So drink to the king, for his soldiers you are.

Chorus.

The answer is honeſt, &c.

Serjeant.	When bullets are whizzing around your head,
	You'll boldly march on wherever you're led.
Second C.	To death we'll rush forward without delay,
	If, good maſter serjeant, you'll show us the way.
Serjeant.	Next, can you swear well?
Second C.	Bluffly, bluffly.
Serjeant.	Handle a Frenchman?
First C.	Roughly, roughly.
Serjeant.	Frown at a cannon?
Both.	Gruffly, gruffly.
Serjeant.	The answers are honeſt, bold, and fair,
	So drink to the king, for his soldiers you are.

Chorus.

The answers are honeſt, &c.

Huzza! Huzza! Huzza!

Enter NELL.

Nell. Well said, my lads. I am glad to see so many good hearts in the country—O, but was not you saying one of your recruits knows me?

Serjeant. O, yes, Nell, a lad from Suffolk. Hark ye, where's the Suffolk boy, as we call him? O, here he comes.

Enter NANCY.

Nancy. Ah, Serjeant, did you not begin to think you had loſt me? but come, will you leave me a few minutes with Nelly?

Serjeant. With all my heart. Come, my lads, let's to the Heart of Oak, where we'll drink his Majesty's health. [*Exit singing,* The answers, *&c. and two huzzas.*

Nancy. Why, Nelly, don't you know me?

Nell. Know you! egad, I do not know whether I do nor not—sure it can't be—and yet, sure it is Nancy Granger.

Nancy. It is her, my dear Nelly, who kisses you now with the truest sense of gratitude for your former kindness and friendship.

Nell. My dear girl—Odso! I must take care of my reputation. —But what in the name of fancy brings you here, and in this dress, child?

Nancy. How can you ask me that question, Nelly? You are no stranger to the love William and I have for each other; a few days would have united us for ever, had not cruel fate separated us; the regiment being ordered to march immediately, no resource was then left, but my flying from my father's house: I procured a dress from one of our neighbours' sons, and that love which induced me to forsake my sex, still supports me under every affliction. Fortunately, on my way, I met the serjeant, and after some entreaty was enlisted, and equipped as you see. What think you, Nell? does not my dress become me?

Nell. Yes, indeed, I think you make a smart little soldier.

Nancy. Why, indeed I am rather under size, but I fancy in action I could do more real execution than those who look bigger and talk louder. But tell me, my dear Nelly, where is William? I long to see him: does he ever speak of his poor Nancy? sure he cannot be faithless.

Nell. Why really, Nancy, I have some doubts.

Nancy. Heavens! is it possible?

Nell. Ah, my poor little soldier, I only did it to try your affection. Your William is true, and worthy of your love.

Nancy. You have made a greater shock on my spirits than even an army of Frenchmen could have done.

AIR.—NANCY.

When war's alarms entic'd my Willy from me,
    My fond heart with grief did sigh:

Each fresh remembrance brought fresh sorrow on me;
  I waked ere yet the morn was nigh,
     No other could delight him,
     Ah! why did I ere slight him,
  Coolly answering his fond tale?
     Which drove him far,
     Amid the rage of war,
And left silly me thus to bewail.

But I no longer thus, a maid forsaken,
  Nor will I mourn like yonder dove,
For ere the dawn to-morrow shall awaken,
  I'll go seek my absent love:
     The diſtant hills all over,
     I'll fly to seek my lover,
  Scorning every threat'ning fear!
     Nor diſtant shore,
     Nor cannon's loud roar,
Shall longer keep me from my dear.

Nell. But, my dear girl, consider, do you think you can cheerfully go through the toil and fatigue, and not repine after your own happy situation you left behind you?

Nancy. O no, I ſtill muſt love, though I should regret the occasion of our difficulties.

Nell. Difficulty!—Why then, marry him at the drum head, and that will end all your difficulties.

AIR.—NELL.

What can our wiseſt heads provide,
  For the child we doat on dearly,
    But a merry soul, and an honeſt heart
    In a lad who loves her dearly;
     Who with kisses and chat,
     And all all that,
  Will soothe him late and early,

If the truth she tell,
When she knows him well,
She'll swear she loves him dearly.

Let the prude at the name or sight of man,
Pretend to rail severely;
But alack a day! unseen she'll play
With the lad who loves her dearly.
Say old men whate'er they will,
'Tis a lover still
Makes day and night roll cheerly,
What makes our May
All holiday,
But the lad we doat on dearly.

Nell. Well, my dear Nancy, you must endeavour to throw off that dress as soon as possible. I'll tell you what, here are some ladies in the camp, who condescend to notice me; I'll endeavour to introduce you to them, and they may be of great service to you: in the mean time, should you by chance meet with William, be sure you don't discover yourself—Hush! here is the serjeant.

Enter SERJEANT.

Serjeant. Why, Nelly, how's this? you have had a long conversation together; I began to think you had run away with my new recruit.

Nell. O, there's no great danger, serjeant; he's no soldier for me; pray is he perfect in his exercise?

Serjeant. O, as handy a lad as ever was. Come, youngster, convince her.

[NANCY *goes through the exercise.*

Nell. Very well, indeed; but serjeant, I must beg of you to befriend him as much as you can, for my sake.

Serjeant. Any service in my power you may command; but a soldier's life is not the easiest in the world, so they ought to befriend each other.

TRIO.—SERJEANT, NELL *and* NANCY.

O the joy! when the trumpets sound,
 And the march beats around,
When the steed tears the ground,
 And shouts to the skies resound,
On glittering arms the sun-beams playing,
 Heighten the soldier's charms:
The fife and the roll of the distant drum,
 Cry hark! the enemy come!
To arms! the attack's begun.

END OF THE FIRST ACT

Act the Second

SCENE I

A Grove near the Camp.

Enter NELL, *speaking without.*

WILLIAM! come to speak to him another time; sure nothing could be more lucky; however, I must obey their ladyships' instructions, and keep him in ignorance, that they may be present at the discovery. Poor fellow, it's almost a pity too, when one has it in one's power to make him so happy.

Enter WILLIAM.

William. I am sorry, Nell, to make you wait, but it was an old friend.

Nell. Aye, aye, some one from Suffolk, I suppose, who has brought you news of your dear Nancy.

Will. I wish it had: it's unaccountable that I don't hear from her.

Nell. Unaccountable! not at all: I suppose she has changed her mind.

William. No, Nelly, that's impossible, and you would think so had you heard how she plighted her faith to me, and vowed, not withstanding her parents were my enemies, nothing but death should prevent our union.

Nell. O, I beg your pardon; if her father and mother indeed are against you, you need not doubt her constancy. But come, don't be melancholy. I tell you, I want to have you stay somewhere near the inn, and perhaps I may bring you some intelligence of her.

William. How! dear Nell?

Nell. Though indeed I think you are very foolish to plague yourself so, for even had Nancy loved you well enough to have carried your knapsack, you would have been very imprudent to have suffered her.

Will. Aye, but prudence, you know, is not a soldier's virtue. Its our business to hold life itself cheap, much more the comforts of it. Show me a young fellow in our regiment, who, if he gains the heart of a worthy girl, is afraid to marry her for want of a little wealth, I would have him drummed out of the regiment for discretion.

Nell. Very fine! but must not the poor girl share in all your fatigues and mishaps?

William. There, Nell, I own is the objection; but tenderness and affection may soften even these; yet if my Nancy ever makes the trial, though I may not be able to prevent her from undergoing hardships, I am sure my affection will make her wonder at their being called so; I wish I could once boast that the experiment was made.

AIR.—WILLIAM.

My Nancy quits the rural train
    A camp's distress to prove,
All other ills she can sustain,
    But living from her love.
Yet, dearest, tho' your Soldier's there,
    Would not your spirits fail,
To mark the hardships you must share,
    Dear Nancy of the dale.

Or should you, love, each danger share,
    Ah! how shall I secure
Your health, 'mid toils which you are born
    To soothe, but not endure?
A thousand perils I must view,
    A thousand ills assail,
Nor must I tremble e'en for you,
    Dear Nancy of the dale.

SCENE II

An open View near the Camp.

Enter O'DAUB.

O'Daub. Well, to be sure this same Camp is a pretty place, with their drums, and their fifes, and their gigs, and their marches, and their ladies in their regimentals; upon my conscience I believe they'd form a troop of side-saddle cavalry if there was any hope of an invasion. But now I am alone by myself, 'tis time I should be after taking my plan; and here I see are some of my directions for it. [*Pulls out a pocket-book and pencil.*] I can't think what it is makes my hand shake so, unless it is Mr. Blaud's wine that is got into my head: so, so! Let me study my orders a little, for I am not used to this business. O. P. and P. S. Who the devil is to understand that? O! here is the explanation: P. S. the prompter's side, and O. P. opposite the prompter. So I'm to mark down the view as it is to be taken on one side, and the other. Very well: P. S. and O. P. Let me see. Somewhere hereabout is certainly the best point to take it from.   [*Retires.*

Enter SERJEANT *and the* Two COUNTRYMEN.

First Countryman. There, you rogues, there he is!

Second Countryman. Aye, aye, that's him sure enough; I have seen him skulking about these two days; if he ben't a spy I'll suffer hanging.

Serjeant. He certainly must be a spy by his drawing figures.

Second Countryman. Do seize him, or the whole camp may be blown up before we are aware.

O'Daub. Prompter's side.

Serjeant. Hush! we shall convict him out of his own mouth.

O'Daub. O yes, the Star and Garter must certainly be P. S.

Serjeant. P. S. What the devil does he say?

Second Countryman. Treason, you may be sure, by your not understanding him.

O'Daub. And then O. P. will have the advantage.

Serjeant. O. P. That's the old Pretender. A damn'd Jacobite spy, my life on't.

First Countryman. And P. S. is Prince Charles, I suppose.

Serjeant. No, you fool; P. S. is the Pretender's son.

Second Countryman. Aye, aye, like enough.

O'Daub. Memorandum—the officers' tents are in the rear of the line.

Second Countryman. Mark that.

O'Daub. N. B. the General's tents are all houses.

First Countryman. Remember that.

O'Daub. Then the park of artillery; I shall never make any thing of that. Oh! the devil burn the park of artillery!

Serjeant. There's a villain; he'll burn the park of artillery, will he?

O'Daub. Well, faith, this camp is easier taken than I thought it was.

Serjeant. Is it so, you rogue? but you shall find the difference on't. O, what a providential discovery!

O'Daub. To be sure the people will like it much, and in the course of the winter it may surprise his majesty.

Serjeant. O, the villain! seize him directly—Fellow, you are a dead man if you stir!—We seize you, sir, as a spy.

O'Daub. A spy—phoo, phoo; get about your business.

Serjeant. Bind him, and blindfold him if he resists.

Second Countryman. Aye, blindfold him for certain, and search him too; I dare say his pockets are crowded with powder, matches, and tinder-boxes, at every corner.

O'Daub. Tunder and ouns! What do you mean?

First Countryman. Hold him fast.

O'Daub. Why, here's some ladies coming, who know me. Here's Lady Sarah Sash, and Lady Plume, who were at the Fête-Champêtre, and will give me a good character.

Serjeant. Why, villain, your papers have proved you a spy, and sent by the old Pretender.

O'Daub. O Lord! O Lord! I never saw the old gentleman in all my life.

Serjeant. Why, you dog, didn't you say the camp was easier taken than you thought it was.

Second Countryman. Aye, deny that!

Serjeant. And that you would burn the artillery, and surprise his majesty—so come, you had better confess before you are hanged.

O'Daub. Hanged for a spy! O, to be sure myself is got into a pretty scrape.

Serjeant. Bring him away; but blindfold him, the dog shall see no more.

O'Daub. I'll tell you what, Mr. Soldier, or Mr. Serjeant, or what the devil's your name, upon my conscience and soul I'm nothing at all but an Irish painter employed by Monsieur Lanternburg.

Serjeant. There, he has confessed himself a foreigner, and employed by Marshal Leatherbag.

Second Countryman. O, he'll be convicted by his tongue. You may swear he is a foreigner by his lingo.

First Countryman. Bring him away. I long to see him hanging.

O'Daub. Tunder and wounds! if I am hanged, what will become of the theatre and the managers; and the devil fly away with you all together, for a parcel of red black-guards!

[They hurry him off.

SCENE III

Part of the Camp.[1]

Enter LADY GORGET, LADY SASH, *and* LADY PLUME.

Lady Plume. O! my dear Lady Sash, indeed you are too severe and I'm sure if Lady Gorget had been here she would have been of my opinion.

Lady Sash. Not in the least.

Lady Plume. You must know, she has been rallying my poor brother, Sir Harry Bouquet, for not being in the militia, and so ill-naturedly.

Lady Sash. So he should indeed; but all I said was, he looked so French and so finical, that I thought he ran a risk of being mistaken for another female chevalier.

[1]The passage in square brackets in this scene is restored from the Greenock Edition of *Sheridan's Plays* (1828).

[*Lady Plume.* Yet, you must confess, that our situation is open to a little raillery: a few elegancies of accommodation are considerably wanting, though one's toilet, as Sir Harry says, is not absolutely spread on a drum head.

Lady Sash. He vows there is an eternal confusion between stores military, and millinery; such a description he gives—On one shelf, cartridges and cosmetics, pouches and patches; here a stand of arms, there a file of black pins; in one drawer, bullet moulds and essence-bottles, pistols and tweezer cases, with battle-powder mixed with marechelle.]

Lady Gorget. O, the malicious creature!

Lady Plume. But pray, Lady Sash, don't renew it, for see, here comes Sir Harry to join us.

Enter SIR HARRY BOUQUET.

Sir Harry. Now, Lady Sash, I beg a truce; Lady Gorget, I am rejoiced to see you at this delectable spot, where, Lady Plume, you may be amused with such a dismal variety.

Lady Gorget. You see, Lady Plume, he perseveres.

Lady Sash. I assure you, Sir Harry, I should have been against you in your raillery.

Sir Harry. Now, as Gad's my judge, I admire the place; here's all the pride, pomp, and circumstance of glorious war! Mars in a *vis-a-vis*, and Bellona giving a Fête-Champêtre.

Lady Plume. But now, seriously, brother, what can make you judge so indifferently of the camp from any body else?

Sir Harry. Why, seriously, then, I think it the worst planned thing I ever beheld; for instance now, the tents are all ranged in a straight line; now, Lady Gorget, can any thing be worse than a straight line? and is not there a horrid uniformity in their infinite vista of canvass? no curve, no break, and the avenue of marquees abominable.

Lady Sash. O, to be sure, a circus or a crescent, would have been vastly better.

Lady Gorget. What a pity Sir Harry was not consulted.

Sir Harry. As Gad's my judge. I think so; for there is great capability in the ground.

Lady Sash. A camp cognoscenti, positively, Sir Harry; we will have you publish a treatise on military virtu.

Sir Harry. Very well, but how will you excuse this; the officers' tents are close to the common soldiers ; what an arrangement is that now? If I might have advised, there certainly should have been one part for the canaille, and the westend of the camp for the noblesse, and persons of a certain rank.

Lady Gorget. Very right. I dare say you would have thought of proper marquees for hazard and quinze.

Lady Plume. To be sure, with festino tents, and opera pavilions.

Sir Harry. Gad, the only plan that could make it supportable for a week; well, certainly, the greatest defect in a general is want of taste.

Lady Sash. Undoubtedly, and conduct, discipline, and want of humanity, are no atonement for it.

Sir Harry. None in nature.

Lady Plume. But, Sir Harry, it is rather unlucky, that the military spirit is so universal, for you will hardly find one to side with you.

Sir Harry. Universal indeed; and the ridicule of it is to see how this madness has infected the whole road from Maidstone to London; the camp jargon is as current all the way as bad silver; the very postillions that drive you talk of their cavalry, and refuse to charge on a trot up the hill, the turnpikes seem converted into redoubts, and the dogs demanded the countersign of my servants instead of the tickets; then when I got to Maidstone, I found the very waiters had got a smattering of tactics, for inquiring what I could have for dinner, a cursed drill waiter, after reviewing his bill of fare with the air of a field-marshall proposed an advanced party of soup and bouille, to be followed by the main body of ham and chickens, flanked by a fricassee, with sallads in the intervals, and a corps de reserve of sweetmeats and whipt syllabubs to form a hollow square in the centre.

Lady Plume. Ha, ha, ha! Sir Harry, I'm very sorry you have so strong a dislike to every thing military; for unless you would contribute to the fortune of our little recruit————

Sir Harry. O, madam, most willingly; and very apropos, here comes your ladyship's protégée, and has brought, I see, the little recruit, as you desired.

Enter NELL *and* NANCY.

Nell. Here, Nancy, make your curtsey, or your bow, to the ladies, who have so kindly promised you protection.

Nancy. Simple gratitude is the only return I can make; but I sure, the ladies who have hearts to do so good-natured a deed, will excuse my not being able to answer them as I ought.

Nell. She means, an' please your ladyships, that she will always acknowledge your ladyships' goodness, to the last hour of her life, and, as in duty bound, will ever pray for your ladyships' happiness and prosperity. That's what you mean, you know.   [*Aside to* NANCY.

Lady Plume. Very well: but, Nancy, are you satisfied that your soldier shall continue in his duty?

Nell. O yes, your ladyship, she's quite satisfied.

Lady Plume. Well, child, we're all your friends, and be assured your William shall be no sufferer by his constancy.

Nell. There, Nancy, say something.

Lady Sash. But, are you sure you will be able to bear the hardships of your situation?   [*Retires up with* NANCY.

Lady Plume [*to* NELL]. You have seen him then?

Nell. O, yes, your ladyship.

Lady Plume. Go, and bring him here. [*Exit* NELL.] Sir Harry, we have a little plot, which you must assist us in.

Nancy [*coming forward with* LADY SASH]. O, madam, most willingly.

SONG.—NANCY.

The fife and drum sounds merrily,
A soldier, a soldier's the lad for me;
With my true love I soon shall be;
For who so kind, so true as he;
With him in every toil I'll share,
To please him shall be all my care;
Each peril I'll dare, all hardship I'll bear,
For a soldier, a soldier's the lad for me.

Then if kind Heaven preserve my love,
What rapturous joys shall Nancy prove!
Swift through the camp shall my footstep bound,
To meet my William, with conquest crown'd;
Close to my faithful bosom prest,
Soon shall he hush his cares to rest;
Clasp'd in these arms, forget war's alarms,
For a soldier, a soldier's the lad for me.

Lady Plume. Now, Nancy, you must be ruled by us.

Nancy. As I live, there's my dear William.

Lady Plume. Turn from him————you must.

Nancy. O, I shall discover myself—I tremble so unlike a soldier.

Enter NELL and WILLIAM.

Nell. Why, I tell you, William, the ladies want to ask you some questions.

Sir Harry. Honest corporal, here'a little recruit, son to a ten-ant of mine, and, as I am told, you are an intelligent young fellow, I mean to put him under your care.

William. What, that boy, your honour. Lord bless you, sir, I shall never be able to make any thing of him.

Nancy [aside]. I am sorry for that.

Lady Sash. Nay, corporal, he's very young.

William. He is under size, my lady, such a stripling is fitter for a drummer than a rank and file.

Sir Harry. But he's straight and well made.

Nancy. I wish I was ordered to right about.

William. Well, I'll do all in my power to oblige your ladyship. Come, youngster, turn about—ah, Nelly, tell me, is't not she?

Sir Harry. Why don't you march him off?

Nell. Is he under size, corporal? O you blockhead!

Nancy. O ladies, pray excuse me!—My dear William!

[Runs into his arms.

Nell. They'll never be able to come to an explanation before your ladyships—Go, go and talk by yourselves.

[They retire up the stage.

Enter SERJEANT, *two* COUNTRYMEN, *Fife, &c.*

Serjeant. Please your ladyships, we have taken a sort of a spy this morning, who has the assurance to deny it, tho' he confesses himself an Irish Painter. I have undertaken, however, to bring this letter from him to lady Sarah Sash.

Sir Harry. What appears against him?

Serjeant. A great many suspicious circumstances, please your honour; he has an O before his name, and we took him with a draught of the camp in his hand.

Lady Sash. Ha! ha! ha! this is ridiculous enough, 'tis O'Daub, the Irish Painter, who diverted us some time ago at the Fête-Champêtre. Honest serjeant, we'll see your prisoner, and I fancy you may release him.

Sir Harry. Pray, serjeant, what's to be done this evening?

Serjeant. The line, your honour, turns out, and as there are pleasure tents pitched, perhaps the ladies will condescend to hear a march and chorus, which some recruits are practising against his Majesty comes to the camp.

Lady Sash. Come, Sir Harry, you'll grow fond of a camp life yet.

Sir Harry. Your ladyships will grow tired of it first, I'll answer for it.

Lady Sash. No, no.

Sir Harry. Yes, on the first bad weather you'll give orders to strike your tents and toilets, and secure a retreat at Tunbridge.

SCENE IV

A View of the Camp.

Officers and Soldiers discovered drawn out in line.

FINALE

SERJEANT.

While the loud voice of war resounds from afar,
    Songs of duty and triumph we'll pay:
When our Monarch appears, we'll give him three cheers,
    With huzza! huzza! huzza !

NANCY.

Ye sons of the field, whose bright valour's your shield,
  Love and beauty your toils shall repay;
Inspir'd by the charms of war's fierce alarms,
  Huzza! huzza! huzza!

WILLIAM.

Inspir'd by my love all dangers I'll prove,
  No perils shall William dismay;
In war's fierce alarms, inspir'd by those charms,
  Huzza! huzza! huzza!

Chorus

May true glory still wave her bright banners around,
Still with fame, pow'r, and freedom, old England be crown'd.

FINIS

A Note on John Burgoyne

OF all English dramatists there is no stranger or more romantic figure than John Burgoyne, the general who surrendered at Saratoga. We have so adopted the American view of the War of Independence that the travesty of his character in *The Devil's Disciple* is accepted as historical in its veracity. We have so accepted the Victorian view of the times of King George III that silence as to his dramatic activities is unbroken, except for the one damning word in the Dictionary of National Biography—"dull." It seems very likely that there will be a mutiny against these traditional attitudes. Burgoyne's reputation as a dramatist was involved, as frequently happened in those days, with his reputation as a politician. The Tories would never allow that the Whig dogs could do anything. The notorious Anthony Pasquin, a blackmailing journalist, is not usually a very reliable witness, but he delivered his opinions upon "the witless *bons-mots* of the studious Burgoyne" with an unaccustomed codicil of candour. "I think his essays in fighting and writing have been equally ineffective, but perhaps" (he had the grace to add) "neither the Minister nor myself can form a proper estimate of the general's merits." Burgoyne's career was chequered. As a subaltern, by no means rich, he married Lady Charlotte Stanley, a daughter of the Earl of Derby. Although the father strongly opposed this marriage, he afterwards relented and left his daughter a considerable fortune. Burgoyne's first attempt at a dramatic entertainment was at the Oaks in Kent, in honour of the marriage between his brother-in-law, Lord Stanley, afterwards Earl of Derby, to Lady Betty Hamilton. The festivities took the form of that favourite Georgian diversion, a Fête-Champêtre. The expenditure was lavish, the scenery costing the unheard-of sum of £1,500—corresponding perhaps to ten times the amount of present money. A few months later this entertainment was adapted to the stage of Drury Lane Theatre as a dramatic spectacle of unparalleled brilliance under the name of *The Maid of the Oaks*. David Garrick was Burgoyne's counsellor in making this adaptation. Mrs. Abington, the original Lady Teazle of three years later, was Lady Bob Lardoon, the fine lady who pretends to be a country wench, Phyllis Nettletop. *The Maid of the Oaks*, like *The Jubilee* of David Garrick, is of no dramatic value; it is a kind of Georgian *revue*, of a type more French than English. It has some little interest to the student of social history as a memorial of the extravagant entertainments in continuation of the Elizabethan masque which were customary at the marriages of the great territorial nobility.

Burgoyne had already enjoyed a distinguished military career. He was virtually the creator in the English Army of the light horse, a more mobile and effective force than the "heavies," and he commanded one of the two new regiments of Light Dragoons. Previously he had been Colonel of the Coldstream Guards, and served in Portugal. After *The Maid of the Oaks* he was so heavily in debt (it is said) that he was forced to fly to France. It was a period of prodigal expenditure, and Burgoyne, like Fox and Sheridan, dissipated enormous sums of money. From France he was sent to America to serve against the revolted Colonies, but returned in disgust at the incompetence of his superior officers. He proposed an expedition from Canada to the Premier, Lord North, and was sent out in command. Its failure resulted in his surrender at Saratoga, and he returned to England on parole, to defend his conduct in the House of Commons (of which he was a member) with great ability. When the Whigs returned to power some five years later he was made a Privy Councillor and Commander-in Chief of the Forces in Ireland. This very short summary of his military career serves only to illustrate the romantic vicissitudes of his life.

With the encouragement of his friend and colleague Sheridan, Burgoyne, after relinquishing office (he was a member of the Whig Ministry) turned his attention again to drama, and wrote *The Lord of the Manor*, *Richard Cœur-de-Lion*, and *The Heiress*. The last comedy went into ten editions during the first year, and gave him a European reputation as a dramatiſt, being translated into eight or nine foreign languages. Nevertheless, it has little to commend it to modern readers or playgoers, even though Sheridan is said to have "given some touches" to it. One little point of intereſt in it is that it gave to the English language that quaint word "niminee piminee" (a forecaſt of Dickens's "prunes and prisms")—a word invented by his fashionable lady to be pronounced before the looking-glass in order to give thelips the coveted infantine "rosebud pucker." *Richard Cœur-de-Lion* muſt have survived on the ſtage as an opera for several generations; at leaſt I remember buying it for a toy-theatre about the end of Queen Victoria's reign. No doubt the plates from which it was printed were designed thirty years earlier, but even that is a long time after Burgoyne's death.[1]

His other play *The Lord of the Manor*, a "comic opera," is delightful and charming. To me, it is better than *Lionel and Clarissa*, though not so good as *The Duenna*—not so picturesque nor so amusing. The music was written by Jackson of Exeter, and has a gracious Georgian simplicity. As a comedy, ignoring the lyrics, *The Lord of the Manor* gives more of the real country-life of the period than any other play I know. It is "taken from the French," from Marmontel's *Sylvain*, but the manners are anglicised. The old manorial England, with its feudal anceſtry, is reflected in it as in a silver mirror. Burgoyne had a passionate love for England which sometimes made him didactic, but in *The Lord of the Manor* his touch, though lively, was lighter. The characters, too, are varied—the familiar "Macaroni," the young blood of the period, is vivaciously depicted from the moment he appears on a game-shooting expedition with a gun in one hand and a silk parasol in the other. Captain Trepan, the recruiting officer, is more bitterly etched; it is the single trace of Burgoyne's military misfortunes in his comedies. The paſtoral quietude of old England, the honeſt, ſtrong, reſtfulness of country-life, is always in the background. Perhaps *The Lord of the Manor* is too gentle for these days.

[1] See also the notes as to Sheridan's ſupposed collaborations in "The Heiress" (Vol. III, p. 324), and "Richard Cœur de Lion" (*ibid.* p. 325).

Bibliography of *The Camp*

1. THE CAMP (1795 Edition.) .

The Camp: A Musical Entertainment. As Performed At the Theatre Royal, Drury-Lane. By R. B. Sheridan, Esq. London: Printed In The Year, M.DCC.XCV.

8vo.

Pagination. P. [1] title; p. [2] Dramatis Personæ; pp. [3] and 4-28 Text.

2. THE CAMP (Cumberland's Edition.)

The Camp: A Musical Entertainment. In Two Acts, By Richard Brinsley Sheridan.... Printed from the Acting-Copy With Remarks, Biographical and Critical, by D——G....London. John Cumberland, 2 Cumberland Terrace, Camden New Town.

12mo. Pp. 32.

"D— G" was George Daniel. Issued about 1833.

3. OTHER EDITIONS.

The Music to *The Camp* by Thomas Linley was "Printed for S. & A. Thompson, London" (1778), oblong folio. *The Camp* was included in The Works of Sheridan (London, John Murray, 1821) which had a general preface by Thomas Moore, who, however, did not "edit" the plays, or even select them. It was included in the Greenock Dramatic Works (1829) and other collections, but on account of Moore's repudiation of its authorship is not found in the Standard Editions, such as Bohn's (1848) Chatto's (1874), and the Oxford Edition (1906), all, of course, reprinted at various dates.

The Forty Thieves,
An Operatic Romance

Note

THE FORTY THIEVES was first printed in 1814 by J. Charles of Dublin under the title of *Ali Baba; or, The Forty Thieves*. The present text reprints that edition, hitherto unrecorded, from the unique copy in my possession. This, however, omitted (in accordance with the practice at the Dublin Theatre) certain scenes concerning Orcobrand, the Enchanter, which have been here restored in square brackets, from "*The Forty Thieves*, by R.B. Sheridan and Colman the Younger," London. J. Duncombe, (?1826). A few variants are noted from *The Forty Thieves*, London, J. Cumberland, (?1828).

R . C . R .

CONTENTS

Introduction

IT is certain that, whether his share in this "grand operatical romance" was limited to that or not, Sheridan wrote the *programme* or scenario of *The Forty Thieves*. Alike in its plot and its success, it was the *Chu Chin Chow* of its generation. While Sheridan was planning it out, his mind must often have returned to his youth of thirty-five years before when he was "adapting to the modern stage" Suckling's comedy *The Goblins*. Out of this version, which he never completed, came *The Foresters*—the comic opera that was also never to get beyond a name, a song or two, some pages of chatter (it was hardly dialogue) and a dream. *The Goblins* and *The Foresters* had alike for their central personages a band of robbers, and one cannot but feel that it was the "perturbed spirit" that had haunted him for so many years which set him at last to take from *The Thousand and One Nights* the story of Ali Baba and the Forty Thieves. It was not the first of these ancient tales to be put on the stage, for O'Keefe had made a pantomime out of *Aladdin or the Wonderful Lamp* in 1788. But *The Forty Thieves* was not a pantomime, it had no dumb-show and no harlequinade, for like Colman's *Blue Beard* this "grand operatical romance" presented a familiar legend as a serious narrative. Nevertheless *The Forty Thieves* is something of a theatrical curiosity: for, in showing its mortals dominated by two conflicting supernatural persons, the powers of Good and Evil, it was destined to become the model of that least literary of theatrical productions, the Victorian Christmas "speaking pantomime."

The Fairy of the Lake and the Enchanter of the Forest were the parents of an innumerable progeny, the Fairy Queen and Demon King of a thousand pantomimes. This does not deny that they, too, had their ancestors, the Adam and Eve of their race being perhaps the ogre and the fairy in *Les Fées* acted at the Hôtel de Bourgogne in 1697. Sheridan took his fable from the

Arabian Nights—from Robert Heron's version of 1792, I suppose, though there were three or four others in the next few years. Moore would restrict Sheridan's share to drafting the plot:

Another of these inglorious tasks of the author of *The School for Scandal* was the furnishing of the first outline or *Programme* of *The Forty Thieves*. His brother-in-law, Ward, supplied the dialogue, and Mr. Colman was employed to season it with an infusion of jokes. The following is Sheridan's sketch of one of the scenes:—

ALI BABA.

Bannister called out of the cavern boldly by his son—comes out and falls on the ground a long time, not knowing him—says he would only have taken a little gold to keep off misery and save his son, &c.

Afterwards, when he loads his asses, his son reminds him to be moderate—but it was a promise made to thieves—"it gets nearer the owner, if taken from the stealer"—the son disputes this morality—"they stole it, *ergo*, they have no right to it; and we steal it from the stealer, *ergo*, our title is twice as bad as theirs."

There is not much trace of this incident in *The Forty Thieves*, but the "moral" argument amended, is transferred to Morgiana:

Morgiana. I have got a basketfull of eatables here: they belonged to your sister, my mistress . . . I stole 'em.
Cogia. Stole them, Morgiana?
Morgiana. Only from the servants—so I can't call it stealing neither; for when they stole them first, 'twas only called peculation.

Genest, in his *History of the Stage*, says that the *scenario* was handed to Ward, who wrote the dialogue so badly that Colman was called in to rewrite it entirely. Hence, no doubt, the attribution of this "grand operatical romance" by Duncombe, in the first London edition, to Sheridan and Colman. But Michael Kelly, who supplied the music, gives the name of the author as Ward, so the songs at least were largely his.

Kelly's only comment is, "I composed the music to the splendid spectacle of *The Forty Thieves*, produced at Drury Lane in April, 1806, which had a very great run. Miss Decamp acted, sang, and danced, in the character of Morgiana, with very great effect." George Daniel, the only editor the "romance" has ever had, ended a curiously uninformative preface by saying, "This piece was first acted at Drury Lane in 1806 with very great *éclat*. Ali Baba, Mustapha and Morgiana were represented by Bannister, Mathews and Miss De Camp. The song, 'Last Week I took a Wife' was sung by Mathews with such comic effect, that it immediately resounded through every corner of the town."

Richard Cumberland in his *Memoirs* has a single scornful sentence : "I am told the spectacle of *The Forty Thieves* was a delicious treat; I did not hear quite so good an account of the dialogue; in like manner I read of forty honest gentlemen at least, who set out exquisite entertainments, but nobody records a single syllable of their conversation."

Dramatis Personae[1]

ALI BABA	*A poor Woodcutter, once in opulent circumstances*
CASSIM BABA	*A rich Merchant, his Brother*
GANEM	*Ali Baba's son*
[ABDALLAH	*Captain of the Robbers]*[2]
HASSARAC	*His Lieutenant*[3]
SELIM	*A Slave belonging to Zelie*
FIRST THIEF[4]	
SECOND THIEF[5]	
[ORCOBRAND	*Enchanter of the Black Rock]*[6]
ZAIDA	*Cassim Baba's Wife*
COGIA	*Ali Baba's Wife*
ZELIE	*A Rich Princess, on a pilgrimage to Mecca*
MORGIANA	*A faithful slave in Cassim Baba's Family*
[ARDINELLE	*The Fairy of the Lake]*[7]
[GOSSAMER	*A Sylph]*[8]

Officers, Soldiers, Female Slaves, Robbers and Attendants. War, Famine, Rapine, and Fraud.

---

[1] *1814 Edition.* [2] *Duncombe's Edition.*
[3] *Duncombe's Edition.* Captain of the Banditti, *1814 Edition* (In the Dublin version the part of Abdallah was merged into Hassarac.)
[4] *Mirza, Duncombe's Edition.* [5] Alcandor, *Duncombe's Edition.*
[6] *Duncombe's Edition.* [7] *Duncombe's Edition.* [8] *Duncombe's Edition.*

315

Act the First

SCENE I

[A beautiful Palace.

GOSSAMER, *with Sylphs and Fairies, enter dancing. They dance round and form on each side.*
ARDINELLE *enters in a splendid Car drawn by Swans. The Sylphs and Fairies pay their homage to Ardinelle.*

CHORUS *of Sylphs, Fairies, Naiads, &c.*

FAIRY of the glassy lake,
Hasten for fair virtue's sake;
Lovely spirit, pure art thou,
As the stream that veils thee now.
While thy chariot glides along,
We tune the choral song—
Thus we tune the choral song,—
Thus we sing and own thy sway,
Friend of virtue's fairest ray.
                    Friend of virtue's, &c.
ARDINELLE *alights from the car and comes forward.]*[1]

Fairy. Fairies, whose feet, when Cynthia towers
    Leave circles in the grass—Sylphs, that, unseen
    Flit thro' the vaults of ether;—woodland nymphs,
    By zephyrs fann'd, in quiv'ring shades at noon;—
    Naiads, with tresses idly willow-bound,
    And glossy limbs, lav'd in the silver stream,
    Attend—and give your aid in virtue's cause.

[1]*Duncombe's Edition.* Not in 1814 Edition, which has instead: *The Fairy* [*i.e.* Ardinelle] *discovered on an eminence. As the curtain rises, she gradually descends.*

Enter ATTENDANT, *dancing.*

Attendant. Hail to our mistress, Fairy of the Lake! [*Salutes her*

Fairy. Where's Gossamer?

Gossamer. Here, mistress.

Fairy. Knowest thou Abdallah,[1] who now heads the robbers—
the fierce banditti that infest this forest?

Gossamer. Full surely.

Fairy. Good—thou knowest too Ali Baba?

Gossamer. Is't the woodman,
    Who, as you oft have told me, when day peeps,
    Comes with his son from Bagdad to this forest?

Fairy. The same—him would I protect.

Gossamer. I ne'er have seen him, gentle mistress.

Fairy. Dull spirit, thou shou'd'st see thro' thought.—
    Observe
Those whom I would protect, for thou must work,
And featly, in my purpose, Gossamer.
Mark Ali Baba, and then note his son;
Two humble woodmen, fall'n from better fortunes,
Still haply doom'd to higher. Thus I draw
Their filmy unsubstantial substances.

[*The* FAIRY *waves her wand, a Grotto descends—through the opening is seen a view of a Forest, in miniature; a little Boy, representing* ALI BABA *leading a profile of an Ass and Panniers, waving his*

[1]Abdallah, *Duncombe's Edition*; Hassarac, 1814 *Edition.* The Dublin version combined the two characters. Apparently the original London version here contained a
passage concerning Orcobrand, the Enchanter, omitted from both these editions.
Cumberland's Edition reads, however (no doubt correctly):

Fairy. Gossamer, you know the potency of my foe.
Goss. What, Orcobrand, Enchanter of the Forest?
Fairy. Yes, Orcobrand, of the Black Forest here.
    Virgins of Bagdad shudder at his name.
Sylph. Your magic art is greater far than his.
Fairy. Haply, but vice has sometimes the ascendant,
    The fierce banditti/Who infest this Forest
    Prowl by his power protected, but their leader,
    (Perforce alive to honour still), he is my care
    Knowst thou Abdallah/that now heads the robbers
Goss. Full surely.
Fairy.   Thou knowst too, Ali Baba?
Goss. Is't the woodman . . . [etc.]

hand for GANEM *to hasten after him; a little Boy, representing*
GANEM, *enters yawning; after which the Grotto retires.*

Attendant. Why does thy power stoop thus to protect
    Such lowly beings?
Fairy. Earth-taught thing!—the hands
    That wield a sceptre, or that hold a plough,
    Are of the self same clay. In virtue's eye
    The good are great—the great not always good;——
    Hence comes it, peasants bless their kings, when kings
    Rule them as fellow-men.—Away!—away!
           [*The* FAIRY *retires to the car, and ascends.*

SCENE II
A Wood.

ALI BABA *enters, leading in a real Ass, with a hatchet on his shoulder*
and singing.
Ali Baba [*calls*]. Why Ganem! faster you rogue, faster! I
thought to have cut a score good logs by this time——Why,
Ganem I say! Zounds! do *you* get on at all events[*beating the Ass*]
you've gone the road often enough to know it.

Enter GANEM, *yawning.*
Ganem. Is the sun up yet, Father?
Ali Baba Up!—Look at it through the branches of the Palm-
trees. [GANEM *yawns.*] Zounds, don't yawn so.
    Ganem. Since you ceas'd to flourish in trade Father, how often
You, Mother, and I wanted a breakfast.
    Ali Baba. That's because when I did flourish in trade, I could
not bear to hear any one say they wanted a dinner,
    Ganem. Aye, when you were a thriving Merchant in Bagdad,
you fed all the poor.
    Ali Baba. Yes to set the rich a good example; but curse em now
that I have grown poor myself, I don't find that they follow it.
    Ganem. No; to be sure they bowed to you, while you were *Ali*

Baba, the generous Merchant.—Now Father they point at you for a *Beggar.*—'Tis the way of the world.

Ali Baba. Then the world points to a dirty crossway, and confounded be the finger-posts. But, what do you mean by a *beggar?* Hav'n't I strength? Hav'nt we hatchets? Don't we cut wood, and live by our honest industry?

Ganem. We do live, to be sure—but all the neighbours say that we are half starved.

Ali Baba. Then I'll give them the lie plump. Hold your tongue, Ganem—I won't have my son tell me he's half starved in my trade; as long as he's with his father cutting wood, I'll maintain it, he's a chopping-boy.

SONG—ALI BABA.

To a woodman's hut there came one day,
    A physician and dancing-master;
"This fellow's hovel must serve," said they,
    "For the rain pours faster and faster."
        Heigh-ho, fal de ral.

The physician was proud, and toss'd up his head,
    And scarce would the woodman mark, sir;
"But, doctor, we're equals," the woodman said,
    "For we both of us deal in bark, sir."
        Heigh-ho, fal de ral.

The master of dance was as grand as you please,
    Till the woodman cried "how now, sir?
You cut but capers—I cut trees,
    And we all know the worth of a bow, sir."
        Heigh-ho, fal de ral.

At last, says the woodman, the weather is good,
    For the rain only falls from the eaves now;
So put out your heads—'twill be carrying wood,
    And pray both be taking your *leaves*, now."
        Heigh-ho, fal de ral.

                    [Exit.

Ganem. My dear Morgiana! how cruel is this suspense; but why should I make myself uneasy for her whose heart is already mine?

SONG—GANEM

Ah! what is the bosom's commotion,
   In a sea of suspense while 'tis tost,
While the heart in our passion's wild ocean,
   Feels even hope's anchor is lost.
Morgiana, thou art my dearest,
   For thee I have languish'd and griev'd;
And when hope to my bosom was nearest,
   How oft has that hope been deceiv'd.
       Morgiana my hope was deceived.

The storm of despair is blown over;
   No more by its vapour deprest,
I laugh at the clouds of a lover,
   With the sunshine of joy in my breast.
Love, made by a parent my duty,
   To the wish of my heart now arriv'd,
I bend to the power of beauty,
   And every fond hope is revived.
       Morgiana, my hope is revived.
                 [*Exit.*[1]

SCENE III[2]

A grand Piazza belonging to CASSIM BABA. *Guests enter, as from an entertainment, who take leave of* ZAIDA, *and depart.*

Zaida. So they are all gone!——broad day light, I declare! I flatter myself my elegant ball and supper will be the talk and admiration of all Bagdad. [*Enter* COGIA.] Cogia, I hope none of the visitors saw you in that horrible dowdy dress of yours.

---

[1]*Duncombe's Edition.* Omitted, 1814 *Edition*, which substitutes: he's a chopping boy. But come boy, let us further into the forest to our morning's walk. [*Exeunt.*]

[2]This scene is found only in 1814 *Edition.* In *Duncombe's Edition*, the song "Ah where can I turn," is sung by Cogia in the Cottage Scene (Act I, scene iv).

Cogia. I kept out of the way as you ordered, I assure you, sister.

Zaida. Well, though I *am* your sister-in-law, you needn't always be putting me in mind of it—I know I am wife to Cassim Baba, who is rolling in riches.

Cogia. And I am wife to his brother Ali Baba, who is pining in poverty.

Zaida. That's the reason I'm so kind and compassionate to you; whenever I give a grand expensive entertainment, an't I always so considerate as to employ you to help the servants? And, provided you keep out of sight of my fashionable friends, that you may not disgrace me, havn't I at all times so much affection for you as to allow you to earn a day's work in my house to keep your brats at home from starving?

Cogia. But if you'd be still kinder, and speak for us to your husband, he'd surely do something for his indigent brother.

Zaida. And what made him indigent? His own folly and extravagance.

Cogia. I thought it had been his charity.

Zaida. His vanity, you mean; while he had money as a merchant, he had the ostentation not to be able to resist any tale of a friend's distress, and now he's obliged to solicit alms for himself.

Cogia. Only from his brother.

Zaida. And that's monstrous mean; whenever he degrades himself to his relations, it makes us quite uncomfortable.

Cogia. Dear sister, consider he is now forced, with my poor son Ganem, to cut wood for subsistence in the neighbouring forest, where, Alla protect them! their lives are in daily peril, from the banditti and evil spirits that infest and haunt the place.

Zaida. All his own fault.

Cogia. Ah, sister! a very little spared from last night's entertainment might have made our perishing family happy.

Zaida. And so you pretend to dictate to me how I am to dispose of my own property! Insolence!—but, remember this, Madam, if I find any more of such pertness and ingratitude, after the marks I have heaped upon you of my pity and affection, not

another day's charing do you get in this house—and so I leave
you to reflect upon it. [*Exit.*
    Cogia. Ah, poverty!—The cruelty of the world is enough!—
it needs not the insults of relations to make it more bitter.

SONG

Ah! where can I turn for relief,
    Since my sorrows a sister disdains?
I have no one to soften my grief,
    My heart in sad silence complains.
How oft have I wept at the woes,
    Describ'd in the poet's sad tale!
How oft did they break my repose,
    When no sorrows of mine could avail!

Compassion's soft tear I have shed,
    When misery stood at my door;
When, who could have thought, or have said,
    I must soon my own sorrows deplore?
Thus friends, thus deserted around,
    New woe can my sister impart?
Yes,—her scorn gives a still sharper wound,
    By ingratitude barbing the dart.

SCENE IV[1]

The interior of ALI BABA's *cottage.*

COGIA *enters, and runs to the bed, where she beholds her infants.*
    Cogia. Thank heaven! my little ones are still asleep.—Sleep,
they say, is nourishing; but, when they awake, I have nothing
——nothing to give them. I wish my sister had paid me for my
last night's work—but, as it is, I——Oh, my heart is breaking!

MORGIANA *peeps in at the door, having a small basket in
her hand.*

    Morgiana. Any body at home?

[1]In *Duncombe's Edition*, this scene follows the Robbers' Scene (Act I, scene v.)

Cogia. Who's that?

Morgiana [*coming in*]. 'Tis I only, your sister-in-law's slave, Morgiana.

Cogia. Morgiana!—my good girl!

Morgiana. I have got a basket here full of eatables; they belonged to your sister, my mistress; and thinking your sweet little children might like 'em—I—I—I—I hope you'll excuse it—I —I—stole 'em!

Cogia. Stole them, Morgiana!

Morgiana. Only from the servants; so I can't call it stealing, neither, for when they stole them first, 'twas only called peculation.

Cogia. But from my sister, Morgiana?

Morgiana. On the leavings of your sister's table—her slaves riot in luxury—your children wanted a meal; so there is no crime in what I am doing. I know where the little rogues lie, let me run in and leave the basket for a scramble among them. [*Lifts up the curtain.*] Here, dears, Morgiana's coming—hear, my loves. [*Goes behind the curtain.*]

Cogia. Why should a sister withhold that relief which the glowing heart of a stranger thus leaps in bestowing?

Re-enter MORGIANA.

Morgiana. I've left the basket among them. How the young rogues, bless their little souls, are pulling it to pieces!

Cogia. How can I thank you?

Morgiana. Pshaw!—don't mention thanks! But isn't Ganem yet returned?

Cogia. Ganem!

Morgiana. I——I mean his father—your husband, you know.

Cogia. No. I never expect him till late in the day; and who knows whether he'll ever return? Whenever he goes into the forest, I feel as if I had parted with him for ever.

Morgiana. But did Ganem ever see any of its terrible inhabitants?

Cogia. Ganem!

Morgiana. Ali Baba, I mean.

Cogia. I don't know; but when I have queſtioned him, he has answered so oddly, that I think he muſt have seen something ſtrange and dreadful.

Morgiana. Dreadful! I pity him! so young as he is to run such risks!

Cogia. Young, Morgiana! Ali Baba so young!

Morgiana. I—I mean so good as he is. I'm sure I feel for him, from the bottom of my heart, Cogia. Oh! would I were your slave, that I might night and day serve you and Ganem—I mean you and Ali Baba.[1]

Cogia. Dear Morgiana, my slave! you would be my friend, as you are now.

DUET

Morgiana. When o'er life's sunshine clouds are caſt,
　　　　　The cheek will loose its bloom,
Cogia.　　But cheering friendship smiles at laſt,
　　　　　And dissipates the gloom.
　　　　　Alas! from early life enslav'd,
Morgiana. ⌠I feel the galling chain,
Cogia.　 ⌡May heaven deſtroy that chain,
　　　　　But love's power soft too long brav'd,
Morgiana. ⌠Inflicts a deeper pain,
Cogia.　 ⌡But love may cure that pain.

　　　　　　　　　　[*Exit* MORGIANA *and* COGIA.

SCENE V

A Foreſt, with high rocks. ALI BABA *discovered cutting wood.*

Ali Baba [*looking at a log in his hand*]. This is the tougheſt morsel I ever met with, except laſt Sunday a shoulder of mutton;

[1]After this, *Duncombe's Edition* reads:
Cogia. Ah, Morgiana, you would not have the means to be so generous then as you are now. [*Exit Morgiana.*]
　　　　　　　SONG—COGIA
　　　　Last night I sat me down and cried.
The scene then continues as in Act I, scene vi, of the 1814 *Edition. Cumberland's Edition* arranges very much as *Duncombe's*, and both omit the Duet, "When o'er life's sunshine."

but I got this—that—and——[*cleaves the log*]—now I've got thro' this Ganem, lad, how dos't go on?

Ganem. I've cut my hand to the bone.

Ali Baba. The devil! then you have done a neat job of journey-work! Go home with the panniers;—is it deep?

Ganem. Pretty well, for that matter.

Ali Baba. Zounds! and wounds mortify! hurry home, and tell your mother—don't affront her, tho; tell her I've a great respect for her salve that cures everything, but I wish she'd sell a few logs, if she can just to get a surgeon to look at your wound.

Ganem. Dear father, it is nothing.

Ali Baba. Don't be too sure of that—I lost my fortune like a philosopher, but I couldn't so well bear the loss of a son.

Ganem. I'm sure 'tis of no consequence, I have bound it round with a handkerchief; and I'm positive 'twill heal of itself.

Ali Baba. Are you? then how dare you, you clumsy rascal, be so awkward to cut your finger,—you did it on purpose, to scare old foolish father out of his wits. However, go home with the load, and then come back, for another; but hark ye, you have another wound, that I ought to have talked to you about.

Ganem. Another wound!

Ali Baba. Yes, made by two plaguing sharp instruments.

Ganem. And what are they, father.

Ali Baba. A pair of eyes and a pretty girl's face is the case for 'em; they chop thro' a young fellow's trunk, into his heart, sooner than I can chip a twig.——

Ganem. I don't understand you.

Ali Baba. Yes, you do, my brother's slave, Morgiana.

Ganem. I—I—I——

Ali Baba. Don't stutter—I know it. But mind, poverty has made me a little proud, not much; I'm like an old oak, a little more majestic, because the storms have shattered me. Don't marry your uncle's slave!

Ganem. Am I to despise the virtues of Morgiana, because she is enslaved by fraud and violence.

Ali Baba. No, surely—virtues are plaguey scarce, and I love 'em if 'tis only for their variety.

Ganem. And to conquer my love for Morgiana is hopeless; her many amiable qualities.

Ali Baba. Don't talk of 'em before your uncle—if you must marry, you must; but if my brother Cassim should hear you, he'll raise the price of his slave, and I shall never be able to buy myself a daughter in law.

Ganem. My kind father, I——

Ali Baba. Psha—get along—away with the first load; I shall have another ready by the time you come back.

Ganem. But why should you stay?

Ali Baba. To cut another load—I tell you; how the boy stares! What can harm me? [*pointing to his dress*]—here is no temptation for a robber, I have nothing to lose but this, [*pointing to his axe*] and this has a sharp argument or two, to offer before it will quit me.

Ganem. That may defend you from a robber—but from evil spirits what can protect you?

Ali Baba. What can protect me? an honest heart here—[*striking his breast*]—and a trust there: [*pointing upwards*]. Come get you gone—I'm very safe.

[*Exit* GANEM *with the ass.*

Ali Baba [*rises and comes forward*]. They say that not only Banditti, but evil spirits infest this forest; it has some strange inhabitants I am certain, for to this place I have traced their horses' footsteps—I must be satisfied.—Here have I heard their horns and voices—and here will I await their coming whatever be the hazard. What have I to fear? the loss of life, well—I will risk it. [*A bugle horn sounds at a distance.*] They approach—where can I be concealed? This tree will hide me.—[*Climbs into a tree.*

[*A bugle horn answers the former.*

[*The Forty Thieves are seen at a distance galloping down the hill. Enter one of the Thieves as a Scout, he looks about cautiously and sounds his horn; on which all the Thieves enter.*[1]

---

[1]*Duncombe's Edition* reads:—

The Robbers are seen returning home through the forest on horseback. They dismount —a march is played—and the Robbers march on singly, headed by Mirza—Abdallah and Hassarac last. They march round and range on each side.

Abdallah.[1] Is all safe?

First Thief. All is safe.

Abdallah. Then brave comrades, secure our booty, we must not lose a moment; I have intelligence that on the edge of the forest, a caravan is passing, loaded with treasure; now for our charm.

The Thieves make obeisance and Chaunt,
"Pronounce the charm and split the rock."

Abdallah. OPEN SESAME!

[*The Rock opens, and discovers Brazen Gates to an inner Cavern. Thieves chaunt*—"Now bid the brasen gates unlock!"

Abdallah. Open Sesame!

[*The gates open with a tremendous crash. Inner passage is discovered; the Robbers enter with plunder into the cavern, followed by the* CAPTAIN.

Abdallah [*at the mouth of the cave*]. Guard the horses.

[*Exit into the cave.*

First Thief. The wood-cutters have been at work to-day,

Second Thief. I've marked one, a prying rascal! if ever I catch him near our cave, I'll chop him to pieces with his own axe.

First Thief. And hang him up on yon tree, as a scarecrow to frighten others.

ALI BABA *peeps between the branches of the tree; but on hearing the threat, draws back, exclaiming—*

Oh! Mahomet!

[2][*Second Thief.* What noise is that?

First Thief. 'Tis Hassarac.

Enter HASSARAC *and his Party, from the Forest.*

Mirza. Well, Hassarac, what think you of our Captain's plan?

Hassarac. Full of danger and treachery.

Mirza. Ha! treachery, say you?

Hassarac. Yes, treachery: you all know the neighbouring

[1]For *Abdallah,* 1814 *Edition* reads *Hassarac,* through combining these characters.
[2]*Duncombe's Edition.* Omitted, 1814 *Edition,* again through combining Abdallah and Hassarac.

Bashaw? his daughter, the beauteous Zelie, is passing through our forest on a pilgrimage. We are to attack the caravan.

Mirza. What's she worth?

Hassarac. Do you forget? this is the girl for whom our Captain jumpt into the Tigris.

Mirza. No, I remember. When the boat was upset with the beauteous Zelie, he plunged into the waves, and saved her without wetting a whisker.

Hassarac. To that beauty he has lost his heart.

Mirza. But where's the treachery?

Hassarac. How dull you are;—with the treasures of our cave, and this girl an hostage, he procures *his* pardon, and our ruin—the destruction of our band.

Mirza. Ha! that must be prevented. We'll support you.

Hassarac. Give me your hand—there are more of your mind. Let this expedition once take place, and then——hush!]

[ABDALLAH *and* ROBBERS *return from the Cave.*]

Abdallah. Shut, Sesame. [*The cave closes.*] Now, my brave comrades, to horses; handle well your sabres, and the greatest treasures we have ever gained is ours.—Comrades, away!

SONG

Like the wind-driven sand
Is the speed of our band;
By night and by day,
We are lords of the way;
Our range is an empire,—its people our prey.
Hence, away to our toils!
Be each bosom prepar'd,
And the traveller's spoils
Shall the bravest reward.   [*Exit* ROBBERS.

ALI BABA *descends from the tree.*

Ali Baba. I shake all over like the leaf of an aspin in a high wind; this is the band of robbers that is the terror of all Bagdad, and here is all their plunder. Shall I venture? I know their charm

—if I am discovered they'll saw off the head of a woodman—if I escape with some of their plunder, I'm a made man for ever!—so here goes!——Open Sesame! [*The rock splits.*] Oh! if "Open Sesame" could split open rocks for the benefit of the poor, I wish each honeſt fellow in diſtress had the charm to unlock all flinty hearts that are shut to humanity! [*Goes into the cave.*] Shut, Sesame! [*Cave closes him in.*]

Re-enter GANEM, *with panniers.*

Ganem. The robbers of the foreſt—thank heaven I have escaped them; tho' faith 'twas narrowly. Where is my poor father? I hope he has not fallen in their way.

Ali Baba [*from within*]. Open, Sesame!

[*The rock splits open and,* ALI BABA *is discovered at the mouth of it, loaded with bags of gold.*

Ganem. His voice!——what can this mean?

Ali Baba. Who's that? robber or devil—if you attempt to ſtop me, I'll knock you down with a bag of gold.

Ganem. Why, father?

Ali Baba. Ganem, is it you? Oh! my dear boy!——

Ganem. What's all this?

Ali Baba. No matter—take this, and chuck it into the pan-niers—and this—and this:—zounds! I'm so flurried. Hey—here's some more. [*Takes up more bags of gold, a gold goblet, &c. &c.*]

Ganem. Well, but I——

Ali Baba. Don't talk, you dog;—if you open your mouth we shall have our throats cut; fill the panniers—there—there—and get along—there—there.   [*Exit* GANEM.
Hold! hold!——Shut, Sesame. [*Cave closes.*] Ha! ha! ha! [*Exit.*

SCENE VI

ALI BABA's *Cottage.*

Enter COGIA.

Cogia. 'Tis long paſt the hour, and my poor husband and son not yet returned! If any accident should have befallen them, what

will become of my dear infants? Heaven knows their lot is hard
enough already.

SONG
Laſt night I sat me down and cried,
  My heart as sad as may be,
For then with hunger almoſt died
  My little darling baby.
Ah! how a mother's heart is griev'd,
  To see her infant dying:
A savage who her pangs perceiv'd,
  Could scarce refrain from crying

Not yet returned! what will become of me?
  Ali Baba [*calling without*]. Hilloo! Cogia. [*Sings*], Toll, lol, de
rol.
  Cogia. Oh! there they are.

Enter ALI BABA *singing.*
  Cogia. Dear Ali, what has kept you so long?
  Ali Baba. My work, to be sure; and it has made me hungry!
give me supper enough to give a thousand bashaws the apoplexy.
  Cogia. Supper! ah, my dear Ali! where can I get you a supper?
  Ali Baba. You'll find supper enough in the panniers.
  Cogia. What! the wood?
  Ali Baba. Burn the wood!

GANEM *enters with the panniers.*
  Cogia. Why it muſt maintain us and the children to-morrow.
  Ali Baba [*snapping his fingers*]. That's for to-morrow!
  Cogia. Mahomet preserve us! his brain is turned! an't you
well, Ali?
  Ali Baba. No;—I've had a violent and unexpeſted attack of
the yellow jaundice.
  Cogia. The jaundice!
  Ali Baba. Gold, you jade!—gold! and I hope it will prove a
chronic disease with me.
  Ganem. Look in the panniers, mother, look into the panniers!

Cogia. Mercy on me! what's here? 'tis gold sure enough; where does it all come from?——

Ali Baba. Showered from the sky; we held our caps and the panniers open while the rain fell.

Cogia. Mahomet! do not deceive me! How much is there?

Ganem. Nay, mother, we never ſtaid to count.

Cogia. But I will.

Ali Baba. Count!——you may as well count the leaves on the trees in yonder foreſt, or the hairs on your cat's back.

TRIO—ALI BABA, GANEM, *and* COGIA.
Happy the day,
Cares flit away,
Sorrow no more shall our pleasure annoy.
As the sky clears,
Sunshine appears,
Danger and grief yield to safety and joy.
Happy the day, &c.

Friendless and poor,
Want paced the floor,
The breath of despair it blew chill on our hearth.
Changed is our lot,
Woes be forgot,
Away with all cares and give welcome to mirth.
Happy the day, &c.

Wealth while it flows,
Treachery knows,
Faithless the poor or the wealthy may prove;
Deſtined to know
Mutual woe,
Mutual, sure, muſt be our love.
Happy the day, &c.][1]

Cogia. I can do it,—I'll borrow a measure from my siſter Zaida. [*Runs out.*

Ali Baba. Let her have her way;—now, Ganem, you shall find

[1] *Duncombe's Edition.* Omitted, 1814 *Edition.*

that the report of our wealth will draw back our false friends, as the tinkling of bells attract bees. Confound all such fair-weather friendship!

Re-enter COGIA, *with a small measure.*

Cogia. Here it is.

Ali Baba. Well—satisfy yourself; Ganem, help your mother —but stay——where can we hide it? Oh! in the cellar. Here, lad, your hand; [*They open the trap-door.*] now, Cogia, empty the measure there—we don't require a charm to hide our wealth; the character of poverty is sufficient protection. [*Knocking without.*

[COGIA *empties the measure, and runs to the door.*

Cogia. They're coming!

Ali Baba. Who?—the thieves! [1]

---

[1]*Duncombe's Edition* reads:—
Ali Baba. Who, the thieves? [*puts all down the trap and shuts it.*]
Cogia. No your brother Cassim and his wife.

Enter ZAIDA, *through door.*
I was just coming home with your measure, sister.
Zaida. And pray what did you want with the measure, sister?
Cogia. Only to measure out a little rice.
Zaida. Gold! to measure out gold, you mean.
Cogia. Measure gold! Lord, how should I——
Zaida. Nay, it is in vain to hide it from us. I suspected something by your eagerness to get the measure, and therefore put some grease at the bottom, by which I discovered what sort of grain you wanted to measure out.

Enter CASSIM, *through door.*
Cassim Baba. Good day, brother Ali.
Ali Baba. How d'ye do, brother Cassim.
Cassim Baba. So, you are grown rich, I find [*significantly*].
Zaida. Yes, so rich that they measure out gold.
Ali Baba. 'Tis plain you think so by your coming to see me.
Cassim Baba. Yes, and like a brother I am come to offer you everything I possess: my fortune is ample, and I now come to share it with you.
Ali Baba. Havn't you been in the habit of thinking that a little unreasonable.
Cassim Baba. Why, Ali, if you had proposed, I——
Ali Baba. I, proposed!—look'ee, brother Cassim, my poor hovel stands within ten yards of your magnificent mansion—I live under a brother's splendid nose, turned up at my poverty. You have known that my poor children have been almost starving for a meal—you have known my wife's patient anguish—you have offered her insult by suffering her to drudge in your house, and then called it charity. And do you think I should have had any success if I had walked in with my hatchet under my arm, and said, "Brother, share your fortune with me?" Oh, no, no.
Cassim Baba. But, consider, my *dear* Ali,—we are as it may be said, one flesh and blood.
Ali Baba. Well, I've no right to be angry with you, Cassim, as you happen to be my

Cogia. Thieves! what thieves? Cassim and his wife, and
Ali Baba. The devil! Ganem, be quick—here! here!——

[*Knocking again.*

[*They hurry the panniers, &c. into the trap-door;* ALI *and* GANEM
take their hatchets, and pretend to work at their logs of timber.
COGIA *goes to the door, and returns with* CASSIM *and* ZAIDA.

Cogia. I was coming to return your measure, sister.——

[*Gives it to* ZAIDA.

Zaida [*examines it, then gives it to* CASSIM]. Would you believe
it? [*Aside.*]

Cassim Baba. Indeed!—I'll find them out—[*aside*]. How do
you do, brother Ali?

Ali Baba. How do you do, brother?—how do you do? [*Aside
to* GANEM.] what do they mean?

Ganem. No good, I'm sure.   [GANEM *retires.*

Cassim Baba. So, brother, you have been cutting wood to
some purpose—you have got rich, I find.

Ali Baba. That remains to be proved—but I'm sure you think
so, by your coming to call upon me.

Cogia. We rich! how should we get riches?

Zaida. Pray, sister, what did you want with this measure.

Cogia. To measure some food for the beasts.

Zaida. Indeed! do beasts eat gold? Look here!—[*Shows the
measure, with a piece of gold sticking to the bottom inside.* ALI *and*
COGIA *seem confused.*] Your eagerness gave me suspicion—I put

brother—unless you were my particular friend—the tide of worldly friendship over
flows the successful, but it runs dry to the needy—the man who is profuse in feasts
will have his larder stocked with presents—but he'll find it empty of gifts the moment
he wants a dinner.

Cassim Baba. How, brother! do you slight my offers of friendship?

Cogia (aside to ALI). You had best not provoke him, for perhaps he'll——

Ali Baba. I know, he'll inform the Cadi; and if the law gets hold of it, good-bye
poor Sesame—so we must e'en give up one half to preserve the other. Well then,
brother I have discovered the secret cave where the robbers conceal all their plunder.

Cassim Baba. Good fortune! let us go there instantly.

Ali Baba. It opens by a charm. Here, this way, and I'll tell you all.

Cassim Baba. You must give me their signals: and it will be best to let me go to
the robbers cave by myself; it will prevent suspicion.

Ali Baba. You shall have them—but mind, be not too greedy, brother.

Cassim Baba. Never fear. Good day, brother; good day, Cogia.

Zaida. Good day, my dear brother; good day, my dear, dear sister. Good bye—
good-bye!   [*Exeunt* CASSIM *and* ZAIDA.]

ε little wax at the bottom, to ſtick to what you were measuring; and you see it shows that it was gold.

Cassim Baba. Come, brother, you have discovered the concealed treasure—is not that the truth?

Ali Baba. And, suppose it was the truth——what then?

Cassim Baba. And won't you let your own dear brother share with you?

Ali Baba. Hav'nt you been in the habit of thinking that rather unreasonable?

Cassim Baba. Certainly not, between brothers; if you had proposed such a thing, my dear brother Ali——I——

Ali Baba. I proposed!—look ye, brother, my poor cabin ſtands within ten yards of your magnificent mansion; I live under a brother's splendid nose, turned up at my poverty;—you have known my wife's patient anguish; you have shown her insult, by employing her to drudge for bread, and then called it charity;—you have heard that my children have been perishing for a meal! Do you think I should have had any success, if I had walked in with my hatchet over my arm, and said, "Brother, share your fortune with me?"

Cassim Baba. Come, come, let us forget all this; you shall remove to my house, and henceforth we will be one family.

Ali Baba. I've no right to complain of you, Cassim, if you did not happen to be my brother, except, indeed, you were a particular friend. The tide of worldly affections overflow the successful —but the ſtream runs dry to the needy; a man who is profuse in feaſts, has his larder ſtocked with presents, but he'll find it empty of gifts the moment he wants a dinner!

Cogia [*aside*]. Dear husband, you muſt consent—you know his temper.

Ali Baba [*alarmed*]. True, he will inform the Cadi, and if the law gets hold of it, alas, poor Sesame!—we muſt give one to save the other. Well—well—know then [*to* Cassim], I have discovered the cave where the robbers conceal their plunder.

Zaida. Have you, indeed!

Cassim Baba. Where is it? I will go this inſtant.

Ali Baba. Hold—[*aside to him*] there is a charm to open it. This way. [*They retire together.*

Zaida [*aside*]. As they are growing rich, 'tis time to alter my tone. [*To* Cogia.] My sweet Cogia—do tell me how are those dear little angels, your beautiful children?

Cogia. O you mean the children you permitted me to work for, that I might keep the brats from starving.

Zaida. Nay, sister, that's unkind.

Cogia. Well—well—sister, I forgive you.

Zaida. Dear Cogia!

Cassim Baba [*coming forward eagerly with* Ali]. Dear brother, I must have your dress; with that I shall pass unsuspected.

Ali Baba. You shall have it—but remember the charm.

Cassim Baba. Yes, yes,—never fear.

Zaida. Come back well loaded, Cassim.

Cassim Baba. Don't doubt that.

Ali Baba. Be not too greedy, brother.

Cassim Baba. Well, well—but draw the curtain, dear brother Ali, you may take cold. [*Draws the curtain, and exit with* Zaida.

Ali Baba. Now, Cogia——oh, what a discovery!

Cogia. Now, my dear husband!

Ali Baba. Where Ganem?—O the sly rogue has stolen off to tell Morgiana of our good luck.

Cogia. Now, my dear husband, we are so rich, I think I ought to order a few under-petticoats.

Ali Baba. There! that is what a woman's head is always running upon.

Cogia. And pray what is yours running upon?

Ali Baba. Money-bags, you little devil—give me your hand. By Mahomet's mule, I am the happiest man in Bagdad!

SONG—Ali Baba *and* Cogia

Cogia.   While poor, the spirit flags,
                   Then we're pining daily;
Ali Baba.   Then drop down money bags,
                   And we'll to supper gaily.

Cogia.	Ah, Ali! my husband dear,
	Oft I've been a starver,
Ali Baba.	Now we'll have dinners here,
	And I will be grand carver?
Both.	O'er dales and mountains stray,
	Spite of wind and weather;
	Rough, smooth, whate'er our way,
	We will march together.
Cogia.	Do not, pray, since wealth's our hap,
	Rove in Bagdad's city,
Ali Baba.	When money's in our lap,
	A wife looks always pretty,
Cogia.	Friends, like bees, when wealth abounds,
	Swarms like metal's tinkling;
Ali Baba.	But when no gold resounds,
	They vanish in a twinkling.
Both.	O'er dales and mountains, &c. [*Exeunt.*

SCENE VII[1]

*The Forest—Rock open—*CASSIM *seen peeping out—steals forward and says—*

Shut————What will become of me? I have forgotten the word! [*He appears in great terror—hears the* ROBBERS' *bugle, and horses galloping. He rushes into the cave.*]

Enter the ROBBERS *from all quarters with booty.*
Hassarac. Ah! treason———we are betrayed—the charm discovered! Surround the entrance, while I explore the cave.
They all form a circle, with sabres drawn; HASSARAC *rushes in, and drags forth* CASSIM, *who exclaims—*
It was my brother sent me—my brother, gentlemen, Mercy, mercy, &c.
[*A confused noise then ensues, the* ROBBERS *vociferating* "Off with his head! throw him into the lake!" *They place him on their shoulders—*HASSARAC *exclaims—*Shut Sesame, *and all depart.*
[1]This scene is found only in 1814 *Edition.*

II. Z

SCENE VIII

A mountainy desart.—A black forest seen at a distance.
[ALCANDOR *enters, watching and listening for the tread of passengers and lays his ear to the ground. A whistle is heard—he rises and answers it.*

MIRZA *enters, and informs him of the approach of the caravan, and their determination to attack it.*

ABDALLAH *enters, and joins them—they all agree in the destruction of the caravan. They all go up the stage and point to it as being in sight, and go off rejoicing to join their comrades.*

ROBBERS

Hark! hark! hush! the camel driver's bell I hear;
Hush! hush! 'tis they, 'tis they, they're drawing near.

Enter the procession of the Caravan.

Chorus. Bid the lively cymbals jingle,
   While we mount the sandy steep,
  Let the bells of camels mingle,
  O'er the mountains as they creep.
   Bid the lively, &c.

At a signal made by ZELIE, *who is borne in a palanquin by four slaves, attended by females and guards,* SELIM *and* ZELIE *comes forward.*]¹

Zelie. Now, Selim, how far are we advanced upon our pilgrimage?

Selim. We are now, lady, not far from the end of it; one day's journey more brings us to the sacred mosque.

Zelie. Then we shall halt here and rest; let my tired beasts be led to the neighbouring well, and pitch my tents among yon olive tree shade; here shall we pass the night, the morning's sun shall guide us on our journey.

¹*Duncombe's Edition.* 1814 *Edition* substitutes:—
 Procession enters. Two elephants, preceded by officers bearing banners. After the elephants come two camels with numerous guards and attendants, music playing. They halt on the stage, at a signal made by ZELIE, *who is borne in a palanquin. by four slaves, attended by females and guards.* [ZELIE] *comes forward.*

Selim. If your slave might advise, we should still proceed. Within that wood, that skirts yon forest's edge, now faintly seen a black and sullen maze, your former foe, fell Orcobrand, resides, nay, more, I'm told a desperate banditti infests this forest, for rapine and midnight murder famed.

Zelie. I fear no danger—my guards are numerous and brave, then rest we here till morning. Oh! Mecca, birth-place of our mighty prophet, now does fancy's eye recall thy visionary shrines, whilst hope, fond hope, whispers to my heart its warmest wish.

[ATTENDANTS *shriek—a general cry of confusion.*

Selim. The numerous banditti—our guards surprised!

[*The* BANDITTI *rush forward—a general combat ensues, in which the Caravan party are worsted, and* ZELIE *borne off prisoner.*
[HASSARAC, MIRZA, ALCANDOR, *and the rest of the Robbers run across to attack the caravan, with loud huzzas. A great noise of fighting and huzzaing.*
HASSARAC *and* SELIM *come on fighting—a desperate battle ensues between them, in which* SELIM *is vanquished and thrown.*
ABDALLAH, ALCANDOR, *and the rest of the Robbers enter, with* ZELIE *prisoner.*

DUET *and* CHORUS

Zelie.	Thus for a lover's safety kneeling,
	Ah, must I plead to thee in vain?
Robber.	Haste away!
Selim.	More than my own her sorrows feeling,
	Duty bids me here remain.
Robber.	Haste away! haste away!
	*Chorus—*Bid the lively, &c.
Zelie.	Ah, must I plead in vain?
Selim.	Duty bids me here remain.
Robber.	Haste away! haste away!

Abdallah. Hold, Hassarac! Fair lady—[*to* ZELIE.]

Zelie. Heavens! my preserver a robber, the captain of banditti?——

Abdallah. Man must bend to strong necessity

Zelie. You saved my life—be not the destroyer of my honour.

Abdallah. Cursed be the villain who would harm the honour of a helpless woman! Lady, confide in me.

Zelie. What, in a robber?

Hassarac. Yes, a robber.

Abdallah. Silence, Hassarac! thou art——

Hassarac. A true robber. I have not the cant of honour and humanity.

Abdallah. Know you to whom you speak?

Hassarac. Yes, to a man—no better than myself.

Abdallah. Audacious mutineer! another word, my scymeter shall cleave thee to the earth.

Hassarac. My sabre bears as sharp an edge as yours.

Abdallah. This to decide it.

Hassarac. Seize him—away with him to our cave, and chain him to the rock.

Abdallah. Take my defiance, villain. [*They fight—the other Robbers seize* ABDALLAH.]

Hassarac. Hear him not—away with him. Zelie shall now be our ransom, comrades. Away to the cave—to the cave!

[*Exeunt* ABDALLAH *and* ZELIE *guarded.*][1]

---

[1]*Duncombe's Edition.* Omitted 1814 *Edition,* which substitutes the direction: *The Banditti rush forward, a general combat ensues, in which the Caravan party are worsted, and* ZELIE *borne off prisoner.*

Act the Second

SCENE I[1]

ORCOBRAND'S *Cave.*

Ornamented with different symbols of his mystic art.—A stand and books—an arch in the centre. [*Thunder and lightning.*]

Enter ORCOBRAND *through the arch, a short wand in his hand, like a caduceus, wound round with serpents.*

Orco-   IN thy black gulph, perdition, be for ever sunk
brand.   the meddling sprite, who dares oppose my will.
           May blasting tempests shiver her airy wings,
and demons shed their murky dew upon her, while thick, pesti-
ferous fogs confound and foil her purposes! Already has this
hated rival of my power, by means unfathomable e'en to the
hellish skill I boast, directed the feeble footsteps of a puny mortal
who, by *her* protection aided, fearlessly has ventured the dark
and gloomy cavern, whose magic portal till then, did never open
but to the cabalistic word my art invented. Ye dread associates,
fell mischief's children—pale-faced Famine,—deep Fraud,—
ruthless War, and unrelenting Rapine, I summon to my aid.

Enter FAMINE, FRAUD, WAR, *and* RAPINE, *two on each side, as they are call'd.*

CHORUS OF DEMONS
Strike the world with fear and wonder,
Rend the poles with bolts of thunder;
Join'd in one fate we'll ne'er give way,
Join'd in one fate we'll ne'er give way,
But combat for infernal sway,
But combat, &c.

[1]*Duncombe's Edition.* Omitted, 1814 *Edition.* Cumberland's Edition agrees (generally, but not precisely) with Duncombe's.

Yes, yes, yes, idolaters of fire,
Revel in the realms below,
Revel, &c.
Revel, &c.

Your infernal train of prowling miscreant votaries, call from the deep abyss of Pluto's realm to aid, with all their powerful enginery, the dark designing measures of thy determin'd master. [*A horn sounds.*] Hark! the watchful gnomes sound their hoarse shells, announcing the approach of mortal footsteps. Whoe'er thou art that boldly venturest to this dread abode, gaunt *Murder*, who guards our brazen portal, will admit and usher to our magic presence.

Enter HASSARAC *through the arch.*

Hassarac. Before you, mighty Orcobrand, I lowly bend.

Orcobrand. Approach, and speak thy wishes.

Hassarac. Since the banditti thrive beneath thy care,—confirm *me* as their leader; for Abdalla, our captain once——

Orcobrand. Your captain!—a puny slave!—a suckling unworthy of a leader's name;—who crouches at a woman's feet, and sighs for love, and all its flimsy blisses;—but he is now within my power: in yonder dungeon chain'd he lies, and to increase the horrors of his fate, within his view, fast bound in adamantine chains, groans his beauteous Zelie.

Hassarac. Yes, with Zelie, our new captive; 'twas to her the milksop sigh'd—now they may groan together. My comrades——

Orcobrand. For you, brave youth, the charge is yet too much: the masterrobber of that mighty band link'd by fate in ties indissoluble, and by my magic power protected, should bear a heart, wherein the germ of cruelty by nature's hand had been implanted; fostered at the breast of knavery, and pruned by deep deceit, until the spreading branches of determined rapine, present a full blown villain.

Hassarac. And with your aid, my head may blossom some years longer.

Orcobrand. Thou hast already proved thyself unskill'd in such deep thought as should preserve thee from the perils of that state. Was it not by your neglect, remissness inexcusable! that your abode was known to mortal man?

Hassarac. It was; but that secret goes no further. I acted justice in our cave this morning, and lopp'd a head off.—'Twas a fool's —who came, I know not by what means, among our treasures; but head and trunk I threw among the palms that skirt our dwelling's mouth.

Orcobrand. Thou canst not think thy secret rests alone with those who are the partners of thy trade;—another now has gain'd the word, and may proclaim it to the curious world.

Hassarac. How! another?

Orcobrand. Yes, another;—protected by a female power, that far transcends in magic charm the influence I lately boasted.

Hassarac. Her triumph shall be short.

Orcobrand. Another lives, I say, that has your secret word obtain'd; a mortal too. If thou wouldst prove thyself worthy the mighty charge you now solicit—'tis thine by *mortal means* to rid thy fears and mine; for in his hand thy life, and that of all thy friends, like the unsteady balance of a quivering beam, stands now in doubtful equipoise.

Hassarac. On me then rest the issue—[*kneels*]—And may sleep never close these eyes, if Bagdad's city hold him, till craft has hunted down my prey and courage plunged this dagger in his heart. [*Rises.*]

Orcobrand. Thy now determined purpose keep—Let me but view the purple die upon thy trusty weapon, and claim of me the bright reward of thy dark deed. Go—hence! pursue the fix'd and steady purpose of thy soul—Be resolute and prosper.

[*Exeunt severally;* HASSARAC *through the arch.*]

SCENE II

An apartment in CASSIM BABA's *house.*

Enter MORGIANA, *meeting* GANEM.

Ganem. Oh! Morgiana, I've been seeking you every where.

Morgiana. No, have you! But this is a very busy night, and we hav'nt time to talk now, my late master just dead, and my new one just taken possession.

Ganem. True: and though close on the heels of a funeral, an entertainment (according to our custom) is preparing for the inheritor. But dear Morgiana, spare me a few moments to talk to you, and no longer keep me in suspence.

Morgiana. Oh, Ganem, this isn't a time—nay, nay, let go my hand.

Enter ZAIDA.

Zaida. Oh, Morgiana!

Morgiana. Don't give way to grief, madam; consider 'tis Mahomet has taken my master from you; do take comfort.

Zaida. I don't know how I'm to find comfort, when Mahomet, in taking away your master, forgot to leave me his money; that low brute, his brother, Ali Baba, inherits house, goods, chattles, and every sequin.

Morgiana. But Ali Baba was here last night, you know, madam, after the fatal event, and promised to be kind to you.

Zaida. He—and must I depend upon him? I never could bear the sight of him—a poor narrow minded, dirty, wood-cutting—

Enter ALI BABA—[*She runs and throws herself in his arms.*] Oh! my dear brother-in-law, how happy am I to see you in the midst of my misfortunes.

Ali Baba. Come, come, chear up; death has always his hatchet in his hand, and, sooner or later, cuts up all families, root and branch.—You have lost a husband—

Zaida. And you a brother. Oh! night and day we must never cease to lament him.

Ali Baba. Then let us split the difference, and four and twenty hours between us; and if he fulfilled the duties of a husband, as he observed the duties of a relative, your lamentations for your losses by night, and mine by day, will be pretty equal. There, go to your chamber, dry your eyes, and be comforted.

Zaida. Alas, chamber, mansion, fortune, every thing now is yours!

Ali Baba. Well, well, I must take possession, but I shall forget that all is my own, on your account, if you won't put me in mind of it.

Zaida. My good, good brother.   [*Kisses his hand. Exit.*

Morgiana [*advancing*]. Sir—sir—

Ali Baba. Morgiana, is it you?

Morgiana. Yes, sir, now your slave.

Ali Baba. My slave! my friend, my benefactress! My wife told me, when I came home yesterday, that you brought her and my poor children a meal, when they were almost starving; I shall never forget it.

Morgiana. We have no time to waste; I have a secret which, if known, might be full of danger.

Ali Baba. Respecting my brother?

Morgiana. Yes.

Ali Baba. His avarice has been his death.

Morgiana. I know it; his wife's joy betrayed to me the charm you had imparted, and I learnt yesterday he had gone on a venture to the robbers' cave.

Ali Baba. Aye, I crept thither in the dusk, to watch the event of his expedition; and my blood curdled when I saw his remains in the stream near the cavern; no doubt they were thrown there by the banditti, but how they were conveyed to this house, the spirits that watch round the abode alone can determine.

Morgiana. Certainly by supernatural means—and last night entering his chamber, there I found his corpse, his severed head lay near it, on his breast was placed this scroll.

Ali Baba [*reading*]. "Morgiana, upon you depends the safety of the family." Well, how did you act?

Morgiana. I remembered to have seen a shrewd merry knave, who whistles over his daily work, in a low shed many streets distant, opposite the fountain.

Ali Baba. I'll be hanged if you don't mean the cobbler.

Morgiana. The same.

Ali Baba. He would do any thing for money.

Morgiana. I thought so—him I engaged. I brought him blind-folded to Cassim's chamber, there he sewed the head to the body; that done, with the same precaution I led him back to his stall, and vanished from his sight.

Ali Baba. Excellent Morgiana, how can I reward you?

Morgiana. Don't mention that; but, dear sir, what has happened to you?

Ali Baba. Just as I reached the forest——

Morgiana. The mourners are at the gate, you must hasten to meet them.

Ali Baba. True: let us go—hold, the Fairy of the Lake gave me this, [*Gives a small phial to* MORGIANA.] one single drop produces instant death; do you, Morgiana, take care of it; and when I visit the cave, we must contrive to give some of the robbers a dose.

Morgiana. No doubt that was the intention of the Fairy.

Ali Baba. Now for a sorrowful countenance. Ah! I'm afraid if the face showed the feelings of the heart, many a mourner would prove a merry one.[1]

[*Exit.*

¹*Duncombe's Edition* here substitutes:

Exit ALI BABA. *Enter* GANEM.

Ganem. Stay, Morgiana. Why do you thus cruelly keep me in suspense? Why thus delay?

Mor. Let go my hand.　　　　　　　　　　　　　[*Takes her hand.*

DUET—GANEM *and* MORGIANA

Ganem.　Ah, cruel maid, too soon retiring,
　　　　　Love's tender vows all fears remove;
Mor.　　Ah, cruel youth, too much desiring,
　　　　　I dare not say how much I love.
Ganem.　Yet why this haste?—
Mor.　　No more delay me, you must not stay,
Ganem.　One moment yet—
Mor.　　You must not stay,
Together.　{Ah, cruel maid, &c.
　　　　　　{Ah, cruel youth, &c.
Mor.　　By love's pure and tender power,
　　　　　This hand and heart I pledge to you;
　　　　　By the blessings of this hour,
　　　　　To plighted vows for ever true,
　　　　　No more delay me, you must away;
Ganem.　Yet why this haste? one moment stay.
　　　　　Ah, cruel maid, too soon retiring, &c.
　　　　　Ah, cruel youth, too much desiring, &c.
Together.　{No more delay, you must away, &c.
　　　　　　{Yet why this haste? one moment yet—
　　　　　Ah, let me stay, &c.
　　　　　Good night, good night, &c.

Morgiana. Ah, dear Ganem! but I forgot that his father is now my master; so he will look down upon the poor slave Morgiana —Ah, love! your only delight is to torment us.

SONG

Ah! little blind boy, much too often you prove us,
    What tricks you delight in, how restless you reign,
To all kind of folly your aim is to move us,
    And pleasure derive from creating our pain,
                    Ah! little blind boy.

To what mischief your malice poor mortals exposes,
    While nothing the sting of your dart can abate,
Yet so strong is the spell that cunning discloses,
    Your absence is worse than the pain you create,
                    Ah! little blind boy.

SCENE III

A Street, with a cobbler's stall—MUSTAPHA *the cobbler discovered working in his stall.*

Mustapha. Pshaw! my stall this evening is as hot as Beelzebub's back-kitchen in the dog-days; there should be something like a breeze between the streets here [*brings out his sign, stall, &c.*] So here I'll work, and if there's no air to be had any where else, I'll sing one.

SONG

Last week I took a wife,
    And when I first did woo her,
I vow'd to stick thro' life
    Like cobbler's wax unto her:
But soon thro' some mishap,
    To logger-heads together,
And when my wife began to strap,
    Why I began to leather.

My wife, without her shoes,
　　Is hardly three feet seven,
And I to all men's views,
　　Am full five feet eleven.
So when to take her down some pegs,
　　I drubb'd her neat and clever;
She made a bolt right through my legs,
　　And ran away for ever.

When she was gone, good lack!
　　My hair like hog's hairs briſtl'd,
I thought she'd ne'er come back,
　　So went to work and whiſtl'd.
Then let her go, I've got my ſtall,
　　Which may no robber rifle,
'Twould break my heart to lose my awl,
　　To lose my wife's a trifle!

Enter HASSARAC, *disguised as an oil-merchant.*

Hassarac. Here will I begin my search; the rash roof, whose head has paid the forfeit of his crime, confessed he had the secret from his brother; yet, in the frenzy of my revenge I forgot to learn his name. Now, by Mahomet I swear, I will not sleep till I have found the knave that knows our secret, and send his body, with his brother's, down the ſtream. I'll queſtion this fellow. Cobbler!

Cobbler. Sir to you! fol de rol [*working*].

Hassarac. What news is ſtirring?

Cobbler. Rare news—we've a tax upon leather, fol de rol.

Hassarac. Do you call that rare news? Why it will ruin the shoemakers.

Cobbler. So much the better for the cobblers: take away the physicians, and there is more work for the apothecaries.

Hassarac. Not so—the apothecaries thrive by the physicians.

Cobbler. Why, that's true; but take away the physicians and apothecaries, I know a third set of men that would ſtarve.

Hassarac. Who are they?

Cobbler. The undertakers.

Hassarac. You have some handsome houses in this quarter; do you know who inhabit them?

Cobbler. Mostly cobblers.

Hassarac. Why you know there is not a single shed in the place but your own.

Cobbler. No, they are cobblers on a greater scale; this neighbourhood is full of statesmen, and lawyers, law-founders, law-confounders, and law-expounders, so they cobble the constitution between them.

Hassarac. You are a shrewd fellow—but how can you manage to work by this light? 'Tis near dark.

Cobbler. By any light, or no light, I am the man for a job in the dark.

Hassarac. Indeed!

Cobbler. What think you, last night I sewed a man's head to his body, there's a job!

Hassarac. Where? Where?

Cobbler. That's past my cunning to find out.

Hassarac. How so?

Cobbler. Why I was blindfolded there and back.

Hassarac [*aside*]. Oh! it must be the same, they have planned it well: blinded, say you? Then you have no idea of the road you took?

Cobbler. Not so bad as that, neither; I am used too to go to bed without a candle, to lose my way in the dark: I counted every turn I made.

Hassarac. Oh, did you? Do you think you could find them again?

Cobbler. Yes, blindfolded; but not otherwise.

Hassarac. I should like to try, for curiosity only. If you succeed [*Shows a purse.*] this shall reward you.

Cobbler. On with the bandage then—I am your man.—Stop, let me shut up my shop first. [*Puts his stool into the stall, and shuts the shutter.*] Now—draw it tighter; if I see in the least, I shall lose my way. Now, fortune, dear blind lady, look down upon your blindfolded cobbler, see that he doesn't lose his way; and he'll run upon your errands for the rest of his life. Now follow me. [*Exit.*

SCENE IV

Another street,[1] with gateways, and door of CASSIM'S *hous*

Enter COBBLER, *followed by* HASSARAC.

Hassarac. You're sure you're right?

Cobbler. Don't puzzle me.—Which way did I turn laſt?

Hassarac. To the left.

Cobbler. That's the right.

Hassarac. And now to the right?

Cobbler. No: the right's wrong.—But let me see—let me see.

Hassarac. Let you see—then I muſt take off the bandage.

Cobbler. Be quiet; I'm like an owl, and see beſt in the dark— [*After feeling at the gateway, goes to* CASSIM'S *door.*] This is the house.

Hassarac. This?

Cobbler. It has one ſtep; I had near broke my neck in coming out.

Hassarac. It has! It has!

Cobbler. Fortune be praised, the purse is mine.

Hassarac. Take it.

Cobbler. I always like to look at my money, so I'll pull off the bandage.

Hassarac. Know you who lives here?

Cobbler [*examining*]. Yes—it is. This was Cassim's, the rich merchant, who, I hear, this morning died suddenly; now his brother has it, he who cuts wood in the foreſt, where the thieves are—you have heard of them?

Hassarac. Yes, yes—often, often!

Cobbler. A pack of rascals! but there's a rope growing for each of them; as for the captain, I would go any length to see him hanged—wouldn't you?

Hassarac. I should certainly be present—damnation!

Cobbler. Farewell, sir. If ever you have loſt your way, or your

[1] *A view of Bagdad; with* CASSIM'S *House, a step at the door. Re-enter* MUSTAPHA *and* HASSARAC.—*Duncombe's Edition.*

heel-piece, I shall be proud of your custom; I work at fixed prices in general, but if ever you wish to employ me in that way again. you'll always find me ready for a blind bargain.   [*Exit.*

Hassarac. Come near, come near [*To a* ROBBER *who enters,*] Where are your comrades?

Second Robber. Concealed, as you ordered, in the oil-jars.

Hassarac. You know the signal?

Second Robber. Yes, all.

Hassarac. This house contains our enemy; to-morrow's sun shall not find an inhabitant alive—away—yet, stay, the stable must be behind the house, there, go wait my coming.

Second Robber. Fear not me.   [*Exit.*

Hassarac [*calls at* CASSIM'*s door*]. Who's there? I have a subtle foe to deal with, and therefore the more dangerous.

Enter a SLAVE *from the house.*

Tell your master a stranger wishes to speak with him.
      [*Exit* SLAVE.

Now for stratagem—A well-told tale makes me and my band inheritors within these walls. and terminates this night the life of the landlord.

ALI BABA [*richly dressed*] *enters with slaves.*

Ali Baba. A stranger did you say?

Hassarac. Under the intrusion, Sir, but—

Ali Baba. No intrusion at all, for you hav'nt yet got into my house: what's your business?

Hassarac. I am a Merchant arrived in the city, with a large and valuable cargo, the Caravansera is too full to admit me, and being a stranger here——

Ali Baba. Why you'd be robbed in the streets; there are a plaguy number of thieves in this town, I assure you.

Hassarac. It struck me that might be the case, the moment I and my followers entered it.

Ali Baba. And you are apprehensive for your merchandise?

Hassarac. Exactly so.

Ali Baba. Then don't be frightened any longer. This is my

door, and while it has a hinge it shall never be shut against a stranger who seeks my protection. Where's your cargo?

Hassarac. At your gate, behind your house.

Ali Baba [*calling*]. Hassan, lead the merchant's mules into the stable, and place his cargo in the court, under the Verandah, it will be safe there.

Hassarac. How can I thank you?

Ali Baba. Tell me I've done the duty one man owes to another; any thing else is mere flummery. What do you deal in?

Hassarac. Oil, from Bassora.

Ali Baba. Oil! why what door could creak on its hinges in opening to you? But I may assist you in the sale. We'll talk of that in the morning.

Hassarac. The morning! that you will never see! [*Aside.*]

Ali Baba. Come! In—In.

Hassarac. I can never return your kindness.

Ali Baba. Yes, you can—show the same to any stranger who requires it, and we are quit. This way—come.

[*Exeunt into the house.*

SCENE V

The veranda in CASSIM BABA's *house. The oil-jars are discovered, a part in sight, the rest supposed to be hid behind the building.*

Enter MORGIANA, *with a lamp, which she sets down, counting as she enters.*

Morgiana. Thirty-one to forty jars[1]—It's lucky they are here, for in the hurry and bustle I have forgotten to provide for the night's entertainment, even this lamp wants replenishing—I'll make free with our friend the oil-merchant, he sure may share a little. [*Goes to a jar, and taking up the lid, a* ROBBER *peeps out.*

Second Robber. Is it the time? Is it the time?

Morgiana [*who has staggered behind the jar*]. Not yet—but presently.

[ROBBER *closes his head.*

----

[1]*i.e.,* she counts "thirty-one; thirty-two; thirty-three"; up to "forty."

Morgiana [*goes to next jar, and so on*]. Not yet, but presently. In every jar there is a robber: their design is plain, it is to murder us! What is to be done? Ah! the charm the Fairy gave my master—it produces instant death! The words of the label then on Cassim's breast must now be verified.—"Morgiana, on you depends the safety of the family."

[*Music—She approaches the jars cautiously, and pours the contents of the charmed phial into them, until she is out of sight, leaving the lamp behind her.*]

Enter HASSARAC *on the Veranda.*

Hassarac. 'Tis time to give my comrades orders for the manœuvres of the night. Ha, a lamp, then the servants are yet on the foot about the court—I must retire and wait a moment.

[*Exit into a house.*

Re-enter MORGIANA.

Morgiana. The groans of the expiring villains have nearly overcome me: now for my master. [*Takes up the lamp.*] My master, oh, a thought rushes on me, the false merchant, leader of the gang, before I reach him, may have plunged his dagger in Ganem's and his father's breast. Alla send I be not too late to preserve them.

[*Runs out with the lamp.*

Re-enter HASSARAC.

Hassarac. All is dark at last. Now for the signal [*whistles*]—no answer. At such a moment sure they cannot sleep? [*whistles*]. Still silent! what can this mean? [*Opens a jar or two, and starts astonished.*] Death and hell! my faithful band destroyed. This is the Fairy's art—brave hearts, you shall be revenged, amply revenged. How shall I act? Shall I, with my sabre, force the rooms? My life I hold as nothing—but no: alarmed as they are it would be vain, I must try art; comrades, brave comrades, an hour shall not pass, ere I avenge, or share, your fate.

[*Exit.*

SCENE VI

An apartment in CASSIM'*s house.*

Enter GANEM *and* COGIA, *followed by* MORGIANA.

Morgiana. This way. This way.

Cogia. Well, but what's the matter?

Morgiana. Where is the merchant?

Ganem. Gone to inspect the jars, as he told me.

Morgiana. Then he has escaped.

Ali Baba. Escaped!

Morgiana. Yes, for in each of these jars was concealed a robber of the cave, brought here by their artful leader.

Cogia. But how were we saved?

Morgiana. By the charm the fairy gave my master, I have locked them up in death.

Cogia. Excellent Morgiana, good girl. What recompense can I offer? You are no longer my slave, you are my daughter indeed.

TRIO—GANEM, COGIA, *and* MORGIANA[1]

Happy this day,
Care flits away,
Sorrow no more shall our pleasure alloy;
As the sky clears,
Sunshine appears,
Danger and grief yield to safety and joy.
Friendless and poor,
Want paced the floor;
The breath of despair it blew chill on our hearth.
Chang'd is our lot,
Woes be forgot,
Away with all cares, and give welcome to mirth.
Wealth while it flows,
Treachery knows,

[1]For this song *Duncombe's Edition* substitutes "Ah little blind boy" from Act II, scene ii.

Faithless the poor, or the wealthy, may prove;
   Deſtin'd to know,
   Mutual woe,
Mutual, sure, muſt be our love.   *[Exeunt.*

Enter a SLAVE, *introducing* HASSARAC, *who is in another disguise.*[1]
   Slave. What visitor muſt I announce, Sir, to my maſter?
   Hassarac. A dear friend returned from travel, whom he has not seen for many years. [*Exit* SLAVE.] A friend who will despatch him on his travels to the other world immediately. But I muſt make him think me his brother's friend, who is set forth on his laſt journey a very little before him.

Enter ALI BABA *and* SLAVES.
   Hassarac [*addressing him*]. My bosom companion, playmate of my tender youth.
   Ali Baba. So, here's a charge, bosom companion, and an old infant playmate I never saw in my life.
   Hassarac [*ſtarting back*]. I—I am miſtaken—yet I cannot be deceived in the house—is not this the house of Cassim Baba?
   Ali Baba. It was until laſt night: but he is now in much more confined apartments; and lodges on a ground-floor—he is dead.
   Hassarac. My friend, Cassim Baba?
   Ali Baba. Yes; and his brother, Ali Baba, who is now alive, and talking to you, inherits the mansion.
   Hassarac. Poor Cassim, while a friend's heart is burſting for you, a brother, I find, can let his family play over your recent grave.
   Ali Baba. And that brother can tell you, he is so punƈtual in paying his debts of grief to a true friend, that he cannot afford the hypocrisy of a tear, when it is not due to the departed. But, ſtill, my late brother's friends are mine—consider this house as much your own as if he were ſtill living. This way, and take refreshment.
   Hassarac. I follow you.

[1] In *Duncombe's Edition* this begins a separate scene, in Cassim's pavilion.

SCENE VII

At Palace[1]*—*SLAVES *preparing a banquet,* COGIA *and* GANEM
inspecting it.

Ganem. Won't it be very pretty, mother?

Cogia. Very—but, ah, my dear Ganem, I can't help thinking
how often this feast might have kept my poor children for a
month.

Ganem. Don't think of that now—see, here comes my father
—and—yes—and a stranger with him.

Enter ALI BABA, HASSARAC, *and* SLAVES.

Hassarac. What, have you an entertainment forward?

Ali Baba. A slight one, quite in the family way.

Hassarac [*aside*]. That may interrupt my plan.

Ali Baba. Wife, this is a very old friend of my brother's.

Cogia. Did you know him intimately, Sir?

Hassarac. Intimately! Was his death sudden?

Ali Baba. So sudden, he had not time to send for assistance.

Hassarac [*aside*]. I believe not, what was his complaint?

Ali Baba. Then, a very strange one—he was attacked with a
giddiness in the head, which made him forget every thing, he
could not recollect a single word, and that caused his death.

Hassarac. Artful evasion—[*aside*] poor man.

Ali Baba. But, come, we must not indulge in mournful reflection. Sit down, sit down.

---

[1]*Duncombe's Edition reads:*—
An elegant Chamber in the Turkish style—At the back an Arch, with folding doors.—
COGIA *and* GANEM *discovered.*
Cogia. Here comes Ali Baba and a stranger with him.

Enter ALI BABA *and* HASSARAC.

Ali Baba. Wife, a friend of my late brother's. Bring forth the banquet.—[*The
folding door opens, and two slaves bring on a round table decorated with an elegant
banquet, and four stools with handsome covers.*]
Hassarac. What, have you an entertainment?
Ali Baba. Only a slight repast, sir, quite in the family way.
Hassarac [*aside*]. This may interrupt my plan.
Cogia. Were you and my late brother acquainted intimately, sir?
Hassarac. Intimately, madam. Was his death sudden?

Hassarac [*aside*]. I did not expect this feast—no matter, it shall not deter me from my purpose.   [*They all sit.*

Ali Baba. Morgiana, what have you there?

Morgiana. Some wine of the finest flavour.

[*Presents a goblet to* HASSARAC.

Hassarac [*observing the goblet*]. As I live, the cavern goblet.

[*Aside.*

Ali Baba. Why, Sir, what perplexes you?

Hassarac. The—the excellence of the workmanship.

Ganem. It is beautiful.

Hassarac. Beautiful indeed, where did it come from?

Ali Baba. From the ca—my brother Cassim.

Hassarac. Oh, it was his—did he purchase it?

Ali Baba. No—no—he left it.

*Hassarac .*Where? [*Eagerly.*]

Ali Baba. In the ca—to be sure to me.

Hassarac. Oh, in his will.

Ali Baba. Certainly; how else could it be? [*aside*] I was just blundering out the cavern.

Hassarac [*aside*]. This goblet is yet to be paid for.

Ali Baba. Come, Sir, fill it Morgiana; I'll give you a toast that nearly concerns me;   I'll tell you before we part—Here's confusion to the memory of the robbers in the forest.

[*During the foregoing part of the speech,* HASSARAC *is holding out the goblet for* MORGIANA *to fill, but upon the mention of the robbers turns suddenly, and drops a dagger from his sleeve; picks it up, confused, and fancies it was not seen.*]

Morgiana [*seeing the dagger*]. A dagger in his sleeve! what can this mean? Allah protect us! [*Looking at him.*] 'tis the pretended merchant, the captain of the banditti. The dagger explains his purpose. Fairy of the lake inspire me!

[MORGIANA *dances with a tambourine, in which, imitating two or three of the passions, she prevents* HASSARAC's *attempt to stab* ALI BABA, *without her intention being discovered.* HASSARAC *has, at length, lifted up his dagger, and is upon the point of assassinating him, when she seizes his arm, and, in the scuffle, forces the dagger into the breast of the robber, who falls and expires.*]

Ali Baba. Merciful Prophet! What have you done?[1]

Cogia.
Ganem. } Morgiana!

Morgiana. Preserved your life—destroyed your enemy—look there that dagger was aimed at you. Know you that face?

Ali Baba. The captain of the banditti!

Morgiana. The last of your foes! [*joyfully.*]

Ali Baba. Unfortunate wretch, this is a just punishment for your treachery.

[*The body of* HASSARAC *descends in fire.*

Ali Baba. To you, then, I owe my fortune, life, every thing.

Morgiana. When I used the Fairy's charm, I vowed obedience to her will.

[*Exit.*

[SCENE VIII[2]

A Landscape.

GOSSAMER *enters sportively, waving her wand to bring on* ALI BABA, *&c. then goes off.*

ALI BABA *enters, followed by* GANEM, COGIA, *and* MORGIANA—*they congratulate each other, and go off rejoicing at their escape from the hands of their enemies.*

ORCOBRAND *enters watching them, full of rage and disappointment—but at length expresses his joy that he shall now have them in his power—follows exultingly, waving his wand.*]

[1]*Ali Baba.* Rash girl! what have you done, Morgiana?

Morgiana. Preserved your life—destroyed your enemy!—Look there—that dagger was aimed at you. Know you not that face?

Ali Baba. [*looking at him*]. 'Tis the captain of the banditti.

Morgiana. [*joyfully*]. The last of your foes.

Ali Baba. It is, it is! Ill-fated man, you have met the punishment justly due to your crimes. Morgiana, you are indeed my daughter. But let us haste from this scene of blood, and seek the Fairy of the Lake, to offer up our gratitude to her for our deliverance from the cruel monster.

[2]*Duncombe's Edition.* Scene omitted, 1814 *Edition.*

SCENE IX[1]

ORCOBRAND's *Cave.*

ALI BABA, COGIA, GANEM, *and* MORGIANA *discovered, guarded by* ORCOBRAND *and Demons.*

Orcobrand. Detested mortals! confederates of my determined foe—whose potent machinations yield at length to my supremacy and all her vaunted powers are vanished in oblivious vapour! you are now within my grasp, and direst vengeance shall await your crimes. [*Strikes the rock, the back of the arch opens and discovers*

A FIERY TRANSPARENCY

FAMINE, FRAUD, WAR, *and* RAPINE *drag on* ABDALLAH *and* ZELIE. There—behold my victims! bear witness to the inventive torments that shall piece-meal tear them. Ye active agents of my fell design, prepare! fast bind the wretches to yon massy rock. Morgiana, in Zelie behold your sister.

Morgiana. My sister!

---

[1]*Duncombe's Edition.* Omitted 1814 *Edition. Cumberland's Edition* (perhaps correctly) reads:—

Scene. Exterior of the Cave. Music and loud thunder.

ORCOBRAND *and the* FOUR DEMONS *discovered.*

Orcobrand. The fairy triumphs in my captain's death—she shall find I am yet to be feared—vengeance will not fall alone. Bring forth your prisoners [DEMONS *rush forth and return with* ABDALLAH *and* ZELIE *in chains.*] Still obstinately bent upon your own destruction—still oppose my will?

Abdallah. Thy threats are vain! we'll never change our faith. Dear Zelie, we will die together.

Orcobrand. Fond wretches! I think not am so ignorant of tormenting,—separate, you shall linger out your helpless days.

Enter MORGIANA *and* ALI BABA, *guarded by* DEMONS.

Morgiana. Ah, we are betrayed.

Orcobrand. Zelie, in Morgiana behold your sister! her fate is linked with yours Seize those devoted wretches, and bind them to the rocks. This is my triumph! away away!

[*Loud thunder, &c. heard—a thunderbolt descends through the Cave, and strikes down* ORCOBRAND.

Enter the FAIRY OF THE LAKE, *descending through the Cave.*

Fairy. Detested wretch! thy power is o'er—the charm is broke! down, down to thy deserved torment!

The Demons rush off. ORCOBRAND *sinks. The Fairy waves her wand and the scene changes.* [to the Palace of the Fairy.]

Ardinelle [*behind*]. Detested wretch, forbear!

Abdallah. To virtue true, we'll live and die together.

Orcobrand. Then take thy wish; this moment ends the doubtful strife, and bitter anguish seals thy doom eternal.

Enter ARDINELLE.

Ardinelle. Hold, blasphemer! and for thy impious threats, now take the death you merit.

[*Strikes* ORCOBRAND *with her wand, and he sinks in a flash of fire—thunder and lightning.*]

SCENE X

A Wood—Enter FAIRY OF THE LAKE—*Thunder, &c.*

'Tis well, my fairy ministers at length
Have closed their mission: vice entangled lies
In the webb which he had darkly woven
To fling o'er virtue. Fortune has remov'd
The erring veil a moment from her eyes,
And seen, in honest Ali Baba's heart,
How gloriously her golden treasures flow,
When a pure bosom is the fount that pours them.
Love, too, has come to twine his gentle flowers
Around Morgiana's chain, and hide each link
Of slavery's bond in wreaths of joy and peace.
Thus ever may the spells succeed that work in virtue's cause

[*The Palace of the Fairy of the Lake; at the back a Transparent Lake, on which Cupids and Nymphs are seen sailing about in fanciful vessels, decorated with flowers.—A Dance, &c. &c.*

FINIS

Bibliography of *The Forty Thieves*

1. SONGS (1806)

Songs, Duets, Trios, Chorusses, &c. &c. &c. In The Grand Operatical Romance Of The Forty Thieves. Firſt Performed at the Theatre Royal, Drury Lane April 8th. 1906. The Music Composed, and Seleɛt ɔd by Mr. Kelly. The Ballets and Aɛtion under the direɛtion o 'Mr. D'Egville. London: Printed by C. Lowndes, Marquis Court, And sold in the Theatre. Price Ten-Pence.

8vo.

[Sheridan did not write any of the"Songs, &c." for this"Grand Operatical Romance." Their author seems to have been Charles Ward—with (perhaps) some assistance from George Colman the Younger.]

2. EDITIONS OF THE PLAY

(i) *FIRST EDITION, DUBLIN*, 1814

Ali Baba; or, The Forty Thieves. A Grand Dramatic Romance, in Two Aɛts; as performed at the Theatres Dublin, Cork, Belfaſt, &c. &c. Dublin: Printed by J. Charles, 57, Mary-Street; Of whom may be had All the Melo Dramas, Printed in a neat uniform manner, so far as published. 1814.

12mo.

Pagination. P. [1] title; p. [2] *Dramatis Personaæ*; pp. [3] and 4-36 Text.

[*Frontispiece*—"Morgiana stabbing the Captain of the Banditti." This Edition, of which my own copy appears to be unique, is eleven years earlier than the first London Edition.]

(ii) *DUNCOMBE'S [FIRST] EDITION. LONDON* (1825)

Duncombe's Edition. The Forty Thieves; A Romantic Drama, In Two Acts. By R. B. Sheridan and Colman the Younger. With all the Original Songs and Chorusses. The only Edition Correctly Marked from the Prompter's Book; With the Stage Business, Situations and Directions As performed at The Theatres Royal. London: Printed and Published by J. Duncombe, 19, Little Queen Street, Holborn; and Sold by All Booksellers in Town and Country.

12mo. Pp. 36.

Pagination. P. [1] title; p. [2] *Dramatis Personae*; pp. [3] and 4-36 Text.

[This Edition is dated, no doubt correctly, as 1825 by Anderson, *Sheridan Bibliography*, p. iv. It is the first to bear Sheridan's name.]

(iii) *DUNCOMBE'S [SECOND] EDITION* (1833)

Duncombe's Edition. The Forty Thieves; A Romantic Drama, in Two Acts. By R. B. Sheridan and Colman the Younger. With all the Original Songs and Chorusses. The Only Edition Correctly Marked, By Permission, From the Prompter's Book. To which is Added, A Description of the Costume—Cast of the Characters—The Whole of the Stage Business, Situations—Entrances—Exits—Properties—And Directions, As performed at the London Theatres. Embellished With A Fine Engraving By Mr. Jones, from a Drawing, taken in the Theatre. London: Printed And Published by J. Duncombe & Co. 10 Middle Road, Holborn.

12mo. Pp. 36.

[This is the *second* Edition of the Duncombe issue, though described as the first by Iolo A. Williams, *Seven XVIII Century Bibliographies.*
The date of Duncombe's removal is suggested by a comparison of these imprints :
The German Jew. A Drama. (acted August 16th, 1830).
J. Duncombe, Little Queen Street, Holborn.
Gustavus the Third, or The Masked Ball. (acted November 11th, 1833).
J Duncombe & Co. 9 Middle Row, Holborn.]

(iv) *CUMBERLAND'S EDITION*

The Forty Thieves. A Grand Melodramatic Romance. In Two Acts. Printed from the Acting Copy, With Remarks, Biographical and Critical, By D—G .... London. J. Cumberland] 6, Brecknock Place, Camden New Town.

12mo. Pp. 40.

[This cannot have been earlier than 1828, since the cast dated as of that year at Covent Garden is given. Since the next play but one in the same series *The Vampire*, (No. 194 of Cumberland's *British Theatre*) contains the cast of the revival on September 26th, 1829, the date given by Sichel, 1829, appears to be correct. It is the only Edition of *The Forty Thieves* he mentions.]

[The three editions by Duncombe and Cumberland follow different texts as acted in the theatres at the various dates.]